KING CONTE

DIARY OF A CHAMPION
by Harry Harris

G2 entertainment

Published by G2 Entertainment Ltd

© G2 Entertainment 2017

ISBN : 978-1-782-81-7574

AUTHOR: Harry Harris

EDITOR: Sean Willis

DESIGNER: Paul Briggs

PUBLISHERS: Edward Adams and Jules Gammond

PICTURES: Action Images

PRINTED IN EUROPE

DEDICATED TO:
Linda, who insisted upon calling our home 'Bridge House'.

CONTENTS

"Antonio Conte is a disciplinarian. I like that about him. The players do what he tells them, no messing. He is one of those fellows who is a no nonsense manager.

At the start of the season, Jose Mourinho arrived at Old Trafford, Pep Guardiola at City, and Manchester was the centre of attention If anyone expected a manager to arrive in the Premier League to win big things in their first season, it was Pep.

But Conte changed the style after a hiding at the Arsenal and changed things around from a very 'iffy' season the previous one. He has done tremendously well.

Until the defeat at Crystal Palace, he led the team on a tremendous run but he bounced straight back with a win over Guardiola and City, the first manager ever to inflict a double over Pep in a season. To beat City under those circumstances was impressive, as Pep and a club with such unlimited resources will always be challenging for titles.

What has impressed me the most about Conte is that he has achieved so much with so little. While the Manchester clubs and others spent heavily in the summer leading up to the season, for whatever reason Conte didn't get the players he wanted, and yet he has still mounted such a fantastic challenge.

He came to this country under the radar as all the expectations were focused on Manchester, but he had played at the highest level, managed at the highest level, and so he knew how to handle the big players. Jose was successful wherever he went, Pep was unbelievable at Barcelona and Bayern Munich, so Conte was naturally lower down the pecking order. Yet even with basically a side he inherited whatever has happened this season has happened because of the manager.

The fans were so disenchanted by what occurred the previous season, I doubt they expected very much at all, so I imagine they have been shocked by Conte's success.

Yet when the team was thrashed by Arsenal the fans could have been excused for saying "what's going on?" But he turned it around. He even brought David Luiz back and turned him into a proper defender. Luiz has blinding pace, is good in the air but sometimes went walkabout when he was first at the Bridge. You have to give Conte credit for transforming him into a far more reliable defender.

I am at the Bridge on match days and see many of the fans and know they would have been delighted just getting back into Europe. But, to win the title - tremendous!"

RON HARRIS

Ronald Edward "Ron" Harris, nicknamed "Chopper", captained Chelsea in the 60s and 70s. He was one of the toughest defenders of his era - along with Tommy Smith and Norman 'Bites Yer Legs' Hunter, and one of Chelsea's greatest ever skippers. Choppers' 795 appearances for the club remains a record. Ron and his brother Allan Harris were teammates at Chelsea in the mid-1960s. Chopper Harris captained Chelsea as they won the 1970 FA Cup against the mighty Leeds after a replay, and the 1971 Cup Winners Cup against European giants, Real Madrid.

CHAPTER ONE

INTRODUCTION

Gary Lineker had famously stated that his beloved Leicester City would NOT win the 2015/16 Premier League title - and paid the forfeit by presenting Match of the Day in his underpants.

Well, clearly not overly concerned about his fateful predictive prowess he was at it again in July 2016. N'Golo Kante had just made his anticipated move from the King Power to Stamford Bridge and Lineker hurriedly took to Twitter:

@GaryLineker - "Inevitably Kante has gone. Fancy Chelsea will now win the title. He's that good!"

Another ridiculous prediction, surely…

King Conte: Diary of a Champion is the inside track of how the flamboyant, gesticulating, non-stop touchline-leaping Chelsea coach took the Premier League by storm in his first season in charge at Stamford Bridge. It is not only a must-read for all followers of Chelsea but also any football fans fascinated by how he came, saw and conquered despite the formidable opposition of Pep Guardiola at Manchester City and Jose Mourinho at Manchester United.

In fact, Conte achieved the impossible, he succeeded Mourinho in the affections of the Blues' faithful; in English football he became the new 'Special One'.

How did he do it? The 'King Conte' diary of the season follows his every move, in every game, to find out exactly how he galvanised a squad that had defended their previous Premier League title with such devastating failure as Mourinho was sacked just before Christmas 2015. There are fascinating insights into what happened on the pitch as well as a look behind the scenes.

John Terry reveals how Conte made his players run for miles in pre-season coupled with far greater emphasis on tactics, more than any of the other former Chelsea managers.

Sessions last in excess of an hour, which were originally met with some resistance from the Chelsea squad. Soon, though, they could see the benefits. "He prepares us precisely about every opposing side, so we go into each game with the correct plan." said Willian.

Conte likes a training routine called 11 v 0; known as 'shadow play'. The team practices attacking combinations without opposition. The exercises are customised to include a cross, or one touch. Repetition of attacking moves is key; as Eden Hazard puts it "automatism". Mourinho's approach to attacking was different to Conte. "Mourinho put in a system, but we didn't work lots." Hazard explained. "We know what to do, because we play football, but maybe the automatisms were a little bit different."

Video analysis is also a cornerstone of his preparation. Conte wrote his coaching thesis on it.

Soon after Jose Mourinho was sacked, as relegation jitters filtered all the way to the door of owner Roman Abramovich and with the title defence in a total shambles, Conte was mentioned as the most likely successor. He would go on to become the fourth Italian manager to win the Premier League in eight seasons but, in reality, few fans in England knew much about his abilities as a player or coach despite a high profile in his native Italy.

CHAPTER TWO

CONTE WHO?

When Arsene Wenger arrived from Japan, it was "Arsene Who?", and to a lesser extent there was some scratching of heads about the appointment of Antonio Conte at Stamford Bridge as the eventual successor to the 'Special One', Jose Mourinho. Either way, it was a somewhat hair-raising appointment.

Ok, he was high profile as coach to the Italian national team and was an Italian legend in his own right with Juve and as an international footballer. However, no one was paying much attention to such a low key Italian side in the 2016 Euros, a team that was over-achieving based on the defensive tactics of their coach. The glare of the spotlight domestically was concentrated on 'Uncle' Roy Hodgson making England a laughing stock once more in a major tournament while losing to Iceland.

The big coaching names were gravitating towards Manchester - Pep at City and Jose at United - but the 'Little Englanders' were soon to discover how much Conte was well respected; certainly in Italy. Juventus and Italy star Leonardo Bonucci backed Conte to be a "big success" with Chelsea, even before the season started. The defender, who impressed under Conte at Euro 2016 and when he was at Juve, discussed his former manager's techniques. "The players in the Italy team nicknamed him 'The Godfather'. That means when he talks, you listen. You do what he says and you don't argue. Players want to listen though. Nobody gave Italy much of a chance in France, and in the end we only got beaten on penalties by the world champions. Conte will be a big success in England. Chelsea are already a very good team, and he will have them challenging both in England and in Europe. He likes leaders, he likes big personalities, but he will not stand for players who think they are bigger than him. He is the boss, and if you listen to him and show him respect, you will see he is one of the best bosses in the game."

It was as a player with Juve and then as a manager that Conte made his name. Before taking over at Stamford Bridge he coached Juventus to three straight Serie A titles as well as twice winning the Supercoppa Italiana. He also helped Bari to win Serie B in 2009 and took Italy to the quarter-finals of Euro 2016.

As he stormed to the summit of the Premier League and with the title in sight Andrea Pirlo said that Conte was the best manager he had played under. Pirlo worked with Conte at Juventus as well as the Italy national team. "Conte for me is the best coach." Pirlo told ESPN FC. "He is a genius. He works every day, every single moment for soccer, for the team, every small detail and in the field the players play with memory and play very good. In Juventus I spent three years with Conte. We won the league but every day training was strong. Maybe now it's the same with Chelsea."

He was possibly as much known for his 'barnet' as he was for his brilliance on the football field or in coaching. The once long-locked midfielder had a hair transplant soon after he ended his playing career. Clearly Conte was as image-conscious as his predecessor, as he 'capped' a distinguished playing career by ensuring he didn't lose any of his dark features.

In fact Conte, who earned 20 caps for Italy during 1994 and 2000, appears as a testimonial story on the website for the Hairloss Improvement Solutions clinic. According to the statement, the former Lecce and Juve midfielder travelled to Vancouver in Canada to remedy his battle with baldness after two botched attempts to reverse the process in his native Italy. Conte was visibly receding towards the latter stages of his career. After retiring as a player he swiftly sported a completely shaved head to allow for the operation. He used his hiatus away from the game to regain his shaggy locks and subsequently look like a well-groomed model manager on the sidelines.

Naturally The Sun newspaper lapped it up as soon as his name was linked with the Chelsea job. They gloated "THREE hair transplants to cover up his bald patch." The same publication also stated that Conte used the Hasson and Wong clinic in Vancouver, Canada to get his dream bouffant. "Antonio Conte's hair transplant is so natural and matches his looks that it is hard to imagine that he went for a hair transplant."

Conte, who was named Serie A Coach of the Year in 2012, 2013 and 2014, is far from alone in opting for a new head of false hair in an attempt to retain a youthful appearance. When he became virtually bald he underwent several costly hair transplants around the world following the same path as Shane Warne, the Australian brand ambassador for Advanced Hair Studio. In the world of football Manchester United and England captain Wayne Rooney is the most famous figure to have a 'syrup'. After the nine-hour operation, Rooney wrote on social media: "Just to confirm to all my followers I have had a hair transplant. I was going bald at 25 so why not. I'm delighted with the result. It's still a bit bruised and swollen but when it dies down you will be first to see it. Anyone recommend any good hair gel. Haha!" Rooney had follow-up treatment in 2013 as part of a £15,000 package. Former Liverpool and Manchester city star Didi Hamann also had a go, saying he wanted to look good on TV. Stephen Ireland burst onto the scene during Manchester City's 2005/06 season with a thinning thatch but as his reputation grew so had his hairline. Referee Mark Clattenburg has also had a hair transplant.

When he enjoyed a full head of his own hair Conte was a tenacious box-to-box midfielder and hugely influential in the dressing room with Juve, as much as Terry has been at the Bridge, and later in management he gleaned the nuances of the job from esteemed Italian managerial 'misters': Giovanni Trapattoni, Marcello Lippi, Arrigo Sacchi and Carlo Ancelotti.

As a player Conte was a powerful figure inside the dressing room who put the team work ethic first; central to Juventus for over a decade. Conte signed for Juventus in 1991 at a time when AC Milan were at the pinnacle of Italian football having won back-to-back European Cups under tactician Arrigo Sacchi. It was also the time of the *Azzurri* finishing third in the world of football while hosting Italia 90 - a tournament I enjoyed first hand with manager Bobby Robson, Lineker, Gazza et al.

Juve had last lifted the Scudetto in 1986 and while Conte did not win domestic silverware at Juventus under Trapattoni he helped begin the resurgence having arrived from US Lecce. The 21-year-old midfield blended with Stefano Tacconi, Toto Schillaci and Italian legend, Roberto Baggio; players he had idolised. Conte was at first overwhelmed, admitting "There was the great Trapattoni. There was Roberto Baggio. I was very emotional. I was a player-fan."

Conte's parents Cosimino and Ade ensured Antonio and his two brothers, Gianluca and Daniele, kept their focus first on schoolwork, but his father was a coach and influential figure at Lecce. Antonio played football in the street outside his house and the priests would allow him to kick a ball around the church's courtyard.

When Conte arrived at Juventus Trapattoni immediately became a major influence in his career. He had come from southern Italy to Turin in the north; cold compared to sun-soaked Lecce. "At the start I thought, why am I doing this, I'm earning more, but I'm away from home, from my friends, from the sea?" reflected Conte. "I only remained because I didn't want to return as a loser.

When I arrived, there was fog, cold and at the time my friends at home were on the beach. It was really tough to adapt to that."

Trapattoni gave him his first start in a friendly against Bayern Munich; a debut match decided when Conte misjudged his backpass to Tacconi, allowing Bayern to clinch victory. "I walked the next day and it felt like I'd be beaten up." Conte remembered. "All of a sudden, Trapattoni appears out of nowhere and it was as if he could read my thoughts. He said, 'You're not still thinking about yesterday's mistake, are you? Oh, come on! Think of the future, you'll be here for many years, it's all fine'. If Trapattoni hadn't been there, I don't know if I would've stayed at Juventus."

In 1994 Marcello Lippi arrived and changed Juve's system to a 4-3-3, deploying Conte on the left side of a midfield trio alongside Angelo Di Livio and Paulo Sousa. Lippi led Juve to league titles in 1995, 1997 and 1998, and three consecutive Champions League finals in 1996, 1997 and 1998, managing to lift the trophy once; Alessandro Del Piero and Fabrizio Ravanelli were the goalscorers that led to Juventus beating Ajax on penalties in 1996, but they crashed to Borussia Dortmund a year later and then to Real Madrid. So, Conte had become a European champion but had watched largely from the bench having been substituted after 44 minutes. He was replaced by Vladimir Jugovic, who struck the decisive penalty in the shootout. Lippi later led Italy to World Cup success in 2006.

In 1996 Conte became captain of a dressing room that contained many big personalities, such as Zinedine Zidane, Edgar Davids, Didier Deschamps and Paolo Montero who, with 19 red cards over 10 seasons, knew how to put himself about. However, his 1996/97 campaign was badly affected by injury and he missed much of Juventus's run to the final; again forced to watch, this time from the stands, as a Dortmund side containing four former Juve players - Sousa, Julio Cesar, Jurgen Kohler and Andreas Moller - outsmarted Lippi's men to win 3-1.

Conte remained on the bench until the 77th minute in the 1998 final against Real Madrid and was unable to stop *Los Blancos* winning their seventh European Cup.

It was Carlo Ancelotti who succeeded Lippi in 1999 as Juventus played in the Intertoto Cup, which they won, with Conte scoring in their two-legged final against Rennes. Ancelotti had secured Champions League football for Parma but some Juve fans were wary of a Milan legend in charge.

Conte, though, was convinced of a domestic league triumph as he played alongside Del Piero, Zidane and Davids to fire Juve into a seemingly unassailable lead atop of Serie A. However, Juve then lost four of their final eight games to allow the 1999/2000 title to fall into the hands of Sven-Goran Eriksson's Lazio by just a single point. Lesson learned, this made Conte extra sensitive in the run-in to Chelsea's Premier League season. As the title loomed the gap widened and then shortened, with Conte steadfastly refusing to take anything for granted, often referring back to his Juve moment when the title slipped from his grasp as a player.

Conte's reaction was as you'd expect: "That was devastating. For seven days I just didn't sleep. Not a wink. We'd lost a Scudetto that we had already won."

Conte lost World Cup and European Championship finals with Italy but relinquishing the league title to Lazio in such an embarrassing fashion has perhaps shaped him most as a manager. "When you lose, you learn." he reflected. "You try to see why you didn't win. You learn a lot about yourself. To win is beautiful. I find the peace in myself when I win. For this reason, I want to work very hard and find solutions and to give options to my players. Only when I win am I relaxed."

Conte retired from playing in 2004 and pursued a managerial career. He began in the 2006/07 season at Arezzo in Serie B and was sacked after nine games without a win. His successor fared even worse so Conte was subsequently reinstated. The team then put together a run of five consecutive wins but were still relegated.

He was given another chance in Serie B in December 2007 with Bari, who he led to promotion in his first full season. After a less than impressive time at Atalanta, ending after 14 games, he moved on to Siena, where he earned promotion to Serie A in 2011.

Conte took over Juve in the summer of 2011 when they were still recovering from the *Calciopoli* scandal (one of the greatest match-fixing scandals of the 21st Century which saw Serie A teams Juventus, Fiorentina and Lazio punished with relegation) and, while they gained immediate promotion back to Serie A in 2007, they were still in need of reinventing themselves with seventh-place finishes in the two seasons before Conte arrived. He certainly exceeded all expectations, leading Juve to the Serie A title, unbeaten for the entire 2011/12 season!

In no uncertain terms Conte let the squad he inherited know that seventh place was simply unacceptable for Juventus. He liked the 4-2-4 system when he first became a manager but, while that had worked for him, he switched to 4-3-3 before tinkering to a 3-5-2 that brought out the best of midfielders Andrea Pirlo, Arturo Vidal and Claudio Marchisio and allowed the wing-backs to effectively support the strikers.

Juve conceded 47 goals under Luigi Delneri in the 2010/11 season; Conte's new system resulted in them conceding a mere 20 (thirteen fewer than runners-up Milan) with Leonardo Bonucci, Giorgio Chiellini and Andrea Barzagli at the heart of the defence wall. Signing Andrea Pirlo, on a free transfer from Milan, was one of the greatest transfers of all time as he pulled the strings and conducted the team from midfield.

Pirlo spoke glowingly of Conte in his autobiography *I Think Therefore I Play*. "When Conte speaks, his words assault you. They crash through the doors of your mind, often quite violently and settle deep within you. I've lost track of the number of times I've found myself saying, 'Hell, Conte said something really spot on again today.' I was expecting him to be good, but not this good. I've worked with a lot of coaches and he's the one who surprised me the most."

In the book Pirlo also casts light on what Conte is like when things displease him. Conte had just been appointed as manager of Juve, and on his first day of training, introduced himself thus: "It's time we stopped being c##p. Every single person here has performed badly over the last couple of seasons. Turning around this ship is not a polite request. It's an order, a moral obligation."

"Even when we're winning, Conte comes in and hurls things against the wall (and thus my little corner). Anything he can lay his hands on... almost always full bottles of water. Fizzy water. Very fizzy water."

Conte had inherited an underperforming squad from Mourinho and has turned it around completely. Conte's philosophy is well known. "Players must put their talent into the team."

Pirlo reveals that at Juventus, Conte used to tape negative newspaper articles to the dressing room door, with the most offensive passages highlighted in red. "We have only one method of proving him wrong. Winning!"

"I love the man; I have nothing but respect and admiration for him. I know if he takes a job, any job, it will have to be on his terms. The players he wants to sign, those he wants to get rid of, the style he wants to play. If you sign him as your coach and then, as the owner, you want to start making decisions, he is not the coach for you. If you let him get on with things and do his methods, then you will have a team that plays attractive football and will, without doubt, be successful."

Pirlo points out his nasty streak. "There is a beast in him. I have been in his dressing room at half-time when we have been winning, but he comes in and will be throwing bottles of water around because of a mistake we made or because he feels we should be further ahead. His life is football. It's a good job Elisabetta is such an understanding wife, and if he takes the Chelsea job then she will have plenty of time to enjoy London, because he has two wives - Elisabetta and football. I have played under a lot of great managers but I can say that Conte is a genius. Like all men who possess genius, he is a little mad. The man can be a beast, a dressing room when he is angry is one of the most dangerous places you can be."

During his three-year reign, Juve finished the 2013/14 campaign with an unprecedented haul of 102 points, 17 above nearest challengers Roma.

He had clearly earned his appointment as Italy manager and was a success, mainly as Italians felt the squad he took to Euro 2016 was the least inspiring *Azzurri* in half a century. But, he got the best out of Emanuele Giaccherini, surplus at Sunderland, Brazilian-born forward Eder and Graziano Pelle.

It was announced that Conte would join Chelsea after the tournament, as Italy enjoyed an opening fixture 2-0 win over Belgium, fancied as potential winners. Italy won their group and then beat reigning champions Spain in the last-16 before losing on penalties against world champions Germany in the quarter-finals.

Interim Chelsea boss Guus Hiddink warned Conte that he faced a tough challenge at Stamford Bridge. Chelsea had endured a poor season and Hiddink highlighted the lack of experienced characters now at the club as an obstacle Conte had to overcome. "That's an extra complication." the Dutchman said. "When I came here the first time in 2009 the team was firm, regarding the personalities. The players knew the culture of English football and the club such as Lampard and Terry. Now it's a bit different and that won't be easy." He further added that Conte would still need to show major progress from the beginning of the next campaign. "The pressure is on. We have to see Chelsea next year again fighting for the title and being on top." said Hiddink. "There are many teams fighting for the title. Five, six clubs must always express their desire for the title, including Chelsea."

Former Italy striker Fabrizio Ravanelli believed his compatriot would deliver a league title during his time with Chelsea. Conte revolutionised the Old Lady after a period of instability and delivered three Scudettos in as many years, so Ravanelli, who played with Conte during his time with the national team, believed the Italian was guaranteed to bring a winning mentality back to Chelsea during his first three years at Stamford Bridge. "Chelsea have made the right choice if they want to win back the Premier League. I think, under Conte, it's a guarantee." said Ravanelli. "He is one of the most meticulous managers in the world - but also a fighter. He always had a great determination. He always had a willingness to make it to the top - and that shows in his incredible rise. Conte needs to be smart and if he wants to change, he needs to do it bit by bit and not rush into it. He brings a wealth of experience, which is important."

Juve defender Leonardo Bonucci called him "The Hammer" because he hammers points home emphatically, with an authoritative voice. He certainly hammered Diego Costa when he stepped out of line. Conte once likened the feeling of defeat to death, so winning was a far better option.

AC Milan and Italy legend Alessandro Costacurta labelled Antonio Conte the "best coach in the world" following his Euro 2016 exploits. Costacurta, who won seven Serie A titles during his 20 seasons at the San Siro with AC Milan, admitted that the Italian players may not be "world class" but Conte certainly is. "The most important thing is the coach, the coach for me is the best coach in the world and I think it's showing at Euro 2016." he told the BBC. "At the end of the year, the team wasn't a unit, it wasn't organised. After two or three training sessions the team improved, it's always about Conte. The players are not world class but the coach Conte, for me he is the best in the world."

Former Chelsea boss Gianluca Vialli praised Antonio Conte after Italy's first half performance against Spain. The Azzurri completely dominated during a brilliant first-half of the side's last-16 clash and went into the break 1-0 up thanks to Giorgio Chiellini's goal. Rarely had Spain looked so ordinary during the last eight years and Conte's side could easily have been three or four goals ahead after the first 45 minutes. Vialli, who was working as a pundit for the BBC, said it was completely down to Conte's tactics.

Asked how Italy had dominated Spain so much, Vialli replied: "Tactical knowledge. I can't believe it. We've been fantastic. We're full of ideas, look much fresher both physically and mentally. Conte's got it tactically spot on. Sometimes we defend our territory, sometimes we go and press them further up the pitch. Sometimes we hold back, sometimes we go forward. We've been fantastic and they've been lethargic and confused."

There wasn't universal approval of Conte's appointment however. Bizarrely, Argentina legend Diego Maradona branded the appointment as "disgusting" and "shameful". Maradona had played in Italy with Napoli. He said: "What happened is disgusting!" he told Italian TV station Piuenne. "The coach of the Italian national team who signs for Chelsea! That seems shameful to me."

So, Conte again had exceeded expectations, this time with the Italian national team, but his arrival in the Premier League was overshadowed by the two big hitters in Manchester. Little to no notice was taken of the Italian and few pundits thought Chelsea would stand much of a chance against the might of Pep and Jose who were throwing vast sums of money at rebuilding their squads.

As the season commenced early set backs against potential title challengers Liverpool and Arsenal made Conte all the more determined, but more significantly made him reconsider his approach and a subsequent switch to a three-man defence proved pivotal.

Conte had to adapt to England more so off the pitch than with the football. It was a challenge to learn the new language and live in a different culture. However, his focus on the football certainly helped to alleviate a troublesome settling in period off the pitch.

Assembling his squad for the Euros, Conte spoke of how he helped create a "family environment" for the players in just 45 days, and he set out to do the same at Chelsea.

In fact, he organised a pre-season barbecue for players, staff and families at Cobham. Marquees were erected and a five-a-side pitch laid out for the children. It set the tone, with Diego Costa joining in with the youngsters for 40 minutes; he was even taken out by a tackle.

When pre-season got under way in Austria and LA, Chelsea's support staff were singled out for warm handshakes and words every day from a manager intent on providing unity.

At the staff Christmas party, the tradition is for the manager to record a message to be played at the event. Conte obliged, and asked if he could also attend the event for about 500 people at the Under The Bridge music venue at Stamford Bridge, staying for more than two hours, spending time mingling with guests and happily posing for pictures and selfies.

Over the festive period there was a family day out at the Flip Out trampoline park in Wandsworth organised for the players' children. Conte ensured staff received wine and Prosecco, with every bottle personally addressed to the individual as thanks, and accompanied by a card with the words of Hannibal as he prepared to cross the Alps by elephant: "We shall either find a way or make one."

Every month, players and staff would go out together for a meal as Conte fostered the Chelsea "family"; ironically being for long spells without his own family, wife Elisabetta and nine-year-old daughter Vittoria who remained in Italy.

Conte's seasonal goodwill even extended to the media on one occasion, with a group invited to a local pub and bought drinks for after a pre-match news conference in the build-up to the Boxing Day game with Bournemouth.

CHAPTER THREE
THE APPOINTMENT

"Antonio Conte: Chelsea appoint Italy boss as head coach."

So rang out the headlines when Chelsea officially appointed Italy boss Antonio Conte as their new first team head coach, on 4 April 2016.

The 46-year-old former Juventus boss would begin a three-year contract after his country had taken part in Euro 2016. "I am proud to be the coach of the national team of my country and only a role as attractive as manager of Chelsea could follow that." he said. Guus Hiddink, who replaced Mourinho, would remain in charge until the end of the season.

Conte was the fifth Italian to manage Chelsea, following Gianluca Vialli, Claudio Ranieri, Carlo Ancelotti and Roberto di Matteo. "We are very pleased to have recruited one of the most highly regarded managers in world football." said club director Marina Granovskaia. "We are equally pleased to do so before the end of the current season. This aids our future planning."

Mourinho's second spell at Stamford Bridge came to an end on 17 December 2015 after a miserable start to the season and what Chelsea technical director Michael Emenalo described as "palpable discord" between the manager and his players. Hiddink restored stability in his second interim spell as boss but Chelsea failed to win a trophy and were set to miss out on Champions League football.

Conte would experience "some problems" adjusting to English football but his appointment will prove to be a "good decision", suggested former Manchester City manager Roberto Mancini at the time of the appointment. "It is difficult when a manager changes championships." Mancini, now in charge at Inter Milan, told BBC Sport. "It is important that he knows the league very well and very quickly. Probably he could have some problems at the start of his job."

The intriguing question is whether Conte was actually first choice. Former Chile manager Jorge Sampaoli felt he snubbed an offer to take over as Chelsea boss. The Argentine tactician, who was widely praised for his work in charge of the Chilean national team, says he had face-to-face talks with Roman Abramovich, but was not convinced by the project at Stamford Bridge. "The proposal that was the closest I've been to accepting was that that of Chelsea." the 56-year-old told Argentine radio. "It was a good project, we met with the president but it did not work." Chelsea later appointed Conte.

Just ten days after his appointment was announced he was acquitted of allegedly failing to prevent a match-fixing scandal when in charge of Siena in 2011. Italian judge Pierpaolo Beluzzi said Conte was acquitted because the accusations of sporting fraud were baseless. Conte, who had already served a ban imposed by the Italian football federation in connection with the case, always denied any wrongdoing but the prosecutor in the case was seeking a suspended six-month jail sentence and a fine.

"It was a full acquittal. What matters is that for him, this story is over." said Francesco Arata, one of Conte's lawyers. "We talked to Conte on the phone and he was very happy." The inquiry followed alleged attempts to manipulate matches in Serie B and the third-tier Lega Pro during the 2010/11 season, with some Coppa Italia matches also involved. Italian football federation president, Carlo Tavecchio, welcomed the decision, telling Italian newspaper Il Sole: "I am highly satisfied with the court's acquittal of Antonio Conte. Finally his position has been clarified and my confidence in him has never been in question. Now we are all the more focused on the Euros."

Conte's stats - courtesy of Opta - make impressive reading:

- Since 1971/72, Conte is the Juventus manager with the highest win ratio in Serie A (72.8%).
- He won 83 out 114 league games as Juventus manager, losing only seven.
- Conte's Juventus scored in 43 consecutive games (February 2013 to March 2014) - a Serie A record.
- Juventus also recorded an unbeaten run of 49 games from May 2011 to October 2012 (with Conte involved in 48 of them) - only AC Milan can boast a longer streak (58 games) in Serie A history.
- Conte won the Scudetto with Juventus in 2013/14, taking 102 points and winning 33 games. both records in a Serie A campaign.

DIARY OF THE SEASON

CHAPTER FOUR

JULY 2016

Hard work and tactics

Antonio Conte was preparing for the European Championships, but he was already Chelsea manager-in-waiting. One of his first tasks was to improve his limited knowledge of the language. "My English is improving because I'm studying. Before, I studied a lot, but now I'm focused with the national team because we're preparing for these Euros in the right way, with intensity. I like the verb, to fight." Conte's word choice shed further light on the managerial style he was to implement at Chelsea; intensity and a close bond between coach and player.

Paolo Di Canio offered Conte one crucial piece of advice - don't be like me! Di Canio's short-lived spell in charge of Sunderland did not go well. "I say (to him) be careful, try to learn the English mentality straight away. Try to learn (the language) and put next to you a good guy, an English guy, with good experience that can help you. You can come with your staff because you trust your members of staff but it's important to have a member of the club who understands everything of English football. Not only in the way you deliver your methodology or your tactics but also in the way you need to deliver the words at the end of the game, before the game, the message during the week. Don't do it like Di Canio!"

Gianfranco Zola backed his fellow Italian to bring with him a new spirit. Zola believed Conte's tactics were very effective. "I wish Conte all the success in the world in this new beginning. Conte's tactical 'creed' is based on good organisation, a lot of support and strong discipline. Chelsea is a different side to Italy but I think we will see all of those elements in Stamford Bridge next season, with a new spirit."

Former Blues manager Carlo Ancelotti had backed Conte to thrive in west London. "Carlo was my coach for two seasons in Juventus and a great brother for me." Conte pointed out. "But we are two different coaches and we live the match in two different ways. I want to play with my players. I want my players to feel me very close. I suffer and I win with them."

Italy were not rated at all highly on the eve of the Euros but defensive midfield international, Daniele De Rossi, was convinced the manager would get the best out of his squad. "The manager strikes the right chord and knows how to motivate you." said the Roma star. "We're aware that we don't start as favourites but we're proud players and, potentially, we can beat anyone."

Manchester United defender Matteo Darmian tipped Conte to succeed in the Premier League: "I think Conte will do well in England." the defender said after Italy drew 1-1 in a friendly against Spain. "He has already proved that he is a great coach and will have no problem adapting to English football."

As soon as the Euros were over, Conte was firmly focused on a good pre-season, universally regarded as the right launchpad to an excellent season.

The previous season, one of the contributory factors to Chelsea's horrific start was a disjointed pre-season, arriving at Cobham in mid-July and jetting off for a North American tour the very next day. The consequence was a slow start that fuelled tensions which eventually bubbled to the surface creating a vicious circle of negativity. Key players were not at peak fitness and suffered.

However, now with a new manager, one renowned for being a task master and with a commitment to training, the players arrived back slightly earlier than last season, despite the Euros, and had a few days to get acclimatised to the new working dynamic before setting off on another North American tour.

Marco Tardelli, (arguably best remembered for his 1982 World Cup Final goal-celebration) who played for both Inter Milan and Juventus as well as earning over 80 caps for Italy, went on to manage a number of clubs including a return to Inter. His last job was to be assistant Giovanni Trapattoni at the Republic of Ireland. Despite never playing or coaching in England, he warned his fellow Italian about England's dislike for tactics. "It'll be a wonderful experience for Conte and he'll settle in well in London." Tardelli told Radio Deejay. "He will have the opportunity to build a team, just as Jose Mourinho did. The only problem is that the English don't really want to understand tactics."

Conte demanded the squad ran more and completed a series of interval training distances to improve their stamina and speed endurance at their state-of-the-art facility in Cobham. Only following these was it when Conte introduced a ball because he believes the players will benefit from practicing their skills while fatigued. He values strategy and ran extra tactical sessions. The players were scheduled to attend two training sessions every day until their opening Premier League fixture.

Pre-season under Conte was not what the players expected. Preparations for the campaign were "very tough". After ten league games, having won the last four, and just a point behind pace-setters Manchester City, Arsenal and Liverpool, Gary Cahill revealed: "It was difficult. I have been there before where pre-season has been very tough and this was the same. But also the way that we work in terms of tactics, analysis of games and things like this alongside the fitness work is something you have to buy into. As a group we thought things would be different. The way he likes to work is different to what I have had before. But when something like that happens, it's important the lads buy into what's happening. Change can sometimes be a good thing or a bad thing, but you have to buy into it and work hard on what he wants. He's had success in the past and he's brought the ideas that he strongly believes in to our club now. It's about the attitude of the players to buy into what we are doing. Yes it's different. Early on in the season we were doing fitness to get us to a level."

It was at the Falkensteiner Schlosshotel on the banks of the Worthersee in the Austrian Alps where the revolution first caught the attention of the players. When they first entered the dining room before the Rapid Vienna friendly match, some walked out on seeing the array of nuts, dried fruit and snacks, assuming they were in the wrong room and went searching for their usual scrambled egg, pizza and sandwiches. However, it wasn't only the food but also the intensity of the work that was different. Not old-school running, but physical work with exercise balls and bands. And then came the video analysis! Everyone knew pre-season would be hard, but there was a level of intensity and then, later, tactical analysis which surprised even Chelsea players.

"Obviously the impression in the beginning with the manager was that we were all going to do a lot of work." said Thibaut Courtois. "There are a lot of video meetings, obviously the things that a football player doesn't like too much. Only physical work and tactical work, you prefer to play little games and have fun."

"He worked us hard." confirmed Nemanja Matic. "Not only in Austria, all season!"

Eden Hazard had a brief chat with Conte before he officially took charge. In fact Conte made a visit to all the players after being named manager, but Hazard says there was only talk of preparing for next season after Euro 2016. "Yeah, I spoke (with Conte) before." he added. "He said 'Good luck in the Euros and we will see after the Euros.'"

Retired Italian international and wide-midfielder, Angelo Di Livio, believed Conte would make wide players a priority at Chelsea. "At the beginning of his career at Juve, he (Conte) told the media that he didn't like to play out wide and that he didn't have fun there." said the ex-Juve ace. "Marcello Lippi publicly scolded him and since that moment Conte embraced his new role despite not liking it. This says a lot about someone who now emphasises the importance of wide players in his teams. It's a real lynchpin of his system. When you become a coach, you understand these things even better."

Chelsea had massively under-performed since winning the Premier League in 2015 but Claudio Ranieri backed Conte to start a revolution at Chelsea. Fresh from guiding the Foxes to the Premier

League title in 2016, he believed his compatriot will "change everything" at Stamford Bridge with his eye for detail. "He is a tough man, he will make a little revolution there." said Ranieri. "I am waiting for it; I await the revolution when he arrives. He changes everything. He is very concentrated in his job, the little things. He wants to care for everything, nutrition, everything."

At his unveiling as the new manager, Conte insisted he would settle on a tactical plan that suited the players at his disposal, rather than attempting to crowbar them into positions to which they are unsuited. He explained: "Usually when you arrive in a new team, I evaluate the right positions for the players. When I was in Italy I liked to say the manager is like a tailor who must build the best dress for the team. You have to respect their characteristics, their talents, and then you decide. In the past I started other seasons with one idea of football and then I changed it, because I saw that the system for these players was not good. Three at the back, four at the back, it's not important for us - what's important is the spirit of the team if we want to compete again for the title."

THURSDAY, 14 JULY 2016

Conte spoke to the media as Chelsea manager for the first time offering an insight into what he had planned for the season ahead and how can deal with the pressures of the Premier League. He also spoke about his tactics and clarified John Terry's role.

He'd had two days of training with his players, as he answered questions on his methods, his response to what he's seen so far, and his plans in the transfer market. Here's a full transcript:

"Good afternoon everyone. It's a great pleasure to be here. I'm very happy. I think that I worked a lot to get here and I'm excited for this moment and to start a new season with Chelsea. This is a new chapter for my life, for my career, for me, and for my family. I'm very happy to start to work in a new country, a fantastic country, in a fantastic league. I think this league is very difficult - the most difficult in the world because there are six or seven teams that can win the title, and Chelsea is a great team. I'm very proud to be the new manager of this great team."

What has he seen in training so far?

"This is my second day of training in Cobham, and I must say it's fantastic to work in Cobham. In these two days I saw players with the right attitude and behaviour, with a great will to fight for this shirt, to fight and to go back soon to compete for the best position, to compete to win the title. After these two days I'm very glad to see these things and I think that this is very important."

On John Terry's captaincy and potential new role...

"John Terry signed a contract as a player, not as a different role. He is captain of this team, he is a great player with a great personality, a great charisma. I like to speak with him because I know he knows the club, he knows the right spirit to play for this club. For me he is an important player, like the others also. All the players know that I'll judge from the training pitch and choose my starting XI. Those who deserve to play will play. When he plays he will be captain, always. I repeat that John Terry is an important player, for me, for the club, for the fans. He signed in May, but all decisions we take together - me, the club - and yes I am very pleased that John Terry signed a new deal with Chelsea. I spoke with him several times and for me it was the most important thing that John, when he signed, was that he was happy."

Does he feel under pressure at Chelsea?

"The pressure for me is not important because I was born with pressure. The pressure is not important for me. It's normal, when you are a player or a manager of a great club, you must play to win, to win the title, or to fight with the other teams to win the title. I know that this league is very difficult, because there are six or seven teams that can win the title and for this reason this situation is very exciting. We know that this year won't be easy for us because if we think of last season - 10th position was a bad season. We know that, me, the players, the club. But I think we must (focus on) the present, to work very hard every day, every week, every month to achieve something important. The fans need to see a team ready to fight until the end, and to compete with the other teams. Only one team can win the title but we must stay there at the end of the season, to fight for the title, for Champions League (qualification). Chelsea belongs in the Champions League, we must stay there."

What tactics can we expect to see?

"We've started to work on different aspects and I think that every manager has their own method, their own philosophy. I want to transfer my ideas to the players. I think that it's important to work on different aspects - tactical, technical and physical, and also on mentality - to become strong and help us to overcome difficulties during training sessions and games. It's important also to have players who have the ability to bring your ideas and methods. At the moment I'm happy about this because I know we have players ready to fight, to play, to transfer our emotion to our fans. I think this is the most important thing this year. Win or lose, but if we are able to transfer our passion to the fans, I think this is a great victory for me, for the players, for the club. I think I can improve my players a lot. It's important, I repeat, that there must be a good ability and I'm sure we can improve a lot through the work."

Is this the biggest challenge?

"I don't know if it's the hardest challenge in my career. When I arrived in Juventus, we had two 7th-place finishes in the previous two seasons, and then we built something fantastic because we won the title in the first year, then the second and third. Also the experience with the national team was fantastic but also very difficult. We had a great pressure from the media and the whole country who follow you and who see what you're doing. I think this is a great challenge. I think this is the right moment for me to arrive in England, in this tournament. (It's) very tough, but I like this, I like the challenge, I like to prove myself in this situation. I'm sure with the players and the club all together we can achieve great satisfaction at the end of the season."

Is he another 'Special One'?

"I'm not very good at finding a different name for myself. I hope during the season I will give you the opportunity to find a new name for me and I hope it'll be a good name. The most important message is that I'm a worker, I like to work, I know only this road to winning - to go back for this club very soon to compete, to go back to play in the Champions League, to go back to winning the title. I know only this verb - work, work work. But I'm very happy because I've seen the right attitude in Cobham and I'm very happy with this."

On the signing of Michy Batshuayi…

"He is a young player, but very strong. Good technique, he uses two feet, great talent. I'm very happy that Batshuayi joined us, and I know that the club bought a great player for the present and for the future."

Will we see touchline antics like at the Euros?

"This is how I am. I don't know if it's a good thing or a bad thing but I have a great passion for football, for my team, for my work. During games and during training sessions I like to stay with my players, to train together, to play with them, to win with them, to lose - I hope not so much - but that's me, I have great passion and I want to transfer my passion onto my players. Also to my fans because I suffer during the game and I want my players and fans to see this because we work during the week very hard to reach our target. When this doesn't happen, I'm not happy, but I find with all my strength to reach with my players the final victory."

What about his intense training methods?

"This league is very tough, very physical. High intensity. Very strong compared to other leagues. If you want to win, you must play good football and attractive football, but must also have a good physical condition. Usually if you have great organisation and great talent you also run more than the others. Then I think you have more probability to win and for this reason I like to work on all aspects. I think that's important."

Why did he leave his job with Italy?

"I decided to leave the national team after our qualification for the Euros because I wanted to go back to breathe the grass, to stay with my players, to improve them and to stay day by day to work with them - for this reason I decided to go back to club (football), and in the new year I had this great opportunity to speak with Chelsea, a great club. I'm very happy that we found a fantastic solution for me and for the club to work together."

How does he feel about becoming the latest 'super-coach' in the Premier League?

"In this league there are many players with great talent, fantastic players. Also there are good managers, and I think that this is very important for the league. I think that a good coach must improve his players and must work to improve all situations in the club. For me this situation is fantastic because it's a great challenge. I'm very happy to compete with them, and in this tournament it's not just a challenge between managers (it's) between great teams, great players. This is the most important thing. Also there are good managers, but I think the most important thing is when there is a game, Chelsea, United, City, Liverpool, Arsenal, Tottenham - it's all (about) teams."

How involved will he be in transfers?

"This question - I prefer to speak always with my club, to take this decision together about players (who can) adapt to our idea of football. It's important to understand this, not to take the champions only because they're a champion; we must take footballers who suit our idea of football, for our philosophy. I think that it's not right to (talk about) names of players because these players are now in other teams and I wouldn't like the other managers to speak about my players and I don't like to do the same."

On the influx of Italian managers in England...

"I think there are a number of Italian coaches that represent our country in the league this season, including (Claudio) Ranieri, who achieved something extraordinary to win the title last season. We all feel responsible for the image of Italy. We're working now in a country now with incredible atmosphere, and I can't wait to experience that first-hand. I feel responsibility for representing Italy abroad. In the coming days I will call Ranieri because he's a lovely man and I will ask for advice. When you move to a new country you do try to come in with respect, a low profile, and try to get a grip of the customs in the country."

How is he feeling about starting at Chelsea?

"First I felt very emotional about coming to Chelsea. Today is my first press conference and it feels incredible. I'm very proud and I know I've worked very hard to get here. I'm aware the league will be very competitive this season and I hope the title winners next season deserve to have taken home the title. I also hope we're slightly underrated, but I hope we're in there, that we can surprise people and this can motivate us further. I hope there's a small flame flickering that can burst into an inferno."

How does he compare with Jose Mourinho?

"I think what I'll bring with me from the experience with Italy is everything I've learned from my coaching and playing career, which makes me extremely proud. I'll also try to represent my country, this is a great responsibility for me. I'll try to make my compatriots proud. For comparisons, it's very tough to compare people. Some managers are winners, I think that regardless of the job they do; there is a winning mentality that some managers have besides their methods or philosophies. I do believe that there are winners in football, and not everyone has that in them. Those who have that are indeed special."

Metro.co.uk studied literally every word of the Chelsea coach's first press conference to see if there were any hidden messages. During the press conference Conte said: "I know only this verb - work, work work." 'Work' the fourth most used word with 16 mentions. The word 'players' used 25 times, more than any other. 'Think' and 'important' were the second and third most used. Conte already has his eye on winning the Premier League. The word 'title' was the sixth most used word with 13 mentions, a place behind 'club' which was used 15. The only other words used more than ten times were 'good', 'know' and 'win'. Draw your own conclusions.

SATURDAY, 16 JULY 2016
SK Rapid Wien 2-0 Chelsea

Conte named a strong starting XI in his first match in the recently opened Allianz Stadion and many first team regulars made up his side in his opening game; Diego Costa, Nemanja Matic, both linked with moves away from Stamford Bridge, and Willian plus Ruben Loftus-Cheek all got the chance to impress. Conte's first selection was an experienced team captained by John Terry. Asmir Begovic began in goal with Branislav Ivanovic, Baba Rahman and Papy Djilobodji in defence. Matic and John Mikel Obi were the central midfielders in the 4-2-3-1 formation. Willian, Loftus-Cheek and Victor Moses supported Costa.

From the very first whistle Conte paced his technical area giving his players instructions and a goal at the beginning of the game and one near the end settled his first pre-season friendly. Chelsea went closest through a Costa shot and a long-range effort from Ola Aina that hit the post. Interestingly, on this trip to Austria the squad was based in the market town of Velden in Carinthia, the same southern region as two years previously when they had played Rapid Wien in July 2014 under Jose Mourinho.

The new manager was anxious to give as many players as possible valuable game time in order to make a comprehensive assessment and this was an ideal opportunity, in the Austrian capital, against a side which had already played a competitive game and had returned to training five weeks previously.

There was a pre-match fanfare to celebrate the opening of the Allianz Stadion, a neat 28,000-capacity arena with an impressive large terrace behind one goal. Live music and a display of Harley-Davidson motorbikes were the highlights before kick-off, along with a match between Chelsea and Rapid's disabled teams that the hosts edged 3-2.

Oscar and Aina were the changes for the second half, replacing Loftus-Cheek and Baba in a stadium now engulfed with green smoke from flares let off by the excitable crowd. Nathaniel Chalobah later came on for Mikel. Conte brought Loic Remy and Kenedy on with a little under 20 minutes of the match remaining.

Aina struck the post with the Blues playing two up front with Remy and recent sub Bertrand Traore the central strikers, and Christian Atsu came on for Moses for the final ten minutes.

Begovic was appreciating the new work ethic and discipline. After their first week under the new coach, he explained: "It's been a good, hard week with lots of training and it was nice to finish it off with a match and get the cobwebs off. We are buying into what the manager wants us to do. We are working hard to try and improve. We're working in a different way so it's going to take a bit of time to process but so far so good, and I think over time we'll get better. He communicates very well, so he got his message across at half-time and before the game. We expect to work hard, that's part of pre-season. We're trying to be very disciplined. The work ethic is very strong. We've got some hard days ahead, we need to get our base fitness and it is something that will do us good in the long run. We're enjoying the hard work."

Conte believed the players were still feeling low about the disappointments of the previous campaign. "It's important to come back with the right enthusiasm. I understand after a bad season there is a bit of sadness with the players, the club and the fans, but I can assure there will be a great passion to change the situation. I know the club will stay with me; we are together with every decision, good or bad. I think that's the most important thing and a good spot to start."

Despite only having worked with the squad for a matter of days, Conte felt the players were desperately eager to put things right. "From these past few days I understand the players are ready to work and fight because they want to play a different way compared to last season." he told the Chelsea FC website. "They know last season wasn't just bad, but very bad. Every single player knows this and wants to change the story."

SUNDAY, 17 JULY 2016

The "speech" from Conte and being convinced by Chelsea's "project" had persuaded N'Golo Kante to sign, according to his tweet. He thanked Claudio Ranieri, his teammates, and the Foxes' fans for their support while explaining his choice.

"The 2015/16 past season will remain as an important season for me as a football player. After a fantastic season, it ended with a final of Euro 2016 with the French National team. We lost, but we can be proud."

"Our team and the fervor of the French people have given us strength and I wanted to say THANK YOU ALL. Of course it has to be appreciated according to the attack that struck in Nice on July 14th and I have at this point a sincere thought for all the victims and their families."

"This season, I also discovered the Premier League championship with FC Leicester. I want to thank the leaders, my teammates and Claudio Ranieri for this fantastic season that saw us winning the title of England. Their confidence and also the fans will forever remain in my memory. And I again thank you all. At the beginning of the 2016/17 season I chose to join Chelsea FC club. It is a great club, which has just recruited a great coach and wants to reach high ambitions I share. The club's project and the coach's speech have convinced me to join this new ambitious adventure. I am now waiting to see my new club and give everything for a successful summer... and season of course!!! We keep in touch! N'Golo."

TUESDAY, 19 JULY 2016

Loic Remy discussed Conte's "intense" and "tactical" training methods as the new coach put the squad through their paces as they began their mini pre-season tour of Austria.

"It's good to be back and for me it's very important that I don't have any more injury problems this season." Remy told the official Chelsea website. "The preparation is very important for me, I feel really well so far but it's a long time since I played. Last year was very difficult for me because I had a lot of injuries, but this is a new page now. I hope to stay free from injuries and to have a better season." he added.

Conte's training methods differ from what the club have become used to. "I feel very good. The preparations are very different to what we did last season and the one before. With the new staff we have been working very hard and even though the result against Rapid Vienna was disappointing I think we will win the next game. All the players want to be involved in the new project, the commitment is there and there is no reason for us not to be ready for the first game of the season. They are very intense sessions but at the same time you have to work on the basics." said Remy. "It's very tactical which is good for us, because as players you need to have direction and know what to do with and without the ball. It's been very tough but all the players are enjoying working with the new manager."

WEDNESDAY, 20 JULY 2016

WAC RZ Pellets 0-3 Chelsea

The first win of the Conte era was in Klagenfurt as goals from Bertrand Traore and substitutes Ruben Loftus-Cheek and Nathaniel Chalobah secured victory.

Conte made three changes, Ola Aina, who performed well as a second-half substitute at the weekend, came in for Baba Rahman at left-back. Oscar and Traore were handed their first starts of pre-season, with Mikel and Loftus-Cheek making way. Those players who only joined up with the squad the day before were not involved at all.

Conte started in the same way as they ended Saturday's match against Rapid Wien, playing 4-2-4. Matic partnered by Oscar in central midfield, with Traore and Costa the strike partnership. Willian, on the right, and Moses, on the opposite flank, were playing high up the pitch, although on the rare occasions when WAC were in possession they dropped deeper, making the formation more of a 4-4-2.

Papy Djilobodji started alongside Terry for the second consecutive game. Baba replaced Ivanovic in what was a solitary change at the break, allowing Aina to move to right-back. Just before the hour, Batshuayi was handed his first minutes in a Chelsea shirt as the Belgian striker replaced Costa, and at the same time Loftus-Cheek and Michael Hector came on for Traore and Djilobodji. Loftus-Cheek played alongside Batshuayi and the England Under-21 man was looking threatening every time he was in possession.

WEDNESDAY, 21 JULY 2016

Former goalkeeper Carlo Cudicini returned as part of Conte's new-look backroom team. Cudicini, who spent nine years at Stamford Bridge, making 141 Premier League appearances, had a dual role as club ambassador and assistant to the first team coach. Another former goalkeeper, Henrique Hilario, joined the coaching staff as assistant to goalkeeper coach Gianluca Spinelli, who had worked for both Italy and Genoa for the past 12 years. Conte had three assistant coaches: Angelo Alessio, who has been with Conte since their Siena days, younger brother Gianluca Conte and Steve Holland, who had worked with the first team since 2011. Additionally, there are three more from the Italian national set-up: fitness coaches Paolo Bertelli and Julio Tous, supported by assistant fitness coach Constantino Coratti.

Conte's brother Gianluca worked as a tactical analyst with him at Bari, Juventus, and Italy.

THURSDAY, 22 JULY 2016

Michy Batshuayi knew he had joined the right club just one day after arriving.

The 22-year-old signed for the Blues for £33 million this month and was already enjoying his time with the team. "It feels fantastic to be here, it's a childhood dream for me so I'm very happy." the Belgian told the Chelsea club magazine. "It's a magnificent feeling. Just being at the training ground for one day I can see it's very big and you feel you've joined a club that really want to win. Everything is new and that is exciting."

On Conte, he said: "It's a great opportunity. He is a manager who works very hard and likes people to work hard for him as well. I am very pleased to come and play for him here at Chelsea."

FRIDAY, 23 JULY 2016

Branislav Ivanovic was ruled out for three weeks with a dislocated shoulder and would now possibly miss the first games of the season including, of course, Conte's first competitive match in charge, against West Ham United.

The 32-year-old had picked up the injury in the 3-0 friendly victory over RZ Pellets, but it had only now been confirmed as a serious issue. Ivanovic was widely criticised for his performances last season, and this setback won't help him to turn it around in the coming campaign as Cesar Azpilicueta would move over to right-back.

SATURDAY, 24 JULY 2016

N'Golo Kante will wear the No.7 shirt, the club confirmed. Kante completed his £32m transfer from Premier League champions Leicester City, just 12 months after he had arrived in England as part of a £4.8m deal from French side Caen. The France international opted for the No.7, a jersey number vacated since Brazilian midfielder Ramires was sold to Chinese side Jiangsu Suning FC for £25m in January. Didier Deschamps, Winston Bogarde, Adrian Mutu, Maniche and Andriy Shevchenko are some other famous No.7 names for Chelsea.

After his Euro 2016 exploits with France Kante was now impressing his new teammates as Ruben Loftus-Cheek explained. "He is a great asset to us." Loftus-Cheek told Goal. "His stamina and how he can get up and down the pitch for 90 minutes (is impressive). He is a really good player so we are lucky to have him. He is a really hard worker and he is a proper team player. We could do with that in midfield and he could really help. Some people's careers take off at different moments, he wasn't on the radar but then for Leicester City he has done really well, won a title for them and now he is going to be playing for Chelsea so I am really happy for him and the club are really happy to have him. We have all met him and welcomed him, he looks good in training. He is quite powerful and it will be good to play with him and see what he can do. We will have to see what happens in the game, I am sure we will link up well. We are doing tactics in training, trying to get used to the movements so I think he will be good. I watched the Euros and he really does look good. He is fast, powerful and can head the ball so we are lucky to have him."

Conte ruled out letting Matic leave following the arrival of Kante. "Matic is an important player for me, a very important player." he said. "In my idea of football he is an important player and he knows this. N'Golo, Nemanja, Cesc, Oscar, Chalobah and Mikel who is in the Olympics, it is not easy to choose. I want this problem."

MONDAY, 25 JULY 2016

Several stars were put through their paces on a YouTube quiz about the USA ahead of the club's pre-season tour to the States. Pedro, Eden Hazard and Asmir Begovic gave some particularly bad answers but every player struggled with knowing how many states there are in America (50); at least Courtois and Begovic were close with 52. Pedro's answer of 32 was a shocker.

Hazard was unaware that Arnold Schwarzenegger was the former governor of California. Pedro attempted a sneaky answer to the MLS club Didier Drogba plays for with a 'yes' while Pedro and Begovic both thought the USA's first president was John F. Kennedy.

Conte promised to give the highly-rated youth prospects a chance. Jose Mourinho had been accused of not promoting youth amid a wealth of high-profile signings - a point Conte subtly pointed out. "There are many players with a good prospect for Chelsea. I don't know why in the past (only) a few players have played with the first team." Conte told ESPN. "It's important because Chelsea has a fantastic academy. I think that the academy is a great source for the manager of the first team. It's important, also, that the young players must show to play in the first team. But I love to play with the young players and to improve them. It's important to have good quality to improve and to show that a young player can play with the first team. I haven't any problem with the choice to take a young player in the starting eleven. For example, Pogba. Pogba arrived at Juventus and he was only 18-years old and after three months he played in the starting eleven."

TUESDAY, 26 JULY 2016

Victor Moses wanted to play as a winger. He was used out wide in the two pre-season games and was hopeful Conte would continue to deploy him in the role. "That is my position really, staying out wide and most of the time going into 1 v 1 situations which I am good at. It is similar to the kind of game I was playing at Wigan and I have really enjoyed the two games. As a winger, you want to get at defenders and make it hard for them. Instead of them going forwards, they have to defend against you."

Chelsea had glamour pre-season fixtures, as part of the club's tour of the United States, against Liverpool, Real Madrid and AC Milan.

Despite the high-profile matches, preparations were no different from Conte's first sessions. "The work has not really changed from Austria." Moses told Chelsea's official website. "We just need to work hard to make sure we are a lot fitter come the start of the season. Everyone is looking sharp, everyone wants to do the work and we are excited; we have got a new manager and we all just want to work as hard as we can. I came back to start my pre-season early with the group of players who had been on loan last season, which helped as well, but to be honest I just want to enjoy my football. I want the fans to be able to recognise I am doing something good for the club but at the same time I want to work hard for the team and make sure we win games. We have played two games so far so we still need to get our fitness up and we have a game coming up against Liverpool which is going to be good for us."

WEDNESDAY, 27 JULY 2016

Atletico Madrid gave up in their pursuit of Diego Costa after Conte refused to sell him. Diego Simeone had made Costa his top target but Conte's insistence regarding his sale forced the Argentine to look elsewhere.

Conte wanted a new centre-half but Roma coach, Luciano Spalletti, reacted quickly to end Manchester United, Arsenal and Chelsea's interest in Kostas Manolas insisting the Greek defender would not be moving. "In my opinion, and especially for those who are here, it is easy to see that there are no problems." he said. "Manolas is a good footballer, like there are many good footballers, and so it can happen that he will be linked in the transfer market - indeed it is inevitable. But his intentions are clear, so there are no issues. Why not talk instead about the problem of writing about issues that are not there? Manolas will stay with us."

Kalidou Koulibaly was chased by Chelsea, according to his agent Bruno Satin but Napoli wanted to avoid offloading the 25-year-old. Conte sanctioned a £37m bid for the Senegalese central defender. Satin claimed his client would not agree a contract extension in favour of a move to England. "I was in Dimaro (northern Italy) on Saturday and we discussed a contract renewal." Satin told Radio CRC. "However, we are not at the point of reaching an agreement. The desire of the player is to leave the club, not renew. We are told by the club that he is a great player but from the renewal on offer, we don't see this. Last year they wanted to sell him, stating he was not focused enough, but then last season he has shown all his quality. To the fans I say stay calm because he won't be joining Juventus. Chelsea and Everton are still interested as they are both searching for a central defender of his quality."

Chelsea, in need of new additions at centre-back with John Terry likely to play less of a prominent role, then switched their focus to Lazio defender Stefan de Vrij after becoming frustrated in their bid to sign Koulibaly with Napoli demanding £45m, while De Vrij was available for £15m. But the Dutchman had suffered from injury problems during his time with Lazio.

Italian defender, Leonardo Bonucci, had already, much earlier in the summer, shrugged off claims he was set to seal a transfer to Chelsea. The 28-year-old Juve centre-back declared himself uninterested in a move. "If I've ever followed Conte, then it's been to get a coffee at most." Bonucci said. "I don't know where he's going to go, but I've signed a new contract at Juventus and I'm only thinking about the Bianconeri (the white & blacks)."

Bonucci had enjoyed a fantastic season in Serie A and his rejection came as a big blow to Chelsea.

With such bad luck at recruiting a centre-half, Conte was running out of options in the summer transfer window. Well… there was always David Luiz. No, surely Not?

John Terry confirmed his plans were most definitely to stay at Chelsea. "I still want to play for a couple of years, hopefully that's at Chelsea." Terry told Brondby TV. "I'm a Chelsea player and that has been my club since the age of 14. I love Chelsea." Terry had made 703 appearances, and clearly wished that to continue.

Chelsea's pursuit of Roma midfielder Radja Nainggolan was over quite early in the summer after the Belgium international stated his intention to stay with the Serie A club. Chelsea held extensive talks with Roma over a possible move and the Serie A giants were happy to let the midfielder leave for the right price but Nainggolan wanted to stay in the Italian capital. "I will stay." Nainggolan told fans at a Sky Italia event. "I'm not moving from here. I'm happy in Rome, I don't want to leave."

Everton striker Romelu Lukaku was determined to return to Chelsea in an effort to prove himself at the club. The 23-year-old believed he had unfinished business at Stamford Bridge after failing to make an impact in a three-year spell between 2011 and 2014 - or at least that was according to The Sun on Sunday, even though the club signed his international teammate and fellow forward Batshuayi.

THURSDAY, 28 JULY 2016
Chelsea 1-0 Liverpool

An early Gary Cahill goal was sufficient to divide the sides in the first of three matches in the United States.

It was quite an occasion for Conte as he had previously been in the Rose Bowl in Pasadena, California, when he was on the subs' bench for Italy's World Cup final defeat against Brazil in 1994.

Cesc Fabregas was sent off during the second half but he was on long enough to deliver the decisive pass for Cahill's goal. Nemanja Matic and the entire defence played the full game. Liverpool had plenty of the ball in midfield but only one effort on target from a free-kick.

The impressive Victor Moses started wide on the left against one of the clubs he had represented on loan, and Bertrand Traore and Ruben Loftus-Cheek were the two 20-year-olds paired together in attack. Cesar Azpilicueta played left-back, Ola Aina right-back with John Terry and Cahill in central defence again.

Chelsea's counter-attacking was showing promise and fresh legs were added when Conte introduced Juan Cuadrado, Michy Batshuayi and Pedro with a quarter of the game to go. However, the Blues were soon a man down when Fabregas was shown a straight red for a late tackle on Ragnar Klavan. Nathaniel Chalobah came on for Loftus-Cheek to rebalance the side and the 10-men held out under the pressure.

To be fair, Fabregas visited the Liverpool dressing room afterwards to apologise for his late challenge on Reds new-boy Klavan, with Conte also issuing an apology. Conte said: "I am sorry and the player is too. I am sorry for him and the Liverpool player. In this period it is easy to go too late into a tackle. I know Fabregas is a good man and a good boy and he is not the type of player to have this situation. When two great teams face each other nobody wants to lose, and for this reason we saw a competitive game."

FRIDAY, 29 JULY 2016

Conte wants "shy" new recruit N'Golo Kante to become one of the most important players at Chelsea.

The Chelsea manager welcomed him to training for the first time and the Frenchman was already impressing him with his quiet determination. "For N'Golo today, it was the first day of training and he started to look at our idea of football, to understand our mentality and we are pleased to have N'Golo with us." Conte told the club website. "I think he is a player that doesn't speak a lot but he does fight and it's very important, a good guy, humble and with a great will to work. I explained to him what I expect on the pitch and I think he's an important player, he can become an important player for Chelsea in the midfield; in the same way like Matic, like Fabregas. I am pleased to have all the players, it's very important because we know that in 20 days we start and we need to start in a good way. I think N'Golo is a bit shy. He just arrived in Chelsea and he must take confidence with the club, his teammates and the manager. But I am pleased he is here. His physical condition is fantastic. He's a runner. He has great stamina. He has fantastic endurance, he's in good shape but we want to respect the time in training sessions, to get him to play with us in the future."

SATURDAY, 30 JULY 2016
Real Madrid 3-2 Chelsea

The attendance in 'The Big House' in Ann Arbor, Michigan, the second largest stadium in the world, was 105,826 as they watched Chelsea, in the new dark second kit, against the white of Real. The European champions raced into a 3-0 lead by half-time, their goals scored by Marcelo, on target twice, and Mariano Diaz. Following the break Hazard calmly netted twice having come on in the second half.

Conte made two changes from the starting line-up two days earlier. One was enforced with Oscar replacing Fabregas, who was serving a one-match suspension, and Pedro was picked in place of Moses.

The rain that had fallen hard during the morning had abated by kick-off, fortunately for those in the uncovered stadium at 3pm local time, but it left the pitch wet.

Oscar, playing in a deeper role than for much of his Chelsea career, had begun the game well and one especially forceful challenge on Mateo Kovacic drew gasps from the crowd.

Changes at the break included the introduction of two of the Euro 2016 quarter-finalists, Thibaut Courtois and Batshuayi. Chalobah and Cuadrado also came on.

After Real had made a raft of substitutions and Hazard come on for Pedro,

Moses, only just on the pitch, was brought down by Zinedine Zidane's son Enzo on the edge of the area. Although Hazard cleared the bar with the free-kick, the Belgian was on target soon after when he beat substitute keeper Yanez to a Chalobah long pass and slotted it inside the near post. Hazard added his second in stoppage time and it was a near carbon copy of his first, with Batshuayi this time supplying the pass.

SUNDAY, 31 JULY 2016

Conte planned to deny Zlatan Ibrahimovic the Premier League title at United - just as he denied him when they were both working in Italy.

Conte's greatest achievement was winning the 2011/12 Serie A, the title in his first season as Juventus manager bringing Ibrahimovic's incredible run of title wins to an end. He had extraordinarily won a domestic title every year from 2003/04, spanning Ajax, Juventus, Inter Milan, Barcelona and AC Milan until it came to an end because of Conte. "It was fantastic." said Conte of the first of three league titles in Turin. "We started the season as the underdog and the press had us down for sixth or seventh place in the table. Milan had Zlatan, it was the only season when he didn't win the championship and I hope this season is the same again."

Conte continued: "Inter had won the Treble in the season before under Mourinho and Napoli had Edinson Cavani and Marek Hamsik. In that period we were the underdogs and we won our first title unbeaten - and the Cup."

CHAPTER FIVE
AUGUST 2016
A flying start, four straight wins,
Hazard back to his best, and David Luiz re-signs.

Conte banned his players from having sauces and fizzy drinks with their food. They were still allowed salt and pepper, but vinegar was replaced by balsamic vinegar and olive oil.

According to The Times, Conte rated diet as an important part of his training system, and has also changed the Blues' pre-match meal. Instead of a carbohydrate-heavy meal of eggs, pasta, and cereals, the team have a small serving of chicken and salad to stop bloating. Despite all the new restrictions and extra work, the players were happy with the new regime. In the past managers have been criticised for taking away certain foods from their players, with Rio Ferdinand losing his rag once as David Moyes took away chips from his Manchester United squad.

THURSDAY, 4 AUGUST 2016
AC Milan 1-3 Chelsea

An opener from Bertrand Traore and an Oscar brace were enough to claim victory at the opening of the US Bank Stadium in Minneapolis.

Burkinabe forward Traore nodded Chelsea in front from a rebound halfway through a competitive first half before Giacomo Bonaventura curled home a stunning free-kick to level the scores before the break.

The pace slowed in the second half as a number of substitutions broke up the play, but one of them, Oscar, took the limelight when he first placed a penalty into the top corner after a Milan player had handled, and then powered a low drive into the bottom corner after good work by Cuadrado.

Diego Costa returned to action from the start of the game following a short injury lay-off while Matic came back with Courtois starting his first game of the pre-season. Kante was on the bench alongside Hazard.

Neither side made changes at the break, as Chelsea's back four started its sixth consecutive half together. Five minutes into the second half Conte made his first changes, Kante, for his Chelsea debut, and Hazard in place of Moses and Traore. There was a change of shape with Kante dropping deep in front of the defence to make a 4-3-3. More changes followed with Ivanovic, back after a shoulder injury, Oscar and Batshuayi all introduced.

Hazard's intended cross was handled by Andrea Poli, and Oscar took the responsibility of side-footing the spot kick beyond the keeper's reach to restore the lead. The Belgian suffered rough treatment from the Italian defenders, becoming the third Chelsea player in need of a jersey change after one overzealous challenge.

Four minutes from time another substitute, Cuadrado, attracted two defenders down the right flank before supplying the unmarked Oscar with a well-weighted pass, allowing the No.8 to smash his second of the night into the bottom corner and put the game beyond their opponents' reach.

Conte took plenty of positives from this victory, plus the fixture attracted the biggest crowd ever for a football match in Minnesota. The squad then flew home before jetting to Germany to complete the pre-season against Werder Bremen.

"There remains work to do before we face West Ham… but things are coming together." was the observation in the club's online match report.

SUNDAY, 7 AUGUST 2016

Werder Bremen 2-4 Chelsea

Hazard, Oscar, Costa and Pedro all scored, ending pre-season with an exciting victory in northern Germany.

The attacking trio of Hazard, Oscar and Oscar linked up sublimely, all getting a goal and an assist each. It was the Brazilian's third goal in his last 40 minutes of football following his brace against AC Milan on the other side of the Atlantic.

Kante played all but the final ten minutes, starting for the first time. He was industrious and effective throughout.

Hazard opened the scoring from range and Oscar doubled it instantly with a cute finish. Former Blue Claudio Pizarro then reduced the arrears from the spot, but Costa restored the two-goal advantage on the stroke of half-time. Sub Pedro completed the scoring right on full-time.

Conte was now fully focused on the Premier League opener against West Ham.

FRIDAY, 12 AUGUST 2016

Conte sometimes sleeps for only two hours the night before matches due to his incessant preoccupation with the upcoming fixtures, occasionally thinking up tactical tweaks in the very early hours.

"When you win, you know yourself about the sacrifices you have made, the many nights you haven't slept. That's important because, when you win the title, you reach a great level with your soul, your mind. You work very, very hard to have this moment. Before games, usually, I don't sleep a lot. Maybe two, three, four hours. Then, when I wake up, I start to think about the game and the situation, and often I have good ideas about the tactical aspects in the first hour of the morning. After the game, when I win, I sleep easily. When I don't win, it is very difficult for me. When I'm awake in the middle of the night I'm thinking, 'Why? What is the reason we lost? What was the situation that made it more difficult? Which players made it more difficult? Was our tactical plan good or not good?' I need to try to find the reply quickly. Lately, I have been lucky because I often won with Italy and Juventus. But when it happened that I lost a game, I needed to think quickly, 'Why did we have that result?' In the Euros, when we lost to Ireland, we had already qualified, but we lost the game. In the middle of the night, I wanted to watch the match again to understand, 'Why, what was the reason we lost today?'"

SATURDAY, 13 AUGUST 2016

Conte assured Chelsea fans that Diego Costa would not be leaving. "I am happy that he (Costa) stayed here and decided to work with us." Conte said. "We know he can improve with the work. I like the spirit of Diego because he always shows a great passion, I am the same, I have great passion for this football. He doesn't want to lose and I like that passion, I want this passion in the team. I know that he is a fantastic finisher and I think that Diego can improve the team a lot. Now, he is a fantastic player but he can improve a lot and I hope for this. Diego is a forward and he knows that in my idea of football, the forward must always be a point of reference for the team. I don't like them to move around the pitch, I like them to stay there because you are a forward, you are committed to score the goals, stay in the right position, to play. You are a forward, not a midfielder or a defender. I never ask this of my striker, never, never. I ask my players to have the right attitude, right behaviour and right commitment. It is important that the players play our style of football. I think all the players need to improve, not only for Diego Costa. My work is to win but also to improve the players. It is important for me to leave him a percentage to improve. I think the coach or manager must improve his players in different aspects, my job is this, to improve my players. Maybe the most important thing."

SUNDAY, 14 AUGUST 2016

A frustrating time in the transfer market led Conte to brand current fees as "crazy".

"I think Chelsea at the moment is waiting for the right solution. The price is too high in general. The market is a bit crazy because when you try to buy one or another player the cost is very, very expensive and not the real valuation of the player. A very strange situation. I speak every day with the club. We have a plan. We know this transfer market is very crazy. We must be patient to find the right solutions for the team. It's important to speak every day with the club to find the right solutions to improve. But I am very happy to work with these players, they show me great commitment every day."

MONDAY, 15 AUGUST 2016
Chelsea 2-1 West Ham United
Premier League

Conte lived up to his reputation of being passionate and animated on the touchline by rushing towards fans to celebrate Costa's winner. "I knew the Premier League only through television. I played against English teams in the Champions League and Europa League, but playing this league is very difficult. There is a great intensity in the Premier League and it's very physical. I don't know if I'll sleep tonight because the adrenaline is high."

The fans loved it as Conte gave a glimpse of the touchline passion he was famed for as Italy manager over the course Euro 2016 and they expressed their delight on social media.

The Italian cut a frustrated figure for much of the second half as Chelsea failed to build on the lead given to them by Hazard's penalty shortly after the restart, and he was almost incandescent with rage when James Collins looked to have secured a point with a late equaliser. But Costa's 89th minute goal sparked wild touchline celebrations for an opening season win.

Costa found the net from 20 yards to spark wild scenes at Stamford Bridge, with Conte celebrating among supporters. Chelsea supporters hugged their new manager in delight as he sprinted along the front of the stands following the late goal. It was the start of things to come!

Hazard had put the Blues in front from the spot after Michail Antonio fouled Azpilicueta. James Collins levelled for the Hammers, but Costa's finish settled it. There were questions of whether Chelsea could mount a title challenge as they dominated possession but failed to finish off the visitors until very late on. But after a disastrous start to last season, which led to Mourinho's sacking and a 10th-place finish, Conte's arrival instantly injected passion into a side routinely accused of lacking commitment under their former manager.

The all-action, energetic performance of £30m midfield signing N'Golo Kante and the vibrancy of Eden Hazard, were positive and encouraging signs. Hazard looked particularly sharp and creative, following an impressive European Championships for his country.

Conte was likely to pursue further signings, with Batshuayi - a late substitute - the only other new arrival to date.

Hazard told Sky Sports: "It was good to be back on the pitch in front of our own supporters. We did very well and we played 90 minutes like tigers. It's not every year I score in my first game. Last season is finished - we are looking forward to the future. We want to bring a lot of emotion to the fans."

Slaven Bilic was disappointed as the Hammers failed to produce a single shot on target until Collins lashed home a loose ball after a 77th-minute corner. Bilic told Sky Sports: "When you lose a game and concede late, of course you are disappointed. Apart from the first 15 minutes until we equalised, they were much better than us. They were better on the ball, in pressing and much more aggressive than us. They had the individual class of Eden Hazard, Diego Costa and Willian. We came back into the game. We played well after 1-1, but we made the mistake in the middle of the park. We gave the ball away and conceded a cheap goal."

Costa was fortunate to still be on the pitch when, having already been booked for remonstrating with the referee, he escaped a second booking after catching Adrian high up on the shin with a late challenge on the keeper. Conte said the referee "made the right decision" in taking no action against Costa. Anthony Taylor did not produce a second yellow card and Costa went on to net the winner. Conte did a 'Wenger' when he said he "did not see" the tackle, adding: "I saw Costa put the pressure on the keeper and then try to stop."

Conversely, Bilic didn't see it that way. "It was not reckless or deliberate, but it was quite late. He could have been booked again and so a red card. I am not frustrated because of that, I am frustrated because of the late goal."

Referees were instructed to book players who protest against decisions and Costa was initially cautioned for chasing Taylor following a penalty appeal. "Diego is a good player and a passionate man - sometimes it happens that he can receive a yellow card." Conte told Sky Sports. "I think in the situation with Adrian the referee took the right decision."

THURSDAY, 18 AUGUST 2016

Costa was fed up being singled out for what he considered unfair treatment by English referees.

He had scored the dramatic late winner against West Ham but earlier in the game Costa was booked for dissent having fallen foul of the FA's new stringent policy regarding the abuse of officials and he felt he was unfairly targeted.

"I can't ask for anything, the crowd here always loved me. It's a support which I always appreciate. It's important to get the three points, it's important to start winning." Costa told ESPN Brasil. "I am aware of (the new dissent law) now. The second time I went to talk to him, he showed me (the yellow card). I even found it a bit weird, but then I understood. I went to apologise at half-time and that's it. But I'll be honest, I am targeted here, by the referees, the people... if I do something, it's totally different than if any other players do. It needs to be seen, that people target me. It's something I have to deal with and I ask God that these things don't disturb me and don't take the sequence of the games from me, which happens sometimes and gives me suspensions."

FRIDAY, 19 AUGUST 2016

Conte confirmed he was still on the lookout for defensive signings.

"I think we need to sign some players. We have too few players in defence and we are working with the club to find a solution. We arrive after a season which was not so good but we are working very hard to improve the situation but, if you ask me, the real target of this squad now is very difficult. We need to pass more time to have a better answer game by game. I have contact every day but I discuss this with the club. We must find solutions." If Conte planned to play with three at the back, as he did at Juventus and Italy, the need became even greater.

Real Madrid manager Zinedine Zidane explained that signing Fabregas would be "complicated".

"If you want to put another central midfielder into the mix then it becomes complicated." Zidane said after Real Madrid's 5-3 friendly victory over Stade de Reims. "Cesc is a great player but it is not very straightforward. I am going to end up with a squad where three or four players do not get selected. To therefore put another player in there makes it difficult."

SATURDAY, 20 AUGUST 2016
Watford 1-2 Chelsea
Premier League

Diego Costa scored the winner for the second game in a row as Chelsea came from behind.

Etienne Capoue put the Hornets ahead on 56 minutes as the hosts looked in control of the game, but substitute Michy Batshuayi equalised with his first goal for Chelsea since his £33m move. Then Costa ran on to substitute Cesc Fabregas's pass and slid the ball under Gomes with three minutes left as Conte maintained a 100% start in the Premier League.

Chelsea seemed to be running out of ideas and with only one shot on target Conte made his first change on 71 minutes bringing on Victor Moses, Batshuayi and Fabregas. Batshuayi opened his Premier League account just seven minutes after coming on, reacting fastest when Gomes spilled Eden Hazard's shot. Hazard collected just his second assist in twenty six Premier League appearances. Fabregas, an unused substitute against West Ham, then found Costa with a perfectly-weighted pass through the Watford defence for the decisive late strike. Since returning to the Premier League in 2014, Fabregas now has more assists than any other player (26).

Conte and Walter Mazzarri had met seven times in Serie A as managers, with the new Watford boss coming out on top only once, back in 2010. The build-up was dominated by the rivalry between the two Italians and Conte admitted the pair fell out during their time coaching with Napoli and Juve.

Mazzarri seemed to have his tactics spot on for eighty minutes of the match. His side pressed well and nullified the attacking trio of Pedro, Oscar and Hazard. Despite Chelsea enjoying almost two-thirds of the possession Watford thoroughly deserved the lead when Capoue controlled Adlene Guedioura's cross with his chest and, with acres of space in the box, rifled a left-foot shot high into the net. Chelsea had now kept just one clean sheet in their past eight Premier League away games.

Conte sparked Chelsea into life with his changes, but, for the second match running, Costa was lucky to have been still on the pitch to score the winner. He was booked for dissent after Watford's goal and ten minutes later dived in the area, but referee Jon Moss waved play on.

Match of the Day presenter Gary Lineker tweeted: "Costa scores the winner in the first 2 games.

Costa lucky to stay on the pitch in the first 2 games."

Conte said: "If every game people find something on Diego it is no good for Chelsea, for Diego, it's better to focus on the game and the match. For me, the first yellow is no good. I don't accept the idea for a second yellow card for a dive but he does have to avoid the first. Diego must be focusing on the game. I don't understand other players, managers or the press that talk bad about him. He must stay very positive on the match because for me the game and the performance are the most important things. It is important to pay attention during the game - only this - because he is an important player and he can score a lot of goals and I want him to put himself in the game and not seek other situations."

"I'm pleased to see the reaction from my players and this win is very important for us as it gives everyone confidence. I don't know what was wrong in the first half - but I repeat that every game in this league is tough. It is wrong to come to Watford and to think it's very simple to win. In the first half I saw a good balance between the teams. I think we showed a great intensity in the second half and we pushed them a lot. I'm pleased for the substitutes. They didn't start but they showed great attitude and commitment with Fabregas and Batshuayi making a real impact."

Mazzarri commented: "I am happy for how we played for 70-80 minutes because we played very well but I am not happy with the result. They scored two goals that could have been avoided. We are a team that still has room to grow and there is margin for improvement. We played very well so the way we played in the first half, we could have scored twice."

Hazard praised the impact of Fabregas, who replaced Matic in the second half and had a decisive impact, setting up Costa's winner with a defence-splitting through ball. "It's difficult because to find the space is not easy. But when Cesc came on he made the assist for Diego and created a lot of situations but we did well and know it's not easy." Hazard said during an interview with Chelsea TV. "We have lots of players on the bench. The manager asks everyone to do a job and when Victor (Moses) was on the pitch, when Cesc came on, they did well."

Conte had now lost just one of his last 32 league games as a club manager, winning 29 and two drawn.

TUESDAY, 23 AUGUST 2016
Chelsea 3-2 Bristol Rovers
EFL Cup, Second Round

Fabregas was back in the starting line-up having been left on the bench by Conte for their opening Premier League fixtures, which had been a cause of concern for many supporters. However, after his quality cameo appearance off the bench at the weekend, where he provided a sumptuous assist for Costa late on against Watford, he got his chance.

Michy Batshuayi was also handed his first start and well and truly grasped the opportunity as he scored twice to edge Chelsea past a spirited Bristol Rovers. The £33m summer signing from Marseille volleyed in after 29 minutes and Victor Moses struck from close range two minutes later. Peter Hartley halved the lead by heading in a free-kick before Batshuayi restored the hosts' two-goal cushion. Ellis Harrison scored a penalty and struck the bar for the League One side, but Chelsea maintained their 100% record under Conte.

The Premier League side had enjoyed the vast majority of possession in the first half but were denied by excellent goalkeeping from Steve Mildenhall as well as being guilty of wasteful finishing.

Batshuayi, initially one of those who missed chances, took his tally to three goals in three games with two smart finishes; Loftus-Cheek involved in the build-up to both. Around 4,000 vocal Rovers fans had plenty to cheer with two goals, in addition to spells in the second half when their side caused problems. That revival persuaded Conte to send on Hazard, Terry and Oscar in an attempt to preserve Chelsea's lead, while Batshuayi was denied a hat-trick in the closing stages by the referee's assistant's flag.

FRIDAY, 26 AUGUST 2016

Conte was concerned about signing his targets after a poor summer for transfers. With only five days left to go in the window, he stated: "I must be honest, I think we'll have a problem to reach our target. But we must think to work, to improve every day. I hope to improve the squad with some new players, but we understand that our targets are very difficult to reach. I think that the most important thing is the work we do, to improve the squad that you are working with now. The league is very tough, it's important to have many players to face this situation. This market is very crazy, we're seeing it's very difficult to reach our targets. But now we have a game against Burnley which is more important than the market. (By the end of the window) I hope to have some more players than now."

SATURDAY, 27 AUGUST 2016

Chelsea 3-0 Burnley

Premier League

It was Eden Hazard who opened the scoring when he burst forward from halfway early in the first half before finishing low into the corner. Willian then added a second just before the break with a clinical strike. Substitute Moses wrapped up the win by sliding home a late finish.

Chelsea were top of the table, level with Manchester United on nine points from three games, but ahead on goals scored.

Two seasons ago Hazard was arguably the best player in the Premier League as his 14 goals and nine assists helped Chelsea to win the title. However, he was a shadow of his former self last season, failing to score in the Premier League until the end of April and his loss of form partly resulting in the departure of Mourinho. Under Conte, though, already he had rediscovered his best form. His second goal in four games was reminiscent of those he scored at his peak, charging at the defence before despatching a perfectly placed strike beyond Tom Heaton's dive. The Clarets had no answer for Hazard, whose clever runs and tricky feet caused the visitors' defence, and in particular full-back Matt Lowton, problems throughout. To win the title, they would need Hazard at his best and already the indications were good.

Conte favoured either a 4-1-4-1 or a 4-2-4 formation, requiring a lot of work from the wingers and Hazard and Willian were successful with a goal apiece. Their replacements, Pedro and Moses, combined for Chelsea's third. Costa had now had a hand in a goal in each of his last five Premier League appearances (three goals, two assists) and Moses scored his first Premier League goal for Chelsea since November 2012.

Burnley had produced the result of the season so far by beating Liverpool 2-0 in their previous game in which they only had 19% possession against the Reds. However, they certainly made the most of their limited time on the ball, while their disciplined two banks of four frustrated Jurgen Klopp's side throughout. That was not the case this time though.

Conte was now unbeaten in his last 30 home league matches as a manager (W28 D2). The Blues ended a run of 13 home Premier League games without a clean sheet, with their last coming in a 2-0 win over Norwich back in November 2015. Conte commented: "I am pleased to see the team play well and create a lot of chances. After 13 games where we have conceded at home, we didn't this time and that is very important. Now we must continue. I want Hazard to be decisive at the beginning and I am pleased because I saw this today. However we must continue with his work and the work of the whole team. I am pleased to work with these players but if we find a right solution, we want to improve this squad."

Burnley's first shot was in the 43rd minute. The Clarets had not won at Stamford Bridge since April 1971, losing six and drawing two games since then. Sean Dyche confessed: "They were far too good today. They are too strong in all areas. We want to take on the challenge and I think the lads got too sucked in with the result from last week. We did not use the ball at all. There were too many sloppy passes and you just cannot do that against teams like this one. They were never in trouble, but we have to learn from these games. This is not really our market, there is a big gap from where they are and where we are. We were not close to getting a result today."

Hazard is back playing his best football, said Match of the Day pundit Alan Shearer. "We are seeing that guy from two years ago. The first thing manager Antonio Conte realised he had to do was get him on side. He knows he's the match-winner."

Ruud Gullit, who helped Chelsea win the FA Cup in 1997 as player-manager, said Hazard had rediscovered his best form. "This was Hazard at his best, when he's facing players one-on-one." the Dutch Euro 1988 winner added. "This is Hazard when he has fun. I don't want him to chase back." The former FIFA world player of the year suggested that the signing of defensive midfielder Kante from Leicester allowed Hazard to focus on attacking. "Kante is like Claude Makelele. He's always there when you need him." added Gullit. "Hazard doesn't need to track back anymore. Hazard enjoys playing and I think that has a lot to do with Kante playing. Kante is a very important piece of the puzzle they needed in midfield. Willian can do the things he likes to do and therefore there's much more balance in the team."

MONDAY, 29 AUGUST 2016

Eden Hazard recognised the impact of the new manager. He believed the Italian's former playing days were the reason why he's able to build confidence in his players. "He's tried to give us confidence." Hazard told Chelsea TV. "He knows players because he used to be one. We had one bad season but we are trying to do better. He tries to motivate us and we are giving everything. He told me to sometimes go inside, sometimes to stay wide and open up the game. He wants me to score some goals and make a difference."

TUESDAY, 30 AUGUST 2016

Chelsea re-sign David Luiz from Paris Saint-Germain for £34m.

The 29-year-old travelled to London for a medical as the Blues also confirmed the signing of left-back Marcos Alonso from Fiorentina for £23m. Luiz returned to Stamford Bridge on a three-year deal. He first joined from Benfica for £21.3m in January 2011, and made 143 appearances before leaving to join PSG for £40m in 2014. Capped 56 times for his country, Luiz won the Champions League and FA Cup with Chelsea in 2012, and the Europa League a year later. "We had a fantastic story during my first time at the club." said Luiz, who went on to lift two Ligue 1 titles with PSG.

Alonso had now moved to the Premier League for the third time in his career. The uncapped Spaniard, 25, played for Bolton 46 times from 2010 to 2013 before moving to Fiorentina, and then had a four-month loan spell at Sunderland in 2014. Alonso is an attacking full-back who could operate as a left wing-back and allow Azpilicueta to move to the right, which also pointed to a long-term shift to a back three. Conte now had cover in the full-back and central-defensive positions, having started the season with just four fit senior defenders. Kurt Zouma was also set to return from injury within the next month.

Conte knew Alonso from his impressive performances for Fiorentina in Serie A. Alonso, who signed a five-year contract, added: "It's a step up in my career and the perfect place for me to continue developing. It's time for me to win some titles. It was an easy decision for me to make when I heard the club were interested in signing me. My family and close friends know Chelsea is the club I have dreamed about playing for, so I'm really excited about the challenge and I'm looking forward to working with my new teammates."

Conte feared he would miss out on landing a centre-back in this window after failing with bids for Napoli's Kalidou Koulibaly and Milan's Alessio Romagnoli. A loan deal was set up for Valencia central defender Aymen Abdennour, with the Blues having seemingly run out of permanent options. However, the club were then presented with the opportunity to re-sign Luiz but it was not until Conte gave his blessing that the move accelerated. Luiz travelled to England via Eurostar to agree personal terms and complete a medical, as Chelsea abandoned their discussions over Abdennour. Chelsea confirmed their agreement with a statement that read: "Chelsea Football Club and Paris St-Germain have agreed terms for the transfer of David Luiz back to London. The move is now subject to him agreeing personal terms and passing a medical." In an inflated and grotesquely distorted market in which Chelsea were quoted £60m for Koulibaly and £75m for Romelu Lukaku, Chelsea believed Luiz represented good value, but there were doubts...

Having earned a reputation for risk filled errors and costly mistakes during his first three-year spell at Chelsea, Luiz did not seem to fit Conte's criteria for a central defender. However, the Brazilian gave Conte the option to switch to three at the back and, crucially, could carry the ball out of defence - something Chelsea had missed since his departure.

So, Chelsea's deadline-day defensive acquisitions were completed and there was still the long-term expectation that 20-year-old Denmark international Andreas Christensen would return on a permanent basis next summer. Christensen started the second season of his two-season loan at Borussia Monchengladbach, but is part of Chelsea's long-term planning.

Chelsea had now signed five players since Conte's arrival, with Kante, Batshuayi and goalkeeper Eduardo the other recruits.

Juan Cuadrado became the latest to join the army of Chelsea players out on loan, completing a three-season-long return to Juventus, where he was a great success last term. Conte wanted to keep the 28-year-old, but Cuadrado favoured a return to Italy and Juventus paid a loan fee of £4m, with the obligation to buy the winger if he made a set number of appearances.

Milan failed with a late enquiry to take Fabregas on loan for the season as he opted to stay and fight for his place. Fabregas had yet to start in the Premier League under Conte and had lost his place in the Spain squad prompting Milan's interest.

To put Chelsea's spending into some sort of context, in total, Premier League clubs had spent more than £155m on transfer deadline day as the summer window outlay reached a record £1.165bn. The League had benefited from a record £5.1bn television deal which came into effect this season.

The biggest summer fees were:

Paul Pogba to Manchester United for £89m

John Stones to Manchester City for £47.5m

Leroy Sane to Manchester City for £37m

Granit Xhaka to Arsenal for £35m

Shkodran Mustafi to Arsenal for £35

David Luiz to Chelsea for £34m

Sadio Mane to Liverpool for £34m

Michy Batshuayi to Chelsea for £33m

Moussa Sissoko to Tottenham Hotspur for £30m

N'Golo Kante to Chelsea for £30m

Chelsea earlier loaned Baba Rahman to Schalke and now a further eleven players had departed on loan, bringing the total out on temporary deals to 38.

Chelsea's deadline day loan departures:

Christian Atsu to Newcastle United (Championship)

Nathan Baxter to Metropolitan Police (Isthmian Premier - tier 7)

Jake Clarke-Salter to Bristol Rovers (League One)

Charlie Colkett to Bristol Rovers (League One)

Dion Conroy to Aldershot Town (National League)

Juan Cuadrado to Juventus (Serie A)

Cristian Cuevas to Sint-Truiden (Belgian Second Division)

Islam Feruz to Mouscron-Peruwelz (Belgian First Division)

Matt Miazga to Vitesse Arnhem (Dutch Eredivisie)

Kenneth Omeruo to Alanyaspor (Turkish Super Lig)

Lucas Piazon to Fulham (Championship)

Premier League Table, Top 6, end of August 2016:

		P	W	D	L	F	A	GD	Pts
1	Manchester City	3	3	0	0	9	3	+6	9
2	Chelsea	3	3	0	0	7	2	+5	9
3	Manchester United	3	3	0	0	6	1	+5	9
4	Everton	3	2	1	0	4	2	+2	7
5	Hull City	3	2	0	1	4	2	+2	6
6=	Middlesbrough	3	1	2	0	3	2	+1	5
6=	Tottenham Hotspur	3	1	2	0	3	2	+1	5

CHAPTER SIX

SEPTEMBER 2016

Crushing defeats, at home to Liverpool and then at The Emirates, prompt Conte into a major, season-defining, tactical re-think.

FRIDAY, 9 SEPTEMBER 2016

Conte believed David Luiz can become one the best defenders in world football. "I think we have improved our squad. We needed two defenders in this transfer market. Two good players arrived who can improve our squad. Now it's important for them to work very hard, to go into our idea of football and to show me that they deserve to play."

Of Luiz, he recognised that there are some aspects to the Brazilian's game which needed improving, but he was delighted with the signing nonetheless. "I must be honest. We need him as a centre-back. In David we took a player with a great personality a great technique. I like a defender that likes to play football. David can improve in defensive situations but I am very happy. He is a good positive guy for the changing room. A great defender must be able to play football and defend. But also a coach must be able to improve players. You have to work on their weaknesses. Every player until the end of their career can improve. Every player. David Luiz is 29. It's a fantastic age for him to become one of the best defenders in the world."

It was, though, unlikely that either Luiz or Alonso would start for Chelsea at the weekend. "I think the new players need a bit of time, the chance to play at the start is not high."

Also, Conte had no plans to play Luiz in midfield. Luiz was occasionally played in a defensive midfield role in his previous time at the Bridge. "I think David Luiz is a centre-back, he's played a lot of games in that position." he told Chelsea TV. "I know sometimes he's played as a central midfielder but in my mind the idea is to utilise him in the right position which, for me, is centre-back. He's played with Chelsea previously and he will bring a good personality."

SUNDAY, 11 SEPTEMBER 2016
Swansea City 2-2 Chelsea
Premier League

Chelsea dropped their first points as Diego Costa struck twice to rescue a draw.

Conte just failed to become the fourth Chelsea manager to win his first four Premier League games, thereby joining Mourinho, Hiddink and Ancelotti.

Costa, who might earlier have been sent off, again, capitalised on poor defending to open the scoring. Gylfi Sigurdsson's penalty and Leroy Fer's bundled goal two minutes later turned the game, only for Costa to score an acrobatic late second to salvage a point as Conte's team stayed second.

Chelsea had total control for almost an hour before conceding two goals in three second-half minutes. The second came after Gary Cahill lost the ball after he was dispossessed by Fer near the edge of his own box - with the England international defender claiming afterwards he thought he had been fouled.

Costa's brace protected Conte's unbeaten record but the team slipped to two points behind leaders Manchester City. His four goals in his first four league games, though, indicated that he was back to his snarling best, as he continued to play on the edge; booked for a clumsy challenge on Fernandez, whose mistake Costa punished for the opening goal. The Argentine defender hesitantly headed the ball to Oscar, whose pass allowed Costa to score with a clinical low finish.

Costa, so far this season, could have been dismissed in virtually every game. Here he clashed throughout with Jordi Amat and was fortunate to escape a second yellow card after diving under pressure from Swansea keeper, Lukasz Fabianski, in the second half. However, he relished the confrontation as well as the adrenalin rush brought on by the equaliser with a bicycle kick after 81 minutes. Interestingly, only five players have reached 35 goals in the Premier League in fewer appearances than Costa (58) - Andy Cole (41), Alan Shearer (42), Fernando Torres (52), Kevin Phillips (52) and Ruud van Nistelrooy (55).

The Swans faced the prospect of three successive defeats under Francesco Guidolin for the first time. The Italian switched to a defensive 5-4-1 formation with a compact midfield diamond aimed at containing Chelsea. Guidolin abandoned his new system after just 41 minutes; left-back Neil Taylor dismayed that he was sacrificed for winger Modou Barrow.

But, Swansea staged a remarkable second-half revival and were awarded a penalty when Sigurdsson was tripped by a stranded Courtois, who was the beneficiary of a rule change which means players are booked rather than sent off if they are deemed to have only accidentally denied their opponent a goalscoring opportunity. Sigurdsson converted the spot-kick. Then Fer appeared to foul Cahill as he dispossessed the Chelsea defender but ran clear before squeezing his shot past Courtois and over the line.

Conte commented: "It's very difficult to talk about the game because we lost two points. We were leading 1-0 and created a lot of chances to score another goal. We are disappointed because the performance was very good in terms of our intensity and because we played good football. People looking at the second goal can see that the referee made a mistake - but this can happen. I've not spoken to the referee. It's a big mistake."

Gary Cahill insisted Swansea's second goal should have been ruled out because there was a foul on him so obvious "you could be sat on the moon and see it".

An animated Cahill added: "It's a clear foul. Come on, seriously. It was clear as day and seeing it back has made me even more angry."

Obviously still smarting from the non-decision, Cahill then posted a clip of the incident on social media labelling it "incredible". He went to see Andre Marriner after the game. "I said to the referee, 'there're three of you that can see that'. There were two fouls on me and between the officials they have said that they couldn't see it. For me that is incredible. I took the touch away from him, he came through the back of me. It's all fun and games for the fans - but it's the players who suffer. That kills me and kills my team. We have dropped two points which is massive in this league."

Conte, though, wanted referees to protect his striker. "Every game the press ask me about the patience of Costa, his behaviour. His behaviour was fantastic. Today he took a lot of kicks. I think the defenders know him and sometimes they try to provoke him. It's football and it's normal in this situation. They try to provoke but it's football, not only in England but in general in the world. The referee must see it and permit Diego Costa to play his football."

Chelsea captain John Terry rather worryingly ended the game limping and left the stadium on crutches. Conte said: "I don't know the extent of the injury. Tomorrow we will see the situation about his ankle. He's a warrior. I'm not worried."

Swansea coach Francesco Guidolin said: "I am happy with the result. My team played the second half with more energy against a very strong team. After Chelsea's first goal I saw my team not playing well and decided to change something before the end of the first half. I am sorry for Neil Taylor (getting substituted) but I decided this way because we needed a reaction."

Chelsea's title credentials would now be severely tested by their next two games, at home to Liverpool and away against Arsenal.

MONDAY, 12 SEPTEMBER 2016

Match of the Day 2 pundit Chris Sutton commented: "Yes, Antonio Conte's side will rue the chances they missed, but the bottom line is that Andre Marriner cost them two points. Marriner's decision to allow Swansea's second goal was an absolute shocker. There is no other way of putting it, because Leroy Fer's foul on Chelsea defender Gary Cahill, before he scored, was as blatant as can be."

"Swansea's first goal was poor from Chelsea's point of view because they were hit on the counter-attack from their own free-kick at the other end of the pitch. But Chelsea were totally in control up until that point and, although they had made a mistake, I still felt they were well in the ascendancy. As Cahill said afterwards, it was Swansea's second goal only three minutes later that killed them - and Marriner's mistake was inexcusable. It is an assault by Fer - there is not one foul, there are two - and it is ridiculous that play was allowed to continue."

"One of the positives that Chelsea can take from the day is that they fought back to rescue a point with Diego Costa's second goal of the game. The Blues have now earned five points from goals in the last ten minutes of games this season, more than any other top-flight team, but they should never have been in a situation where they were chasing the game. Costa now has four goals from four Premier League appearances this season and I was really impressed by his movement, his confidence and his all-round play. He was a focal point all game. He was showing for the ball, and held it up really well to buy time for his team to advance up the pitch. The Spain striker wasted a big chance to put Chelsea 2-0 up before half-time when he missed from close range but he was a real handful and looks like he is back to his best form. His first goal against Swansea, a first-time shot from Oscar's pass that he caressed into the corner, was a superb finish and his second was acrobatic and exceptional. We know he plays near the edge - he was booked for the third time this season - and oversteps the mark sometimes, but that is part of his game. Swansea tried to rough him up at the start of the match but he does not mind that side of things. He should have had a hat-trick and he looked very sharp, which is a worrying sign for Premier League defenders."

"Chelsea had 14 shots in the first half and looked in total control against a Swansea side that were poor and did not look a threat. It was astonishing that the Blues ended up dropping their first points of the season and they will feel like they actually lost the game because they had made such a good start. Chelsea still have ten points out of 12 and they can be pleased and positive with the way they have started the season, but it will be very frustrating for them to lose their 100% record like that."

"I like the way Conte manages - he is all about graft and it already looks like he is getting a lot out of his players. This is a Chelsea team that under-performed last season but N'Golo Kante was the only player to start against Swansea who has joined since, and you could not accuse them of not working hard enough in Wales."

"Chelsea's three league wins this season have come against West Ham, Watford and Burnley. You could argue they should be beating those teams, but they did not manage it last season - they only took two points from the same games against the Hammers and the Hornets. They are clearly going to do better than their 10th-place finish last time out, but the question is how much of an improvement will there be. They will want to get back in the Champions League and they probably have title aspirations too."

"Manchester City look a different class to everyone else so far, but the rest of the top four looks wide open. We will find out a lot more about Chelsea's prospects in their next two league games - at home to Liverpool on Friday and away to Arsenal the following weekend. Those head-to-heads will be very important but I can see all the top teams taking points off each other when they meet. The race for the top four threatens to be very close, so it is even more disappointing for Chelsea that they slipped up against a team like Swansea, because those are the games they definitely should be winning."

Former Chelsea manager Gianluca Vialli spoke of his admiration for Conte and believes his fellow Italian was already doing well at Stamford Bridge. "I think Conte is already doing a great job at Chelsea." said Vialli, who managed the London club from 1998 to 2000. "He arrived at the right moment after a disappointing season. He has had a very good team in his hands and he tried to bring in more quality players. I think players have no choice but to follow him. They are used to working with managers with a strong personality like his. I think he has to adapt to his players as much as they have to adapt to him. I'm positive they will find a compromise. He is already doing a great job."

Former England boss Fabio Capello believed Chelsea could win the Premier League title thanks to Conte. The ex-Real Madrid and AC Milan manager was impressed with Conte. OK, Pep Guardiola's Manchester City and Jose Mourinho's Manchester United were favourites to win the Premier League, but he said: "Don't forget about Antonio Conte. His team lacks in creativity but makes up for it with strength and determination. I think they will battle for the title until the end."

TUESDAY, 13 SEPTEMBER 2016

John Terry was out for ten days after straining ligaments in his foot.

He had left the Liberty Stadium on crutches and later posted a video on his Instagram page showing him having treatment. A scan revealed he would miss Friday's home match with Liverpool.

David Luiz would start against Liverpool, Conte confirmed. Luiz was an unused substitute and remained on the bench during the draw with Swansea but the injury to Terry made it almost certain he would play against Liverpool. Discussing Terry's injury, Conte said: "He has strained the ligaments in his ankle. The doctor told me after ten days he can come back, he is working very hard and had a training session today to recover. David Luiz will play with us for the first time and we are confident."

WEDNESDAY, 14 SEPTEMBER 2016

Conte appeared to warn Costa about his first team place, criticising his aggressive style, picking up three yellow cards already. Whereas he hailed his passion he wanted him to go about things "in the right way."

"He must pay attention because he has three yellow cards but I am not worried about this. He is growing in this situation, in the last game he showed a great attitude despite it being very difficult for him. We all know him, he's a passionate man and we want to put his passion in the football when he plays. It is important to have passion in the right way. He is an important player but in our squad there is also Michy Batshuayi and he is waiting for the right moment to show quality. And we also have Ruben who can play in this position."

THURSDAY, 15 SEPTEMBER 2016

Conte considered having a bed installed at their Cobham training ground because he was working such long hours.

"When there is my wife and daughter, then I am allowed to go in together and visit and enjoy London and it is a fantastic city." the Italian told Sky Sports. "And when I stay a long time here, it is very difficult for me because I stay at Stamford Bridge for eight or nine hours, I prefer to work here (Chelsea's training ground at Cobham). But in the future I want to ask for a bed here because there could be a situation that happens where there is the possibility I want to stay here!"

He warned his side that Liverpool were "the worst team to play now." Klopp's side were inconsistent; an opening-day 4-3 win over Arsenal but a shock 2-0 defeat to newly-promoted Burnley.

Conte told Sky Sports: "I think it will be a very tough game because at this moment Liverpool are in a very good shape and we must pay great attention. I consider Liverpool the worst team to play now and we must prepare the game in the right way, but it will be a good game."

Jurgen Klopp was highly complimentary of his opposite number, describing Conte as "a great manager" and "the Pep Guardiola of Juventus". He commented: "I watched the game (against Swansea), whoever was the broadcaster, they showed when they missed the goal and he's always involved in the game. That's not the important thing though, he's a successful manager. He was the Pep Guardiola of Turin. He created a special style of play. He was very successful there and with the (Italian) national team too. Quite impressive, but I don't play against Antonio Conte."

Conte repaid the compliment. "He is one of the best in the world." he said. "He is showing at Liverpool great capacity to be a great manager. I know him but not too much but we only play with our teams only once, I am very glad to see him on Friday."

Conte made the point that he would not tolerate any of his Chelsea players disrespecting him or the team, insisting he would rather "kill" that player than have him in the squad. He explained how important respect is when it comes to forming a winning side. "From my experience as a footballer, I think this is the right way to manage a changing room." Conte told Sky Sports when asked about his strict management style. "I think that when I start a season, I speak with my players and I always talk about education and respect. And I demand this, but I give this. And if someone does not have a good attitude during the training session, or good behaviour in different circumstances, I prefer to kill him than have 22 players. Because I repeat, from my experience as a footballer, if a manager closes his eyes, he does not want to see the bad situation and he loses the changing room."

Cesc Fabregas's lack of defensive qualities were keeping him out of the team, playing only 26 minutes in the Premier League and his single start coming against Bristol Rovers in the League Cup. Conte, though, was pleased with Fabregas's work-rate but Oscar was currently a better option in midfield. "Cesc is in my plans and in Chelsea's plans. We all know Cesc is a fantastic player. I see him in every training session with great work and effort. If he continues in this way, it will be very difficult for me not to choose him in my midfield. But I want this from a player, putting many doubts in my mind over choosing someone else. Cesc is a great player. We all know Cesc, a great technical player. Now I'm starting to get to know him as a man. A great personality. I'm pleased with him. He's working very well. He's improving a lot on many aspects, above all the defensive situations. I'm very clear with my players: when a player deserves to play, I put him in the team. I always thought that this team needed to find a good balance when you have the ball and, above all, when you don't have the ball. Last season Chelsea conceded 53 goals. Now, we have found the right compromise between defensive and offensive situations. Oscar is a good player, great technique and can do both facets: both offensive and defensive. I asked him to stay always focused on the game, to stay in the game. He's an important player for Chelsea."

FRIDAY, 16 SEPTEMBER 2016
Chelsea 1-2 Liverpool
Premier League

Conte's first loss of the season was inflicted by a Klopp side on the march as title contenders. It was also his first home league defeat as a manager since January 2013, ending an impressive run of 30 games.

The meeting between Conte and Klopp meant eyes were trained on the technical area, on two of the game's most charismatic and animated managers. It was an eventful evening for fourth official Bobby Madley, who crossed swords with both, delivering an early warning to Conte for straying outside his designated area as well as being in regular conversation with Klopp. Conte prowled his technical area throughout, dark-suited and with shiny black shoes, Klopp in a black Liverpool tracksuit.

Conte was all agitated, nervous action, while it took Klopp until the 13th minute to even leave his seat. Klopp was unleashed when Henderson's long range effort curved and dipped beyond Courtois after 36 minutes. He leapt from his dugout with the exclamation "boom" as the shot flew in and Liverpool then took control. It was a control they never relinquished.

In the end Conte was as subdued as his Chelsea side and at the final whistle it was Klopp who embraced his Liverpool backroom staff before going around all of his players, back-slapping, bear-hugging and chest-beating before pumping his fists in the direction of their fans.

Klopp had also won at Stamford Bridge the previous season - and Liverpool fully deserved to add to their 4-3 win at Arsenal on the opening weekend of the season, a 1-1 draw at Spurs, and 4-1 thrashing of champions Leicester at Anfield.

Liverpool over-ran Chelsea to take control by half-time through Dejan Lovren's close range finish and captain Henderson's spectacular 25-yard strike.

David Luiz made his first appearance as replacement for the injured Terry, and whilst Costa pulled one back this was a laboured performance. Chelsea, without the injured Terry, lacked direction and leadership in defence.

Conte's animated touchline body language screamed 'frustration' as Chelsea struggled. He had previously needed late winners from Costa against West Ham and Watford before a convincing win against Burnley.

There was even a question mark over Conte's approach, taking 83 minutes to make a change when it was apparently clear that something needed to be done. When it finally came, it was a triple substitution as Moses, Pedro and Fabregas came on for Willian, Oscar and Matic, although there was widespread surprise that £33m striker Batshuayi was not given an opportunity.

Liverpool have now won five of their last nine Premier League visits to Stamford Bridge, having won only one of their first 16 trips there. Chelsea have not kept a clean sheet in any of their last seven home Premier League games against Liverpool, last doing so in October 2009. The Blues were two goals behind in a Premier League game for the first time since December 2015 (against Leicester), Mourinho's final match in charge. Klopp is the first manager to win his opening two visits to Stamford Bridge in the Premier League since Arsene Wenger, and only the fourth manager overall to do so along with Mike Walker and Harry Redknapp.

Conte commented: "We conceded the goals in a strange way. They took the free-kick quickly for the first goal and it was a great shot from a long distance for the second but if we are in the right position he must not receive the ball unmarked. When you want to think like a great team you must pay attention in every moment."

"We played with good intensity and anger in the second half. We scored a goal and could have scored another with Diego Costa. We played a good second half. I must work more to improve my players. Defeats are never good. We know this, we must work and keep our concentration."

"Every single game is very tough. We must not forget last season. Last season was a bad season. I don't want to repeat last season. When you finish a season in 10th, there is something strange. It's not simple. It means you have to work hard to improve."

Klopp remarked: "From the first second we had unbelievably good movement. We were quick in mind. We did really well. We deserved the lead at half-time. So often this season Chelsea scored in the last few seconds with a direct style. But I can't remember too many chances from them. We had a few moments where we weren't so good but that's normal against a good team. We played football like hell. It was really nice to watch. In the second half it was a bit more difficult. After their goal, we managed it well."

Goalscorer Lovren added: "It is always a tough game here but I thought we did brilliantly. In the first half, I thought it was our best football of the season."

TUESDAY, 20 SEPTEMBER 2016
Leicester City 2-4 Chelsea
EFL Cup, Third Round

Cesc Fabregas scored twice in extra time as Chelsea came from two goals down to beat 10-man Leicester and reach the fourth round.

He had so far been unable to establish himself under Conte, restricted to appearances from the bench in the Premier League and his only two starts coming in the EFL Cup - but he was arguably the standout player for Chelsea in this game. Criticised for a lack of goals in the past; he scored six the previous season and five the campaign before. But he took both his finishes well and also provided the assist for Cahill's goal; a performance to give Conte food for thought.

Conte commented: "It's important when I call someone to play and they show me my choice is not wrong. I am pleased for Cesc because he played a good game, he showed me great commitment in the training sessions. I am satisfied when I see this behaviour. This is the right way and I want my players to create good competition and, game by game, give me the opportunity to choose the best line-up."

Okazaki's double-strike had put Leicester in control, but Cahill nodded in before the break. Azpilicueta equalised with a long-range effort before Marcin Wasilewski was sent off. Fabregas's clipped finish put Chelsea ahead early in the first extra period and a powerful shot sealed a pulsating cup tie.

Wasilewski's dismissal for elbowing Costa proved costly. Chelsea had come back to win from two goals down for the first time in a game since 17 August 2002, against Charlton.

Chelsea had now scored in every game this season and their attacking strength came to the fore towards the end. However, defensive frailties continued to cause concern for Conte. Only once in their previous 14 games in all competitions had the Blues kept a clean sheet.

"Chelsea's decision-making when under pressure was poor." said BBC Radio 5 live summariser and former Leicester defender Gerry Taggart. "We are talking about basics. Clear the ball first, then ask questions. Some of Chelsea's decision-making was abysmal."

Claudio Ranieri said: "I am happy with our performance until 2-0. We started very well and we were in control of the match. Chelsea had more possession but we were very smart and clever to score twice. The key was when we conceded a goal on the last corner of the half - we lost two dangerous men, Luiz and Cahill. In extra time I said stay together and close the space, but Fabregas scored and it was very difficult for us."

WEDNESDAY, 21 SEPTEMBER 2016

Experienced centre-half Terry Butcher believed David Luiz caused problems with Chelsea's defence and wanted the Brazilian to just "focus on being a good defender". Asked why Chelsea have started conceding more goals in recent matches, Butcher candidly replied: "David Luiz is back." The former England defender, Butcher, renowned for being a tough defender added: "I could not believe Chelsea took him back. All of a sudden it is panic stations and there are goals flying in."

Butcher's advice: "Just be good defenders. Stop pulling your socks over your knees and stop wearing these bloomin' under-shorts and the big hair."

Conte expected to welcome Kurt Zouma back to training next week. The Blues centre-back had yet to feature under Conte after he tore his anterior cruciate ligament in February and missed the last seven months. Another international break was fast approaching, with the start of October taken up by World Cup qualifiers, and Conte was optimistic that by the time Chelsea returned to competitive action on 15 October he would have Zouma available to play. "For Zouma, I hope to see him in the training sessions next week. He's in good shape and I hope to see him next week in training, to start counting on him. Possibly (he will return after the international break). Probably - we will wait one week more."

THURSDAY, 22 SEPTEMBER 2016

Conte knew it would take time for him to get his side playing how he wants. "It is normal when you start work in a new team and you bring a new idea and method of football you need time, but I'm confident about this and trust in the work. We can improve a lot."

Conte was the 12th Chelsea manager Arsene Wenger had faced in the Premier League. "It is fantastic if someone is able to stay for 20 years in the same club. There is satisfaction in both sides. Sometimes I think it is important to value a manager not only if he wins, loses or draws. Sometimes if you judge only if they win you make a big mistake and you pay for this in the future."

Chelsea had conceded 53 league goals last season, and so far kept just one clean sheet in seven games this campaign. "When we concede a goal, all the team concede a goal, not only the defenders." said Conte, who would be without John Terry against Arsenal. "It means we must work together to improve the defensive situation. This problem was already there last season. We must work a lot on this aspect because if you want a great championship you must not concede so many goals."

Conte believed Arsenal would be among the main title challengers. The Gunners had not won the coveted trophy for 12 years now, but finished second to Leicester City and look an improved side with some astute summer signings. "I'm sure Arsenal will fight until the end to win the title because they're a very good team. They have young players, great technique, good players with good physical potential and organisation."

Both sides were level on points with Arsenal in slightly better form having won three games on the spin to make up for a slow start. Chelsea, conversely, had won their first three before setbacks against Swansea City and Liverpool.

FRIDAY, 23 SEPTEMBER 2016

Match of the Day pundit and former Chelsea manager Ruud Gullit observed: "Seeing Liverpool dominate Chelsea at Stamford Bridge in the Blues' last Premier League game was very difficult for me to swallow. Antonio Conte's side were very passive defensively as they lost 2-1 at home and I think they were left exposed a little bit. That has to change. But, although I am very curious about how Conte will approach Saturday's game against Arsenal, I am not worried."

"Up until now I think he has been playing the 'Chelsea way', rather than his own, since taking charge over the summer. For me, Conte is still searching for a system he can rely on - what he sees as his ideal way of playing in the Premier League, and the best team he can pick to execute it. He will need time to find out what he wants to do, and also whether it works. It means there are a lot of questions about Chelsea right now - but we will soon get some answers. I am analysing this weekend's game against the Gunners for Match of the Day and I am looking forward to seeing what Conte tries next, and how he gets on. When Conte took charge of Italy, he adapted the national side to the 3-5-2 formation he favours, which he used predominantly as Juventus manager."

"But a system on its own is not the key to success. Conte himself has said it is important to find out what works best for a specific team, and that is exactly what he is doing now. So far at Chelsea he has always set up with four at the back and used a shape close to either the 4-2-3-1 or 4-3-3 that the Blues played under Jose Mourinho in his two spells as Blues' boss. Playing the way Chelsea have played for a long time has its advantages - it suits N'Golo Kante in the centre of midfield, Eden Hazard is back to playing well on the left too, and up front Diego Costa is getting plenty of chances, even if I think he is too isolated at times."

"Conte will not be happy with the number of errors his side has made at the back, however. That is something he might try to change this weekend by reverting to what he knows works for him. At the start of the season I don't think he had the players to play a three-man defence, but signing David Luiz gave him that option, and he can do it now that John Terry is fit again."

"Will it work for Chelsea? I don't know but, until now, Conte has not even had the opportunity to try it. Conte has another decision to make in midfield. Will Cesc Fabregas play against his old club Arsenal after the Spaniard has not started a Premier League game this season but showed against Leicester what he can do? The fact he did well in that game does not mean he will play on Saturday but whether he is picked or not will tell us more about how big a part he plays in Conte's plans. Fabregas is very creative of course, but he is not known for chasing back or tackling, which might be why he has spent most of this season on the bench. But, with Kante in the team, Chelsea have a player who does that side of the game really well, so I can understand why many Chelsea fans want to see Fabregas start against the Gunners and increase their attacking threat."

"I would like to see Ruben Loftus-Cheek in the Chelsea team too - he has not played at all in the

Premier League so far this season, and I don't know why. But of course I do not watch him or Fabregas in training and without seeing either player every day it is difficult to demand that he has to play - that is for Conte to decide. Saturday's trip to Emirates Stadium is going to be tough because Arsenal look stronger than they did last season, right the way through their team."

"Chelsea have some other big games coming up too, against defending champions Leicester and then Manchester United. How the Blues get on will tell us more about their current strengths and weaknesses but we should not judge Conte as a Premier League manager on those results. He has only just arrived in this country and has just started his job - he should be given six months to settle in. Sadly, that does not seem to happen anymore. I was the first Chelsea manager that Arsene Wenger came up against as Arsenal boss 20 years ago - Conte will be the 12th. Things are very different now to when Arsene first came to England. Because of the amount of money involved, people demand instant results and nobody gets a honeymoon period in a new job. It is the same for everyone - look at the criticism that Mourinho is already getting at United. I fear that Conte will get similar treatment if Chelsea have a bad spell over the next few weeks, even though he is still adapting and working out how he wants to play."

SATURDAY, 24 SEPTEMBER 2016
Arsenal 3-0 Chelsea
Premier League

Arsenal produced a devastating first-half display to dismantle Chelsea and secure a fourth successive Premier League win.

Chelsea fell to their second league loss in a row as rampant Arsenal moved third in the table, five points behind Manchester City, who had won all six. Wenger, who would celebrate his 20th anniversary as Arsenal manager next week, remarked: "The quality of our performance confirmed that we are on the way up. There's still room for improvement. Now let's continue to improve."

If you had to pick a title contender between these two London teams at this early stage, it wouldn't have been Chelsea! Meanwhile Arsenal's fans shared, at this time, the optimism expressed by Wenger. He wrote in his programme notes: "We feel as though we are on the way up."

Chelsea, however, looked on the way down. Conte said: "I think that we didn't have the right attitude from the first minute. After today we are thinking we must work a lot because we are a great team only on paper. It is always a team problem rather than individuals. When nothing works it is very hard for a player to play well. I don't want to talk about the mistake (from Gary Cahill). It is not right for the player. We win and lose as a team. If someone thinks this team is ready to fight, I think we must wait to improve a lot to come back a great team on the pitch, not just on paper. We have not got the balance and now is the moment to consider everything. It is incredible to concede three goals. We must have last season present in our mind to not repeat the mistakes. We must reflect a lot to find very soon the right way."

Alexis Sanchez took advantage of Cahill's error to race clear and lift a composed finish over Courtois after only eleven minutes, and Theo Walcott completed a brilliant move to steer in Hector Bellerin's pass three minutes later. Mesut Ozil then left Kante trailing to expose Chelsea on the counter-attack and steer home Arsenal's third five minutes before the break, following a neat exchange with Sanchez.

There was a damning assessment in the BBC's match report: "Chelsea looked an old and jaded side when faced with Liverpool's intense, aggressive approach at Stamford Bridge last week, their first loss under Antonio Conte. This was, arguably, an even more harrowing experience and a stark illustration of the job the Italian must do to revive Chelsea. Conte will know the pressures that come with managing under demanding owner Roman Abramovich, but the man who impressed so much in charge of Juventus and Italy must be given time to address so many problems. Chelsea still rely so heavily on 35-year-old captain John Terry, out injured here, while elements of the side that looked so strong winning the title the season before last are crumbling."

Cahill was involved in an arm-waving spat with Courtois after a breakdown in communication in the second half as Chelsea looked all over the place, while in contrast the Gunners were rampant. Wenger inflicted Antonio Conte's heaviest league defeat since October 2010, when he was manager of Siena (3-0 loss to Empoli). Chelsea found themselves three goals down at half-time in a Premier League game for the first time since May 2012 (vs Liverpool, 4-1 FT). This was the first time since October 2012, against Manchester United, the Blues had conceded twice in the opening 15 minutes of a Premier League game. It was Wenger's first win over Chelsea in the league since October 2011 (drew three, lost six). Chelsea's first shot on target didn't come until the 82nd minute.

Wenger purred: "It was an outstanding team performance. We played with spirit and collective pace and movement, always in a positive and committed team way. Our defenders have done extremely well. You cannot say one player was not at the right level from Petr Cech to Alexis Sanchez. We wanted to start strong in a high pace and committed way. Ideally you want the perfect game and you never get it. We got nearly the perfect first half and that is not bad. Football doesn't care for history and the anniversaries, just the result on the day. Today we had a good performance. It's one of the games where what we wanted to do worked very well. It's one of those moments in your life as a manager where you think 'today is a great day'. We played with style, with pace, with movement - and that's the kind of football we want to play. It's one of the best performances in recent years."

MONDAY, 26 SEPTEMBER 2016

Branislav Ivanovic, one of many to under-perform, admitted the players hadn't believed in Conte's plan at the beginning of their game against Arsenal.

"We didn't start the game in the way we wanted. We didn't believe in what we were doing at the beginning and we were punished." the Serbian told Chelsea's official site. "As a team we didn't answer anything the manager asked of us, we have to be honest with ourselves and put more attention on the small details. We have to be more focused and concentrated on the game. I know it's very disappointing and it hurts all of us, but the opinion of everyone in the dressing room was in the same direction. We have to build on that, stay together, work hard, and believe in what we are doing. I am sure we can come out of it stronger. We have to stick together. Nothing in life or in football comes easy, you always go up and down, but we know when you're in a difficult position you have to work hard and prepare for the next game. I hope we are mentally ready for the challenge."

Ivanovic felt it could change but only *if* the new boss's methods start working. "In this league every game is a different story, but it doesn't mean you have to change your philosophy if you win or lose a game. We have worked very hard on different ways. Our way of playing has changed a bit and you always need time. In the last two games it has not been the usual Chelsea way, but if it starts working it will be very good for us. We will be very, very dangerous. We have another week to prepare for a very hard away game. We know how difficult it is to play a team with a different shape to yours.

We have to work hard but this is something normal. We have to be on top of our game and our performances week-by-week to get points from every game. We have to believe in what we are doing and the results of that will come."

Chelsea fans not enjoying the first half against Arsenal, voiced their opinions and some wanted Guus Hiddink back!

Conte was already under some early pressure!

TUESDAY, 27 SEPTEMBER 2016

Such was the disappointment and concern that Conte couldn't sleep following the drubbing by Arsenal. "I don't sleep, sure. I don't sleep. After this game, this defeat, it's normal for me not to sleep. Not only one night, but for two nights. When I don't sleep, I reflect. And it's important to reflect. When you have a bad performance we have a bad performance together - me first, my staff second, and then the players."

WEDNESDAY, 28 SEPTEMBER 2016

Conte was not giving the January transfer much consideration but instead his thoughts were concentrated on improving the players at his disposal. "I don't see January as an opportunity to spend money. Now I see the present and the opportunity to improve. We must think about the present now rather than think about spending money in the future."

THURSDAY, 29 SEPTEMBER 2016

Conte confessed he had already held talks with Roman Abramovich over the Blues' poor run. Clearly Chelsea needed to improve and he had conversations with Abramovich concerning as much.

"Mr. Abramovich is passionate about football and to talk to him about football is very interesting. To have a *confrontation* is very interesting - I like this."

Conte clarified shortly afterwards that he meant "conversation" and not "confrontation."!

"We haven't the magic wand to change the situation in one, two, three months. We must work hard together and we are doing this." Conte added.

Perhaps worryingly for Conte - enough to lose sleep maybe - Abramovich has a reputation for brutally sacking managers, overseeing ten managerial changes in eleven years.

FRIDAY, 30 SEPTEMBER 2016

Conte, to be fair, had fairly low expectations as he inherited a team with a number of problems. He had already said, when coming into the job, that he knew he had work to do to lift a side after such a poor campaign.

"I am not surprised (about poor results) because, usually, when you change manager it means you have a problem. When you arrive in a place for you to solve the problems then you know you must face this situation. The expectation is to improve compared to last season. The expectation comes from me. I have that expectation, not only the club or the fans because I decided to be the manager of a great team like Chelsea."

Conte confirmed that John Terry and John Obi Mikel would miss the trip to Hull as the manager aimed to avoid three defeats in a row. Terry had not been involved since hobbling off in the draw with Swansea, while Mikel was struggling with a small muscular strain and had yet to feature after spending the start of the season on international duty with Nigeria in the Rio Olympics.

Premier League Table, Top 6, end of September 2016:

		P	W	D	L	F	A	GD	Pts
1	Manchester City	6	6	0	0	18	5	+13	18
2	Tottenham Hotspur	6	4	2	0	10	3	+7	14
3	Everton	7	4	2	1	11	5	+6	14
4	Arsenal	6	4	1	1	15	7	+8	13
5	Liverpool	6	4	1	1	16	9	+7	13
6	Manchester United	6	4	0	2	12	7	+5	12

(Chelsea in 8th place on 10 points)

CHAPTER SEVEN

OCTOBER 2016

'Antonio Gone-te'. Several bookmakers suspend betting on Conte being the next Premier League manager to lose his job. Humiliation for Jose at the Bridge.

SATURDAY, 1 OCTOBER 2016
Hull City 0-2 Chelsea
Premier League

Chelsea stopped the rot after successive Premier League defeats, grinding down Hull at the KCOM Stadium.

Conte promised "a solution" after his side went down with a whimper against Arsenal and he found his answer in a strategy he used at former club Juventus, opting for a three-man defence during much of this trophy-filled time in Turin, deploying Cahill, Luiz and Azpilicueta at the back.

It did not initially appear to have stabilised a side who had conceded nine goals in their previous four games in all competitions. Luiz lost track of Mbokani as he apparently struggled with the extra space he and his teammates had to cover and was fortunate that the Hull striker's control betrayed him. But the defence, along with the team as a whole, improved markedly after half-time and never looked like blemishing only their second clean sheet of the season.

The chief beneficiary of Conte's reorganisation was Victor Moses. The 25-year-old's last Premier League start for Chelsea was in a 2-1 win over Aston Villa in May 2013 when Ashley Cole, Frank Lampard and Juan Mata were among his teammates. Loan spells at Liverpool, Stoke and West Ham followed, but the Nigeria international, playing as a right-sided wing-back, was industrious and inventive and might have earned a first-half penalty when his trickery lured Hull forward Adama Diomande into a rash challenge. Willian and Costa's precise efforts decided the three points, but Moses was a tactical revelation.

Conte commented: "Every game is very tough in England and I am pleased with our performance because we scored two goals and got a clean sheet. I saw the right pressure and the right intensity from the players. After these two defeats it's not easy to work because two defeats for Chelsea are heavy defeats. But this was a good answer. I saw many of the players with great commitment, attitude and will to change the situation. I am pleased for them. We must follow this with work, work, work!"

Chelsea kept their first clean sheet in eight away Premier League games since a 4-0 win at Aston Villa in April. Kante made more passes (79), more successful passes (70) and had more touches (95) than he had in any of his previous 43 Premier League matches.

Azpilicueta, Luiz and Cahill made up the three at the back and Conte was delighted to see the defence keep a clean sheet. "I'm pleased for all the players because I think in this championship it is the second time we have had a clean sheet and it is important after two defeats." Conte told Sky Sports. "In the last four games we have conceded always two or three goals so to finish the game with a clean sheet is very important. We scored twice but we could have scored more."

The hosts enjoyed the better of a cagey first half but went behind when Willian swept home a curling shot following good work from Diego Costa after the break. Costa himself then found the top corner with a similar strike to double the lead after Matic's powerful run. Hull never recovered and could have been further behind but for Pedro's poor finishing from only six yards out. Since Diego Costa joined Chelsea, only Aguero (55) and Kane (48) have scored more Premier League goals; Costa on 38.

Had Robert Snodgrass's early deflected effort not been brilliantly tipped over the top by Courtois it might well have been different. Caretaker manager Mike Phelan remarked: "We were quite pleased we created a few issues for them in the first half but we expect a team like Chelsea to ramp up the pressure a little bit. It has been difficult to get forward but we're not playing Mickey Mouse teams here. We have to be sensible with our approach and can't just be open against these teams." In all competitions, Chelsea were unbeaten in their last 13 meetings with Hull, winning eleven and drawing two.

Costa had now smashed in six goals in the Premier League, one of the standout players under Conte.

It was Costa's work-rate in particular that pleased the manager the most.

"We're working very hard. This is the right way. We must follow this. We must know we have to improve a lot. Only one way and that is to work. Costa is fantastic: scored six goals for us, but it is important not only that he scores, but that he works. This is most important."

Chelsea were now due to play Leicester City, the defending champions, when they returned from the international break.

MONDAY, 3 OCTOBER 2016

Swansea City appointed Bob Bradley as their new manager but ABC7 News (the ABC outlet in Los Angeles) reported it incorrectly as they rather awkwardly believed that the 58-year-old American coach had in fact replaced Antonio Conte!

TUESDAY, 4 OCTOBER 2016

Conte praised Victor Moses for justifying his selection against Hull. Most fans were surprised that the manager had named Moses in his starting line-up in place of Fabregas as he moved to a 3-4-3 formation.

The Nigeria international played at right-wing back in his first Premier League start for The Blues in over three years and put in an all-action performance. Conte described his display as "incredible" and hoped to see similar outings from the Nigerian in future weeks. "Moses played an incredible game - in defensive situations and offensive situations, he was fantastic because he was working very hard. He deserved to play, and he showed me my choice was right. If he plays in this way it's fantastic. I also think Pedro (can play there). It gives us the opportunity to use wingers - if we have wingers who can play in this role, it gives us great options."

Moses, though, was replaced by Fabregas late on after picking up a hamstring injury.

The new formation and system pleased Conte, though he was reluctant to suggest he might use it every week. The game was Marcos Alonso's first start for the club since signing from Fiorentina as well as Azpilicueta's first ever game as a centre-back. "Alonso played in this role at Fiorentina. This was his first Premier League start, but in the same way as the other players he must work. He played a good game but he can improve." He added, "I saw a lot of things that I like to see. We work to put pressure to win the ball quickly, to try to play football, to put high pressure. I like this, but to do this we need a bit of time and we must change the habit of the past. The mentality is important. The work is good and we must continue."

As well as defensive changes Conte's midfield was set up vastly differently with Kante deployed in a far more advanced position, regularly finding himself breaking into the box, while Hazard, usually a starter off the left, was given a free role in behind Costa. "Now we have another solution, another tactical system. It depends on the game and the opponent, but I think it's a good way and in this game I'm very happy for the players because when you finish with a clean sheet after you concede two and three goals in the last four games it is important to find more confidence. Now I think we must continue to work. We know that to change the past we need to work a lot, together, and to understand there is a road to improve. Then to play games against Liverpool, Arsenal, City, United or Tottenham in another aspect."

WEDNESDAY, 5 OCTOBER 2016

Branislav Ivanovic would fight to try and win back his position.

While Ivanovic started the campaign as a regular, the 32-year-old now found himself on the bench. "I was fully fit and healthy for the match with Hull, but I never got the chance." Ivanovic said. "I'll always put myself below the interests of the team, be that national side or club. When the team is successful and when they win, it's quickly forgotten when you make mistakes. It's been a while since I was a back-up, but I do not mind. I'll sit on the bench whenever the coach decides, and not for the first time in these eight years at Chelsea. I think that the status of players cannot be concluded on the basis of an un-played 90 minutes. Today's football means that every day you have to fight and prove yourself. There is no past, no future, only the present. It is normal to be on the bench, especially in clubs that over and over again are going a step further."

THURSDAY, 6 OCTOBER 2016

Conte introduced open discussions during post-match analysis sessions, giving players a chance to air their views. Ruben Loftus-Cheek told Metro.co.uk that the sessions had been one of the most notable changes installed by Conte. "A real benefit that we do differently (since Conte's arrival) is that we sit down and analyse the games. I think that helps. As a team we'll analyse the game, good stuff and bad stuff, which I think helps massively. That's one thing that he's brought in that I think everyone's impressed about."

Speaking at the launch of EA Sports' FIFA 17, Loftus-Cheek added: "After a game when we're next in we'll analyse the game together and it's like a discussion, it's really open. It's really good for the team, it's an open discussion."

Another interesting and challenging change was switching formation. "We've been trying different systems and I think we're doing quite well. The manager likes to implement his ideas and we're trying to do that to the best of our ability. I know sometimes it takes a while to get used to them but I'm sure we will because we're working hard on the training pitch and whatever formation the manager asks us to play we'll play. It always benefits, if we need to switch formation in the game, if we need to chase the game we can switch so it's all the better."

Conte quickly saw in the England Under-21 international the attributes that could see the player shift from midfield to attack and tried him in an advanced role in pre-season. "At first it was a bit strange but I think I adapted quite quickly. I had never played striker before he came. He said to me I think striker kind of suits you because I'm strong and I'm fast and I'm good technically so he said it might suit so he asked me to try it and if I'm playing I'm going to take that. Even though I do enjoy playing midfield more, if that's where the manager wants me to play I'll play it."

Loftus-Cheek had made just two appearances, both in the EFL Cup, but was determined to break through. "Right now for me it's just game time on the pitch that I need. I'm working hard on the training pitch and trying to give the manager confidence to play me more. And I think the more game time I get the more I will improve."

He insisted the club must aim for the Premier League title this season. "I think the manager said we want to win titles and I think being at Chelsea, it's a massive club so I think that has to be the aim, to win titles. And that's what we want to do, that's why we're on the training pitch every day working, trying to improve what we need to improve. I think everyone in the team thinks we can."

John Obi Mikel revealed they were aiming to win the Premier League with Conte. "I can only see Chelsea winning trophies with this guy and hopefully we can achieve that." he told Goal. "The manager knows what he wants, we are behind him, we support him as players and we have to go with him, so I think that everyone is looking forward to this season. It is going to be a very interesting season with the likes of Manchester City, Arsenal, Liverpool, Everton, everyone has spent a lot of money and it is going to be very difficult. We want to be, at the end of the season, on the top and, if we can win it, why not (go for it)."

He continued: "Yes, (Conte shouts a lot) in training. In games I don't even need to say, you can see how passionate he is and how passionate he is about winning, it is just the passion he has for the game and the way he thinks that he can get his message across to the players on the pitch. Sometimes the manager needs to communicate with the players even when they are on the pitch, to do what he needs them to do. I have never seen anyone that passionate, but yes, he is very, very passionate about winning games. A lovely guy to talk to and he listens to what you say. I don't think any player has a problem telling him how they feel because I think he listens quite a lot and I think it helps that he also played football and he knows what we go through and players like to be listened to sometimes, and I think that Antonio does that really well."

WEDNESDAY, 12 OCTOBER 2016

Eden Hazard would prefer to play as the No.10. He excelled in a central attacking role in the win over Hull and he felt he would thrive if given that role for the rest of the season.

"I like to play as a No.10. I think I have more freedom offensively. For Belgium, we have full-backs who run hard and create a lot of space, which is good and I like to play there. I don't know if I will play there for Chelsea. You need to ask the manager! I play on the left hand side and I try to do the best I can. It's true I like to play as a 10. Sometimes at Chelsea we don't play a system with a No.10, too. I don't think Chelsea wants to change just for me (to play) as a 10. I did well in the past as a left winger and for now, I am trying to get back to that best again."

THURSDAY, 13 OCTOBER 2016

Perhaps surprisingly and prematurely, several bookmakers suspended betting on Conte being the next Premier League manager to lose his job.

Here's how The Sun put it, in their headline:

"ALL BETS OFF Antonio Conte sacked by Chelsea? Three leading bookies suspend betting on Italian boss being axed by Roman Abramovich. SunSport understands Conte has been at Stamford Bridge today, with rumours circulating about his future."

The Sun continued: "Following a flurry of bets this afternoon, the former Italian boss is now firm favourite to be the second manager to lose his job. SunSport understands that Conte was not at the Cobham training ground today, as rumours persists surrounding his future. A spokesperson for Sun Bets said 'We've currently suspended the next Premier League manager to go until the rumours about Antonio Conte's future at Chelsea settle down.' The shift in the odds, backed down from 16/1 to 4/1 favourite, suggests that Conte's future at the Bridge hangs in the balance. Diego Simeone is Sun Bets 7/2 favourite to take over the reins."

A spokesman for Paddy Power added: "It sounds like 'Antonio Gone-te', according to our bettors at least. Atletico manager Diego Simeone, who recently reduced his contract with La Liga leaders, is our favourite to be next Blues boss - with Bournemouth's Eddie Howe the leading English contender."

Betfair slashed their odds from 33/1 to 6/1, Ladbrokes from 20/1 to 6/1. William Hill had Conte as fourth-favourite to go, at 4/1.

It was already the sacking season as two weeks earlier Swansea boss Francesco Guidolin was the league's first casualty. American Bob Bradley was immediately installed as his successor. The Daily Express reported that the Italian "went from being an outsider in the market to an odds-on favourite". At the start of the week he was around 25-1 to be the next manager to lose his job but all that has changed according to reports on website The Sack Race. "Betway and Paddy Power are both no longer taking bets on the Italian, while he is as short as 6-4 with BetVictor and 2-1 with Sky Bet." it said. But it also suggested that the run on Conte "is likely the result of one or two monster bets".

Well, as the soon-to-be new President would have put it - Fake News!

Chelsea were forced to insist that Conte was not about to be sacked and stated that their manager "still has Roman Abramovich's trust" three months after his appointment on a three-year deal, while Chelsea sources told Sky Sports that rumours of Conte's impending departure "are absolute nonsense."

Since becoming the tenth manager of Abramovich's 13-year reign, Conte had struggled to re-establish Chelsea as a serious force in the Premier League. The nadir had come in the 3-0 defeat to Arsenal coupled with only one win in four games which had left them in eighth place and eight points behind leaders Manchester City. However, a home clash against Leicester City offered the chance to relaunch the season after the two-week international break but lose and the pressure would only increase on their manager, the media reports suggested at the time.

Meanwhile, Chelsea announced a record kit deal with Nike, somewhat overshadowed by the 'sacking' story. According to The Guardian the agreement was "worth an estimated £60m per season for the next 15 years". Chelsea had been in negotiations with the American sportswear giants throughout the summer after they opted to end their partnership with Adidas six years early, costing £40m, offset by the deal with Nike, which begins next season. Describing the partnership as "the largest commercial deal in the club's history", Chelsea said all their teams - including academy and women's - will wear Nike kits until 2032, by which time they will have received a staggering £900m from the sportswear company. The Nike deal will bring in double what the Adidas contract was worth but it's still chickenfeed compared to the £106m that Real Madrid pocket each season from Adidas; who also signed a deal with Manchester United two seasons ago worth a minimum £750m over ten years.

FRIDAY, 15 OCTOBER 2016

Conte was poised to give a momentous press conference where the media were salivating at the prospect of enquiring about his relationship with Abramovich, which some believed had already hit the rocks. However, Conte laughed off the rumours and took rumours of him being sacked as Chelsea manager very much with a smile.

"I am trying to find out who put the money on, it's very difficult!" he joked.

Conte was asked if the pressure on managers in England is more extreme than in Italy. As a former Juve manager Conte dealt with some of the highest expectations in Serie A and denied feeling under increased scrutiny on these shores. He added: "The pressure is the same. It's normal to live with the pressure. Also, the players, you want to win, you want to do good work. Pressure is a part of our job. It's normal. The same as in the other countries."

The build-up to Saturday's game was naturally dominated by talk about Conte's position. "It is difficult to talk about the situation because I am focused about my work and improving the team." he said. "I have a good relationship and communication with the club. We are working very hard to change the situation of the past. We are trying to build something important for the present and future."

N'Golo Kante was up against his former club for the first time and Conte commented: "Kante is an important player. He is a fantastic player with good stamina, technique and personality. He brought a great will to fight and he is a humble man. I like him and these types of players, those who put the team before himself."

John Terry had completed a full week of training. "He is available because he came back in training sessions in the middle of the week." confirmed the Chelsea boss. "He has recovered from his injury. For the line-up, I prefer not to give it away. I will try to take the best decision for the team. Now I have four central defenders and I have to take the decision for three. I have to evaluate the situation. I love the players that always show good spirit. I prefer the English spirit because it very strong."

Conte also took the opportunity to send his thoughts to Willian after the death of the Brazilian's mother. He was given compassionate leave, missing the Leicester game. Conte confirmed: "We are very sad. We knew the problem with his Mum. We are very close to our players and we are with him and his family."

Following the training session Courtois took to Instagram to share a picture of the day's events - including a jovial, scarf-clad shot of Costa, who kept his teammates in high spirits by combining his neck-scarf and hat to create a mysterious look during the attacking drill.

SATURDAY, 15 OCTOBER 2016
Chelsea 3-0 Leicester City
Premier League

Sacking! What sacking?

Chelsea condemned defending Premier League champions Leicester City to a fourth consecutive away defeat with a dominant display.

Ahead inside seven minutes when Nemanja Matic flicked on Eden Hazard's corner for Diego Costa to smash home, this turned out to be yet another turning point in the season.

A David Luiz free-kick struck the post, before Pedro played in Hazard, who rounded Kasper Schmeichel to slot in.

Luiz hit his own post when clearing a cross but Victor Moses' finish after a one-two with substitute Nathaniel Chalobah completed the scoring.

Leicester, who left Riyad Mahrez on the bench for the first time in 36 league games, failed to register a shot on target as they struggled to cope against Chelsea's aggressive pressing and quick passing. Defeat left Claudio Ranieri's side with eight points from their first eight games - the joint second lowest haul by a defending Premier League champion, along with Chelsea's team of the previous season.

Since joining Chelsea from Leicester, Kante had found himself doing slightly less of the defensive work that established him as such a prized midfielder at the King Power Stadium. But he continued being in the right place at the right time and this was another excellent performance - clearly missed by Ranieri's side.

However, much of Chelsea's success came from their wing-backs. When Alonso - making his home debut - harried Danny Drinkwater high up the pitch to win the ball back and deliver a dangerous low cross, he was repeating the pattern set by Moses on the opposite right flank.

Kante would have scored Chelsea's third had it not been for captain Wes Morgan, who made a brilliant block after a Costa cross spilled off Schmeichel's legs to leave the goalmouth exposed. And his perfectly weighted through-ball deserved a better finish from Moses, who eventually did settle the points when latching on to a delightful flick by 21-year-old English midfielder Chalobah - making his senior home debut after six loan spells away from the club.

When several bookmakers had suspended betting on Conte being the next Premier League manager to lose his job it had left doubts whether there would be a sign of weakness in his side's performance. There was not! Chelsea began with a swagger and Costa's early goal was the end product. The Premier League's top scorer gambled on a late move to the back post and, as Morgan did not stay with him, was left with an easy finish for his seventh goal; it had taken him until January to reach that total the previous season.

The dipping Luiz free-kick that crashed against the post would have been a fitting second, so when Hazard found himself through on goal after a slightly lucky bounce it was hard to deny that a 2-0 lead was deserved. The Belgium winger showed superb composure for his third goal from eight matches, compared to four from 31 the previous term. Also, Matic (three assists in eight appearances) has made more Premier League assists this season than in the entire 2015/16 campaign (two assists in 33 apps). What a difference a season makes.

One of the finest flourishes, however, came from Conte. There was a huge round of cheers from the home crowd when he brilliantly trapped a misplaced long pass that plummeted down into his technical area. The fans found it hard not to have been incredibly impressed by their team's performance - especially after what they had witnessed the previous season.

Ranieri commented: "When you concede a goal from a corner again it is clear: you come to Chelsea and your attention must be at the maximum. We made mistakes. We tried to react and the second half was much better. If we scored the goal when we create a chance we can re-open the match. But our approach to the match was not good. Maybe we were a little nervous. We miss him (Kante) - but we have to play better."

Conte observed: "It was a good game. From the start I asked them to play well with intensity and to try to do what we are doing in training. I am very happy because I had a good reply. This is the best game for us. I saw good commitment. When you work hard it is important to have a good performance. In the week, we tried a lot to find a solution that gave us more compactness. For this team and squad this system is the right fit. The coach must understand and find the right suit. We are like a tailor."

Demonstrating a wonderful spirit throughout the squad teammates were quick to congratulate Ola Aina on his debut. The win was dedicated to Willian and his family as well as to Oscar, who was also allowed to fly to Brazil because of a family illness.

SUNDAY, 16 OCTOBER 2016

Gary Cahill worked harder within matches because of the ground he had to cover in Conte's 3-5-2 system. Due to the nature of the attacking wing-backs, Cahill was often tasked with covering ground on the flanks, but insisted the formation was an enjoyable one within which to play. "I feel like I do more running. I have to come inside as well as go outside when we go out wide so I'm covering more ground. But I am enjoying it and ultimately it is working for us as well. The last four games have been brilliant. I heard the manager speak the other day and he said that when you get the results it gives you belief that it is working and you're going in the right direction. For me it's been different but enjoyable. As a player you take the best out of every manager and learn that to move forward. We have had a lot of great managers at this club. We are seeing the results on the pitch. It's a long season, a long way to go, but it's important we stay in and amongst the front runners."

N'Golo Kante praised Conte's new 3-4-3 system. He had so far featured in every game and, within the new system, was deployed in a far more advanced position and regularly found himself breaking into the box as Matic was tasked with the deep-lying defensive role. "The new system is working well." said Kante. "We have been better with and without the ball, and we have conceded fewer chances. Personally I like the system too. My job in a defensive central midfield position is to cut off attacks against us, but it has been a bit different in the past two games as I have been able to get forward a bit myself."

Kante was Man of the Match in the victory over Ranieri's Foxes. "We needed the victory but to score three goals too is really good for our confidence. I am so happy with the win." added Kante. "Getting Man of the Match was good for me but winning and playing well as a team was more important. I had a formidable season at Leicester and so it was a special match for me. Before the game I spoke to my old teammates but I am a Chelsea player now and once it started it was just another game. I wanted to help my team get the three points. That's what we did."

MONDAY, 17 OCTOBER 2016

It emerged that Costa and Conte were involved in a heated row in the Chelsea dressing room following their victory over Leicester, according to reports in Spain. Costa was caught making a substitution gesture towards the manager in the second half and it was assumed that the striker wanted to be taken off in order to avoid another yellow card, which would have seen him suspended for the clash with Manchester United. But it emerged that Costa was reacting angrily to Conte's constant instructions, as the Italian was unhappy with his side's lack of pressing after the half-time break. According to Spanish newspaper, Marca, the argument between Costa and Conte turned into a shouting match in the changing room after the game. Costa reportedly told the Chelsea manager that it's "the last time" he was to be pointed at on the pitch and Conte should "get him out" of the club if he was unhappy with his performances. Costa reacted angrily to Conte's outburst and the pair had to be separated. The row was the biggest between the pair so far since Conte arrival at Stamford Bridge. However, the disagreement was over quickly and Costa was seen laughing with teammates shortly after the game.

Conte was in no mood to defend Costa after the game when he was quoted as saying "I know that in football when you are winning 2-0, in ten or 15 minutes you can be losing. For this reason, I always stay (on edge) to maintain the right atmosphere on the pitch for my players."

The club, however, gave Costa a warning about his behaviour according to the Daily Telegraph.

The incident brought back memories of a similar exchange between Costa and Mourinho last season resulting in the then Chelsea boss leaving his frontman out for the next game as punishment for the disobedience.

WEDNESDAY, 20 OCTOBER 2016

Former Chelsea player and manager Gianluca Vialli was amazed by Conte's start, being particularly impressed by his ability to convince the squad to play in his style so quickly.

"It is the most difficult job for the manager to convince players of that talent, that creativity, to actually work hard for the team when it's not in possession of the ball." Vialli told the club's official site. "You build a team and you become successful when you are defensively solid. He switched to three at the back and they look much more solid, not conceding goals. The rest comes. I'm amazed by the ability of Antonio; in two or three weeks, he's already been able to make them play the way he wants. They are still a work in progress, you can see they are not perfect, but I think that is the way to go. Antonio will get them to where they belong, which is the top of the table."

THURSDAY, 21 OCTOBER 2016

Jose Mourinho, as an opposition coach, had been back at the Bridge for the Champions League match which paired his Inter side with Chelsea in 2010. Before the 1-0 victory, which would confirm Inter's place in the Champions League quarter-finals, he had been able to boast an incredible record at the Bridge. "Mourinho does not lose at Stamford Bridge." he proclaimed after a 2-1 first-leg win at San Siro. "We can go there with a legitimate ambition to go through."

"I have big emotional connections with Chelsea." he said shortly before returning to west London for a second spell in 2013. "One day I think I have to go back to English football, to Chelsea or another club. Chelsea are in my heart." He ended up doing both, cementing his position as the

Blues' most successful manager of all time with the 2015 Premier League title before a calamitous defence led him ultimately towards the Manchester United job.

"Working in England, staying in the Premier League, I knew that sooner or later I had to play against Chelsea and I had to go to Stamford Bridge. The computer has decided that it is now, and here we go. When I played there with Inter, before that I had never lost a match at Stamford Bridge because I had that home record. Now I have lost already a few matches at the Bridge, last season I lost two or three matches in the Bridge so I cannot use the same words because now I lost there."

Manchester United's 4-1 Europa League win over Fenerbahce occupied Mourinho's mind and left little scope for sentimentalism in such a hectic week. He was now back to his usual mind games and suggested he wasn't really well prepared to take on Conte. "I don't have to analyse their start to the season. You just look at the table and you see where they are, and they are in a good position. So their start to the season cannot be bad if they are where they are."

So, the eyes of the footballing world would definitely be on 'the Big One' - Mourinho's return to Stamford Bridge. Should Chelsea win, they would be five points clear of United after only nine games. Costa had already netted several match-winning strikes under Conte, in such good form in fact that new £30m signing Batshuayi had yet to start a league game, and the team would be confident ahead of the clash. Defeat for United, however, threatened to cut them adrift early in the title race but a win would add a vastly different complexion.

Mourinho did not expect a negative reaction from supporters who had continued to back him last season despite Chelsea's on-pitch struggles, and he would attempt to treat this game the same as any other. Who was he kidding? No one! "To say I care is not true. I am more focused on the game. I try to prepare myself for the match, so I cannot say that I care. What can I expect? I don't know. They can think about me and remember our great relation and have a good reaction. They can look at me and say for 90 minutes he is Manchester United manager and he is playing against us, so he is not someone we like at this moment. I did my job (at Chelsea). They gave me their love and they gave me their support. That is the most important thing. If now I go there as Manchester United manager and they decide to have a different approach, I will always respect them. I played there with Inter. I tried to do my job. If you ask me, if my team scores a goal, am I going to celebrate like a crazy kid? No. I think I can control the emotion of that situation. Am I going to have a negative reaction if the crowd has something negative with me? No. I have the maturity enough to control the emotion. I have lots of respect. What Manchester United fans can expect from me is more important. What Manchester United fans can expect from me is to play against Chelsea the same way I play against Fenerbahce, Liverpool, anyone, because that is my job."

Mourinho's second departure from Stamford Bridge was officially portrayed as mutual consent but he now admitted he was sacked. No hard feelings, though, and he was looking forward to seeing some of the lifelong friends he made at the club. Again, no hard feelings. Really?

Abramovich was not among those he would be seeking out. "He was never my friend. We always had the relationship of owner-manager. Very respectful relationship. We were never friends. We were never close to each other. When some managers leave clubs, they like to, I don't know the right saying, but in Portuguese it is 'wash the dirty clothes'. Go back and speak and speak and speak. I leave clubs with a very good feeling, the feeling of doing everything to succeed. I gave everything to the club. I don't like to go back and speak specially about the bad things. I want to keep the good things - and at Chelsea I had so many good things, in terms of results, friends I have for life, an amazing empathy with the supporters. The supporters didn't change their relationship with me because of last season and a couple of months of bad results."

Chelsea's start to last season was shocking, losing nine of their first 16 Premier League games while Mourinho's position was undermined by a dispute with former club doctor Eva Carneiro. Mourinho does not feel it has affected him: "That period came in a part of my career when I was already a grown man. I was not a kid. I was lucky to have a big club like Manchester United, who focused on my career and not my last three months. I was lucky enough to have the chance to stay in the competition I most love and to stay in a big club like Manchester United, with a big project, with a big challenge like I have in my hands. Everything is positive."

FRIDAY, 21 OCTOBER 2016

Conte aimed two digs at Mourinho.

"When there are these types of very bad seasons - because we finished 10th in the table - it's normal that something remains in the players. In their minds. In their heads." Conte explained. "In this situation, the risk is to lose confidence. Also, it's very difficult because you must change what happened last season, and that's not easy."

In a further thinly-veiled attack, Conte said that he would never set up his side to play like United did at Liverpool in Monday's bore 0-0 draw. Asked if he could envisage adopting similar tactics, he said: "No. I think it's right always to play for a win and to start a game trying to win. I try and transfer these thoughts to my players always. If you play at home or away, it must be the same. You must start the game with only one target: to win. Not to play for a draw. I don't like this. It's not football. I think that it's also important to win in the right way. Because sometimes I've won in the past with other clubs but I wasn't satisfied with the performance. When you win it's important to put in a good performance for our fans. To win is important, but it's important also to play good football, to play with good intensity, to show always the will to win, the passion."

Victor Moses revealed that during Mourinho's second reign at Stamford Bridge he never spoke to him. Moses was sent out on loan for the entirety, firstly to Liverpool and then to Stoke. "He never spoke to me." Moses told ESPN FC of Mourinho. "I thought in my head, 'He's got his own players already.' I think we chatted a couple of times on the phone - he asked if I was alright at Liverpool, but that was it."

Moses, however, was treated differently by Conte. "The manager came to me and said: 'I feel that you're working hard, I really enjoy watching you play and I don't want you to go out on loan'. When he said that to me I was really pleased. To be honest, I just want to go out there, enjoy my football and work hard for him. He's played the game before, he understands it and he understands how players feel."

SATURDAY, 22 OCTOBER 2016

Conte emphasised that he was consulted over the deadline day purchase of David Luiz. "Never do we take the decisions (alone)." Conte told reporters. "We take the decisions together with the club. In every situation, we make the decisions together. Never (just) me or the club, always together. I think this is always the right way, you want to build something important for the people."

He also revealed that Paul Pogba dreamed of returning to Manchester United. He coached the midfielder at Juventus but believed the 23-year-old always had his eyes set on a return to Old Trafford. "He was born in England in a football aspect and he came back. When we took him from

Manchester United he was a fantastic player. He deserves it all. For him to come back to Man United was his dream. I wish for him only best - but only after the game."

SUNDAY, 23 OCTOBER 2016
Chelsea 4-0 Manchester United
Premier League

Jose Mourinho was humiliated on his return to Chelsea as his former club blew away his Manchester United side.

In what turned out to be a season-defining game, the Blues led after just 30 seconds when Pedro capitalised on slack defending. The tone was set when Chris Smalling hesitated in dealing with a long ball, allowing Pedro to nip in and around David de Gea - and United never recovered. Gary Cahill smashed in the second after the defence allowed Eden Hazard's corner to bounce in their box. United offered little sign of making a comeback, falling further behind when Hazard drilled in a precise 15-yard strike. Hazard had now already equalled his goal tally from last season in the Premier League - four - in just nine games. N'Golo Kante skipped around a static defence to slot in and seal victory as Chelsea moved to within a point of Premier League leaders Manchester City.

Suddenly, Chelsea were proper title contenders.

The comprehensive win lifted the Blues above Tottenham into fourth with only one point separating the top five. United stayed seventh as the gap between them and the early pacesetters widened to six points, with almost a quarter of the season gone.

Mourinho said before the match he was unsure and unconcerned about the reception he would be given. Having delivered seven trophies in his two spells, it turned out to be positive. Hundreds gathered to greet Mourinho as he walked off the United team bus, while he received a warm embrace from former skipper John Terry before kick-off. That is where the hospitality ended. The fans could not resist chanting "you're not special anymore" after his team were torn to shreds.

Mourinho said before the game he would not "celebrate like a crazy kid" if his new team scored at the Bridge; there was precious little sign of that being put to the test.

United were ripped open by Pedro's opener without even having a touch and the severity of the scoreline was emphasised by some startling statistics: Pedro scored the fastest goal in the Premier League this season after 30 seconds, he was also booked after 59 seconds for his celebration, the quickest yellow this season in the Premier League. This was only the sixth time United had conceded in the opening minute of a Premier League game; Gus Poyet, Jason Euell, Marlon Harewood, Jermain Defoe and Edin Dzeko were the other scorers. Only twice before had Jose Mourinho seen his side concede inside the first minute - both to Southampton while at Chelsea (James Beattie in 2004 and Jay Rodriguez in 2013). Chelsea had gone eight league games - winning four and drawing four - without losing against United, their best run against the Red Devils in their history. Far more consequential though, this was the heaviest defeat for Mourinho in all competitions since Real Madrid's 5-0 defeat by Barcelona in November 2010. It was United's heaviest Premier League defeat since the 6-1 loss against Manchester City in October 2011. This was the first time since 1999 that they had lost a Premier League away match by four or more goals - also at Chelsea.

The basic ability to defend a set-piece eluded them for Chelsea's second, two deflected touches helping the ball on to the unmarked Cahill, who lashed in.

United, without the injured Wayne Rooney, looked unrecognisable from the side that had kept a clean sheet at Anfield on Monday. Always expected to be well organised and difficult to break down they certainly did not look like a typical Mourinho team.

A stony-faced coach watched his static defenders allow Hazard and then Kante to skip into space and score after the break, leaving Conte lapping up the acclaim of a home crowd revelling in their former boss's misfortune.

"We made incredible defensive mistakes." admitted Mourinho. "And then you pay for that."

Conte was tasked with restoring Chelsea's fortunes, but his start was not smooth, as the back-to-back defeats by Liverpool and Arsenal had led to some criticism, forcing him to laugh off rumours of his imminent sacking. But, after making a tactical switch to a 3-5-2 formation following those defeats, Conte's team was now flourishing.

Three successive victories had pushed the Blues back among the frontrunners, with the Stamford Bridge crowd showing their appreciation for the new manager as he urged them to make more noise during the second half.

"It is important for the manager to find the right solution for your team." said Conte on his team's recent revival. "It was not a good situation when Chelsea conceded in every game - we change and now we are playing good football."

After this emphatic and highly significant win Conte commented: "We made a fantastic start. We scored the early goal but we continued to play good football, intensity and possession, create many chances. Today we didn't concede, which was important. It was a type of win that increases the confidence. We wanted to show our ambition and give the satisfaction to our fans and show last season was very bad."

Mourinho reflected: "You come with a strategy, you cannot concede a goal in the way we did. We were coming to have an offensive approach. We wanted to create chances; we showed that after the 1-0. The second and the third were counter-attack goals. It is one of those days when you give the advantage to opponents by doing nothing. In terms of points, we got zero points, we lose three points. We are six points from the top, three from the top four, we now need to win matches. We need to win our matches now, which are not easy. We need to win to close that gap - after these last three matches, we made two out of nine. We now need points."

MONDAY, 24 OCTOBER 2016

The recriminations from Mourinho began to bite.

Conte, though, insisted he was "not mocking anyone" after appearing to antagonise Mourinho by the manner of his celebrations at the fourth goal.

Conte had encouraged fans to make more noise in the closing stages but reports emerged that, at the final whistle, when Mourinho whispered into Conte's ear it was not words of praise or respect but anger and dark mutterings of envy.

Mourinho told Conte that his actions had "humiliated" United.

Conte said: "I've been a player too and I know how to behave. I always show great respect for everyone, including Manchester United."

Reports in the Italian media claimed Mourinho told Conte: "You don't celebrate like that at 4-0, you can do it at 1-0, otherwise it's humiliating for us."

Neither manager confirmed what was said in their post-match media conferences. "There was no incident, it was just a normal thing to do. I wasn't mocking anyone, I wouldn't do that." said Conte. "Today it was right to call our fans in a moment when I was listening to only the supporters of Manchester United at 4-0. The players, after a 4-0 win, deserved a great clap. It's very normal. If we want to cut the emotion we can go home and change our job."

"To the millions of fans we have around the world they have a bad feeling and I am so sorry for that." stated Mourinho. "I have to apologise as the leader of the dressing room and the only thing I can say is I'm 100% Man Utd, not 99% for Man Utd and 1% for Chelsea. I feel deeply about the situation but there is only one answer, training on Monday and keep fighting."

Conte added: "It is important for the manager to find the right solution for your team. It was not a good situation when Chelsea conceded in every game, we change and now we are playing good football."

Conte revealed after the match that he felt the supporters were not applauding his team enough. "We were 4-0 up and our crowd was flat." the 47-year-old told Sky Italia in a post-match interview. "I wanted our supporters to applaud our team because they deserved it."

Former Manchester United and England defender Phil Neville commented: "After the first six games of the season, which saw them struggle defensively and lose to Liverpool and Arsenal, I was wondering what their new manager Antonio Conte was doing. His team looked like the same old Chelsea who struggled last year. But then Conte changed to the 3-5-2 formation that has brought him such success with Juventus and Italy, and they have not looked back. While Chelsea look like they have found the formation and system that suits them, United are still searching for theirs. It looked like they might have found it against Liverpool at Anfield on Monday night when they were hard to beat, solid, aggressive and a threat going forward. They still created chances against Chelsea on Sunday but pretty much everything else went out of the window - they were opened up far too easily and did not have the same aggression."

So, the previously titled 'Special One' was now the 'Humiliated One' and social media was quick to react:

Former Chelsea striker, Eidur Gudjohnsen, cheekily stating that "Jose still knows how to get the best out of @ChelseaFC"

Stand-up comedian, Benji Waterstones, "A painful Chelsea return for Mourinho. It's like when you meet up with an ex and they look better than when you were together."

TUESDAY, 25 OCTOBER 2016

Conte dismissed accusations that he had humiliated Mourinho insisting his behaviour on the touchline is simply "normal" for him.

In his press conference, Conte was asked if he felt he needed to apologise to Mourinho but the question was batted away by Chelsea's head of communications.

However, Conte was keen to stress that he meant no disrespect with his animated behaviour in his technical area and that he acted in a similar fashion during his time at Juventus. "I think everyone must show respect for me, for my work, for my job, I think in every game I show myself." said Conte. "I have a history and you can see my history, my past, my behaviour on the bench, it's normal, I'm a passionate man. I want to stay very close with my players, especially when they are struggling. I always show respect to my opponent."

Mourinho's criticism of Conte was justified, at least according to former Spain manager Vicente del

Bosque, who masterminded Spain's 2010 World Cup and Euro 2012 wins. He believed Mourinho has every right to feel aggrieved. "It did not seem like a wrong message from Mourinho to Conte." Del Bosque told AS Espana. "Sometimes Conte has to be a little more considerate when he celebrates victories, really. I was also hurt when we played against Italy at Euro 2016. I'm not saying don't express joy, there's no need to be as dull as me, but express a moderate joy. It is not that I am a defender of Mourinho, but he had a point."

Conversely, West Ham manager, Slaven Bilic, defended Conte. "I know what Jose thought of that, but I don't think that's the reason Conte did it, to humiliate United." argued Bilic. "He just wanted the crowd to praise the team because they were winning, and for what they had done in the game. From my point of view I don't think he wanted to humiliate United. On the touchline many managers just sit and watch the game, others are like they are playing. You have to be yourself. During that game I saw nothing wrong from Conte or nothing he hasn't done since he started. It was typical Conte, aggressive, but in a good way."

Conte, moving onto tactical issues, explained why his three-man defence worked so well. "The central defenders on the right and the left must be very fast and aggressive. The players that play in the middle of the three defenders must be more tactical, must reflect more and find the right position, and also call the line up and down. In these last three games we did very well. It's normal when you play with the same players. They take confidence in the role to play together. It's important also for example in this game, the cup, to find a new solution. If you have during the season an injury, then it's important to have a good solution ready."

Cesc Fabregas was still struggling with a thigh problem, picked up ahead of the Manchester United game, which now ruled him out of the trip to West Ham. "He's not still well. We must wait, he had a muscular problem and we are waiting." Conte confirmed. "We must be patient because the muscular problem was tight. But I hope to see him soon with the team in the training session."

John Obi Mikel spoke about his lack of game time. The Nigerian was out of favour and yet to make a single appearance for Conte, competing with Matic and Kante for a spot in defensive midfield. He confirmed that he'd spoken to Conte about his frustrations at the club. "I hope I will get some playing time against West Ham (in the EFL Cup), but it is down to the manager." said Mikel. "He has been open and honest with me. I respect him for that. He has explained the situation and I totally understand. When you have been at a club for a long time, these things happen where a club wants to move forward. I just have to be professional, work as hard as I can to try and get into the team. I work twice as hard every day and it's because I appreciate this club. I have been here a long time, have a lot of trophies and memories that will never go away. If I don't get back in the side, I will respect it. I always respect the football club's decision. The club is more important than me."

WEDNESDAY, 26 OCTOBER 2016
West Ham United 2-1 Chelsea
EFL Cup, Fourth Round

Crowd disturbances marred the conclusion of West Ham's EFL Cup fourth-round victory at the London Stadium. Plastic bottles and seats were thrown towards the end of the match as hundreds of fans were involved in ugly scenes.

The flash points were a blot on what had been an entertaining night on the pitch as a much-changed Chelsea were beaten by a cohesive West Ham. A superb Cheikhou Kouyate header before the break and an 18-yard Edimilson Fernandes strike a few minutes into the second half secured West Ham's place in the last eight and a tie against Manchester United who beat Manchester City 1-0.

Gary Cahill swept home from close range in injury time but it was only a consolation at the end of another difficult evening off the pitch for the Hammers. Security was boosted for the high-risk derby and an alcohol ban imposed as part of a "robust policing plan", with West Ham's new home dogged by disturbances.

Prior to this tie there had been nine arrests outside the stadium and 23 banning orders issued by West Ham in what has been a traumatic start to life in the former Olympic Stadium.

Chelsea were allocated more than 5,000 tickets, making this the biggest test to the police and stewards but once again trouble stirred. An ugly atmosphere was brewing throughout the match and as the game neared the end riot police were deployed to maintain order as home and away fans came together in a section of the stadium concourse.

Conte commented: "I must be honest, because I didn't see the situation. We were playing and I didn't see this. I don't like this type of situation. It's important to see always the right atmosphere. Above all in England, we are used to seeing the right atmosphere. This country is fantastic in this aspect. I'm sorry about this situation."

Slaven Bilic said he did not notice the disturbance but added that the club was "totally against it". In a statement, West Ham said fans found to have "acted improperly" would be banned for life from attending West Ham games.

Chelsea made seven changes, the most notable inclusion was that of captain John Terry, returning from injury to the centre of a three-man defence. Terry had last played on 11 September and in his absence Cahill, Luiz and Azpilicueta had formed a backline that registered three consecutive clean sheets. Azpilicueta was moved to wing-back to make room for Terry and the former England international's lack of match practice played a part in the visiting defence's weakness. Terry was beaten by Kouyate as the midfielder headed home for only his second goal of the season and the 35-year-old also played a part in the Hammers' second as Fernandes threaded his strike through his legs on the way to goal.

Conte brought on Costa, Hazard and Pedro early in the second but they failed to spark a comeback. Costa put through by the bright Willian, making a return following compassionate leave, was one-on-one with Randolph in the closing stages, but chipped inches wide.

Chalobah's first-half effort was tipped over by Randolph and Kante also went close.

Bilic said his team were "buzzing again" after back-to-back victories in the league following a shaky start to the season and they carried their recent form into the tie against Chelsea.

Bilic: "It was a good game of football, it deserves to be talked about. I can't say we were perfect but we had a plan and the guys executed it in a great way. We were good in defending as a unit. We were really good in keeping the ball and stretching them and playing wide. In the first half it was great and I think we deserved to be more than one up."

Conte was giving the club's young stars the chance to impress. England Under-21 star, Chalobah, who had been loaned out to Watford, Reading and Nottingham Forest was clearly delighted, "It's fantastic to see the manager is giving young players a chance. For me it's just about trying to improve and trying to learn from the experienced players that we have here. I've got to keep going and not get too complacent, keep working hard and see how things go. It's been a dream come true. I've been a ball boy at games like that in the past. I always thought about what it would feel like to step out on the pitch against teams like Manchester United. I'm ever so grateful to everyone at the academy, my family and obviously the manager."

Conte tipped young striker Tammy Abraham to become the future of the club. The 19-year-old joined Bristol City on a season-long loan and has hit eleven goals in 16 appearances for the Championship club. He has yet to make his first team debut at Stamford Bridge but Conte confirmed that Abraham has "great potential" and will be the club's future. "Abraham is another young player, he's the future for Chelsea, for sure." said Conte. "He's very young, I saw him only one week during the pre-season in America, there we decided to send him to play every game, to get experience, and then come back with us. Abraham has a great potential. I think the academy is working very well. Next season… I think now it's important to look to the present."

FRIDAY, 28 OCTOBER 2016

Conte admitted the stress of managing Chelsea is not good for his health.

When asked if he was worried about his heart rate and the stress of the job, he replied while laughing: "I worry a bit. Every day I try to run, to keep fit."

The Premier League title in his first season might help alleviate the pressure… perhaps.

But Conte believed five or six teams can win it this season. "This league is very difficult. Every game anything can happen, you can win or lose. It's important to give continuity, to trust in the work. Now there are five teams very close, but we shouldn't look at the table. We must be focused on the work on the training pitch and take it game-by-game, step-by-step. It's important to improve and trust in the work, these are the most important things."

SUNDAY, 30 OCTOBER 2016

Southampton 0-2 Chelsea

Premier League

Chelsea kept pace with the leading pack as they moved into fourth place with an impressive win.

The fourth win in a row - a feat they last achieved in April 2015 - put them one point behind Manchester City, Arsenal and Liverpool. Chelsea now had exactly double the number of points (22) that they had after ten games last season (11).

Chelsea took the lead when Hazard capitalised on poor marking before cutting inside Steven Davis and powering a shot through the legs of keeper Fraser Forster.

Southampton had plenty of the ball but could not find a way through a well-drilled Chelsea, who looked the more threatening and went close when strikes from Hazard and Costa were saved. Costa, however, beat Forster at full stretch with a wonderful curled effort from 22 yards.

Hazard was the 2014/15 Premier League Player of the Season during a campaign in which Mourinho said the Belgian had outperformed Ronaldo! Hazard, though, had struggled to maintain those heights managing four goals and rarely showing the pace and trickery that made him such a threat. Suddenly the magic was back, just as easily and quickly as it had gone.

He had already scored five goals and looked like he'd regained the confidence to torment defenders, scoring in three consecutive Premier League games for the first time, then provided the pass from which Costa added Chelsea's second. Costa had now reached 40 Premier League goals in 64 games, the sixth fastest player to do so and seven games faster than it had taken Manchester City's Sergio Aguero.

Chelsea had been exposed defensively in consecutive league defeats by Liverpool and Arsenal but, since then, they have kept four consecutive clean sheets, for the first time since August 2010 (a run of six), and scored eleven goals.

Conte's move to a formation with three centre-backs had the duel effect of making his team more secure at the back and threatening in attack.

"We've worked hard in training." said Gary Cahill. "We've worked hard on the shape that the manager has brought and we are getting the rewards. It's OK having the shape but it's about having the mentality of the players to go out and dig in and do the business when you need to."

Saints had accumulated 55 shots on target this season before the game, but could muster only one against Chelsea despite 55% of possession; Dusan Tadic's low effort comfortably palmed wide by Courtois.

Southampton manager Claude Puel: "We played very well in the first half with so many possibilities and good play. But it's difficult to play against this team when you concede a goal after a few minutes. They can play their game with a strong defence and counter-attack. It was difficult to find solutions. It's a disappointment because we tried to play good football. We can do better."

Conte commented: "We knew today was a test against a strong side in good shape and form. It's important to win games like this - people can increase their confidence and will to work and trust in the work. We created many chances. It's the perfect game when strikers score and defenders don't concede. The players deserved this; they work hard in training. When you see this type of game and commitment from your players, it's fantastic for a coach."

Premier League Table, Top 6, end of October 2016:

		P	W	D	L	F	A	GD	Pts
1	Manchester City	10	7	2	1	24	9	+15	23
2	Arsenal	10	7	2	1	23	10	+13	23
3	Liverpool	10	7	2	1	24	13	+11	23
4	Chelsea	10	7	1	2	21	9	+12	22
5	Tottenham Hotspur	10	5	5	0	14	5	+9	20
6	Everton	10	5	3	2	15	8	+7	18

CHAPTER EIGHT
NOVEMBER 2016
Chelsea go top and stay there.

TUESDAY, 1 NOVEMBER 2016

Conte needed imported Italian sweets to help soothe his throat from all the shouting he does at his players, according to the Daily Telegraph.

Conte is known to be one of the most vocal and demanding managers in the game, and is often seen barking out the orders from the touchline during matches. He is the same in every training session, and he's relying on Ambrosoli al Miele - a chewable honey sweet not widely sold in the UK - to ensure he doesn't completely lose his voice.

THURSDAY, 3 NOVEMBER 2016

Antonio Conte admits that Chelsea owner Roman Abramovich is a "demanding boss" who takes a keen interest in how he manages the team.

After an early wobble, Conte established Chelsea as firm contenders for the title.

Speaking to Sky Italia, Conte said of Abramovich: "He's a very demanding employer but a great football enthusiast. He went to Austria to follow our training sessions. He comes to Cobham to spend time with us and watch the videos I show to my players, because he really wants to understand. I think this is wonderful."

FRIDAY, 4 NOVEMBER 2016

David Luiz believed Chelsea were like "snipers" under Conte, winning their last four without conceding a single goal since switching to a 3-4-3 formation. Luiz thinks that this more cautious approach has been perfect for the team. "You need to prepare and plan for each game in the best way," he told the club's official site. "Sometimes, when you play away, you need to understand that the opposition might have more possession of the ball. The home team can often be more excited playing in front of their own fans so you have to play with intelligence and wait, like a sniper, for an opportunity. Southampton was that type of game. We found ourselves in good positions and we shot to kill. It's important to understand when you need to play that type of game and when you need to impose yourself and be more dominant. For me, the key is to try to understand the best plan for each specific game."

Chelsea legend Pat Nevin believed the back three of Luiz, Azpilicueta, and Cahill were as good as Juventus's was when Conte was in charge at the Old Lady. Giorgio Chiellini, Leonardo Bonucci, and Andrea Barzagli were rock solid for the Serie A side in their 3-4-3 formation. "In most games with only a goal advantage away from home in the Premier League you can never feel really secure." Nevin wrote for Chelsea's official site. "I have to say I absolutely did feel relaxed throughout and when Diego struck the second, I could have pottered off to get a cup of tea in the secure knowledge that if anyone was going to score in my absence, it would be the Blues. Not that I would walk away while watching the team in such form, but it was an ultra-disciplined performance from start to finish. Even though we have lost no goals in the past seven hours of league football, it is unsurprising when you defend with that level of organisation and concentration. What it underlined was a subject

I was writing about on this page a few weeks ago. Antonio has a plan A for sure, but other plans stretching way down the alphabet are sitting there ready to be utilised when needed."

And, on their likeness to the famous Juve defence: "The defending was not unlike Juventus at their best (without some of the cynicism) and that is high praise indeed. At the end, when the back line of Cesar (Azpilicueta), Gary (Cahill) and David (Luiz) hugged in celebration of yet another clean sheet, the indulgent moment was richly deserved from this team within a team. Everyone around them gave a huge amount of help as well of course, from Thibaut Courtois behind and N'Golo Kante and Nemanja Matic ahead of them, it was nothing less than a living, breathing, impenetrable blue wall."

Conte's training sessions are "back-breaking" according to former Juve star Fabio Quagliarella.

The winger won three Serie A titles under Conte from 2011 to 2014, and also revered the coach's tactical work as "phenomenal". Conte gets angry "very, very often" during the workouts. "With Conte, it was back-breaking both in training and in games." Quagliarella told Mediaset television. "The intensity was so high, and you could see that also in our games. He is phenomenal in the way he prepares you tactically. There were a lot of rules to adhere to - if he gave us a day off, we weren't allowed out of Turin. He got angry very often - very, very often."

SATURDAY, 5 NOVEMBER 2016
Chelsea 5-0 Everton
Premier League

Eden Hazard scored twice as Chelsea climbed to the top of the table for the first time since August with a stylish victory.

Chelsea moved one point clear of Manchester City as Hazard put the Blues ahead with a low, angled shot, before Marcos Alonso added a second when he slotted through Maarten Stekelenburg's legs. Diego Costa made it 3-0 just before half-time, and Hazard scored the pick of the goals after the break. Pedro put the gloss on the result when he tapped into an empty net.

Conte commented: "It was a great game, a good performance. It is important for confidence to be top of the league. We have to continue as Everton is now in the past. The players deserve this because they show me great commitment and I can tell they are working very hard. The team has more balance defensively, but we don't lose our offensive situation. We are creating more chances to score goals."

On Eden Hazard he added "He played an impressive game. We all know he is a talented player. I see he is working a lot for the team and his teammates are very happy for this. He must continue - he is showing his talent in every game. I know the great talent of Eden and he must continue to work and to improve all the time. In this moment, he is putting his talent and himself in the team. This is fantastic and the right way to become one of the best in the world. If you ask me the difference between Messi and Ronaldo, I don't want to reply. The only thing that I want to do is work with him, and my players, to try to improve and support them."

Conte continued "I don't like to speak about last season and a single player. I repeat, I think when you have this type of bad season, many players of the team didn't perform in the right way. Now it is another season and I am pleased he performs with the commitment and the work rate for the win that I see during training. It is important in this type of modern football that you have the talent and technique, but you must run with intensity and the strength to have the contact. Here in

England, we play with an intensity that is supersonic."

For the first time Hazard had scored two or more goals at Stamford Bridge in the league since February 2014. He now had seven goals, but Conte focused on his all-round contribution. "The most important thing I'm seeing with Eden is he's fantastic with the ball and without the ball. He's a complete player, when he plays in this way - with the ball and without the ball. He must continue because he has great talent and he's showing this in every game."

Conte's side have been in searing form since switching to the Italian's favoured 3-4-3 system. "I'm pleased because when you win in this way it is fantastic." he added. "All the players played in the right way with the ball and without the ball. We created many chances to score and it is also the fifth clean sheet in a row. That is fantastic because you look at the past and you can think that this is incredible to reach this result. It's a pity that we have to stop now for the international break. I wanted to continue."

Everton spent the majority of the game penned in their own half and did not manage a shot on target in the entire 90 minutes as Chelsea produced a stunning performance. Many of the visiting fans left well before the end, those that stayed applauded Chelsea off the pitch.

The biggest ovation by far from the home fans was reserved for Hazard, who capped a brilliant display with his two superb goals.

Hazard's transformation was now complete, as he scored for a fourth consecutive league game. Costa had how had a hand in more goals than any other Premier League player, with nine plus three assists, but Hazard was compulsive viewing with the ball at his feet.

Conte claimed Hazard was on the right track to becoming one of the world's best players. BBC Match of the Day pundit Ian Wright heaped on the praise too: "Eden Hazard was world class against Everton. I think Ronald Koeman picked the wrong day to pick three at the back."

"It was one of the most dominant displays of football I have seen." former Tottenham midfielder Jermaine Jenas added, also on Match of the Day. "It is unbelievable how fast this Chelsea side has adapted to the way Conte wants them to play. The freedom they play with is scary so you can't say they are not title contenders."

Hazard, himself, revealed how Conte has got him back in to form. "He has not changed a lot, it is just that I have a little bit more freedom when we have the ball and without the ball. Because I don't need to defend against the right back, because Alonso is there, I just focus on staying in my position. And when I have the ball I have more freedom and I can go where I want to go, and be decisive."

In an attempt to stifle the 3-4-3 system that yielded and impressive four consecutive Premier League wins, Ronald Koeman reverted to three men at the back to match-up Conte's tactics. But the tactics were negated as Conte's team out-passed them in a master class first-half display that suddenly brought the realisation that Chelsea were genuine title contenders. Incredibly, there were 23 passes in the build-up for Hazard's second goal, the most before a goal in the Premier League this season.

In the five games since the formation change, Conte's side had scored 16 goals and conceded none. Chelsea had won five of their six Premier League home games, as many as they managed in the whole of the 2015/16 season.

Romelu Lukaku was desperate to impress against his former club but hardly got a touch as Chelsea dominated. He had now played five Premier League matches against his former club, but was yet to score.

Koeman accepted: "The difference was too big between Chelsea and Everton. The one positive thing is it is only three points. This system is very difficult to play against and really the Chelsea manager has brought a winning mentality to the players. They are hungry and they will fight for the title for sure. I expected more from my team. It was a big difference in every aspect. It was not about the system - the difference was the mentality to win the game. With five defenders we control it, after 2-0 it was over."

Koeman was in awe of the way Conte's team pulled this system off. "Chelsea showed us today a very high level of football in every aspect of football." the Dutchman said. "How they work, how they run, how they press - we can learn from them. It's a big lesson what happened today. I never saw a team playing so well this system. This system is very difficult to play against, the movement of the players, Hazard."

After the international break Chelsea faced Middlesbrough at the Riverside Stadium and, as Conte said, he didn't want it to end.

TUESDAY, 15 NOVEMBER 2017

David Luiz had not conceded in any of his last five Premier League games, as Chelsea took maximum points to propel themselves to second.

The 29-year-old has made seven appearances in the Premier League since returning to England. Luiz told Chelsea TV: "I have a great relationship with the Brazilians and with the other ones. It's important for us, the group and for the atmosphere to pass some time together also outside because it can make the difference in the details inside the pitch. The team spirit can make the difference when you pass during the season through some bad moments, it can help to change these kinds of things. So it's important for us to have a great relationship with everybody."

Conte welcomed back Kurt Zouma from a long-term injury; out of action since picking up an anterior cruciate ligament injury back in February. He had made his comeback in the Under-23 side.

Zouma has an important role due to a shortage of options at the back, with Terry and Ivanovic now past their peak. But Conte wasn't rushing Zouma back, and commented: "I'm happy to have this ability of central defender. It's important Kurt is with us. The training session show he's in a good form. When you arrive after a bad injury you need a bit of time to recover your best form and for this reason we prefer Kurt to play with the U-23s. He did that on Monday and it's important to have game time in this period. He's good and (it's) fantastic to have another player available like Kurt."

WEDNESDAY, 16 NOVEMBER 2016

Eden Hazard was ready for action as he posted a picture from the Cobham training ground, showing the dark purple sky which had descended on their Surrey base.

He posed alongside Oscar and Alonso on his return to training as the nights begin to draw in and the fixtures start to come thick and fast. Ahead of their trip to Middlesbrough on Sunday, the No.10 posted the picture on Twitter, along with the message: "Afternoon training gets really dark soon @ChelseaFC ! Ready for the weekend!!"

Hazard was forced off late on after scoring in Belgium's 8-1 win against Estonia in their World Cup qualifier. Manager Roberto Martinez confirmed after the game that Hazard had received a kick to the calf but that the injury was not that serious; and so it has proved as he was ready for action at the Riverside. Conte was hoping Hazard could pick up where he had left off before the international break - during which, incidentally, he played alongside his brother Thorgan for the first time in their professional careers. Hazard was currently in scintillating form, scoring seven times in eleven league appearances since Conte had taken charge.

The upturn in his form coincided with Chelsea laying down the foundations for a genuine title push, one point behind Liverpool at the top of the table.

Hazard revealed that should he ever depart Stamford Bridge, it will be after winning the title again. He told the Guardian: "Back in March I'd spoken (to Conte) about the difficult season I'd had up to then, and what he expected of me in the year to come. I'd not scored many goals, but he saw me as a goalscorer. He spoke to me about his preferred systems, the 3-4-3 or even with two up front. His passion and enthusiasm for the job were obvious." Hazard added: "I made clear I had no intention of leaving after such a poor year. I didn't want to go out like that. If I ever leave, it'll be after winning a championship. You need to go out on a high so that people remember you for the right reasons."

THURSDAY, 17 NOVEMBER 2016

Conte had turned Chelsea's form around and in recognition of his achievements he won the Premier League Manager of the Month award, beating fellow nominees Jurgen Klopp, Mark Hughes, and Arsene Wenger to the prize after guiding the Blues to four straight victories during October.

Chelsea hadn't even conceded a goal since he changed their formation to the 3-4-3 system but it hasn't just been a defensive masterclass. Eleven goals for Conte in attack had been scored in their four fixtures against Hull City, Leicester City, Manchester United, and Southampton. Among those results was the stunning 4-0 win over former manager Mourinho's Manchester United side, a victory which had helped the Blues climb into the top four.

Conte told the Premier League's website: "It's a great honour and I will share this with my players and the club. It is the first time I work in another country with a different culture, and when you want to bring your own philosophy it is not easy, but now I am glad for this choice."

Conte became the sixth Chelsea manager to win the award after Claudio Ranieri, Jose Mourinho, Avram Grant, Carlo Ancelotti and Rafa Benitez.

Hazard was named Player of the Month following his exceptional form, including goals in the victories over Leicester, Manchester United and Southampton and had followed up that goalscoring form by netting a brace in the 5-0 win over Everton earlier in the month.

Hazard told chelseafc.com: "It means a lot. We played a very good month. I scored a lot of goals and all the team played well. We scored a lot of goals and we didn't concede a goal. I'm the best player this month but the most important thing is at the end to win the league and to do that we have a lot of things to do from now until then."

Conte believed Hazard has the potential to do "great things" after returning to form. "I'm pleased for Eden he is playing fantastic football." Conte said in a press conference. "He's working very well in the training session and with attitude and commitment."

Conte was asked if he thought Hazard can be considered at the same level as the likes of Messi and Ronaldo. "He is a fantastic player in this moment he's a great player - he's working a lot for the team and this is fantastic when someone of this talent believes in the team. It's great for the team. I think we have to go with the team step by step. Eden is showing his talent but it's not right to compare with other players at this moment - he has the potential to do great things in his career, now it's important that he puts himself in the team and he's fantastic. That's the best situation."

FRIDAY, 18 NOVEMBER 2016

Conte praised Diego Costa's new found anger management. Costa, who had scored nine in eleven Premier League appearances, started to show greater self-control when curbing his anger despite picking up four bookings.

Conte believed Costa was developing into one of the world's best with his new-found attitude. "Diego is showing he can control himself, it's fantastic." Conte said. "Diego is improving a lot under a lot of aspects. For me now, Diego is one of the best strikers in the world. He must continue that, working in this way, with his commitment and work-rate. It's fantastic to see his work during the games, but also in training. Diego is a very good player. The same for Eden. It's important for me, for their teammates, to see that in every game, Diego works a lot with the ball and without the ball. He's an example for all. And I want to continue this way. If he continues to score, I'll be very happy. But I'll be happier to see this commitment, this work-rate during training and in games, to work with the team with and without the ball. If all the players are able to think in this way, it's fantastic and we'll be a good team, a very tough team to play."

SUNDAY, 20 NOVEMBER 2016

Middlesbrough 0-1 Chelsea

Premier League

Diego Costa's 10th goal of the season moved Chelsea back to the top with their sixth straight win.

They leapfrogged Liverpool and Manchester City to go a point clear. Chelsea had won six Premier League games in a row without conceding - the 10th time it had happened in Premier League history, the fifth time for Chelsea.

After an even start Chelsea upped the tempo and deservedly led at the break when Costa reacted quickest to drill in a loose ball inside the Boro box. Costa was the first to reach double figures in Premier League goals. He had scored in six of his past seven league away games, netting seven goals in total in that run.

Conte had been effusive in his praise of Costa before the game, labelling him "one of the best strikers in the world".

Pedro smacked a rising drive against the bar. Alvaro Negredo's 78th-minute volley was the only time the home side forced Courtois into a serious save as they lost for the first time in four matches.

Boro failed to deal with Hazard's inswinging corner just before half-time, Costa reacting quickest to instinctively stab in an angled effort from inside the six-yard box. With Hazard comparatively quiet, Costa was the fulcrum of the attack. He also teed up chances for Pedro, Alonso and Hazard, showing once again he is back to the form which had helped the club win the Premier League title 18 months earlier, in his first season.

Middlesbrough had lost their previous six matches against Chelsea without managing to score, and there looked little hope of getting anything from a ruthless team with their focus and ambition set on the title.

Conte told BBC Sport: "I knew this game would be difficult because this team is well organised and they are in good form. But we deserved to win because we scored the goal and created many chances for a second goal. The first five minutes wasn't good for us. Middlesbrough started very well and we started badly but during the game our possession got better and we started to move the ball quicker. We didn't concede and stopped any opportunity for them to score."

THURSDAY, 24 NOVEMBER 2016

Conte responded to speculation linking Victor Moses to Barcelona. He was aware of the gossip that has seen the Nigerian ace tipped for a move to the Camp Nou but Conte hoped Moses was focused on his own game at Chelsea. "It's important to be focused on the present." he said. "I'd like to think my players are looking at the present."

John Terry was ruled out through injury and was set to miss the next three weeks of action. The Chelsea club captain did feature for the Under-23s against Southampton on Monday but was now set to miss more action. Conte also revealed Obi Mikel was unavailable.

FRIDAY, 25 NOVEMBER 2016

A big test of Chelsea's title credentials now loomed... Tottenham Hotspur at Stamford Bridge were next.

Conte refused to rule out splashing the cash in January, with his side just one point above Liverpool and Manchester City at the top. He was coy when asked what his plans for the New Year were, and the futures of stalwarts Obi Mikel and Ivanovic were up in the air.

Conte insisted he was more than happy with his current squad, although he would consider his options in January. "I have a squad that I'm very happy with. In January, we will see."

Conte then praised his squad and believed they were "very happy" under his management. "After the change in system we found more balance. It's important we continue to work. I see the players are very happy."

Conte now demanded that his players to stay focused during their game with Tottenham. The Blues and Spurs played out a feisty encounter towards the end of last season, with the 2-2 draw effectively putting an end to the latter's Premier League title chances, and Conte didn't want to see similar scenes again. Instead, he was looking for his players to keep calm when facing their London rivals "This type of game is not normal and it is a special derby. In London there are a lot of teams but this game is special for our club. The supporters feel this and there is a fantastic intensity during the game. Our behaviour, our attitude, must always be perfect and to think only about the game because this match will be very tough. But during the game, every single player must be focused on their job and then to put the passion into it. The right passion. I want my players to play with great intensity, with the right passion, but in the right way."

SATURDAY, 26 NOVEMBER 2016

Chelsea 2-1 Tottenham Hotspur

Premier League

Chelsea returned to the top after coming from behind to inflict Tottenham's first Premier League defeat of the season.

Spurs had aimed to recover from their midweek Champions League exit and all looked encouraging when Christian Eriksen's superb 11th minute strike put them in front. Pochettino's side was dominant until the closing seconds of the first half when Pedro curled in a spectacular right-foot effort.

Spurs' poor record at Stamford Bridge was extended to 30 games without a win - dating back to February 1990 - when Victor Moses scored the winner six minutes after the restart. Hugo Lloris and Jan Vertonghen both got touches on Moses' goal-bound strike but the ball flew in as Chelsea recorded a seventh league victory in succession. So, Moses' transformation continued and he fully deserved the standing ovation when he was substituted.

It was hard to believe that when Chelsea lost 3-0 to Arsenal on 24 September Conte's side had dropped to 8th, eight points behind then leaders Manchester City. Since that moment, however, the coach had masterminded a remarkable transformation: switched to three at the back, no place for Terry, made Luiz look less error prone, reinvented Moses, brought the best out of Pedro, and returned Hazard and Costa to their formidable best with seven straight league wins.

Conte commented: "I am satisfied with the way we fought back. These games are difficult. It was a tough game with a lot of intensity. Tottenham started well. It's not easy to go down 1-0 but I am pleased with the performance and reaction. Now it's important to continue the work. It's too early to talk of the title. This league is very tough. Tottenham showed in this league there are six or seven teams that can win the title. It's important to continue in this way and improve the confidence."

Pochettino was bitterly disappointed: "If we analyse the game we were better. We competed very well and we were a bit unlucky to concede... never 1-1 at half-time. The second half we conceded a goal very early. We are disappointed but we need to be pleased for the performance and the way we competed against a very good team."

Pedro was warned by Conte that he had to maintain his form to keep Willian out of the starting line-up. He was back into Conte's side following the decision to give Willian time off after the passing away of his mother. But, he had now scored in victories over Tottenham and Everton and Conte recently described him as "perfect" for his 3-4-3 formation. However, with Willian back in the frame, Conte told Pedro he must reproduce his performances over the last month to stay in the team. "Pedro played a good performance and scored a great, fantastic goal. It was a great finish but he must continue in this way. (At the moment) he deserves to play and start but it's important that he continues."

Chelsea next travelled to Manchester City for a clash between first and joint-second in the Premier League.

Premier League Table, Top 6, end of November 2016:

		P	W	D	L	F	A	GD	Pts
1	Chelsea	13	10	1	2	29	10	+19	31
2	Liverpool	13	9	3	1	32	14	+18	30
3	Manchester City	13	9	3	1	29	12	+17	30
4	Arsenal	13	8	4	1	28	13	+15	28
5	Tottenham Hotspur	13	6	6	1	19	10	+9	24
6	Manchester United	13	5	5	3	18	15	+3	20

CHAPTER NINE

DECEMBER 2016

Top of the Tree at Christmas.
Clean sweep of December, six straight wins.

THURSDAY, 1 DECEMBER 2016

Conte certainly believed Spurs would challenge Chelsea for the title despite masterminding a victory over them last weekend, recovering from 1-0 down against Mauricio Pochettino's side.

The defeat had left Spurs seven points off the top, four behind Arsenal in fourth place. Pochettino's team had only won once in their last ten matches in all competitions and were in desperate need for a win against Swansea. But Conte was not concerned about their chances this season and believed they will be right up there challenging for the title.

"Tottenham can fight till the end for the title." Conte said at his press conference ahead of Saturday's clash with Manchester City. "The first half was very difficult. Usually when you have this difficulty you can learn a lot. This week we've studied a lot."

Chelsea had now won all seven of their Premier League games since the switch to a 3-4-3 system and only conceded their first goal after 601 minutes against Tottenham last Saturday. Conte's side struggled in their first half against Spurs and he believed their clash against Guardiola's side will represent another key test for his formation.

"I think tomorrow it's a really tough game, a great test for us, for our formation to continue this way. We know that it won't be easy, tomorrow we will face a really great team with great players, with a great idea of football, great organisation. We are growing, tomorrow is another step to show if something has changed since the start of the season."

Thibaut Courtois believed the stunning Premier League run was indeed down to the new system. He told Sky Sports: "I think it's the system. It not only gives cover for the goalkeeper, in general it's a good system. When one guy can drop down and you can still have four at the back, when one guy can put pressure high up and you still have a solid shape that's quite good. We've played it a few times with Belgium now too and it's a system that's very hard to play against. In the summer we were working on another system. It was after the Arsenal game that we decided to go to three at the back. Since then we have trained it constantly."

Courtois suggested the new system gave him far more options to play out from the back: "With a three you can put two in the middle, two wide and have your wing-backs open. If the opposition full-backs close them they risk leaving the winger alone. Then I can maybe go to the winger. So it's hard for a team to really put you under pressure high."

FRIDAY, 2 DECEMBER 2016

Pep Guardiola branded Conte as "maybe the best coach in the world right now."

Manchester City were only one point behind Chelsea heading into an intriguing battle of two tactical minds at the Etihad.

"Conte is, without doubt, one of the best, maybe the best coach in the world right now." Guardiola said "They were contenders to win the Premier League from the beginning. Now, maybe more than before. It's a good test for us. It is the first time we are going to face each other. It's good to play against him. He made an exceptional job in Turin (with Juventus) and in the national job. It doesn't matter if it is Serie A or the national team, you realise his strengths. He has started here with maybe not good results, but they have won the last seven games, conceding one goal. That says a lot about how good they are."

Conte, conversely, felt that Pep was currently the better manager of the two due to his profile in the game and for what he has achieved in his career so far. "Who is more famous? Pep, for sure. Pep won a lot in his career. He won international trophies, not only in Spain but also in Germany." Conte was keen to point out. "Now he's in England. For sure Pep is. Now he's the top. Can I walk the streets here without being mobbed? Yes. In England it's very different if you compare it with Italy. In Italy you can find a lot of friends who say 'Come with me, have a photo, come and eat with us…' The fans come and sit and want to eat with you. This is a great difference. Here, if I go for a walk and someone asks for an autograph or a photo, I'm very pleased."

This mutual admiration society would stop for sure come kick-off, and after flying starts in the Premier League for both teams it was Chelsea who stood to be overtaken by title rivals City

SATURDAY, 3 DECEMBER 2016
Manchester City 1-3 Chelsea
Premier League

Chelsea's eighth successive Premier League win cemented their place at the top but the game ended in chaos as both Sergio Aguero and Fernandinho were sent off in injury time.

This was the most compelling result to indicate that Conte's team was capable of winning the title. Chelsea had now won eight consecutive Premier League games for the first time since the 2006/07 season, when they won nine in the row during Mourinho's first spell as manager.

Conte's side delivered an impressive statement of intent as they cut City apart on the break after going behind to Gary Cahill's own goal on the stroke of half-time, when he diverted Jesus Navas's cross beyond Courtois.

The game turned on Kevin de Bruyne's 56th-minute miss with City in control, crashing Navas's cross against the bar from inside the six-yard box.

Chelsea were level on the hour when Diego Costa outmuscled Nicolas Otamendi and ahead only ten minutes later when substitute Willian raced clear to beat keeper Claudio Bravo with ease. Eden Hazard completed a magnificent win with another goal on the break, showing too much pace for Aleksandar Kolarov to wrap up three vital points.

This was the second week in succession they had come from behind to beat a team regarded as realistic title rivals. They were tested by periods of City domination but tore Guardiola's side to shreds in the closing 20 minutes.

City, however, felt there were a series of injustices by referee Anthony Taylor culminating in matters boiling over in injury time when Aguero caught Luiz high and late; this happening after the Argentina striker clashed with the defender at an earlier corner. Chalobah joined in and was lucky not to see red, while Fernandinho was sent off for grabbing Fabregas and had to be forced to leave the pitch. Fortunately Taylor was able to blow the final whistle seconds later. Both clubs would inevitably be censured for a failure to control their players, the only question would be the severity of the punishment and how that would affect Chelsea's march to the tile.

Guardiola said on Sky Sports: "Congratulations to Chelsea - they won. We played really good, had a lot of control and created chances - but the ball in the box was not strong enough. Chelsea's approach was really different but that is part of the game. You don't expect Chelsea to create 25 chances - they created three and scored three."

When asked about Aguero's challenge on Luiz at the end of the game, Guardiola added: "Both players were strong there - that's all."

Guardiola later apologised for his team's part in the mass brawl.

"It is a pity the game finished like this." Guardiola said. "I don't like that and I apologise for what happened. I don't think Aguero's challenge is intentional. Both players were strong, that is all. Then Fernandinho went over to defend his teammate because of what the opponent did to Aguero. When Nolito did that against Bournemouth, it was a red card for him and a three-game ban. That is why Fernandinho went to defend his teammate, that is all. I have not spoken to him about it - if it is on TV, we will see about it."

Guardiola refused to blame Taylor for the defeat, his first at the Etihad Stadium since he took charge of City. "We didn't win because we missed a lot of chances, not because of the referee's decisions. I am proud of my team and how we played - I came here to try to play the way we played in this game. You have to remember who we were playing, and that we created more chances than we did in our last two games against Burnley and Crystal Palace, when we won. But in the boxes we are not strong enough. When the opportunities arrive, we have to score goals because when we don't it is tough mentally for the players. It is a problem we have had all season. It is difficult for us to score goals and we concede them very easily."

Conte commented on Sky Sports: "Today was very tough and the game was open until the end. There were lots of chances for both teams to score. I saw lots of character from my team and that's very important to grow - but we must continue to work and improve."

Speaking about Costa's, perhaps unexpected, role as peace keeper at the end of the game Conte added: "Diego is showing he is using his passion in the right way and I'm very happy about that."

Jason Roberts, former West Brom striker, on Final Score remarked: "Chelsea were incredible. They went behind but they kept their heads. I think Pep got it wrong and I think Conte got everything right. The performances from Willian, from Costa, from Fabregas - who came on and showed he has that bit of guile. This is the best game I've seen this season."

Former England winger Chris Waddle was also suitably impressed. "Chelsea have been clinical. Where they had opportunities to punish Manchester City, they have. They're well organised, they're well drilled and they look fresh." he commented.

Emotional Tribute

Matches in England and Scotland had paid pre-match tributes to the victims of the Colombian plane crash that killed 19 members of Brazilian side Chapecoense. Support staff and journalists covering the club were also among the 71 who died in the crash outside Medellin.

Chelsea's Brazil defender David Luiz was noticeably touched by events after one of the most significant victories for his club and said: "I give this victory to the people who died."

Luiz's former teammate, Arthur Maia, was one of the victims of the crash. "It was a difficult week for us, especially emotionally." added Luiz, who held up his black armband alongside teammate Willian when the latter scored against Manchester City. "It was difficult to prepare the head for this type of game. Now we pray for the families, for comfort they have as it is a very hard time for them."

Willian said he "wanted to do this for them, to say they have to keep strong."

Brazil-born striker Diego Costa added: "We pray for them, that God comforts their hearts. We have this job and sometimes we travel a lot. We need to pray for everyone inside the plane - the journalists as well as the players. I had some friends there also. It's a sad moment for everybody and we hope we can help them somehow."

MONDAY, 5 DECEMBER 2016

Manchester City and Chelsea were, not surprisingly, charged by the FA for failing to control their players. Both clubs had until 6pm on 8 December to respond to the charges.

THURSDAY, 9 DECEMBER 2016

Match of The Day pundit and former Chelsea manager Ruud Gullit gave a full assessment of the system and tactics so far: "A lot of people questioned Chelsea's decision to re-sign Brazil defender David Luiz from Paris St-Germain on transfer deadline day, but he is proving to be the perfect fit for their 3-4-3 system."

"I understand why there were doubts - while Blues manager Antonio Conte is known for his teams' defensive discipline, Luiz's problem is that sometimes he will switch off and he can be a little bit complacent. At 29, he has not changed and he is still that same player who can make mistakes, but the formation Conte has used during their eight-game winning run allows him to play to his strengths because of the players he has got around him."

"In front of him, Chelsea's defence is protected by N'Golo Kante and Nemanja Matic, but the key for Luiz is that when Chelsea play three at the back, he does not have to mark anybody. Gary Cahill and Cesar Azpilicueta do that, and do the dirty work for him. When Luiz plays in a four-man defence and he needs to mark, that can be a problem for him. In this 3-4-3 system, however, he is more of a sweeper and makes fewer challenges than Chelsea's other defenders. That suits him more, firstly because he rarely finds himself in trouble so is not in danger of making a mistake, and also because he is the player with the most freedom in that Chelsea team. Luiz can bring the ball out or play it forward and he uses it very well, which is so important when Chelsea look to break quickly."

"Playing him alongside Cahill and Azpilicueta means they have the ideal combination at the back. Captain John Terry cannot get into the Chelsea side because of how well they are playing, particularly defensively. He has not made a fuss about it, however. I am not surprised by that. As well as the fact the team are playing well and winning without him, Terry sees himself as a worthy captain and also a team player. He is part of the squad, and I think he understands the situation. Of course he would like to be involved - he is 36 and at his age will know he does not have much of his career left - but he is handling it the right way and he still has a part to play. There will be injuries and suspensions and moments when Chelsea need him in their title bid. At the moment he has done well just with the way he has handled the situation. Terry is not the only Chelsea player who is having to wait for a chance. Conte did not change his line-up very often even before he altered his formation to play 3-4-3 at the start of this winning streak. Players like to have consistency because then they know what they have to do. If you change too much then you get confusion. Of course what helps Conte here is that Chelsea are not in Europe."

"One of the good things about the run Chelsea are on is that they are doing things the Italian way, by conceding hardly any goals. That's not down to luck, because Conte's tactics are designed to put the defence first and make his team solid behind the ball. Look at Victor Moses - he was a right-winger in the games where Chelsea dominated possession but against City he was playing as a right-back in and around his own area for much of the game. He drops into the back-line whenever Chelsea don't have the ball which is another thing that helps Luiz - when you are one of five at the back there are not really many mistakes you can make. But when Chelsea do win the ball back they also have the right players to attack quickly and hurt teams. Eden Hazard, Diego Costa and Pedro are all clever enough to create their own space, and dangerous when they get it. Put all of that together and you have a very good plan because you don't concede anything and are dangerous going forward too."

"In September, before Conte had switched to the 3-4-3 formation he used with Juventus and Italy, Chelsea took one point from three Premier League games. He needed time, and I said that people should judge him after six months, not six weeks. It turns out he has not even needed that long to demonstrate again what a good coach he is. Conte has come to a different league and had to adapt to it like everyone else but, as soon as he could play his own system because he had the players to do it, then suddenly everything changed for him. So I am not surprised by how well he is doing. He has a game plan that works and some very good players at Chelsea who he uses in the best way, and things have just clicked for them."

"Can Chelsea carry on winning? I hope so, but there will come a moment when they get injuries or tiredness. Look at the next few weeks and the number of games everyone plays. There will be days when they don't play well. When that happens the most important thing is not to lose and, with the way they are defensively, even on difficult days they will always have a chance."

SUNDAY, 11 DECEMBER 2016
Chelsea 1-0 West Bromwich Albion
Premier League

Chelsea moved back to the top, three points ahead of Arsenal, with their ninth successive league win as Costa scored the winner against a stubborn West Brom.

Costa took advantage of a rare mistake by a hesitant Gareth McAuley in the 76th minute to rob the defender and curl a brilliant left-foot shot past Ben Foster. Albion had looked like earning a point after restricting the Blues to just one other shot on target, a 30-yard Luiz free-kick. Chelsea also came close through a Kante shot that deflected off Pedro and rolled just wide of the post. The Baggies had early chances through a Chris Brunt shot that fizzed wide and Salomon Rondon shooting across goal.

Chelsea had scored 22 goals in their previous eight league victories but Tony Pulis's side were doggedly defensive until Costa struck. Taking advantage of McAuley's error, who had plenty of time to clear a hopeful Fabregas pass down the line but delayed, Costa forced him off the ball and ran inside for his 12th league goal, matching the previous season's total.

Fouls on Costa have resulted in nine cards shown in the league, more than any other player. He has been involved in 17 goals in the league so far this season (12 goals, five assists); more than any other player. Costa has either scored or assisted in 15 of his last 17 league games - only failing to do so against Manchester United and Arsenal.

Conte observed that Diego "is showing his passion in the right way". Costa was booked four times in his first seven games, but had not been shown a yellow card in his past ten league and cup appearances. If he was cautioned in Chelsea's next four games he would receive a one-match ban, as the cut-off date for a suspension after accumulating five bookings is 31 December.

"January is arriving, no? It's incredible." said Conte of Costa's run without any bookings. "If you ask me why in the past I don't know. But now if you ask me about Diego I can talk well about his work-rate, commitment and behaviour. For me, it's fantastic. I always say to my players, 'stay focused on the pitch'. I don't like the provocation. I want to have players with great behaviour."

Costa was booked nine times in domestic matches in 2014/15, his first season at Chelsea, and was shown eight more last season, plus a red card in the FA Cup defeat against Everton in March. His punishment for that dismissal at Goodison Park was a two-game ban, with an additional one-match suspension for his reaction to the red card. Costa also served retrospectively-awarded three match bans for stamping on Liverpool's Emre Can in a League Cup semi-final in January 2015, and violent conduct in altercations with Arsenal's Laurent Koscielny and Gabriel in September 2015.

Conte told Match of the Day: "For sure there was relief, it was a tough game and we prepared for this situation. West Brom is a tough team, a physical team who are difficult to break down. It was a good win and now we must continue. We have won nine in a row which is fantastic because this league is very tough. We are working very well. I think West Brom prepared well defensively and tried to close every space. This game, if you find the goal quickly, you can have an easier game. When you don't find the goal, it becomes more difficult but we were very good to find in the right moment to do it."

The Baggies had now failed to win at Stamford Bridge in the league since September 1978.

Chelsea had won at least nine Premier League games in a row for the fifth time, more than any other team in the competition and in this match recorded their highest share of possession in a league game this season (66.9%).

Conte laughed off suggestions his side could face a Premier League points deduction. After previous incidents, an FA appeal board warned Chelsea in July that "the time cannot be too far distant when... the only proper sanction is a points deduction".

Asked about the possibility, Conte said: "Are you joking? Are you joking?"

Chelsea had been fined five times by the FA for failing to control their players since February 2015. They were originally fined a record £375,000 following three charges resulting from the 2-2 draw with Tottenham at Stamford Bridge in May. An appeal board reduced it to £290,000 but referenced the club's "lamentable recent record for failing properly to control its players". The last top-flight teams to be docked points for disciplinary issues were Manchester United and Arsenal following a brawl at Old Trafford in October 1990.

The FA commission which ruled on the charges that followed the Tottenham game said Chelsea's record of failing to control their players was "abysmal" and that "there is a recidivist nature to the club's offending". The commission said it considered imposing a points deduction then but decided not to, with one of the reasons given that Chelsea have yet to receive "a final warning that such transgressions simply cannot continue if a future regulatory commission is not to resort to other more draconian penalties". Chelsea, along with Tottenham, were warned as to their future conduct but there was no mention in the commission's report of a "final warning" for the Blues.

"Manchester City and Chelsea, at the end of the game, my players tried to keep their calm. I don't understand this. I repeat, I don't understand this." added Conte. "You must be honest and understand which team is at fault. We had a bad record in the past, but now we are different."

WEDNESDAY, 14 DECEMBER 2016
Sunderland 0-1 Chelsea
Premier League

Chelsea moved six points clear at the top as Cesc Fabregas's first-half goal beat a stubborn Sunderland.

It was a hard-fought and important win for Chelsea after Arsenal slipped up against Everton on Tuesday meaning Conte's side would be top of the table at Christmas. Six of the past seven teams to top the Premier League at Christmas went on to win the title. Chelsea went on to win the league title on each of the four previous occasions they have been top of the league at Christmas (2004/05, 2005/06, 2009/10 and 2014/15).

So, home and dry then? No way as far as Conte was concerned as he demanded that no one, for one minute, thought it was all over, despite the stats pointing to a Chelsea title.

Chelsea had become the 10th side to win 10-plus Premier League games in a row, the third occasion the Blues have done it (more than any other side). Conte was only the second manager in Premier League history to win 13 of his opening 16 games in the competition (after John Gregory at Aston Villa in 1998).

Chelsea had to fight hard for their second consecutive 1-0 win. Sunderland keeper Jordan Pickford saved from former Black Cat Marcos Alonso and Willian to prevent Chelsea from winning by a bigger margin. The home team had few chances although they could have snatched a point in injury time but Courtois superbly denied Patrick van Aanholt.

A key element was consistency with Conte having named an unchanged side in eight of the nine games prior to the trip to Sunderland. Liverpool boss Jurgen Klopp recently suggested that Chelsea's good run could falter when either Hazard or Costa picked up an injury. Hazard did not travel after picking up a knock against West Brom at the weekend, replaced by Willian. Hardly a shabby replacement! Conte also rested Nemanja Matic as Fabregas made a rare start. In fact, Fabregas has scored more goals at the Stadium of Light (four) than he has at any other away ground in the Premier League.

Initially, the team missed Hazard's creativity as they struggled to find a way to break down a packed Sunderland defence, but Fabregas highlighted the Blues' strength in depth as he managed to find the gap to sneak a shot into the far corner.

Chelsea had kept a clean sheet in five of their previous seven games but their inability to put the game out of Sunderland's reach was a cause for concern for Conte. For the third time in four games, they won by a single goal and Conte wanted his side to improve their finishing. "When you have the possibility to kill the game you must kill the game." he said. "We had this possibility but we didn't and at the end Courtois made a good save. I hope in the future we can improve."

Costa, the joint-top scorer in the Premier League, was kept largely quiet by a well-organised and disciplined defence. The Black Cats have now lost ten Premier League games at the Stadium of Light against Chelsea, more than they have against any other side at the ground.

David Moyes said: "Don't say commiserations, it sounds bad, they deserve more than that. We don't have the quality of Chelsea but we did a really good job. I thought we would get a goal, but Courtois made two great saves, and it would have been a really good point."

Chelsea returned to London, not having long to wait for the next game, a visit to Crystal Palace.

SATURDAY, 17 DECEMBER 2016
Crystal Palace 0-1 Chelsea
Premier League

Chelsea equalled a club record, beating Crystal Palace to secure their 11th successive Premier League win, moving nine points clear at the top, while Conte became the first Premier League manager to win 14 of his opening 17 games in the competition.

Chelsea previously won eleven matches between April and September 2009, with the Premier League record held by Arsenal's 14-game winning run in 2002.

Costa put the Blues ahead with the first attempt on target, heading in from Azpilicueta's floated cross with Scott Dann failing to get off the ground and challenge. He had now scored 50 goals in all competitions for Chelsea. Alonso nearly doubled the lead, striking the underside of the bar with a curling 25-yard free-kick.

Several fine saves from Crystal Palace goalkeeper, Wayne Hennessey, denied Chelsea a wider margin. Palace did not have a shot on target in the first half and Chelsea defended superbly to deny them any clear-cut opportunities in the second. Conte's side had now conceded only two goals in eleven Premier League matches since changing to three at the back.

Palace had won only one home league game against Chelsea since 1990. Cahill was making his 300th Premier League appearance. Chelsea became the third team to win 500 Premier League games, after Arsenal (512) and Manchester United (593). Palace were now winless in nine Premier League London derbies since a 2-1 victory at Chelsea in August 2015 (drew two, lost seven).

Pardew commented: "It was a strong performance but they did not give us anything and that was as good a defensive display that we have seen. Once we conceded, it was very difficult. For our offensive players, it was the toughest game they have had. We have all come up against this system before but it is with outstanding players. They ask questions and do not make errors. N'Golo Kante gives so much energy like he had at Leicester and fills holes which goes unnoticed. You don't really expect a centre-half (Azpilicueta) to have that quality - it was a Cesc Fabregas-type ball for the goal and it was a crucial one before half-time. I take heart from the last two performances. We deserved something."

Conte observed: "The run is fantastic. Congratulations to my players, not me. I am pleased for them because they deserve this. I see every single moment, every day. It is commitment, the way we prepare for the game and the way they fight. I am pleased for the fans who are fantastic home and away and who push us. We can improve though. You can always improve in different aspects. I am pleased with this level we have reached, but it is important to understand we are only at the 17th game in the season. We must not look at the table. We must not look at our rivals and continue working hard ourselves. We have reached a good balance between offence and defence. In some moments, our goalkeeper has been decisive. We dominated the last game but Thibaut made a fantastic save. After last season when he conceded lots of goals, this season is very good for him. We attack and defend as a team."

Conte's side now had 43 points but had played a game more than Liverpool in second and third-placed Arsenal, who were both on 34 points. Arsenal were due to meet fourth-placed Manchester City on Sunday, before Liverpool visited Everton in the Merseyside derby on Monday.

The Chelsea team now appeared to have all the attributes of champions: creating plenty of chances, a goal scorer on devastating form, a tight defence, and a system which the squad all seemed to understand.

However, they would now be without two key players for the Boxing Day game at home to Bournemouth: 13-goal top scorer Diego Costa picked up his fifth yellow card, following a foul on Palace's Joe Ledley, as did N'Golo Kante resulting in a one-match ban for both players.

SATURDAY, 24 DECEMBER 2016

Conte could do no wrong on the pitch and he endeared himself off it by taking some journalists out for a pre-Christmas drink in the local pub near Chelsea's Cobham training ground in Surrey.

BBC reporter John Southall explained how Conte invited journalists who attended his press conference before the game against Bournemouth for a pint afterwards. He said: "We spent a very enjoyable hour in his company. A handful of journalists were invited for a pre-Christmas drink with the manager after his press conference. So we all adjourned to the local pub around the corner from the training ground, The Plough, and he bought us a beer. It was all very pleasing. He was very engaging, personable and open with us, reflecting how he has transformed the club on and off the pitch. The players know exactly where they stand with him, they know what is expected from them, his man management appears to be good and I think that reflects the way he carries himself in front of the press and his players. Remember this time last year, they were three points off the relegation zone, they were treading water horribly under Guus Hiddink, and he has transformed it."

MONDAY, 26 DECEMBER 2016
Chelsea 3-0 Bournemouth
Premier League

Chelsea moved seven points clear by setting a club record 12-straight Premier League wins and Conte was the first Premier League manager to win 15 of his first 18 games in the competition.

Cesc Fabregas set up Pedro to break the deadlock with a deflected shot that looped into the top corner. Hazard capped an impressive display, making it 2-0 from the spot after he was brought down by Simon Francis. Chelsea added a third deep in injury time when Pedro's shot hit Steve Cook and the ball spun over the line.

Bournemouth's best chance saw substitute Benik Afobe denied by Courtois.

Liverpool would reduce Chelsea's lead to six points if they beat Stoke on Tuesday.

Chelsea were missing two key components, Costa and Kante both suspended, but it made little difference. Without Costa to lead the line, Batshuayi again left on the bench, Conte went with a front three of Hazard, Willian and Pedro. It took time, but the trio eventually proved an effective combination, happy to swap positions throughout.

"This is the first time we played without a real forward." Conte explained. "We tried this in training and I think for us at the moment this situation is the best, but I don't forget Michy because he is a young player with great talent. He is adapting to this league and its football. In the future, I trust in him."

Kante's absence saw Fabregas recalled to partner Matic at the heart of Conte's midfield. Again they took time to settle, giving Wilshere too much room on occasions before the break, but they were far more assured after half-time.

Bournemouth boss Eddie Howe switched to a 3-4-3 formation to match Chelsea's shape and, initially, it worked. Even when Pedro put the hosts ahead, Wilshere got on the ball in some good positions, going close twice. Bournemouth enjoyed more possession but were unable to do much with it, and in constant danger from counter-attacks. "You can't be too upbeat about getting beaten 3-0 but there were fine margins and many elements of our game-plan worked." Howe said. "They scored their first goal out of the blue, without any real sustained period of pressure, and the second goal just after half-time was the decisive moment."

Howe's side remain seven points above the relegation zone so having some breathing space, but their away form is becoming a cause for concern.

Eden Hazard became the sixth player to score 50 Premier League goals for Chelsea after Frank Lampard, Didier Drogba, Jimmy Floyd Hasselbaink, Gianfranco Zola and Eidur Gudjohnsen. Only Hasselbaink (84), Drogba (106) and Gudjohnsen (153) reached 50 Premier League goals for Chelsea in fewer games than Hazard (155).

Fabregas has now provided 98 assists in the Premier League; only Wayne Rooney (101), Frank Lampard (102) and Ryan Giggs (162) have more in the competition's history.

Former England captain Alan Shearer commented: "Chelsea look so strong in every department, so confident in every department. The win was without two of their biggest hitters - N'Golo Kante and Diego Costa. Once they got that first goal it was just a matter of how many. Their one-touch and two-touch play was just brilliant at times. Eden Hazard is in such incredible form and Willian had a fantastic game. Chelsea are red, red hot at the moment."

Chelsea were next at home to Stoke City looking to move closer to Arsenal's record of 14 successive Premier League wins, set across the 2001/02 and 2002/03 seasons. "To win 12 games in a row is not easy in this league." added Conte. "It's a fantastic run but it's important to continue that now. In four days we have another tough game and we have to prepare very well. Because now every team wants to beat you."

TUESDAY, 27 DECEMBER 2016

Shanghai SIPG FC general manager, Sui Guoyang, explained that Oscar's lack of recent opportunities at Chelsea coupled with a desire to return to the Brazilian national squad were the chief motivations behind his big-money move to the mega-rich Chinese Super League (CSL).

Oscar had been capped 48 times for Brazil but was left out of the squad for the Copa America Centenario in the United States.

Rumours of a lucrative £60m switch to Shanghai first began circulating earlier this month and Oscar himself later told Brazilian cable television network, SporTV, that such reports were "90% right" and that the deal hinged on some details. Chelsea subsequently released a statement confirming that terms had been agreed for a permanent transfer, with The Times claiming that the 25-year-old was set to quadruple his weekly wage and follow Lionel Messi and Cristiano Ronaldo as the third highest-paid player in world football with an annual salary of £20m after tax. Clearly the money wasn't the major motivating factor then, eh?

Incredibly, his lofty status as the third highest paid superstar in the world would immediately drop down one in the pecking order as Boca Juniors striker Carlos Tevez completed a move to Shanghai Greenland Shenhua FC on a staggering £615,000 per week. Clearly, again, the money wasn't the major motivating factor then, eh?

Oscar had started the first five Premier League matches of Conte's reign, but lost his place following the 2-1 defeat to Liverpool in September and had been limited to fleeting substitute appearances since. Conte's effective shift to a three-man defensive system accelerated his decline and such a frustrating lack of first team football was crucial to his decision. Guoyang explained: "Oscar has fallen out of favour with Conte because he has no place in Chelsea's 3-4-3 formation. It played a key part in his desire to leave. He felt terrible to sit on the bench and not be involved. He is so young."

Interestingly, Andre Villas-Boas, the former Chelsea manager, who succeeded Sven-Goran Eriksson at Shanghai SIPG FC on an £11m per year deal in November, had attempted to bring Oscar to Tottenham from Brazilian football club SC Internacional in 2012 but was pipped to the £25m signing by Chelsea. "Oscar wants to come back to the Brazil national team." Guoyang added. "Some of his compatriots play in the CSL and they still get called up to the national team. So it helped him to make the decision to move to China. And of course, the appointment of Andre Villas-Boas is a plus. Oscar knows we are an ambitious club."

Guoyang confirmed that the fee was actually €60m (£51m, $62.6m) and that Shanghai SIPG's senior management team personally flew to Paris to complete negotiations. Justifying the mammoth price, he insisted that it is "unrealistic" to expect the club to go about such a deal in a different manner given the "huge gap" that currently exists between Europe's major leagues and the CSL. "If we don't offer €60m, do you think he will bother to come?" he said. Perhaps that suggests that money is indeed a major motivating factor then, eh?

While Conte described Oscar as "an important player", the offer was too good for Chelsea to turn down. The club had profited from the financial power of the Chinese Super League during the last January transfer window selling another Brazil midfielder in Ramires to Jiangsu Suning FC.

Oscar joined the growing fraternity of established South American stars plying their trade in the Far East, with Alex Teixeira, Ezequiel Lavezzi, Jackson Martinez and Fredy Guarin all having joined Chinese Super League clubs in the last year, and former Manchester City and Manchester United striker Carlos Tevez joining Shanghai Shenhua.

Michy Batshuayi would not be sent on loan Conte confirmed as it would be a failure for the club and the manager if the striker was shipped off to another club to adapt to the Premier League even though he had yet to start a game in the league. He had made the match day squad for all 18 games, but all his eleven appearances came from the bench, yielding one goal, which was against Watford in August.

West Ham tried to buy him in the summer and were plotting a loan move, but were denied the opportunity by Conte's keenness to keep him at Stamford Bridge, confident that Batshuayi, given time, would prove his potential. However, the Belgian's frustrations intensified after he was left out of the starting lineup for their game against Bournemouth on Boxing Day despite Costa's suspension. Conte, instead, decided to play Hazard as a false number nine with Batshuayi only coming on as a substitute in the final seconds of the game.

"Because this player is a new player for Chelsea and to go on loan now is a defeat for the club and above all for me." Conte explained. "I think that Michy Batshuayi is a really good player. But he's young and he's trying to adapt to this league, this football. I'm sure Michy could (have) the possibility to show his talent in the future. I wanted to give him the opportunity to play and to have another appearance this season. It happened at the end, but I think that we have to continue to work with him every day to try together to improve him. Every decision I make is because I want to win and I have to take the best decision."

SATURDAY, 31 DECEMBER 2016
Chelsea 4-2 Stoke City
Premier League

Chelsea equalled the top-flight record of 13 consecutive wins in a single season.

Chelsea had a six-point lead over second-place Liverpool, who defeated Manchester City 1-0 in the late Saturday game, and were now just the second Premier League team in history to win 13 consecutive games in a single season, following Arsenal in 2001/02.

Conte had no time for records unless it meant going on to land the title. He explained: "Congratulations go to my players. To win 13 games in a row in this league is very difficult. Stoke played very well. They hit long balls to Crouch and fought for the second ball. My players showed they can adapt to the different kinds of game we face. They showed great commitment, work-rate and will to win. I'm delighted for them. Now, it's important to celebrate the arrival of the New Year, then to think of the next game against Tottenham. Numbers are not important if you do not win the title. Now, they are fantastic and we are proud, but we must concentrate on the second part of the season."

An exceptionally entertaining second half included five goals as the Blues were twice made to retake the lead by a Potters side who gave them one of their toughest tests.

Gary Cahill gave Chelsea the lead when he headed in shortly before half-time but Stoke defender Bruno Martins Indi levelled only a minute after the break when he poked in from close range. Willian handed the Blues the advantage again only for Peter Crouch to level with a side-foot effort high past Courtois.

Stoke barely had time to celebrate, as moments after the restart Chelsea drove towards goal with Willian applying a fierce, angled finish. With five minutes remaining the Blues all but sealed the three points when Costa shrugged off the attentions of Martins Indi to fire in the fourth.

This was a brutal test for Conte's team. Stoke were organised and disciplined and until Cahill's goal they were the better team.

There was a moment late in the second half when Costa was involved in a minor altercation with a Stoke defender in the opposition area. That 'moment' was, however, ended by the alert refereeing of Bobby Madley.

Martins Indi was given that task of shackling Costa and did a good job until the 85th minute when he lost his grip of the striker, who subsequently punished him with Chelsea's fourth. Costa had now had a hand in 19 Premier League goals (14 goals, five assists) and in only three games had he failed to either score or assist a goal.

Conte acknowledged it would be "difficult" for his side to repeat their run, which began on 1 October. "The first part of the season was incredible for us but the next half will be very hard for us." he said. "We started the season as underdogs and now we have the light on us, we must know this and work more to find the right solution to try to win in every game."

Conte praised his players for coping with the Potters' aerial and physical threat. "They showed great character because it's not easy when you take the lead and concede, and do it again. I was a player so I know this type of situation. You look at the clock and see you don't have much time to win the game. It's not easy because, after so many wins, you face teams who want to beat you for many reasons and we must know this. When you have these types of players you can go to sleep happy."

Cesc Fabregas registered his 100th Premier League assist - the fourth player to achieve this feat (Ryan Giggs - 162, Frank Lampard - 102, Wayne Rooney - 101). Fabregas was the quickest player to reach 100 Premier League assists, however (293 apps). It's the first time Fabregas had assisted in back-to-back Premier League games since January 2015.

Mark Hughes commented: "It's a similar story to our efforts at Liverpool. We got back level, but then conceded poor goals. We've made mistakes and good teams punish you. I thought we did really well, showing courage to get back in the game. I thought we were good value to get a draw, but we can't keep on making the mistakes we are at the moment because it's hurting us. We were positive, got back level and it was up for grabs. For their third goal, the ball went through about four of our players. We can't keep defending as we are in key moments. If we take that out of our game, we will be fine. Mistakes happen, the opposition can affect what you do. You have to understand the time, the moments of the game."

Former Manchester United and Everton defender Phil Neville on BBC's Match of the Day observed: "This was probably the most difficult game Chelsea have had in their run. Stoke played really well and matched their system which might be the first time that's happened. From kick-off at 2-2, Chelsea ploughed men forward, Eden Hazard went for the jugular. Teams usually retreat but Chelsea don't. Teams can't live with their intensity. That comes from Antonio Conte. Sensational!"

Former Newcastle United striker Alan Shearer also on Match of the Day added: "Costa's goal today summed up his displays this season - it had aggression, power and a great finish. He was angry, but in the right way. He's the player of the season so far."

Premier League Table, Top 6, end of December 2016:

		P	W	D	L	F	A	GD	Pts
1	Chelsea	19	16	1	2	42	13	+29	49
2	Liverpool	19	13	4	2	46	21	+25	43
3	Manchester City	19	12	3	4	39	21	+18	39
4	Arsenal	18	11	4	3	39	19	+20	37
5	Tottenham Hotspur	18	10	6	2	33	13	+20	36
6	Manchester United	19	10	6	3	29	19	+10	36

CHAPTER TEN

JANUARY 2017

Spurs become the main title challengers.

MONDAY, 2 JANUARY 2017

Conte faced one of the toughest tests of his title credentials at Spurs.

He confirmed Alonso would be available for the eagerly anticipated showdown at White Hart Lane. The versatile wing-back featured for the full 90 minutes against Stoke City on New Year's Eve but provoked concerns over a potential injury blow in a Snapchat post that appeared to show him receiving treatment. Fears over Alonso, however, were alleviated after Conte confirmed, at his pre-match press conference, that Chelsea had no fitness concerns as they chased a record 14th consecutive top flight victory.

Captain John Terry returned to training last week following a buttock injury, while Pedro was back after missing the victory over Stoke due to a one-match suspension.

Conte also claimed that David Luiz's physical condition and pain was improving. He had been playing with heavy strapping around his left knee after falling victim to a hideous late challenge from Sergio Aguero during last month's win at Manchester City, which had earned the Argentine a straight red card and a four-game ban.

Conte inevitably faced more questions regarding reported interest in Wolfsburg defender Ricardo Rodriguez and Bayern Munich midfielder Arturo Vidal. He confirmed there were one or two positions in his squad that could be strengthened should the right opportunity arise. "There are some positions that, if we are able to find the right solution, it is important to take them. This championship is long. Also, I know the difficulty of the market and finding the right player. But we are talking about this." Asked specifically about Rodriguez and Vidal, he added: "I answer always in the same way - that I don't like to speak about players that are playing with other teams. It is about respect for the players and the clubs."

Diego Costa made headlines earlier this week revealing he did indeed come close to rejoining Atletico Madrid during the summer. However, he made it clear that he only wanted to leave due to family reasons and Conte, who insisted there was no news regarding the potential exit of long-serving midfielder John Obi Mikel, had no concerns over his commitment to Chelsea. "When Diego decided to stay, he said he wanted to fight for this club and for his shirt. I wasn't concerned. He is showing great patience in the right way, in every moment of the game. We are happy for this. He is completely focused on the game."

WEDNESDAY, 4 JANUARY 2017
Tottenham Hotspur 2-0 Chelsea
Premier League

Tottenham ended Chelsea's attempt to make Premier League history.

Conte and his players were bitterly disappointed they could not achieve a 14th successive win that would have matched the mark set across the 2001/02 and 2002/03 seasons by Arsenal. However they remain in prime position in the title race and hold a healthy five-point lead over Liverpool in second place.

Conte had not seen his side drop points in 101 days since defeat at Arsenal but said he must be satisfied with his team being five points clear at the top after 20 games. "We knew that defeat could happen before the game. It is a pity to stop this run, but Tottenham fought last season and they can fight also this year. Don't forget we lost to a good team. They are one of the six teams who can fight for the title. We must work hard and be pleased with our position in the table, but know this league is tough until the end."

Spurs moved up to third place as headers from Dele Alli either side of half-time made the difference.

Alli rose to meet Eriksen's cross in first-half stoppage time and the same pair combined to put the game out of Chelsea's reach in the 54th minute. Tottenham scored with their only two shots on target in this match.

Eden Hazard had Chelsea's two best chances in each half as Spurs displaced Arsenal out of the top four and were now seven points off the top after their fifth successive league win. Tottenham's season was at a tipping point after a disappointing Champions League exit at the group stage and a poor performance in defeat at Manchester United in early December - but they had responded superbly.

Pochettino said before the game that he regarded Alli as "the most important player to emerge in English football in recent years." The £5m signing from MK Dons backed up his manager's confident words with an all-round display crowned by the two towering headers.

Pochettino said: "It is a massive victory, a very important three points to reduce the gap at the top of the table. It was a very tough game, we were playing one of the best teams in Europe, so the value of the victory is massive. It makes us very proud and we showed character and were competitive. It is one step forward for the team and is important to keep going. Football is about belief. We have shown we can challenge for the big things. We are in a good position, Chelsea is in a very good position, but we are fighting to get points and to reduce the gap above us."

Conte commented: "I saw a game with a great balance. It is not easy to play against Tottenham. But we played with a good personality to create the chances to score a goal, but we could not take them. It is strange for us to concede these goals because we are defending well, and they are in a crucial moment. At the end of the first half and then in the second half after we miss the chances to score, but this can happen. We must work hard and be pleased with our position in the table, but know this league is tough until the end for the title."

Conte felt Tottenham can challenge for the title. "Tottenham are a really strong team and are, for sure, one of the teams that can fight for the title."

Tottenham were Leicester's closest title challengers for much of the run-in last season - moving to within five points with four games left - but eventually finished third behind Arsenal after a stuttering finish. They are unbeaten at home in the Premier League and Pochettino felt consistency will be the key to success at the top of the table. He said: "The top four is very competitive. There are a lot of games to play but this result is very important for us. We showed in our performance we can be competitive and we can achieve big things but it is also true you have to do this regularly and show consistency during the whole season."

This was only the fourth occasion in the Premier League where Diego Costa has failed to produce a goal or an assist. Chelsea have not won at White Hart Lane since a 4-2 victory in October 2012 (drawing two and losing two since).

THURSDAY, 5 JANUARY 2017

Headlines: "It's payback and DELirium as the title race is blown wide open". Time will tell…

SATURDAY, 7 JANUARY 2017

Conte believed Nathan Ake was ready to fight for a first team spot as the Dutchman can play as a centre-back as well as at left-back - and Conte was eager to find out if he's a natural at wing-back. The 21-year-old had featured 12 times for Chelsea's senior team since joining in 2011, but Conte believed he was ready to become a first team regular after spells at Watford and Bournemouth in the top-flight. "I called him back because I think he's showing that he's ready to stay in the squad of Chelsea." Conte said. "Chelsea is his home. In the last season he played with Watford, and this season he was with Bournemouth. He's shown he deserves to stay at a great team like Chelsea. I'm pleased he's come back. Ake gives me an important option because we are playing with three central defenders. He can play on the left and in the middle. It's important to see in training sessions if he can also play wing-back."

SUNDAY, 8 JANUARY 2017
Chelsea 4-1 Peterborough United
FA Cup, Third Round

Chelsea captain John Terry was sent off on his first start since October.

Conte made nine changes for the third-round tie against League One opposition and almost trailed when Asmir Begovic was forced into a fine save from Lee Angol's close-range header. However, his side had amassed 20 shots by half-time, with Pedro's curled finish and a drilled Michy Batshuayi effort giving them a comfortable lead at the break, before Willian drove in from 18 yards soon after the re-start.

Terry saw red for bringing Angol down as the last man and Tom Nichols scored the penalty, only for Pedro to restore a three-goal advantage from the edge of the box.

Conte felt Terry was hard done by, claiming the decision was "not right". But Terry, who was making his 50th FA Cup start but only his eighth appearance in all competitions this season, clearly impeded Angol and he had now collected three of Chelsea's last six red cards.

He instantly put his hands on his head and protested with referee Kevin Friend but to no avail. Before his dismissal Terry completed 100% of his 30 passes, though winning only 20% of his duels, less than defensive partners Cahill (50%) and the fit-again Zouma (60%). "John played a really good game." added Conte. "For me, in this season he has shown me great ability."

Zouma's return after eleven months out with a knee injury was a positive for Conte, who recalled Nathan Ake from his loan at Bournemouth on Sunday. Ake was available for future cup ties, having not turned out in the competition for the Cherries and Chelsea's central defensive options were now bolstered without spending a penny yet in the January transfer window.

Chelsea were impressive in responding to defeat at Tottenham, their first in eleven matches in all competitions. Nathaniel Chalobah and Ruben Loftus-Cheek impressed in midfield as Chelsea reached round four for the 19th season in a row having not lost in the third round since 1998.

Batshuayi converted a smart Loftus-Cheek lay-off to clinically end a four-versus-two situation but had now only played just 82 minutes of league football since his £33m summer move. Conte was keen not to let him leave on loan and his display endorsed that decision. He had claims for an early penalty and managed eight shots in all, drawing two good saves from Luke McGee and a fine last-ditch deflection from Gwion Edwards.

Conte said: "I am pleased. When you change nine players it is never easy to play a good game and to be a team. Today we showed we were a team. I'm pleased for those who have played less as they have showed me good form." On the return of Kurt Zouma, Conte added: "I am very happy. It is a first game after a really bad injury and he is fully recovered. He played good. We know he can improve a lot."

Conte was pleased with Batshuayi's performance as the Belgium international got on the scoresheet in only his fourth start. "Michy played a good game." Conte said. "During the game he stayed with our philosophy and idea of football. He showed me great commitment and work-rate and it's always important for a forward's confidence to score. He has to continue to work in this way. He's young, he's improving and he showed that today. It's important for him to give me the opportunity to have another solution."

Peterborough manager Grant McCann said: "I thought we were excellent. I thought we had two or three really good chances. I couldn't believe Begovic's saved from Angol. The biggest difference is how clinical they are. It is something we need to work on. I thought the boys were outstanding and in the second half we matched them."

John Terry would now miss Chelsea's trip to reigning Premier League champions Leicester City.

TUESDAY, 10 JANUARY 2017

Swansea City boss Paul Clement pledged to keep hold of prized assets Gylfi Sigurdsson and Fernando Llorente which could largely determine whether they win their survival fight.

Spain striker Llorente was Swansea's top goalscorer with six and was at the centre of feverish speculation that he will rejoin his former Juventus boss Antonio Conte.

Clement - who would take charge of his first Premier League game at home to Arsenal on Saturday - said: "You need to keep your best players and Gylfi and Fernando are two of the best players the team has got. You'd possibly expect interest in them, but they're signed and contracted here and I want to keep them. I've enjoyed working with both of them already and they appear to be very motivated and focused on what we need to do to move this team forward. I can't say anything will or won't happen, and there's a lot of speculation and gossip. But there's been no conversation between me and the players, the players and the club, or the players and other clubs. So it's just business as usual, getting down to work."

Clement's first league game will also see former Chelsea and France midfielder Claude Makelele in the Swansea dugout. Makelele joined the coaching staff and Clement believed the 43-year-old will have an immediate impact on the squad. "He will bring a different dynamic to the backroom staff." Clement said. "I knew him briefly as a player at Chelsea, but much better when we worked together as assistants at Paris St-Germain. We both assisted Carlo Ancelotti and worked together for 18 months, he has a wealth of experience of playing at the highest level. He understands the game. He knows and smells football and is very good with people as well."

WEDNESDAY, 11 JANUARY 2017

Former Chelsea midfielder Michael Ballack met with Conte on a visit to the club's Cobham Training Centre. Ballack spent four seasons at Stamford Bridge after joining the club on a free transfer from Bayern Munich in 2006. The midfielder won six major trophies during his time in west London, including the Premier League title during his final season with the Blues in 2009/10. The former Germany international believed Chelsea were well equipped to claim yet another league crown under the guidance of Conte.

"Amazing to be back today at the @chelseafc training's ground in Cobham… nice to see the team in great shape and always good catching up with Antonio Conte." Ballack posted on Instagram, alongside a photo of himself and Conte.

THURSDAY, 12 JANUARY 2017

Conte became the first manager in Premier League history to be awarded the Manager of the Month award three times in a row. To mark the occasion Conte posed with the award and ten of his backroom staff, including his brother Gianluca and former goalkeepers Carlo Cudicini and Henrique Hilario.

Conte oversaw victories in each of his side's six games in the final month of 2016, with Manchester City, West Brom, Sunderland, Crystal Palace, Bournemouth and Stoke all beaten by the league leaders.

The award for December comes on the back of previous successes in November and October, and a winning streak of 13 consecutive league wins.

The three prizes, in only the first five months of his job, put Conte in the record books and also saw him draw level with another former boss at Stamford Bridge, Jose Mourinho, who collected his awards in November 2004, January 2005 and, amazingly, the most recent one way back in March 2007. This present lack of recognition has troubled the current Manchester United boss throughout the years, and in Rob Beasley's book - *Jose Mourinho, Up Close and Personal* - he was convinced there was a campaign preventing him from picking up the award. Beasley wrote that Mourinho asked him: "Do me a favour, try to (find out) who decides that s*** Manager of the Month. I don't care (about) that s*** but till the end of November I was, from day one to the last day, top of the league and zero defeats. (But) I didn't win in August, September, October or November! The last one was Pardew - lost in November against West Ham and I won all, including Liverpool away and drew at Sunderland. This isn't normal! I need to know who are the people? Four years in Premier League, two titles, two seconds and I won manager of the month twice eh, eh, eh."

While Conte caught up with his Manchester United rival, he still had some way to go to catch those at the top of the Manager of the Month hall of fame. Claudio Ranieri is the next former Chelsea boss in the Italian's sights with five awards. But ahead of him, amongst the current Premier League managers, are Sam Allardyce on six, David Moyes ten and Arsene Wenger with 15.

During his time at Manchester United, Sir Alex collected 27 Premier League Manager of the Month awards to go alongside his 13 league titles.

Claudio Ranieri urged Leicester fans to give N'Golo Kante a champion's reception when he returned to the King Power Stadium for the first time since moving to Chelsea for £30m.

Ranieri also told Kante that his performances for Leicester were better than under Conte because he no longer owns the spotlight. He believed Kante's contributions were more valuable for Leicester than they have been at Chelsea, where Hazard and Costa lead a collection of higher-calibre talents. "I hope our fans give him a warm reception because he was our champion." said Ranieri. "It's important to remember what he gave us. In the summer, after the international matches, he came to me and said he wanted to go and I could understand. When a big club arrives it is normal a player takes the train. Of course I tried to keep him with all my strength. I am not surprised how well he has done at Chelsea. He's very good player. But I think here he was more able to play better than Chelsea. Here all the light was on him. At Chelsea there are so many champions and he's (just) another one. I told him that last summer but it's normal that a young boy comes from France wins title and then goes to a big team. It's human. With N'Golo we played with 12 players and the referee never counted! This season it is not the same - I found a Plan B where I change formation and players."

FRIDAY, 13 JANUARY 2017

Diego Costa's future was thrown into doubt after a furious row with Conte over his fitness amid a mammoth offer from a Chinese Super League side.

Costa believed he was suffering from a lower back problem, which could be linked to his history of hamstring injuries. This sparked a series of blazing arguments and had led to a rift between Costa, Conte and the Chelsea physios, with Conte backing his medical team. The Chelsea staff were cautious with Costa, taking extra precautions to ensure his hamstring issues do not flare up. However, the striker did not agree with their methods and pointed to his impressive record this season, 14 league goals.

Representatives of Costa were in China and, of course, Oscar and John Obi Mikel had already quit Chelsea for mega-money deals there in recent weeks. Sky Italia reported that Conte had shouted at Costa, "Go to China!" during their heated exchange. As news broke of the row, Costa uploaded a picture of him scoring against Tottenham on Instagram, with the caption: "Come on Chelsea!!!"

Conte remains unconvinced by Costa's £33m understudy Michy Batshuayi and was in the market for a striker, with Swansea's Fernando Llorente a target. This latest issue with Costa could see him step up his search.

Speculation in the media was rife that the clash with Conte could now see him leave Stamford Bridge. But Costa was prone to such fallings-out and the club felt the matter would be resolved.

Liverpool legend and Sky pundit Graeme Souness insisted Chelsea must find a solution to get Costa back onside, or risk throwing away the title. He said: "You have to sit down with him and you have to find common ground. You cannot have him sit there and not play for the rest of the season. West Ham are talking about that with Dimitri Payet but I don't think Chelsea can afford to do that. If I was Conte I would be saying, 'We've got to resolve this, we've got to get him back playing like he has been for the previous six months.' They'd be losing their biggest threat. He gets them goals - that's the hardest thing in football. He's a warrior and he makes people play. He is the biggest loss Chelsea could have… they cannot afford that. I would imagine that the owner will be up for a fight. He'll be saying to Costa, 'You're staying here, you're going nowhere'."

SATURDAY, 14 JANUARY 2017
Leicester City 0-3 Chelsea
Premier League

Marcos Alonso scored twice as Chelsea moved seven points clear at the top, despite Diego Costa's absence - he'd been left behind in London after not training with the team during the week.

Chelsea had now already picked up more points this season (52) than they managed in the whole of 2015/16 (50). Conte did not allow Costa's high profile absence to affect his team at the King Power Stadium with Hazard setting up Alonso to fire home after only six minutes. Chelsea had now scored five goals in the opening ten minutes of Premier League matches - a division high. The wing-back added his second early in the second half when his shot from the edge of the area was deflected in. Pedro made sure of the points with a deft header from Willian's cross.

Costa had been suspended for their 3-0 victory over Bournemouth on 26 December - the only other league game he has missed in 2016/17 - and again Conte used Hazard to lead the line rather than turn to Batshuayi, who was left on the bench still awaiting his first league start.

Chelsea's dominant performance was further evidence that it was now going to be hard to dislodge them from top spot. This was Chelsea's 12th clean sheet in 21 games and, even without Costa, they remained difficult to break down and dangerous on the break.

Leicester City, lining up in a new-look 3-5-2 formation to match up with Conte's style, struggled to find a way back. Ahmed Musa tested Courtois before his side fell behind but the defending champions did not manage another shot on target. Ranieri, named FIFA's Coach of the Year this week, attempted to match Chelsea's formation by playing with wing-backs of his own - but his experiment did not pay off. Jamie Vardy was back from suspension to lead their attack but he made little impression apart from playing one dangerous cross and did not manage a single shot.

Spurs' emphatic win over West Brom earlier on Saturday had reduced the Blues' lead to four points, but Chelsea brushed aside any pressure in the title race. Their form was ominous for the chasing pack, and Liverpool - their nearest rivals before the weekend - could ill afford to lose any more ground when they faced Manchester United at Old Trafford on Sunday.

Before kick-off, Conte played down the Costa row, claiming he was not in his squad because of a back injury. Whatever the reason behind Costa's absence, Conte showed again he can win without his top striker (currently on 14 goals and five assists).

Conte was unsure when Costa would return from injury. "I don't know how long it will take, I don't have his pain." explained Conte. "We'll see about this next week."

BBC Match of the Day pundit Ian Wright said: "For Costa to come out at this stage when they need him so much feels very strange. He's scored 14 goals this season - you need someone like that in this team. It seems like it's derailed what's going on." Asked if a move to China would surprise him, Wright said: "Absolutely not. Costa doesn't seem like the sort of person who cares what people think. Whatever happens - if it's his back it's very hard to detect - something has turned him."

But Conte was repeatedly questioned about the rumours surrounding Costa. Asked whether Costa has a future at Stamford Bridge, he said: "I can't be concerned about this because today my players produced a great performance and showed spirit. I can't be concerned with nothing."

He was then asked whether Costa would feature again for Chelsea and responded: "Why not?"

He added: "There are a lot of 'if' questions - I don't like to answer these types of questions."

On reports of interest from China, Conte told BBC Sport: "I don't know and the club doesn't know anything about the reports of Costa to China. The truth is what I told you before."

Alonso added: "You guys (journalists) made up the story. Diego wasn't feeling well because of his back. He's very happy and will have a great season at Chelsea."

Former England defender Danny Mills on BBC Radio 5 live commented: "Why shouldn't Diego

Costa go to China? There is no loyalty from clubs in football. He's already defected from Brazil, his native country, to play for Spain and has no real affinity with England and the Premier League. I'm sure he likes London but he doesn't have any real affinity here. Brazilians move around all the time; they will go wherever the money is."

BBC football expert Mark Lawrenson added: "Well done Conte. If you get £60m, then let him go. He's at his peak, the team is built around him totally. He is a top, top player, but if he wants to go to China and be bored 18 hours a day, good luck to him. If he went - and I don't think he will - they don't win the league."

Former Arsenal defender Martin Keown on Football Focus remarked: "Conte is reasserting himself. Costa has football utopia at the moment - top of the league, top of the scoring charts, what is wrong in his life? He will come back quietly with an apology. I don't think it will derail Chelsea. He is a quality player who they can't do without. People tell me he goes off on ones like this, but he will see sense. It is a very difficult dressing room at Chelsea and the manager has done very well this season."

SUNDAY, 15 JANUARY 2017

Conte is adamant John Terry will not be leaving Chelsea this month, despite his decision to recall defender Nathan Ake from his loan at Bournemouth.

Ake's return to Stamford Bridge would appear to push Terry even further down the centre-half pecking order, with the 36-year-old having failed to start a league game since September.

Bournemouth were keen on a loan move for the former England captain this month but Conte emphasised, several times, the importance of Terry and insisted he is going nowhere

Conte labelled Terry a "great man" and hailed his importance in the dressing room. He said: "I didn't know about Bournemouth interest for John. John is an important player for me and if he doesn't play he is a really important man in the changing room. This squad needs him. John, I repeat, is an important player for this team, this squad, for me. His work on the pitch and in the changing room outside is fantastic. This shows he is a great player but also a great man. For me it is fantastic to have a person like him to help me in my first season in Chelsea. For this reason I repeat, John will stay with us in my squad. When I see a situation for him to start to play he will play. But he is a really important player for me."

Ake's recall follows some excellent form on the south coast under Eddie Howe, which in turn came after spells at Reading and Watford.

Conte added: "Nathan, I am very pleased he is back with us. I think in his one year and a half (on loan) he has improved a lot. That shows it is important when a player comes from the academy and goes out to play on loan that they can be ready to come back and play with us. Ake is a really good example. He is a good player - very young but with a good personality. For me he can play as a central defender, left, also as a wing-back. It's important now for him to work with us. He has been with us for only a few days. It's important now for him to go into our type of football. To adapt."

TUESDAY, 17 JANUARY 2017

According to reports in Spanish daily sports newspaper, Sport, via media company, Sport Witness, it is claimed that Conte has asked the Chelsea hierarchy to "make an effort" to sign Alvaro Morata from Real Madrid this summer. Sport also claimed that Chelsea would not be put off by the striker's £61.5 million valuation. Could Chelsea be looking for a replacement for Diego Costa this summer?

SUNDAY, 22 JANUARY 2017
Chelsea 2-0 Hull City
Premier League

Diego Costa scored on his return as Conte's team moved eight points clear at the top.

Interestingly, Conte had now accumulated the same number of points (55) from his first 22 Premier League games as Jose Mourinho had in his.

Costa was cheered throughout the game as he had an early impact, sending an effort from 20 yards fizzing just wide after only ten seconds, and collecting the opening goal when he converted Moses' low cross from eight yards in the seventh minute of first-half injury time. The long stoppage was a result of an injury to Hull midfielder Ryan Mason, who went to hospital after being carried off on a stretcher wearing an oxygen mask following a horrible clash of heads with Cahill. Hull later announced he had fractured his skull.

In his 100th Chelsea game, Costa scored his 52nd goal for the club. Costa's strike was the latest first-half goal in the Premier League since exact times have been recorded by Opta, coming at 51' and 35 seconds. He has now scored in all four of his Premier League games against Hull City.

The Tigers played well but lacked cutting edge without the injured Robert Snodgrass. At 1-0, Hull could have had a penalty when Alonso kicked the back of Hernandez's foot, but nothing was awarded.

Cahill sealed the win when heading home Fabregas's free-kick. Only Ryan Giggs (162) and Frank Lampard (102) have provided more Premier League assists than Fabregas (101, same as Wayne Rooney).

Last weekend, Chelsea's position at the top was looking far from secure, five points clear after their long winning run was ended by Tottenham and Costa's future in severe doubt. Eight days later, however, Costa was back and the team now eight points above second-placed Arsenal, the only other team in the top six to win at the weekend.

Conte's side were far from spectacular against the Tigers with Costa - six shots - the only Chelsea player to have more than one effort. But a 15th win in their past 16 league games - and a 13th Premier League clean sheet - took them closer to a sixth title. No team has failed to win the title after picking up 55 points or more in their opening 22 games. This is the fourth time a team had 55 or more points after 22 Premier League games - and Chelsea have now done so three times (also 2004/05 and 2005/06).

Conte told BBC Sport: "This game was very difficult for us. It is not easy to play this type of game. I think our opponent played very good, had good organisation and made it difficult for us. We are in the second part of the season and every game is now very tough for us and also for the other teams. You can see today the difficulty all of the teams have."

Conte was happy, and no doubt relieved, to see rumours about Costa come to an end. "I am pleased for him and for the fans and club. Today finished all types of speculation." Conte told BBC Sport.

Conte repeatedly insisted that Costa had told the club he could not train in the build-up to the Foxes game because of a back problem, and also denied any bid from a Chinese club. "In this situation I told always the truth." Conte added. "I am happy for him and to finish this speculation. He played and played very well. A lot of people asked me about his form, his attitude, and I said I took the best decision for the team. I think I made the best decision after this performance."

Costa's celebration of his 15th Premier League goal involved moving his hands to imitate speaking, aimed at the media for discussing the reasons for his absence. Conte said: "Honestly, I was very happy to see his celebration because I was celebrating the goal on the bench. The most important thing was he scored."

Gary Cahill said: "He is delighted to come back. There has been a lot of talk. If he misses one game you are hearing about all the different stories. It gets a bit tiring and the best way to respond is to get a goal. We are delighted to have him back in the team."

Hull City manager Marco Silva: "It was not what we wanted from the game. We came here to compete, to take points. Chelsea are in a very good moment but we try. In some moments we controlled the game. Chelsea had more ball possession but our team tried and conceded in the last minute of the first half which was cheap. If we changed some things the result might have been different. It was a good performance but I want more."

Chelsea had now won 1,002 Premier League points at home, becoming the third club to reach four figures in the competition (Manchester United 1,116 and Arsenal 1,019).

Next up were London neighbours Brentford in the FA Cup fourth round and then a visit to Liverpool, who were ten points behind them in the league.

SATURDAY, 28 JANUARY 2017
Chelsea 4-0 Brentford
FA Cup, Fourth Round

Chelsea swept aside west London rivals Brentford to reach the fifth round of the FA Cup.

Conte made nine changes but still had far too much for their Championship opponents, effectively killing the game after 21 minutes with Pedro finishing a sweeping move after Willian's free-kick had put them ahead. The third was scored on the break by Ivanovic, who was later fouled to allow Batshuayi to add a fourth from the penalty spot.

Loftus-Cheek had two shots saved and chipped a third against the bar, while Batshuayi had an effort cleared off the line and another ruled out for offside.

Conte had now won 14 of the 15 home matches in all competitions and been victorious in ten successive games at Stamford Bridge.

Pedro and Willian had been the chief architects of the 4-1 third round home win over Peterborough and the pair shone again, with both once more getting on the score sheet and Pedro claiming another assist. Willian's precisely executed 22-yard free-kick was his fourth goal in his past four starts and capped a typically incisive display, while the equally effective Pedro now had eight for the season following his close-range finish, set up by Batshuayi's accurate pass.

Willian has scored in three of his past four FA Cup games (three goals), with all the goals coming at Stamford Bridge. He has scored seven times from free-kicks in all competitions - more than any other Premier League player. Pedro had already equalled his goal tally from last season (eight in 40 games) after just 24 appearances this season. Batshuayi was involved in six goals in three starts at Stamford Bridge for Chelsea (four goals, two assists).

Costa made a late appearance off the bench but Hazard and Kante had a complete break ready for Liverpool, who also fielded an under-strength side themselves on Saturday, in the FA Cup, and then suffered a shock home defeat to Wolverhampton Wanderers.

TUESDAY, 31 JANUARY 2017
Liverpool 1-1 Chelsea
Premier League

Chelsea had to settle for a draw against a much-improved Liverpool side after Diego Costa's late penalty was saved by Simon Mignolet. Some viewed the penalty save as keeping the title race alive but, the fact was, Chelsea had still extended their lead at top to a cushion of nine points.

"When you have a good chance with a penalty in the 76th minute then you think you could win and take three points but Mignolet made a great save." said Conte. "We had two chances to score the second goal but it didn't happen but we must be pleased. It wasn't easy to play with the same intensity of Liverpool so we must be pleased. It was a very tough game. Both teams tried to play with intensity. I'm pleased. We saw a different game to when we played Liverpool and lost at home. It's a pity Diego Costa missed the penalty because he played very well. We had different chances to score goals, but we must be happy with the result and the performance because it is not easy to play away at Liverpool."

Mignolet made amends for his first-half embarrassment when he had been caught off guard by Luiz's superb free-kick from 25 yards, scoring his first Premier League goal for Chelsea since April 2013 - 1,386 days ago. Georginio Wijnaldum's close-range header eleven minutes after the break gave Liverpool a draw they fully deserved, ending a run of three successive home losses, two of which had knocked them out of the EFL Cup and FA Cup.

Costa went to ground under a challenge from Joel Matip 14 minutes from the end. Referee Mark Clattenburg pointed to the spot but Mignolet dived low to his right to save the Spain striker's spot-kick. The keeper has now saved six of the 14 penalties he has faced in the Premier League as a Liverpool player, more than any other keeper for the Reds. Firmino wasted Liverpool's two best chances, shooting high over an open goal and heading straight at Courtois in the closing seconds.

Conte disguised his disappointment about Costa's late penalty miss with his reaction at the final whistle. He knew Chelsea faced a wounded Liverpool after three damaging defeats and he viewed this as a point gained rather than two lost as he went straight to the visiting fans and pumped his fists in delight.

Chelsea were not at their best and yet showed the resilience of old as they were dominated in possession but kept Liverpool at arm's length. N'Golo Kante was outstanding; perpetual motion as usual. In fact he made a season-best 14 tackles and if the tackle stats are collated from the beginning of the 2014/15 season then Kante has made more than any other player, with 253, despite having only being in the English top-flight since August 2015.

Costa had an off-night but carried more of a threat after Pedro came on as a late substitute.

Results elsewhere for Arsenal and Tottenham made this a good night for the leaders, while Liverpool's hopes of a first title since 1990 receded as they remained ten points behind Chelsea. Tottenham's failure to win at Sunderland and Arsenal's abject display that saw them lose at home to Watford meant Chelsea actually gained ground on Arsenal, who started the night in second place, as well as not losing any ground to Tottenham. Conte, however, was already celebrating even before he learned of those results.

"What Antonio Conte is doing is outstanding - but Chelsea without Costa this season?" said Klopp, adding "If I had played against Costa I could never be friends, that's how it is, but when you have him in your team it's much more fun. He is a warrior."

Former Liverpool midfielder Danny Murphy, speaking on Match of the Day: "In the second half Liverpool's bravery and courage was brilliant. Against probably the best counter-attacking side in the country they could have got done. But they committed many men forward - a huge risk, but one they had to take. It was a really, really courageous performance from a side that had only won one of the previous eight games. Jurgen Klopp deserves credit, as do the players who came out under huge pressure and deserved the draw."

Former England winger Trevor Sinclair, also speaking on Match of the Day, about Luiz's goal: "It was an unusual free-kick by David Luiz but the technique is absolutely brilliant. It has pace and dip. A super finish. If there were two goalies in there I'm still not sure they would have stopped it."

Chelsea are unbeaten in their past five Premier League trips to Anfield, last losing there in May 2012.

Premier League Table, Top 6, end of January 2017:

		P	W	D	L	F	A	GD	Pts
1	Chelsea	23	18	2	3	48	16	+32	56
2	Tottenham Hotspur	23	13	8	2	45	16	+29	47
3	Arsenal	23	14	5	4	51	25	+26	47
4	Liverpool	23	13	7	3	52	28	+24	46
5	Manchester City	22	13	4	5	43	28	+15	43
6	Manchester United	22	11	8	3	33	21	+12	41

CHAPTER ELEVEN

FEBRUARY 2017

The lead at the top is extended. The team reaches the last 8 of the FA Cup. Revenge over Arsenal.

WEDNESDAY, 1 FEBRUARY 2017

Eden Hazard picked Arsenal and Manchester United as main rivals in the title race, as he expected Spurs to fade away due to their relative lack of experience.

Chelsea had won 15 of their last 17 league games and looked uncatchable with a nine-point gap over second-placed Tottenham and third-placed Arsenal, while Manchester United were sixth, 14 points behind the leaders after 23 games.

In an interview with Sky Sports, the man of the moment Hazard said: "I think Arsenal and Manchester United (are the biggest title rivals). United had a bad first part of the season and I think for a couple of games now, they played well. They have good players and the squad is very good. The manager is good, so they will be second or third. Tottenham also are strong. We lost there, but for me it is more Manchester United. They are more experienced. That is my opinion, maybe I'm wrong."

Hazard felt Conte has a stronger focus on tactics than Mourinho, explaining "In tactics and training we do more with Conte. We know exactly what to do. With Mourinho, he put in a system but we didn't work lots."

Ryan Giggs had wanted Manchester United to sign Kante after his performances had helped Leicester City to their incredible title triumph last season. The Old Trafford legend, who was assistant manager to Louis van Gaal, described him as a "nightmare" for opponents. Writing in his Daily Telegraph column, Giggs said: "All I can say is that last season I hoped United would sign Kante, and in the end his buy-out clause looked very good value at £29m. Kante hunts the ball down. He is so quick to cover space, get to the ball and make the tackle. I have played against that kind of opponent over the years. They are a nightmare - you cannot shake them off."

Arsene Wenger twice tried to bring N'Golo Kante to the Emirates - once when he was still at French club Caen and again last summer. Wenger suggested Chelsea's financial muscle was behind Kante's decision. "I cannot explain everything but it is quite obvious when you look at where he has gone. Was it the money? I do not want to talk about that. Transfers are transfers - you cannot explain absolutely everything."

Chelsea icon Didier Drogba was one of the main sources of inspiration that drove Kante towards a career in football. "The professional world makes a lot of young amateurs dream, and to go from one to the other can inspire others, like me, when I heard stories of Didier Drogba and Adil Rami, who went from being amateurs to becoming pros." Kante told French telecommunications company, SFR. "It was a source of strength, and told me that it was possible, even if you start from a long way off. My failures were something for me - my first contact with professional football. Though it didn't go all that well, it's not a regret, it's just like that. But looking back, those failures helped me consider football differently, consider the professional game differently. Perhaps I would have been different, I would have left my home earlier, my family, my friends. I grew up just as my friends did until 19 before leaving home, and it's because of that I am who I am now."

Conte commented: "If it is so simple, next season I think every team would pay £100m for N'Golo and would be sure to win the title. First of all, we didn't win the title this season (yet). I hope (we do). If this happens, for N'Golo it would be a great achievement. But I don't trust in the theory that you can win only because of one player. Win, lose or draw, the team is together."

Kante had been left trailing by Ozil in the loss earlier in the season at Arsenal, but was consistently brilliant since and was "outstanding" at Liverpool on Tuesday night, said Conte, who added: "I think he can improve a lot still, to try to look always forward, to try and play forward."

FRIDAY, 3 FEBRUARY 2017

In the lead up to the forthcoming London derby Conte urged his players to remember their heavy defeat to Arsenal at Emirates Stadium back in September.

"I'm sure, it will be a really tough game and we must pay great attention. Arsenal beat us already in the first game, and they have the possibility to repeat this in this game. For this reason, we must be focused, stay in great concentration, and have the same anger, the same will to fight and try to win. It's important. I like to repeat to my players: look at yourselves, not at others."

Conte accused Pep Guardiola of playing mind games after the Manchester City manager insisted the title was "Chelsea's to lose" with a 9-point margin to second-placed Tottenham and a further one point over City in fifth after the midweek fixtures. That provoked Guardiola into claiming: "The gap is too much - he's ten points in front of us. Only Chelsea can lose the Premier League. I don't think (City can pressure them)."

Conte dismissed that idea that the title was a foregone conclusion ahead of a potentially pivotal fixture. "It's normal, a mental strategy that every single coach tries to use for the players, for his players. Also to try and put a bit of pressure on the others. But normal. A normal strategy. I like to respect every decision for the other coaches. If we win the game against Arsenal, for sure, it's a good hit for us. To improve your own place in the table, take three points and also to have Arsenal 12 points (away from us), that's very good. If someone thinks that the league is finished, I'm not so sure. Anything can happen. It's important to keep the antennae very high. I want to have this tension, this right tension. There are 15 games to play and there are a lot of great teams behind us."

Conte watched City's 4-0 win at West Ham on Wednesday, which only further highlighted the quality of those chasing Chelsea. He added: "We all know the real potential of Manchester City." City had led Chelsea by eight points after six games, following the losses to Liverpool and Arsenal in September. Now Guardiola was 13 points behind Conte's side. "The situation can change very quickly." he said. "In that moment City had seven (sic) points more than Chelsea. There are 15 games (left) and we must pay great attention to reply to Pep."

The next fixture marks a rematch of the clash in September, which saw Arsenal crush Chelsea 3-0. Since that game, Chelsea had stormed the division, thanks to a 13-game winning run that started in the very next game. Conte reminded everyone: "This defeat seems far (away), but it's important to remember the defeat against Arsenal because it was a bad defeat, 3-0 after the first half, and in my mind it's always present, this defeat. I hope also it is in the minds of my players. Tomorrow, for sure, this game will be very difficult and I think it's important to remember the first game against Arsenal. I think a lot of things have changed now. But, for sure, we are a team. We want to have a good game tomorrow against Arsenal and try to win. We play at home and we have our fans to push a lot. For these reasons, we want to play a good game, to win, but it will be a really tough game and we must play great attention."

Conte reiterated that he cannot guarantee Diego Costa's Chelsea future beyond this season. Asked yet again about the reports linking his striker to a move to China, Conte said: "I don't know. Every week, though, I hear a lot of news, a lot of speculation about Diego. I think now the most important thing is to be focused on this championship. We are in a good position and Diego is an important player for us, very happy to stay with us. For me, these are the most important things: not what happens in the future, or what happens in the summer. The summer is far away. We have to think about the present to prepare a good future for us."

Victory at bitter rivals Chelsea would see Arsenal close the gap on the league leaders to just six points. Defeat will mean a 12-point gap with just 14 games remaining. Arsenal's league record at the Blues in the last ten years was one that made miserable reading: Played 10, won two, drawn one and losing the other seven - including a demoralising 6-0 drubbing in Wenger's 1,000th game in charge of Arsenal. Recent history suggested defeat No.8 was the probable outcome but with four games in 16 days over three competitions, Wenger knew it was important to begin that run well by bucking the trend at Stamford Bridge. "Yes but that's competition." he said when asked about the Gunners' crucial upcoming fixtures. "When you accept competition and want to be at the highest level you have to accept you have defining moments and games. We have accepted this job and the beauty of it is that you can have highs. First of all we want to recover from this disappointment (the home defeat to Watford) and the team is healthy and united. We're all focused on tomorrow's game."

The Emirates defeat had now famously prompted the change of formation to 3-4-3 and was the catalyst to a 13-game winning run in the Premier League for Chelsea. "For me it was a shock." said Conte. "Usually, my teams are not used to conceding three goals after the first half. I tried to transfer this shock on to my players, to avoid it happening again in the future. It was a bad defeat, 3-0 after the first half."

Referring to that change in formation Conte explained "We'd never tried this solution in our training sessions. The first time (was) during the game. In my mind, there was this option. I'm very happy to change the system because now we are top of the league."

SATURDAY, 4 FEBRUARY 2017
Chelsea 3-1 Arsenal
Premier League

Chelsea tightened their grip on the title race by delivering a blow to Arsenal's aspirations with a convincing victory.

Wenger, watching from the stands as he served the third of a four-match touchline ban, was hoping Arsenal could respond to the shock defeat by Watford. Not so. They faced a vastly different Conte team to the one they beaten at The Emirates, leaving the Gunners 12 points behind the leaders.

Marcos Alonso gave Chelsea the lead after 13 minutes, heading home after Costa's header came back off the bar. Arsenal were unhappy with Alonso's challenge on Hector Bellerin that saw the defender take a heavy blow to the head which forced his substitution, but referee Martin Atkinson saw nothing wrong.

Eden Hazard made the decisive contribution with a magnificent solo goal eight minutes after half-time, leaving a trail of Arsenal players in his wake in a run from the halfway line before beating Petr Cech. Chelsea had now won all nine Premier League games in which Hazard scored.

The goalkeeper's poor clearance then gifted substitute Fabregas Chelsea's third, five minutes from time - it was his first ever Premier League goal against Arsenal. Olivier Giroud scored a late consolation goal for the visitors and, despite Courtois saving efforts from Gabriel, Ozil and Welbeck, they were well beaten.

Chelsea looked like Premier League champions in waiting!

Conte commented: "It was an important game. I consider Arsenal one of the six teams that can fight for the title until the end of the season. To put them 12 points behind is very important for us. In four days we have had two games against two great teams. I think we are showing we deserve to stay on top of the table. I am very pleased for my players. In every session they show me great attitude and great will to fight and win this league. Was the first goal a foul? In England never. No."

Arsene Wenger disagreed: "It was a foul. If you look at a number of games recently we can feel sorry. It was 100% a foul, it was even dangerous play. That doesn't take anything away from the performance of Chelsea. We had a strong start but didn't take the opportunities and after half-time the second goal was the killer for us."

Wenger then added: "That defeat against Watford had bigger consequences, maybe, than expected. We didn't create enough. In the final third we didn't look dangerous enough. That was difficult to watch from upstairs. I'm not subdued. I'm disappointed and angry because we lost a very big game." On his team's predicament, he said: "The title's slipped further out of our hands and there's no hiding that."

A single banner saying "Enough Is Enough. Time To Go" was held aloft in the Arsenal end during the defeat.

Chelsea had now won nine successive Premier League home games and the aggregate score in these matches is an impressive 27-4!

Chelsea's lead at the top of the Premier League had been 12 points at the conclusion of this victory although Tottenham moved back to within nine points following a win against Middlesbrough.

Contrast the current position with the 3-0 loss to the Gunners back in September that had left Chelsea in eighth place, eight points behind then-leaders Manchester City after six games. This proved to be a watershed moment for Conte. In the intervening 18 games, after Conte switched to his preferred three-man central defensive system, they won 16 league games, lost at Spurs and drew at Liverpool; an incredible run that has effectively brought a 20-point swing in the title race.

N'Golo Kante was again a tireless midfield influence, but Hazard scored a wonder goal, and Conte's celebration showed how much the win meant to him.

Conte believed the midfielder can get even better: "Kante is extraordinary. He brings a lot of quantity, ok, but what quality too, even if he should improve in his build-up play. His first pass is always horizontal and he needs to make that vertical. I was just like him, so I do understand. He's a really good lad, always helping his teammates. He's been a great buy, though he's often tired by the time he gets to the goal. He's still young and can improve."

Hazard reflected on a special goal after tearing through Arsenal to score his 10th goal of the season. "I score a few goals, a few beautiful goals." Hazard told Chelsea TV. "But this one is special. It's against Arsenal and we won the game. This one is one of the best."

Conte praised Hazard's all-round display and wanted him to repeat the performance. "He played very well. I hope he play always in this way. He has great talent and we need this talent." Hazard may have lit up Stamford Bridge with a delicious solo goal which started in his own half but his manager was more impressed with his attitude and discipline. "A great goal, yes." said Conte. "We all know his talent and his strength. He is a really, really talented player and a good man. Today I am pleased for his work above all without the ball, defensively. He played with great attention and with great concentration. When we are able to work together in this way it is simple to try to win."

Hazard showed great strength to shrug off challenges by Koscielny and Coquelin before firing past Cech. "Eden showed he is in great form and great shape." added Conte. "If you are not in great shape you cannot score this type of goal." The goal took the Belgian into double figures for the Premier League season. Conte continued: "He has incredible talent and really balances the phases of the game."

Conte vowed to avoid complacency, relying on his own experience as a player and manager and the pedigree of his players; many had won the 2014/15 title and Kante was a champion last term with Leicester.

Hazard, who was Chelsea's Player of the Year in the title win of two seasons ago under Mourinho, made it clear the Blues were focusing only on next Sunday's trip to Burnley. "The gap is more big now. We want to stay there, top of the league forever. We are full of confidence. We don't want to focus too far (ahead). We take game after game and be ready for the next one. The next one is next week, so now we have a good week for training to get ready for the next game."

Hazard felt Chelsea could have won more convincingly against Arsenal while also sounding a warning for Burnley. "We could score two or three more goals. We didn't. We keep it for the next game, I think."

After Pep Guardiola and Arsene Wenger had both anointed Chelsea champions this week, Conte was having none of it and insisted the title race was not yet over. "There are 14 games to play before the end of the season and there are 42 points to take. Now it's important to celebrate this win, but then it's important to think about the next game against Burnley, a really tough game, because Burnley when they play at home are dangerous."

Conte, as expected, refused to take anything for granted. "There is no one particular team that worries me more. The experience of being a player really helps. I won the Champions League, but I also lost other finals and that made me more determined to win. You can't talk about the title yet, as anything could still happen. Just look at us, Chelsea were struggling at the start and turned the whole season around. We've got to stay calm. Manchester City beat Swansea with two minutes to go and I would've preferred that game end in a draw."

Hazard discussed their motivation: "We are motivated by being in a good position, but also because last season was so bad. We want to be there again, to be at the top again, for the fans. This is why we are top now. At the start of the season, everyone was thinking: 'Chelsea are a good team with a new manager but I don't know if they can contend for the title'. Within the team we knew we were ready to win. When you are top of the league you want to stay top of the league, it's simple. If you keep winning games, your opponents can lose some points, like they did recently, and if you concentrate on yourselves, you can be top of the league all season."

Conte's touchline antics were as interesting as his team. He often gets caught up in the moment, usually at the expense of his assistant first team coach. For example, even with Chelsea a goal up, Conte was suddenly incensed late in the first half grabbing at the jacket of his assistant Angelo Alessio and bellowing at him to get down the touchline to sort out the issue he had identified. "I was angry because Kante was supposed to track back in place of Moses, who had gone into the box to mark the sixth Arsenal man on the corner. He didn't do that and I took it out on Alessio. He's been my right hand man and thus, unfortunately, my victim for many years."' he confessed afterwards. "When I see something that isn't going right, I am capable of murdering anyone."

Meanwhile, John Terry might not have had a playing role - although as an unused substitute in the win over Arsenal he did take part in a post-match training session for those on the bench - but he had the best seats in the house for two of the events of the weekend in London. Terry followed his spot on the bench at Stamford Bridge with another prime seat, this time, at the O2 Arena watching Drake's show at the Greenwich venue before meeting the rapper afterwards. Posing in an image with wife Toni, Terry wrote: "Good to see you @champagnepapi. Unbelievable show tonight @toniterry26. What a pic this is."

Conte, despite rarely having used Terry in his league campaign, heaped praise on the Chelsea skipper while also hailing his current stand-in with the armband, Gary Cahill. "I want to underline that our captain is John Terry." Conte confirmed. "He's our captain and he's doing the job very well and helping me a lot. Not only me but also his teammates. His attitude and behaviour is fantastic. Gary is vice-captain and he's captain on the pitch when John doesn't play. I think he's playing very well and he's showing his quality. He's a really good defender and I'm happy for him."

SUNDAY, 5 FEBRUARY 2017

The rumour mill was rife with speculation that Inter Milan planned to prise Conte from Chelsea by offering a £250,000-a-week contract. According to Italian sport newspaper, Tuttosport, Inter's Chinese owners identified Conte as the man they want to bring the glory days back to the San Siro. The Suning group, which owns the club, would also hand him a £350million transfer kitty.

Conte had turned leaders Chelsea from an "ugly duckling" into a "swan" so it was easy to see why he was coveted back in his native Italy. He had taken over a club that finished 10th with their top stars inexplicably under-performing. Asked by Sky Sports Italia about Chelsea's transformation, Conte said: "I have blind faith in what I do. We had won the first three games, but I didn't like the performances. It was a delicate time, but not dramatic. Looking at last season, when Chelsea had practically the same players, you cannot immediately transform from ugly duckling into a swan. At the end of the day we found our balance. The blind faith in my ideas helped. I made some strong choices."

Conte felt Costa was back on track. Officially described as a back injury, the reason behind his absence following the Leicester game, the manager conceded there had indeed been a row. In an interview with Sky Italia, Conte said: "I was clear with him. I raised my voice and the player understood."

In addition to the 'disagreement' during the Leicester game the two had also clashed in the United States during the pre-season tour but Conte clarified: "Now everything is perfect."

Atletico Madrid remained in pursuit of their former striker but club president Enrique Cerezo did not think Chelsea would sell. The Atletico supremo felt that Chelsea would stand firm over Costa. "They (the media) say he will go to China, but Chelsea will not allow him to leave." he told Spanish radio station, Cope. Cerezo further clarified his stance, on Costa, to Spanish media company, Cadena Ser radio, confirming that he would be very interested in a reunion with the player he sold for £35m back in 2014. "I would love for Costa to return but it's not easy. He plays for a strong team, a team that is likely to win the Premier League. I don't think the big teams will allow their top players to leave."

Conte was, as expected, confident of keeping Costa but admitted clubs face an uphill battle stopping their top stars from going to China. Conte, asked by Gary Lineker on the BBC's Premier League show if Costa was likely to stay, said: "Yeah... Diego is a really important player. The situation is very clear, he is very happy to stay with us and fight for the title."

Costa is contracted until the summer of 2019 and Conte believed he will stay at the club. "I think (he will stay for some time)." Conte said, "I see him every day and his commitment and behaviour. He loves this club."

Conte, however, feared the growing attraction of China and their vast reserves of money. He cited the example of Oscar's big-money switch to Shanghai SIPG. "It's very difficult to manage these situations. £51m for Oscar, also a lot of money for the players. I think it's not the right way to pay a lot of money. The players to keep them in a club we must always have the right vision, the right vision, and stand the right way and not lose the right way because if we lose the right way it's not a good example for the young players (and) for the people in general who have to work every day."

Asked whether he thought the title race was over, he emphatically replied: "No, no. Now we are top of the table but this league is very tough. For me now it's very important to continue to push and to exploit this momentum but of course if you send the right signal it is very important."

Juan Cuadrado's sensational strike for Juventus impressed Conte but, perhaps frustratingly, he does not have the option of bringing the on-loan winger back because of the unusual three-year loan contract between the two clubs which did not have a recall clause built into it, unlike Nathan Ake's loan contract at Bournemouth.

Conte was in Turin to watch his former club beat Inter Milan 1-0 courtesy of Cuadrado's goal, who was seen as surplus to requirements at Stamford Bridge. The promising winger had been signed by Chelsea back in February 2015 but, after playing sparingly and wanting first team football, was loaned to Juventus,

The 28-year-old's stay at Juve sees Chelsea paid £4m per season and another £8.4m should the Italians look to make the deal permanent. The Colombia international has scored twice and made four assists in 13 starts for Juve so far this season.

MONDAY, 6 FEBRUARY 2017

Jose Mourinho was apparently miffed by the praise received by Conte and it was naturally billed as 'jealousy' in the media.

Mourinho oversaw United's 3-0 victory at Leicester on Sunday as his team were finally able to turn a succession of draws into victories, taking them into a challenging position for the top four, although way off the top club Chelsea.

'The Old One' of the Bridge took exception to the adulation of the 'New One's' counter-attacking tactics at his old club.

Mourinho was not happy by Conte receiving lavish praise for a style that he had previously employed at Stamford Bridge; the same style, different response. "My team is playing very well but for many, many years in my career, especially in this country, when my teams were ruthless and phenomenal defensively, and very good in the counter-attack, I listen week after week that it was not enough in spite of winning the title three times." he said after victory at the King Power Stadium. "It looks like this season to be phenomenal defensively and good in counter-attack is art, so it was a big change in England. But my Manchester United, I don't want to change the profile of our play, this is the way the fans want us to play, this is the way the club wants us to play. But I also don't want to be a manager of a team who plays very well, creates a lot of chances and doesn't win matches. We need to score goals."

Willian revealed that Mourinho had shown interest in signing him in the summer. The Brazilian won Chelsea's Player of the Year award at the end of the 2015/16 season, during which Mourinho was fired by the club for the second time, and upon the Portuguese's appointment at Old Trafford it appears he was keen to work with Willian again. "Concrete I do not know, right? But there was interest, yes." he said during an interview with Brazilian media outlet, Globo Esporte. "It was (from) Manchester United, because Mourinho is there too. Other clubs I do not know, but there are always some things on the internet. But I'm glad to know that clubs have to admire my work." Asked if he would consider following fellow Brazilian and former Chelsea teammate Oscar to China, Willian said: "To make this decision, we end up thinking our future, our children and family. I do not know if I would or not. What I can say is that I'm happy at Chelsea, I feel very good there, as if it were my home."

TUESDAY, 7 FEBRUARY 2017

Conte rewarded his players with extra time off to relax and recharge their batteries and gave permission for them to travel abroad. Conte confirmed: "After the Arsenal game I wanted to give them one day off more. Because I thought they deserved this. We had an intensive week with three games in seven days and it's important. There are different moments: there are moments when you must work very hard and this season you had this a lot of time. But sometimes there's a moment when it's important to have one or two or three days off, to relax, for your family and to come back fresher and restart to work very hard. We know our results depend on our work. If the players want to relax in different countries, the most important thing is that they come back in the right way with the right attitude and behaviour."

Having declared that two-day holiday Conte chose to spend them… yes, watching football, including making a flying visit on Sunday to the match in Turin. "Honestly, my wife when I told her I'm going to watch Juventus and Inter she wasn't happy." Conte said. "She told me, 'Why? Stay with us and your daughter and your wife.' But sometimes it's not easy to explain to my wife my choice when I have a day off, to watch a game for example. The passion for the football is great. My wife didn't know football before me. Her parents never watched a game and on Sunday would go for a walk or a bike ride. Now I have involved her family and they are the first supporters."

Conte's trip to Turin was purely for fun, to visit the city he used to call home and to watch the club where he played and managed. "Only fun, a bit of relaxing after an intensive week. It was good for me to watch a game in total relaxation and to come back to a stadium I know very well. It was very good. An hour and a half of complete relaxation."

He felt obliged to organise a dinner for his wife Elisabetta on Valentine's Day as part of his apology!

Meanwhile, David Luiz visited his former Paris Saint-Germain teammates at their training ground. The Brazilian left Parc des Princes in quite a hurry last summer as he completed a shock deadline day return to Chelsea.

In particular, he returned to reunite with former teammate and close friend Marco Verratti. Luiz snapped a selfie alongside the Italian midfielder, who was hard at work ahead of PSG's Ligue 1 tie against Lille on Tuesday, and posted it on his Instagram account.

Eden Hazard had been the star of the show as they swept the Gunners aside, scoring a wonder-goal in the second half that Luiz later compared to another former PSG player. "It was fantastic. It reminded me a bit of Ronaldinho - it was amazing. I love Eden's talent and I love him as a person so I enjoy having this kind of person in my team."

Courtois chose to take in an NBA game followed by the Super Bowl and shared his sporting adventure with his 3.2 million followers on Instagram. He watched the basketball at Madison Square Garden as the New York Knicks were downed by the Cleveland Cavaliers 111-104. Having flown into New York, Courtois then jumped on another flight down to Houston for Super Bowl LI where Tom Brady led the New England Patriots to an improbable overtime victory after the Atlanta Falcons had led by 25 points in the third quarter.

Courtois, not complacent, was still striving for perfection, seeking more from his own performances. "I want to improve myself to reach a higher level." he told Sky Sports. "I think I am on a very good level, but I know that I can improve myself. I think in everything you can improve. Everything you can improve every day and search for perfection and that is what I will try to do."

Conte's new system, a back three with Marcos Alonso and Victor Moses as wing-backs, allows Courtois the chance to play the ball out short from the back and the Belgium star admits that is one aspect he is working hard on. "When I was in Belgium, I played a lot of balls short." he continued. "At Atletico Madrid, the trainer preferred only long balls, so you forget to play short a little. So maybe that might be the biggest point of improvement. It is good if you have a manager who is demanding a lot. You have to be at your top every week, and that is what makes you champions. If you have a manager who is not demanding then sometimes you relax and you lose games."

Courtois had helped Chelsea keep 13 clean sheets so far, and only a stoppage time header from Giroud prevented the tall Belgian from adding to that. He benefited from having a consistent defence, with Cahill, Azpilicueta and Luiz ever-present since Conte made the tactical switch to three at the back last September.

Recently departed Oscar scored and starred on his debut for Shanghai SIPG as they waltzed into the Asian Champions League group stages by beating Thai side, Sukhothai FC. Andre Villas-Boas' first competitive game ended in a comfortable victory for SIPG, with their £51m January signing netting the opener before fellow Brazilian Elkeson made it 2-0, and an own goal from Kiattisak sealed their progress. They faced South Koreans Seoul, Japan's Urawa Red Diamonds and Western Sydney Wanderers of Australia in the competition proper. Oscar was subbed after 80 minutes to an embrace from former Chelsea and Tottenham boss Villas-Boas.

Newly-retired Frank Lampard had been in regular attendance at Chelsea's academy over the last few weeks as he started his coaching badges with the B licence.

WEDNESDAY, 8 FEBRUARY 2017

N'Golo Kante was the latest to insist that the race for the title was not over as virtually every pundit was now predicting.

Tottenham kept themselves within touch with a hard-fought 1-0 win over Middlesbrough and Kante believed Spurs, along with a number of other clubs, still had a chance. Aiming for a second title in a row with a different club, he commented, "Every season is different - this season, there are a lot of competitors for the title and there is still a long way to go. We can't say we are close to the title, we just have to fight for every game. It's not finished and a lot of things can happen. It was an important week for us with Liverpool and Arsenal, we took four points out of six, and this was a good win for us."

Cesc Fabregas was concerned about a prevailing trend for physically gifted players to be preferred to those with natural, technical ability; "talented" players increasingly overlooked by managers in favour of fitter, faster and more powerful teammates. Fabregas had to up his work rate in order to stay relevant at Stamford Bridge. "Today it's more difficult for the more talented players to succeed." he told Chelsea TV. "I don't think my physical abilities are the best - I'm not the quickest, I'm not the strongest, I'm not the sharpest, so you have to be ahead of the game if a player like me wants to succeed in football. To be a football player today... if you are very strong or you run a lot or stuff like that it's easier. That's why I try to get even better because football is growing in a way that before I don't think it was. Every day you see less talent and more power and players running around."

Conte revitalised the club with an infectious enthusiasm and Kurt Zouma puts Conte's excellent relationship with his players down to their shared love of the game. "He's a really nice guy. He thinks, eats and sleeps football. He talks football, everything is football with him. He's so passionate and he wants to give that to the players." the defender told the Daily Mirror. "Tactically we watch a lot of videos and we learn. Details are important to him. He says, 'you can't be there, you need to be there because if the ball goes over you there you're dead, so just anticipate.' You learn a lot with him, a lot. The Italian style is very good for defenders." A title triumph would erase the memories of the desperately disappointing 2015/16 campaign. "It was a bad season, now we are doing well again." he added. "Conte loves what he does. He wants to give that special feeling to us. We need to love football like he does, to breathe football. That's what he wants."

Former Chelsea defender, Marcel Desailly, observed that for John Terry it was "time to go" having watched him fall out of favour - saying it's just like when Terry ousted him 13 years ago.

Desailly left Chelsea in 2004 having been surpassed by Terry and William Gallas towards the end of his glittering career. Chelsea's last club captain before Terry, can see parallels. Terry had played just six minutes in the Premier League since mid-September. "I left because they were faster than me, better than me and it was my time to go - their time to shine - and now it's his time." Desailly told Sportsmail. "It's great to see that he's been able to handle it. You are the captain, you have been put to the side a bit because other players are more suited for the tactics required, but you're still there present, you are still there focused. You remind one of the players when he's not training well 'Oh, what are you doing?' so these are the small important details that John is going over. I'm happy because it's a different phase for John - leader as a first-choice but also leader as a second-choice. He's there to boost and to be present in the group so it's a different approach of John." Desailly was 35 when he left Chelsea and, despite being in and out of the side in his final season, was a big influence in Terry's career. The World Cup winner was named as a mentor to Terry in the early years of his professional career.

"His new role is more about putting pressure on the central men in Antonio Conte's title-chasing team. He's good because he gives a lot of pressure to the first choice that Conte has selected - Kurt Zouma or Gary Cahill." Desailly continued. "When you have John Terry on the bench I can tell you that when you come on the pitch you want to perform because you know that he can change you (out of the team) at any time." Desailly was speaking at the TAG Heuer Premier League Pressure Test.

Kenedy celebrated his 21st birthday on Wednesday night. The young Brazilian, who recently returned to Stamford Bridge from his loan spell at Watford, spent the evening with his closest friends as he posted an image of the occasion on Instagram. He featured once for the Vicarage Road side and has also only played one game back at Stamford Bridge - the 4-0 victory over Brentford in the FA Cup. In attendance was Diego Costa, who himself ran into an old friend, Arda Turan, while out celebrating the birthday of his younger colleague. They were together at Atletico Madrid as they won La Liga, the Copa del Rey and finished as runners-up in the Champions League between 2012 and 2014. Costa, who was dressed in a grey t-shirt and jeans for his evening out, posted an image of the pair on Instagram captioned: "My bro arda turan!!!el craque", with the latter part translating as 'the ace'.

Willian wrote: "Congratulations brother Kenedy. God bless and keep you."

THURSDAY, 9 FEBRUARY 2017

The Gunners last won the league in 2004 and their fans were up in arms about the prospect of missing out again as their team slipped to fourth after defeat at Chelsea. Arsene Wenger's side hosted Hull City next up having lost four of their past nine league games.

"It is never over." insisted Wenger. "Even if you (the media) think it is, I don't - we can't think like that." Just five points separated second-placed Tottenham from Manchester United in sixth. We're in a pack that is very tight and the fight for every position will be massive, maybe more this season than before. If it is over for us, it is over for everyone else as we are all in the pack. Chelsea have an advantage, they do not play in Europe, they play for nothing, they do not play midweek games and are in a strong position."

Jurgen Klopp like Wenger refused to give up. The Liverpool manager was dreaming that Liverpool can win their remaining 14 games. No chance!

The German boss had endured a nightmare start to 2017, with a dreadful sequence of one win in ten matches, seeing Liverpool slump from second to fifth and exit both the FA Cup and the EFL Cup. Even a top four spot and Champions League football was in the balance as they faced a home game with Tottenham. "In my dreams we can win 14 games. I know how it sounds but I cannot change my dreams and that is what I am working for and after these 14 games, it is another moment when we watch back and we use all these experiences and all the things we learned about each other. Then we will make decision that will help us in the next season."

Liverpool had slumped to 13 points behind Chelsea and Klopp reflected: "We recognised that at one point we lost the flow. In this moment you have this player out, this player is coming back but with no rhythm, this player is injured and coming back after how many days and another two players are ill or injured. That is how it is. In a good moment it is not a problem but it is rare one player is out and the other player who comes in is then in a world class situation because of playing not for a long time. That is all clear. I am more interested in what will be and what we can do and what results we can get and performances we can show and where and when we can deliver."

Cesc Fabregas and his partner Daniella Semaan were pictured with Hollywood film legend and Oscar-winning star Colin Firth. They were attending the BAFTA Gala Dinner in London. The event, held ahead of Sunday's main BAFTA ceremony, was in Piccadilly at the academy's headquarters. It didn't take too long before Fabregas had uploaded an image onto social media.

FRIDAY, 10 FEBRUARY 2017

Conte had celebrated Hazard's glorious goal against Arsenal by diving into the crowd, he had pushed around his assistant, Angelo Alessio, when Kante did not track back on a set-piece, and he joked he is "capable of killing anybody" when the intensity reaches its peak! It was therefore of no surprise when he was asked to discuss his touchline habits. "It's not easy for me to see me in this situation because I don't like to see myself again after the game. It is not because I have a strange attitude or strange behaviours but because I don't like to see it. Sometimes I'm a bit ashamed to show all this passion. It's my enthusiasm. I live the game in this way and not only in England. If you remember during the Euros, if you remember in my past with Juventus, when I started my career, I live the game with great passion and enthusiasm. Sometimes for me it's very hard to keep this passion under control. Sometimes I want to share my passion with fans, with my staff, with players. When I was a player and I scored always I showed my passion with great celebrations. I scored not a lot but when it happened, I showed great passion. I live football with great passion and great enthusiasm - I put a lot of myself in my work. It's funny. My daughter watches every game and stays five metres behind me in the stands. I want this. For me it's a great support - my daughter and my wife. I think it's important for my daughter to see my will to win. I try always to transfer the right education to my daughter. As a manager this is my way. It's not good to judge someone who is always sitting during the game. And it's not good to judge if one manager stands up for all the games. The moment you see me staying seated, you must be worried. Above all my club must be worried, because I think I finished my passion."

Chelsea's next fixtures looked like a good opportunity to secure the title; Burnley, Swansea, West Ham, Watford, Stoke and Crystal Palace, leaving Conte in pole position to land the club's fifth title in 13 years under Abramovich. That would also exceed Conte's brief of a top-four finish in his debut season.

He was paid £6.5m a year and only eight months into a three-year deal with rumours circulating in Italy of interest from Inter Milan's wealthy Chinese owners who were prepared to offer nearly twice as much.

Jose Mourinho and Pep Guardiola might not have their teams in pole position but they do top the managers' earnings league with £15m a year, while Wenger and Klopp are on £7m - £8m. Conte had rejected an offer of £25m a year to coach in China in order to prove himself in England. He has certainly proved himself so far, and quickly, so much so that a new improved contract was hastily being drawn up to ward off Inter.

Conte was already committed to a strong summer recruitment drive for next season with the subsequent challenge of the Champions League, a trophy he has yet to win as a coach.

Conte discussed Fabregas's situation, conceding that he has the luxury with this squad to leave out a "football genius" and offered little reassurances. "Cesc is a top player and is a genius at football. I can talk in the same way about Andrea Pirlo. Cesc, if he doesn't run 100 metres in ten seconds, I can allow him this, because he's a genius with the ball. His velocity is in his mind. Sometimes you must make the decision and to look at the balance of the team. Don't forget in his place is playing Kante and lot of people say he is the best player in the league. Then there is Nemanja Matic and he too is playing in an outstanding way. When you have two players playing in front so well it's not easy. But I prefer to have this type of problem."

They are the kind of problems that will certainly not keep Conte from dancing along the touchline.

After having given his players two days off, Conte warned them against complacency. "I always like to keep the right level of tension in my players." he explained.

Chelsea faced a difficult trip to Burnley who had defied most people's expectations, heading into this game 12th in the league, largely thanks to their solid form at Turf Moor. Sean Dyche's side had won their last seven games at home in all competitions and in the league had picked up 28 points out of a possible 39 at home, although they failed to record a single victory on their travels this season. "There are teams at the bottom who win and draw so you must have the right concentration. If your ambition is to stay in the top four or top six, you can have highs and lows. If you want to win (the title) you must have concentration and focus and know that in every game you can lose points. It will be a tough game." said Conte. "The stats show Burnley is a really strong team at home. Top of the table of home games is Chelsea, then Tottenham and third Burnley. They are in good form. For sure, they will want to beat us because we are top of the table. We are preparing very well. My players know really well the game we face. It won't be easy."

He still refused to rule out a title challenge from the teams immediately below. "Honestly, I think there are six teams very strong and can fight to win the title. This is the truth and we must know this. If we think we have nine points and we are close to the title it is a great mistake. There are 14 games to play. There are five teams and Chelsea who can fight until the end to win the title. It is important not to make a big mistake in this race. Until the end of the season you have to live with this pressure. If the opponents win they close the gap. If they don't win you have the opportunity to take more points. But we have the experience to live with this situation."

Mourinho was not out of it. "Manchester United? Yes! They have a great squad." added Conte.

Burnley defender, Michael Keane, believed that Chelsea's title credentials would be given a tough examination at fortress Turf Moor. Keane was confident they can upset Chelsea and potentially blow the title race wide open again. "We believe we can beat Chelsea. Our home form has been unbelievable. They are in for a tough game. They have a lot of great players in good form. It will be tough but when we are at home in front of our own fans we have belief we can beat anyone. We showed that against Liverpool. The fans are brilliant at Turf Moor, they always stick behind us, never on our backs and are really positive. That feeds into the players. Every time we play at home we feel we are going to win, no matter who it is against. That just comes with games and more wins."

Conte has the chance to get a first-hand view of a potential summer transfer target as the Burnley defender has only 12 months left on his contract come July, having rejected the offer of fresh terms. Burnley are resigned to losing the 24-year-old but were expected to demand a £20m fee.

SATURDAY, 11 FEBRUARY 2017

Nearest challengers Spurs faltered, and Mauricio Pochettino was highly critical of his team's performance at Anfield.

Sadio Mane scored twice in 138 seconds as second-placed Spurs disappointed, losing 2-0. "If you start a game like we start then it is very difficult." said Pochettino. "It is difficult to fight for the Premier League if you show that lack of desire to play for a win."

It meant Chelsea could extend their lead at the top if they beat Burnley at Turf Moor, as Pochettino added: "If Chelsea go 12 points clear, it is a big problem."

Spurs had won only twice on the road since 24 September, including defeats at Chelsea and Manchester United in addition to draws at fellow top-six rivals Arsenal and Manchester City. In their past 17 meetings with the other top-six sides away from home, Pochettino's team had won once. "In the first 45 minutes you saw a team that is not ready to fight for the Premier League." the Argentine told BT Sport. "We are in a position that is up to us. But if you show like today that you cannot cope with the pressure then it is difficult to challenge and fight for the Premier League."

Arsenal and Manchester United both won to make it a massive fight for the Champions League places but it was generally accepted, outside of Stamford Bridge, that Chelsea were running away with the title.

John Terry was out of the trip to Burnley after a training ground injury following a challenge with Diego Costa. He shared a graphic photo of his ankle being stitched via his Instagram account. Nice.

Terry accepted he is no longer first choice. However the club captain recently told Soccer AM that whenever he is needed he is ready to step in. "I think as a player, you have to adapt and you have to adjust as you get older. Realistically can I play every week? Yeah, I'm in great condition, I'm feeling great and I'm back fit, but the boys that are playing at the minute have been unbelievable. As a player you have to accept that, more importantly, the team's top of the league and flying, so as a fan, let alone a player, I'm delighted at the moment."

SUNDAY, 12 FEBRUARY 2017
Burnley 1-1 Chelsea
Premier League

Ahead of the kick-off former Arsenal defender, Martin Keown, said "Antonio Conte is a winning machine. People underestimated him. If you put good players with him it is a recipe for success. He is a serial winner of trophies. He understands the system and gives a clear message. Contrast that with Man City, Pep Guardiola is an artist and it is about creativity. It is lot easier to just be told a job to do."

Kerry Dixon, speaking on Chelsea Fancast, shared his cautious optimism, "They are totally dominating their title rivals. Nothing is won in February but we have put ourselves in a wonderful position. We have to keep our foot on the pedal. But Burnley, given their home form, will give us a game. We have to match them in the physical department because they are a big hard working side."

However, Chelsea missed the chance to move 12 points clear as they were held to a draw by a resilient Burnley.

Conte commented: "It is one point and for sure we must be disappointed. We tried to win. We started very well and scored a goal and created chances to score the second goal. We tried to win but we know Burnley at home are not easy. They have taken 29 points at home. Now it is important to continue to work. I think we tried to build and do our football for sure. Burnley tried to disrupt our play. They played long balls and the second ball is not easy. It is not easy to play against this team. It is very particular. At home they are very tough. The pitch is small and this is better for the team that has to defend and play this long ball. You have less pitch to cover and then there is a good atmosphere with the supporters and I think it's good. We found a team that thought to disrupt our football, to play this long ball and to fight the second ball. We must be very disappointed that we have only taken one point but I am sure of the commitment. Sometimes there are tough games and this was very tough."

Burnley had won all four of their previous homes games without conceding but fell behind early on when Pedro finished off a sweeping counter-attack. The visitors dominated possession and it seemed only a matter of time before they added to their advantage. However, Burnley's record signing Robbie Brady - making his full debut following a January move from Norwich - equalised with a stunning free-kick. Despite Conte's disappointment the Blues moved ten points ahead of Tottenham but Manchester City could close the gap to eight points if they beat Bournemouth on Monday.

Cesc Fabregas came off the bench but with 20 minutes remaining all he managed was a yellow card. Chelsea (19) have scored the first goal of the game more times than any other Premier League team this season and have yet to lose (W16 D3). Pedro had scored nine times in all competitions this season, surpassing his total of eight in 2015/16. Brady was the first player to score a direct free-kick against Chelsea, in the Premier League, since Rickie Lambert in March 2013. Costa has failed to score in three consecutive Premier League appearances for the first time since April-May 2016.

Burnley boss Sean Dyche commented: "Chelsea are a fine side. They are the market leaders for a reason and we limited them to two shots on target and that is tough enough. We made four or five really good chances. I am very pleased overall. The mentality here, I am pleased about the growth in the side. We are maturing as a side as individuals and as a team. You need assuredness in the Premier League. I was super impressed with our reaction to their goal. We were not disappointed or stepping on the back foot."

Conte, as usual, insisted the title race was not over. "There are 13 games before the end. If someone thinks this league is finished, I can tell you now, no. There are six teams that can win the league and anything can happen."

He then responded to Jose Mourinho's "joking" that Chelsea cannot be caught because they are a "defensive team". Mourinho, known for mind games with his rivals, said his former team would not slip up because they win with "counter-attacks".

"He's playing," replied the sage Conte, "I have the experience to understand this." Mourinho was speaking after United beat Watford 2-0 on Saturday to extend their unbeaten run to 16 games, sixth in the table, and 12 points behind Chelsea. Wenger previously accused Mourinho of playing mind games, as did Sir Alex Ferguson. Conte said: "I don't like to reply about the other coaches."

MONDAY, 13 FEBRUARY 2017

Ruud Gullit analysed Chelsea in his online BBC column. The former Chelsea manager observed: "Not many teams have tested Chelsea's three-man defence this season, but Burnley showed there is a way to get at Antonio Conte's side. The Clarets were extremely clever, especially in the way they targeted Chelsea's left flank, which is far less disciplined defensively than their right side. Eden Hazard always wanders inside from the left - far more than Pedro does when he starts on the right - which is what happened at Turf Moor. That leaves Chelsea's left wing-back Marcus Alonso to advance up the pitch and give them an option wide on that flank. But, with Hazard often on the opposite side of the pitch, Alonso is sometimes left isolated when the Blues lose possession. Alonso is also not as strong as their right wing-back Victor Moses when it comes to getting back to help his centre-halves. I look at him and think he is more of a left winger. It is a weak spot because it leaves space to exploit if teams can get the ball into that channel behind Alonso, but you usually have to do it quickly. Burnley managed it early on by playing long balls up to Andre Gray that forced Gary Cahill and David Luiz to come out wide, out of their comfort zone."

"The Clarets had more success in the second half when Ashley Barnes intercepted a Chelsea header down that flank, with Alonso further up the pitch, and Hazard over on the right. Cahill should have done better with his challenge on Barnes inside the Burnley half, and Luiz should have cut out the cross after Barnes had burst forward - but the ball still found Gray, who missed an excellent chance to put his side ahead."

"Burnley got their tactics exactly right on Sunday. Their attitude was spot-on too. Their game plan, and the way they executed it, was an example of how the right system and attitude gives you a chance when you are facing a side with more technical quality."

"Chelsea are always well organised under Conte as well, of course, but they struggled to control the game because of Burnley's approach. I think it was a good result for Chelsea too, because they could have lost. They did not play particularly well, but they still picked up a point, and they still have a very healthy lead at the top of the table."

Gullit then paid tribute to Conte's defensive organisation. "The Italians, they always think about the defence first. At the beginning of the season, when they were winning 3-0, 4-0 or whatever, the first thing he said is I am content that we did not concede any goals, that's a typical Italian, he wants to have that solid base."

Speaking as a pundit on Match of the Day 2, Martin Keown commented: "The whole game was compelling stuff, very much so. They are the best two managers I think in the Premier League at the moment, Sean Dyche and Conte. Two different styles, two different systems, and Burnley really took Chelsea out of their comfort zone today and they worked their socks off, but with intelligence and good quality. Conte knows his tactics, every player goes on to that pitch knowing his role, but you have to say equally for Sean Dyche's team, they did as well, and maybe we don't shout enough about our English coaches. You look at the resources he has there and what he is achieving, four or five of those players went down before, he has come back this time and he is using that extra knowledge. He is using a system that I doubted at the start of the season, 4-4-2, but that was a tactical masterpiece today from his team."

Chelsea had led early at Turf Moor but failed to muster a further shot on target all game after that. Captain Cahill reflected: "We could have played a lot better but the most important thing is we stay focused. Maybe that was a little wake-up for us where we realise it's going to be tough to cross the line and there's plenty more football to be played. We just have to keep working, keep focused and believe in what we've been doing all season. Maybe that's a big point for us, who knows? We didn't lose. If it was going to be this game, then it was important we didn't lose. Everyone makes mistakes. But we have not made that many this season, hence the clean sheets. That comes from work on the training ground and that's what we have to keep doing. It's not hard to focus if you want to achieve what we want to achieve. We've done so much hard work this season to put ourselves in this position. We can almost see the finish line now. We've got 13 games now and it's important that we tick the games off with the right results. I think we should be even more focused because the games are getting closer and closer and be even more determined."

Looking ahead, Cahill added: "It's time to press on and it's a time where the motivation to finish the job should be there for everyone. There's light at the end of the tunnel and it's important we keep working and keep focused, as we have been for 95 per cent of the season."

Michy Batshuayi amusingly dealt with a West Ham fan on Twitter. The Belgian has struggled for game-time under Conte and the Hammers supporter quipped that even, on loan at West Ham, Simone Zaza had played more league minutes this season. Batshuayi used his critic's own phrasing against him to put a stop to the exchange:

@mbatshuayi - "Have a good evening everyone, thanks for all the messages and support."

Hammers fan - "Zaza has played more minutes in the league this season than you have, let that sink in."

@mbatshuayi - "...and I still scored more than him...let that sink in, good night bro."

Pep Guardiola feared it was unrealistic to expect Chelsea to slip up, despite Manchester City moving to within eight points of the leaders. City shifted up to second with a 2-0 win at Bournemouth - having watched Chelsea drop points at Burnley the previous day. Guardiola said: "It is so close. This result takes us from fifth to second, but it will be a good battle to qualify for the Champions League. The gap is too big (to catch Chelsea). Yes they didn't win their game this weekend, but they still played so solid. It is important to keep the focus on our game. Our performances have been much, much better and my only regret is that we created so many chances but didn't turn more of them into goals."

Gary Neville, like Conte, thought that Jose Mourinho was being "mischievous" when he accused Chelsea of being "very defensive". Neville thinks Mourinho is actually jealous of Chelsea, and will be looking to copy the balance of the league leaders in coming seasons. Speaking on Monday Night Football, Neville said: "He's probably envious, probably saying it as a compliment, because when I watch Chelsea they look balanced to me, the right mix of what you would like. I've never watched Chelsea this season and thought they were really boring. I've seen them go away to City and be absolutely outstanding. I've seen them be resilient when they needed to be. I've seen them play great football. When I've watched them this season they have a look of a team that's got the right balance, and if Jose Mourinho is saying that, maybe he is being a little bit mischievous, but he'll be thinking that is the balance of a champion team. Jose will be searching for that balance, understanding that at United you need to be a little bit more expansive in the way in which he plays."

Chelsea had scored 52 goals, United managed 38. Chelsea had 60 points, eight ahead of second placed Manchester City, 12 ahead of Mourinho's United who were sixth.

TUESDAY, 14 FEBRUARY 2017

David Luiz was limping during the draw at Burnley. He was later treated by medical staff after leaving Turf Moor and was sure to be rested for their trip to Wolves in the FA Cup fifth round. He had struggled with his knee since being fouled by Sergio Aguero at the Etihad Stadium in early December, which had resulted in a red card for the Manchester City striker. From then on he'd been wearing strapping on his right knee and was spotted grimacing in pain during their game against Burnley.

Luiz posted an amusing photograph on social media on Sunday night showing himself in hospital attire alongside a picture of a syringe, with the written message: "Let's do it", possibly to the immediate concern of some fans.

Joking aside, Conte declared Luiz a "warrior" for playing with a problem. "He is showing his real value. It's important for him, for Chelsea and for me."

WEDNESDAY, 15 FEBRUARY 2017

Marcos Alonso revealed that regular team dinners helped create an "amazing atmosphere". He told Chelsea's official site: "We have been going out for dinner once a month all together as a group, just enjoying each other's company off the pitch as well. It's been a great help and the atmosphere within the squad is amazing. You can see that when we're on the pitch. It's organised by the manager and the captain and it's good fun for everyone."

Additionally, Alonso credited compatriot Pedro for helping him settle in to his new surroundings. "Pedro is a very good friend and I like to catch up with him after training. I didn't know him before I came here but he's been a great help since I arrived. We go for dinner quite regularly and we went to the NBA at the O2 together. I'm not a massive basketball fan but I follow some of the Spanish players."

Bayern Munich's Arturo Vidal dismissed reports linking him with a move to the Bridge in the summer. The Chilean international played under Conte when the Italian was in charge between 2011 and 2014 and won three Serie A titles with Juve. Despite his relationship with Conte, Vidal, 29, said there was no reason for him to depart the Allianz Arena. "They are only rumours that come about quickly. Ultimately, I played four very successful years under coach Conte at Juventus. But there's no reason for me to leave Bayern. I wear this jersey with pride. I feel good, my wife feels good and the children are happy. And I still have big goals in Munich." Chilean newspaper El Mercurio reported last month that Chelsea would launch a £56m move to sign Vidal and suggested the midfielder had already begun learning English in preparation for the switch.

THURSDAY, 16 FEBRUARY 2017

Pedro had struggled to adapt to the Premier League in his first season in English football after joining from Barcelona and looked set for a return to his native Spain. Now, however, he had no regrets that a potential move fell through. "This is the best moment for me at this club and also the best moment for the whole team since I've been here." he confirmed. "I'm very happy here. It's a good situation when you are top of the League and progressing in the FA Cup. We are on the right path. Last year was a difficult one for me, for the club, for the team, but this year is different. With this coach, all the team is focused on the fight for the title, with more confidence for every game and this is good. It's a completely different season."

The 29-year-old had scored six goals and had five assists in 16 league starts.

At the Cobham training ground, England manager Gareth Southgate dropped in to watch how the Premier League leaders prepare, and was warmly welcomed by Chelsea boss Antonio Conte.

Nathaniel Chalobah hoped of a senior call-up and enjoyed a friendly handshake with Southgate. Southgate knows Chalobah well, having regularly picked the defensive midfielder while he was in charge of England's under-21s team. He has closer ties to Chelsea than with many other Premier League clubs through Steve Holland, Southgate's assistant manager who will continue in his role as a coach at Stamford Bridge until the summer.

FRIDAY, 17 FEBRUARY 2017

Conte defended Wenger and stated that Arsenal would be losing "one of the best" if they decided to part ways.

Wenger was under severe pressure to step down after Wednesday's Champions League 5-1 defeat to Bayern Munich.

"I have great respect for Arsene Wenger as manager and as a man." said Conte. "He's done a good job for 20 years and is doing a great job in the present with Arsenal. When you are the coach in a great team, you are under pressure in every moment. But I think Arsene is a really good manager, one of the best in the world. I have great respect for him and his team, they're strong and have a good idea of football. Results at the moment are not good but it's important not to forget the work the coach has done in the past and in the present."

Conte confirmed that the injury to David Luiz was not too serious but that he would be rested for the fifth round match. "For Luiz, we have the opportunity to give him a week to recover very well and to prepare for the next (league) game." the Chelsea boss said in a press conference. Conte added that the 29-year-old's condition was improving and that a week of work with the medical staff should have him ready to go again in their next league match against Swansea.

Conte admitted that young forward Dominic Solanke was likely to leave the club when his contract expires in June. The club refused to meet his wage demands, with the 19-year-old's representatives asking for a £50,000-a-week salary; a substantial increase from his current £7,000 per week.

Solanke made his senior debut at the age of 17 in 2014 but had failed to break through since and spent last season on loan at Vitesse Arnhem. Now, after failing to reach a compromise with his representatives, Chelsea appear resigned to losing the young English forward. Conte spoke with Solanke and believed the player wants to leave. "I think this is his will." Conte confirmed. "This question is better to ask him. I think for a young player to stay in a great team is a great opportunity. We have to respect every decision. Obviously I have spoken with him to try and understand his will. I repeat we must respect every decision. His contract expires in June. I wish well for him and his family in the future." The club would be entitled to compensation of £8m due to rules governing the transfer of academy-trained players and the fact that Solanke was younger than 24. Everton, Sunderland and Newcastle were amongst those likely to be interested but only if the striker is more realistic with his wages.

Conte was likely to include academy prospects Nathaniel Chalobah, Nathan Ake and Ruben Loftus-Cheek in his squad for the FA Cup tie at Wolves.

The kids reached the FA Youth Cup final for the eighth year in a row this week. "The academy is doing a really great job." Conte said. "In my squad, I have a lot of young players from the academy.

Chalobah, Ake, Loftus Cheek, Ola Aina. A lot of young players are in my squad. The young players who stay with me because they deserve it. It is not a gift. It's important to be clear about this."

SATURDAY, 18 FEBRUARY 2017
Wolverhampton Wanderers 0-2 Chelsea
FA Cup, Fifth Round

Chelsea kept alive ambitions of a domestic Double as they eased into the quarter-finals with second-half strikes from Spanish pair Pedro and Costa.

There were 30,193 in attendance, Wolves' highest home attendance since 1981; some way short of their all-time record of 61,315 set in February 1939 for an FA Cup fourth round clash against Liverpool.

After starring in Wolves' shock 2-1 win over Liverpool in the previous round, Helder Costa was out to overshadow *the* No.1 Costa. No chance. Diego had the last laugh when he doubled Chelsea's lead and made sure of their passage to the quarter-finals in the dying minutes. Pedro gave the Blues the lead in the 65th minute, his fourth goal in the cup and his tenth of an increasingly prolific season.

Conte could afford to rest Luiz, Kante and Matic and still field £176m worth of talent from the start, resulting in 'only' £158m and 38-places separating the two sides in the football pyramid.

Batshuayi and Loftus-Cheek were omitted from the starting line-up, in favour of Hazard and Costa, despite featuring in each of the previous rounds.

Chelsea survived an early scare when George Saville hit the post but their quality told. "It was important to continue to play with Costa, Willian and Hazard. Our target is to win, not to try to make all the players happy." said Conte. "In the first game I made nine changes, the second game I made nine and against Wolves I made seven but I tried to make the best decision to win, and then when we have the game in the quarter-final I'll decide the line-up. I repeat, it is important to find the best solution, so then why not start the next game with Ruben or Michy?"

Conte stated that Lincoln's victory at Burnley in the cup had helped concentrate the minds of his players and Asmir Begovic stressed that Chelsea always approach lower-league opponents seriously. "I think the competition is getting tougher every year because every year all the divisions are improving. We have a very good squad so any changes that are made we have ready-made players to come in. I think it's important to give it the respect it deserves because it's one of the best cup competitions in the world."

Conte further added: "A very difficult game but we all knew this. It was important to suffer in the moments and then in the second half we deserved to win because we scored two goals. We had many chances but this is the FA Cup. The results this afternoon show there is no easy games. Don't forget, I changed seven players. It is good to have a good answer from the players who are not playing a lot. We showed great commitment to fight, to win and to continue in this competition. I am pleased because we scored a good goal with the situation. I am pleased for Pedro, for the team and now we must continue in this way."

Wolves manager Paul Lambert said: "I could not ask for any more. The game plan was unbelievably performed and we were up against a world class side. Not just class, world class. They have won the Champions League, so many honours, but we gave it a good go. In big moments, we have to score. If George Saville's shot goes in, we have something to hold on to. We played with intensity but needed breaks to go our way. Big players make things happen. They are most dangerous when we have the ball. They have so much pace on the counter-attack. This was no disgrace, I thought we played great."

Former England winger Trevor Sinclair spoke on Match of the Day: "Antonio Conte has started something at Chelsea. There is a culture at the football club. Players on the periphery are still fit and when they play, they do a job. They may be favourites for the FA Cup too."

Ex-Republic of Ireland midfielder Andy Townsend said on BBC Radio 5 live: "It was a very good game and very competitive, the top third was the difference between the sides. Wolves had lots of half-chances but when Chelsea had theirs they took them. Chelsea made lots of changes today, but their attitude was good, they have passed a test today. You do not question Diego Costa's work-rate. He is running everywhere but he has the knack of being in the right place at the right time. The best striker in the Premier League at the moment."

John Terry's future beyond this season was up in the air but Conte replied enthusiastically when asked about the prospect of the defender ending this season by lifting a sixth FA Cup. "I'd sign now for this!" he said.

However, he was less clear-cut about whether Terry might be able to continue into next season, given the inevitable addition of Champions League football. "The most important thing is the present - to work and build a good future. Then for sure we will see the situation of every single player."

He added: "I want to be very clear. I'm pleased to give the opportunity but not because there is a sentiment. John Terry is my captain and he's important on and off the pitch. He played very well. He's helping me a lot."

Asmir Begovic was unequivocal about Terry. "Absolutely he's still got it, he's the best defender in Premier League history." said the stand-in keeper. "We don't play regularly so when we are called upon we have to show what we can bring to the team. He trains like he always has. I can see him continuing to play and I don't see why he should quit but maybe if he lifts two trophies that's a great way to go out as well."

SUNDAY, 19 FEBRUARY 2017

With Manchester United drawn away to Chelsea Jose Mourinho started the mind games soon after the quarter-final ties were made. He suggested Chelsea had the Premier League title wrapped up and could afford to pay more attention to the FA Cup than United.

United had to come from behind to see off Championship strugglers Blackburn in their fifth round tie, with goals from Marcus Rashford and substitute Zlatan Ibrahimovic cancelling out Danny Graham's opener.

The draw followed shortly after the full-time whistle and pitched Mourinho against his former club at Stamford Bridge - a first cup meeting between the teams since the same stage four years ago. Chelsea edged that tie 1-0 in a home replay after drawing at Old Trafford, and Mourinho suggested their eight-point lead in the league meant they could begin planning for a repeat performance now. United, on the other hand, continued to balance a Europa League campaign, an EFL Cup final and their battle for the top four.

Mourinho initially offered no reaction to the draw but could not resist an early start to the psychological battle. "Probably Chelsea can only think about that (the FA Cup) because I think they are champions and they have nothing else to fight for." he said in a clinical and brief press conference. "The FA Cup is something I believe is important for them. I have to play St Etienne (on Wednesday), I have to play the (League Cup) final, I have to play hopefully another opponent in the Europa League. I have to fight for a top-four position in the Premier League. I have so many things to think about."

He then added: "The match is in one month's time. I don't want to be speaking about it."

Kerry Dixon told the Chelsea Fancast: "I think it's a fantastic draw for us and from the point of view if you've got a hard team you might as well have them at home. I don't believe that any previous result like the result earlier on this season will have any effect at all. I think United are a better side now. They've got more confident, they're playing better. I think Mourinho wants the cup. He's already in one cup final. We'll know by then if they've got one trophy in the cabinet. It's going to be a great game."

MONDAY, 20 FEBRUARY 2017

Thibaut Courtois pulled out of appearing on French TV on Sunday at the last minute. He was absent from the cup tie where Begovic played with third-choice Eduardo on the bench.

Courtois had been an ever-present in the league but was ruled out of the cup with a severe stomach bug. Telefoot presenters Christian Jeanpierre and Frederic Calenge said: "All we can say is that to let us know like that at the very last minute is not very 'Courtois'." - his name translates in French to courteous. The station's editor-in-chief Marc Ambrosiano also tweeted: "Unfortunately Thibaut Courtois is suffering from gastroenteritis, and has had to withdraw from appearing on Telefoot this morning. We wish him a speedy recovery."

Courtois had bumped into a familiar face during a recent night out on London's nightclub scene in the form of British boxing icon David Haye. The pair met up at London's Tape nightclub, posing for photographs which the former heavyweight champion later uploaded onto Instagram. Courtois, a self-confessed boxing fan, smiled alongside Haye while sporting a Muhammad Ali t-shirt bearing the iconic fighter's catchphrase – "Float like a butterfly, sting like a bee". Haye took to Instagram to treat his 350,000 followers to the snap of himself and the Chelsea stopper.

"Chillin at @TapeLondon with boxing fan & all round great guy Thibaut Courtois" Haye wrote alongside the image.

TUESDAY, 21 FEBRUARY 2017

In an interview with Chelsea Pitch Owners - the company with the freehold of the land on which Stamford Bridge stands - Conte spoke of the vital ingredients needed to shape a successful side, having done so previously at Juventus. "I think to win, not only one game, but to win… not one (battle) but the whole war it is important to create a good spirit." he said. "To create a team, and to try to exploit every single player, the talent of every single player in the best way. And for this reason to find the right solution, the right system, to create a family spirit, a good spirit. And then in the negative moments it's important to have a family. If you have a family you solve the situation and then can go forward. I think this is very important to win the league: to create a team, to create a good spirit with your team, and for sure to have good players."

Conte says the fans have played their part. He enthused: "They are incredible! I remember my first game against West Ham they prepared the flag with three colours, the Italy flag, the Tricolore. And then they showed me very soon great enthusiasm, great passion. For me it's fantastic to hear my name during the game, at home or away. Sometimes I'm embarrassed, but it's fantastic. Honestly the first time it happened, with Everton, my assistant coach called me to tell me, 'Mister, the crowd are singing for you.' And then I understood: 'Antonio Antonio Antonio…' Away, (the fans) are incredible. In Liverpool - believe me, it is very difficult to hear the other fans, the opposition fans - and there were 3,000 of our fans, and they pushed a lot our team."

WEDNESDAY, 22 FEBRUARY 2017

Conte and his staff paid a visit to observe the England rugby union squad's preparations for the weekend's international. Back in April 2016, the England head coach Eddie Jones and his forwards coach Steve Borthwick came to Cobham to observe Chelsea's training and facilities when Guus Hiddink was in charge, and a reciprocal invitation for a similar fact-finding visit was accepted by Conte.

Twenty-four hours after Chelsea take on Swansea at Stamford Bridge, Conte's native Italy were the next to try their luck at Twickenham. Bizarrely, England were thoroughly confused by Italy's tactics, especially in the first half, but eventually won by 36-15.

England Rugby's training base, Pennyhill Park, in Bagshot is situated 14 miles across Surrey from Cobham. Among those meeting Conte and his assistants was England fly-half George Ford, who is a big Chelsea supporter and had spoken to the official Chelsea website during one of his visits to a home game. Jones, apparently, is a bit of a Blues fan too.

Conte spoke about how he benefited from the visit: "For me it was very interesting to observe another sport and the differences between the two such as the physical aspect to their training as well as speak with Eddie Jones about the analysis side to the game. It is important for me to compare my work and experience with another sport to gain inspiration and tactical ideas for the future. I learnt about how detailed the preparation is in rugby through video analysis as well as the physical element to the sport."

Conte was full of praise for Jones, who was unbeaten since taking charge of England. "We spoke about our experience and it was very interesting to speak to him. Eddie is a winner and he is transferring that mentality onto the team."

THURSDAY, 23 FEBRUARY 2017

Former goalkeeper Carlo Cudicini was helping Conte improve his English and get his message across. Cudicini, 43, spent nine years on the books at Chelsea and was regarded as one of the finest 'keepers in the Premier League on his day, and is now playing a vital role as Conte's assistant.

Speaking to the club's official site, Conte explained just how much he's enjoyed working with him. "Honestly Carlo is helping me a lot." Conte confirmed. "He is staying with me a lot of time in my day. He is also my teacher in English. After every press conference or interview, he always tries to tell me the mistakes to correct. Then sometimes to explain the situation in the right way, or with the players, with the club. He is helping me a lot and he's a really good guy. He's a really good professional."

FRIDAY, 24 FEBRUARY 2017

Conte was "ready to take the risk" (of the sack) if Chelsea are crowned champions, despite it appearing to be a poisoned chalice to win the title.

He planned to contact Claudio Ranieri in the coming days after the Italian was sacked by Leicester, the 5,000-1 title winners from last season. Ranieri's dismissal followed Jose Mourinho and Manuel

Pellegrini, who both lost their jobs at Chelsea and Manchester City respectively after winning the title the previous season.

Conte added that it is an indication of a "poor club" if it is true that Leicester's players played a part in Ranieri's sacking behind the scenes. Conte said it would be wrong for any club to allow its players to decide a manager's future. "It is a lack of respect for Claudio because I think it is not right." Conte said. "The players don't decide if a manager must be sacked or not. Because if this happens it means the club is poor. It is poor without power. I don't believe in this, I don't trust in this and I don't want to listen to this type of story because it is frustrating for a manager. Also to imagine that the players can decide your destiny."

Chelsea were eight points ahead as Conte said: "If we are able to reach this dream, for me, for the players, I am ready to face this risk. I am happy, very happy to face the risk next season. I am really focused, me, the players, about this season. It won't be easy but I am ready to take this risk if it means we win the league."

Conte joked that bookmakers were offering odds on him to be sacked before Christmas. "If you remember very well I was already sacked this season with the bookmakers and I was lucky to keep the right concentration and continue the work." Conte added. "It's nonsense to say Chelsea have won the league when there are 13 games to play. We must be focused and take it step by step. I watched Swansea's games against Liverpool and Leicester and the coach has had a great impact on the team. We must pay great attention."

The media revisited Conte's playing days for Carlo Ancelotti's Juventus in the 1999/2000 season when they looked to have built an unassailable advantage in Serie A. At one stage they were nine points clear with only eight games to go but would lose four of their final fixtures to surrender the title to Sven-Goran Eriksen's Lazio. On the final day, when Lazio beat Reggina at home, Juventus needed an away win over Perugia. On an almost flooded pitch they lost 1-0. "When we lost the title in the last game against Perugia, I was the captain and I remember it very well." Conte said. "After this game, I had to go to Euro 2000 with the Italy national team and I didn't sleep for six days because it was such a shock to me to lose the title."

Conte had a better experience involving Lazio at the end of the 2001/02 season. His Juventus team had to win on the final day at Udinese and see Internazionale lose at Lazio in order for them to leapfrog Inter to the title… and that's exactly what happened.

Conte was asked about facing Manchester United at home in the FA Cup quarter-final, but his thoughts were only for Swansea as he prepared his team for the threat of the striker, Fernando Llorente, with whom he worked when he was the manager of Juventus.

"Thirteen (remaining) games is an enormous space of time and 39 points." Conte said. "If we take 32 points, we win the title - otherwise, anything can happen. We must be focused and go step by step."

Referring back to his visit to the England rugby union camp he emphasised how interesting and beneficial it had been to have shared ideas with their head coach. "It was fantastic to see his methods, like the video analysis, and to compare the different ways we work during the week - when you work very hard and find the day to work less, to give rest to the players." Conte said. "It's important to compare the physical work, the mental work and see the way they face the game through individual analysis. I like to have this type of meeting with the coaches of other sports. It is very interesting and useful. I have invited him to come to Chelsea so that we can spend another afternoon together."

Now looking ahead to the Swansea game, Kante commented: "It's a good opportunity to extend the gap at the top because we play first. We are working hard in training and the desire of the team is to win every game. Our last league game against Burnley was tough and we know Swansea are on a good run. It's going to be difficult and we're going to have to fight and work hard."

Paul Clement had no problems finding his way around Stamford Bridge. He returns along with assistant Claude Makelele, twice a champion with Chelsea. Swansea's 45-year-old boss spent two spells with Chelsea's coaching staff, including a spell as Carlo Ancelotti's assistant when the Blues won the title in 2010. Clement's previous experience of Antonio Conte came during his time as Ancelotti's assistant at Real Madrid when they faced Juventus in the Champions League. "He has done a really good job at Chelsea." Clement said. "They have looked really strong home and away with the new formation they are playing, there is a lot of confidence."

SATURDAY, 25 FEBRUARY 2017
Chelsea 3-1 Swansea City
Premier League

Chelsea extended their lead to eleven points after a victory that was anything but emphatic yet still yielded the required points.

With Manchester City having a weekend off - they were due to play rivals United who were playing in the EFL Cup Final - the league leaders took full advantage to keep the pressure on the chasing pack of City, Spurs and Arsenal. Chelsea now had 63 points from 26 games, three more than at the same stage in 2014/15 when last crowned champions of England.

Fabregas marked his 300th Premier League appearance with a class finish. But Chelsea were rocked in stoppage time at the end of the first half when Swansea, rejuvenated in recent weeks under Clement, levelled; one-time Conte target Llorente heading in Gylfi Sigurdsson's free kick with their first meaningful attempt. Chelsea had conceded in consecutive home league games for the first time under Conte.

The champions-elect got their act together in the second half, although they were made to wait until the last 18 minutes to make their overall dominance pay. Pedro continued his rich vein of scoring form with the second after 72 minutes and the Premier League's second leading scorer, Costa, secured the points.

It could have been a different outcome had Swansea not been denied a penalty when Azpilicueta handled inside the area at 1-1. Referee, Neil Swarbrick, didn't spot it and neither did his assistant.

Cesc Fabregas could have had four goals on his return. He had a goal-bound shot deflected behind shortly before he opened the scoring, was denied by former Arsenal teammate Lukasz Fabianski and also rattled the bar.

Fabregas made only his sixth start and later explained how he was still learning and happy at Stamford Bridge. "In the beginning when I didn't play I told people not even to speak to me because I was really upset. I can understand there are doubts, the philosophy of the manager. He came in, wanted to see if I could adapt and I understand that. As a player I'm someone who wants to play with the ball, maybe not so much the defensive side. But I adapted to the way he wants to play and hopefully I can play more. Now with Conte, I'm learning new things, new football. It makes it entertaining. I know sometimes I didn't play as much but even in training I'm learning and sometimes you think if you've been playing for a long time, won a lot, you've done everything and then you realise that in football you can never know everything. Hopefully I've reversed the situation from the beginning of the season to now and hopefully I can keep playing like that to keep my place."

"I'm happy. It's a proud moment for me, a fantastic three points for us. We're getting closer to the end of the season and we want to be at the top for as long as we can. We showed great character, great fight and we had the three points. Now the most important thing for me is that Chelsea win the Premier League and hopefully we can make this happen."

He will not be departing. "China?! I'm 29!" the Spaniard laughed. "For sure, it's Chelsea I'm thinking about. Until the day Chelsea tell me they don't want me, I can leave, and it happens to everyone, then you have to move on. When my brain says you can't do it anymore then I will move, probably away from Europe. But for now it's all about Chelsea and performing here."

Fabregas had justified his return to the side in place of Nemanja Matic. Conte explained that, aware Swansea play a compact game, Fabregas's superior passing ability was the reason for the change. "Swansea play very, very compact." Conte told Chelsea's official website. "Probably in this game it was difficult to find the space to play between the lines. I'm very happy, for Cesc, but also Nemanja. When I called him to play off the bench, he played really well. N'Golo is playing fantastic. This is why we are top of the league - all my players are playing very, very well."

Despite concerns of upsetting players, Conte would continue to rotate. "For me, it's always difficult to make these decisions. But I have to do this. Sometimes I make a mistake, but I try to do the best for the team because I want to win. Against Swansea I decided to start with Cesc, but don't forget Matic is playing a fantastic championship, Kante the same. We must continue in this way. Our target is more important than a single player. We played very well, it was a good performance, and we created many chances to score. We conceded at the end of the first half, after the time was finished, so in this case there was a bit of luck, but we showed great character in the second half. We deserved a lot to win the game, now it's important to continue in this way."

Conte believed the trophy-winning experience in his ranks would prove key to the leaders' pursuit of the title. Chelsea's win was their twelfth in succession at Stamford Bridge, equalling a club record. "Keeping that focus is not easy over the whole championship but I have a lot of players who have won (titles) in the past. They know very well the way that we must continue to try to keep at the top of the table, to try and win the title. For this reason I'm lucky. I'm lucky to have a lot of players who, in the past, won a lot of trophies. If, sometimes, I can see some of them relaxing, it's right for me to try and help them be focused for every moment. But, honestly, it hasn't been necessary for me to keep the concentration and focus of the players yet. I have a team who, until now, have deserved to stay at the top of the table. Above all I think we deserve to stay there at the moment. We are playing good football, with good intensity, scoring a lot of goals. Trust me, I'm very happy above all for my players. They are deserving this. Every day I see them during the training sessions, the commitment and behaviour. They deserve this. Today we were a bit frustrated to be 1-1 at half-time but I told them: 'We are playing very well, dominating the game, creating chances but it's 1-1. We don't deserve this but that's the reality. So go into the second half and push because we need to win.' They did this. In these situations, when the tension starts to increase, you've got to see the right answers from my players. Today I saw a lot of right answers from my players."

Fernando Llorente was wanted by Conte in January as a back-up for Costa. "I wasn't always confident we'd keep him but I'm certainly glad we have." said Paul Clement. "I didn't have to fight to keep him but we did have some discussions together and in the end (the move) didn't happen. Fernando's still very pleased to be with us and very motivated to do well at the club. He's a key player for us and will be a big help for us in the run-in."

Conte was in reflective mood following the brutal sacking of Claudio Ranieri and he knows that a title will not guarantee him long-term security in the Chelsea hot seat. "In this type of modern football, it is not easy to start a project or to be sure you will stay in for a long time in the same team. It is not only for me but for all coaches. Then for sure if you have the possibility to stay for many years in the same team, you can work to improve your idea. But the results... the results in football are very important. We all know this and it can happen that one season you win the title and the next you can be going on your way."

Chelsea had nine days to prepare for their next game away to West Ham United. Hazard believed the title-winning experience of two years ago would help them get over the line this season. Chelsea last won the title under Mourinho in 2015 and Hazard felt the know-how from that campaign will stand them in good stead in this season's title race. He said: "We are professional. We won the league two years ago so we know what to do. We have been first for a few months, we want to stay at the top and we have to take it game after game." Hazard brilliantly set up Costa for his goal but failed to get on the score sheet himself. "For me it is the same if I score, don't score or assist. Even if I don't make an assist or score goals - if I play a good game and we win, I will be the first man happy on the pitch. In the second half we created a lot of chances and scored two more. At the end, the result was 3-1 and it could maybe have been 5-1."

Frank Lampard returned to say goodbye to the supporters, taking the microphone during the half-time interval and addressing the fans.

@ChelseaFC - "Frank Lampard is our half-time guest and the cover star of a very special edition matchday programme today."

211 GOALS

648 APPEARANCES

13 TROPHIES

UNFORGETTABLE MEMORIES

THANKS FOR EVERYTHING, FRANK

MONDAY, 27 FEBRUARY 2017

Chinese Super League club Tianjin Quanjian FC, managed by World Cup and Ballon D'Or winner Fabio Cannavaro, bid £90m for Diego Costa, and offered him £85m in wages over a three-year contract, according to SFR Sport (a division of French telecommunications company SFR).

Chelsea had rejected the offer which would have made Costa, who was interested in the move, the second most expensive player in the world behind Paul Pogba. Tianjin owner Shu Yuhui confirmed in January that talks had been held between himself and Jorge Mendes, Costa's agent, while Conte refused to discuss the striker's future until the end of the season.

Costa, though, was back among the goals and seemingly happy.

TUESDAY, 28 FEBRUARY 2017

Conte's players remained grounded despite their commanding advantage at the summit. David Luiz told Chelsea TV: "(We) need to go game by game. Premier League everybody knows is difficult.

So keep the feet on the floor, with humility, working hard. That's the way."

The 12-match winning run had equalled the club record. Conte commented: "To have ten wins in a row in the league and 12 in all competitions shows it's very difficult to play at Stamford Bridge for the opponents. It's fantastic to have this record. Now it's important to continue this record."

As for their lead at the top: "(Ten points) is not the reality." Conte warned. "The other teams have to play the game. For sure we have to look at ourselves, to play game by game and to continue to show we are deserving to stay at the top of the league. Next week we have to prepare (for) a really tough game against West Ham."

Premier League Table, Top 6, end of February 2017:

		P	W	D	L	F	A	GD	Pts
1	Chelsea	26	20	3	3	55	19	+36	63
2	Tottenham Hotspur	26	15	8	3	50	18	+32	53
3	Manchester City	25	16	4	5	51	29	+22	52
4	Arsenal	25	15	5	5	54	28	+26	50
5	Liverpool	26	14	7	5	55	33	+22	49
6	Manchester United	25	13	9	3	38	21	+17	48

CHAPTER TWELVE

MARCH 2017

Two out of two in the league.
Through to the FA Cup semi-finals.

WEDNESDAY, 1 MARCH 2017

Conte was on course to take Chelsea back into Europe's premier club competition; Chelsea had played in the tournament for 13 successive years until this season. He was soon expected to be offered a contract extension, and said: "A great team and club like Chelsea has to play in the Champions League every season. It is important for us - the Champions League has to be our house to stay. It's important to think now about this season and go step by step. We have 12 league games till the end of the season to try to reach a dream for me, for the players and for the club. Then we will prepare for next season. But when your name is Chelsea, you must always fight to win the Champions League, the Premier League, the FA Cup, all the competitions."

Cesar Azpilicueta had been utilised by Conte on the right side of a three-man defence since the beginning of October; a move which had more than paid off. Conte singled out wing-back Victor Moses and defender Azpilicueta for their importance to his team in the 3-4-3 set-up - labelling the former as "fantastic" and the latter "incredible".

"This system (3-5-2) was in my mind when we planned the season with the club." Conte said. "We have two systems 4-2-4 and 3-4-3. When I switched this system, I felt it was a good fit for our players.

We don't lose offensively but we are better defensively. We found players not to adapt but to play in different roles compared to the past. Like Moses and Azpi - he's incredible in this new role. He is one of the best in the world in this role. Moses too. To run for the whole game with this quality is fantastic."

Moses had a successful loan spell at West Ham to thank for his reversal, playing regular Premier League football with the Hammers in the 2015/16 campaign. He was grateful for the chance to impress during their final season at Upton Park. Now, though, he was enjoying life at Stamford Bridge as Chelsea headed to the Hammers' new London Stadium for Monday night's London derby. "I had a great time there last season, it's a nice memory but now I'm a Chelsea player and I'm enjoying my football." Moses told Chelsea's official website. "I can't wait to go to the London Stadium and hopefully we'll get three points. I've always wanted to play for this big club, it's one of the best clubs in the world at the moment and I'm enjoying every single minute. I just want to keep on working hard and helping my teammates out."

Chelsea had continued their run against Swansea and Moses reflected: "I thought we did well and showed great character. Swansea did well in the way they tried to sit back and frustrate us but we kept on playing and as soon as we got the second goal we started to enjoy it. We're not looking at the table at the moment, we still have 12 matches to play and we just need to take each game as it comes. We just want to stay grounded and win as many games as we can between now and the end of the season. We're going to stay focused and keep working hard together as a team, as everyone can see we're doing."

He committed his long-term future by signing a new deal - a two-year contract extension, recommitting to the club until 2021. Moses, who spent the last three seasons on loan at Liverpool, Stoke City and West Ham, confirmed: "I feel very excited. I'm delighted to be here for another few years now and to sign a new deal. Now it's time to concentrate on the team and keep working hard to make sure we win games and try to win the Premier League this season. We're having a great season, I'm enjoying my football and we have a good manager here that has given every single one of us confidence. I just want to keep on enjoying it and working hard for the team."

Chelsea technical director, Michael Emenalo, added: "We are extremely pleased Victor has chosen to extend his contract with us. He is enjoying an excellent season and, under Antonio's leadership, has proved to be an important member of the squad. This new contract is a testament to Victor's hard work and dedication to succeed at Chelsea and we believe he will be a big part of our future success."

Conte effectively reinvented Moses into a marauding right wing-back in his 3-4-3 formation. "I realised quickly that Victor could stay with us, I saw his potential quickly. I knew of him, but to see him live is very important to judge a player. I always saw him as a winger, very good in one-versus-one, but a bit poor defensively. Then, when I decided to change the system, I wanted to try him in this new role. Now we have a complete player."

THURSDAY, 2 FEBRUARY 2017

Jose Mourinho hailed the passion of his Manchester United supporters as "unrivalled" by any of the sides he has managed before - including Real Madrid, Inter Milan - and on two occasions Chelsea.

"The crowd at Old Trafford must play its part." Mourinho said in a brochure for prospective season ticket holders. "I have to say I've been impressed by your dedication and commitment, as season ticket holders here at United. I've managed several clubs and I have never seen such unrivalled passion. The stadium is full every time we play and the support the players receive is special."

Frank Lampard responded to the "jealous" backlash John Terry faced after famously, or infamously, wearing a full kit to lift the Champions League trophy in 2012.

The club captain had been suspended for the final and watched as the Blues came back from a goal down to beat Bayern Munich on penalties at the Allianz Arena and win the competition for the first time. Terry had then rejoined his teammates for the celebration, changing out of his club suit to a full strip to start an internet meme of the defender celebrating victories of which he played no part. 'Lamps' blamed "jealous" people for the negative response, adding that Terry could have worn whatever he liked including Speedos. "Can I answer first?" Lampard asked presenter Holly Willoughby on ITV's *Play To The Whistle* after the incident was raised. "It's not easy for John to say, right. Firstly, because of social media, it all exploded because of the jealous people, who didn't like that Chelsea won it, that John won it. Secondly, he was our captain for ten years before that, roughly. If he had wanted to go up there in his Speedos and pick it up he could have done what he liked."

N'Golo Kante won London Premier League Player of the Year after having been in the capital for only a few months, picking up the gong at the London Football Awards. He won the prize ahead of Blues teammate Diego Costa, Arsenal's Alexis Sanchez and Tottenham's Dele Alli. He was also one of the favourites to be named PFA Player of the Year. Conte was named as the Manager of the Year, beating off competition from Pochettino, Millwall's Neil Harris and Fulham's Slavisa Jokanovic. Frank Lampard was recognised for his services to football in London. Lampard, who won three Premier League titles and one Champions League crown during his 13 years at Stamford Bridge, picked up the prize for his outstanding contribution to Chelsea. Former England manager Roy Hodgson helped present him his award.

Former Chelsea cult hero Dennis Wise likened Kante to club great Claude Makelele. Wise believes comparisons can be made between Kante and his compatriot Makelele, who played over 200 games for the Blues. "He is very much like him (Makelele). He breaks things up really well and his passing is impressive." Wise, who himself made over 300 appearances in eleven years at Chelsea, told the club's website. "He's an unsung hero and people are recognising what he is doing for the team. He closes people down and he shuts holes, protects the back three and I think he's done fantastic ever since he's come in."

Wise believed his former side had no trouble dealing with the pressure, having won the title in 2015. "Some of these players, they're big players, they've been in this situation before so I can see them coping quite easily with the pressure coming towards them."

Burglars broke into the Surrey mansion owned by John Terry while he was on a family skiing holiday. A spokesman for Surrey Police said: "We can confirm that a burglary took place at a property in Moles Hill, Oxshott, overnight 25/26 February." Thieves forced their way into the house and escaped with valuables while he was away with family and relatives.

FRIDAY, 3 MARCH 2017

Conte's family was finding it difficult to cope without him but he had no plans to quit London and return to Italy, despite being linked heavily with Inter. "I think my situation is very clear. I have a contract with Chelsea. We are trying to build something important with the club, for the present and for the future. I am happy here. The only problem for me this season was the family missing me. My family stayed in Italy. I am working, and working for the future to try and bring them here and to stay together. My family is missing me, this is the truth. This is my first season away, in a new country, with a new language and new habits, and it's totally different from my past. For sure, to arrive here is not easy. It's not. It's not easy to stay alone and live this experience with my family still in Italy. I hope to live this experience with my family next season."

Conte's wife Elisabetta and their daughter Vittoria originally intended to move to London in January but those plans were delayed until the summer, which only served to fuel the rumours of a return to Italy. But, he wished to stay at Chelsea for many years. "If you ask my opinion, I hope to stay and work a lot for this club, to win a lot with this club. Every coach, when you start working at a new club, you hope to stay many, many years because it means you are working very well. You have the possibility to improve your players, to improve your team, and to grow together. I think this season we are doing this. We are putting great foundations down for the present and, above all, for the future. So it is normal for every coach to hope to stay many years in a club, and to work to improve your players and reach great results and to win. But you know, especially with memories fresh from Claudio Ranieri, you have to be ready for anything."

Claudio Ranieri was fired only nine months after winning the Premier League, a reminder of the uncertainty of a manager's life. "The story tells us this." said Conte. "But I'm not worried about this. I want to work very hard with my players. We have to continue this way and try to do something important this season. We are in the right position and we have the possibility to continue in this way."

Conte will manage somewhere other than Italy when he leaves Chelsea as his intention is to work in different countries. "In my mind, there is the will to find different experiences in different countries. I think it's fantastic to find these experiences. When I was a footballer, I played only for two teams: Lecce and Juventus. Now I am having this great experience in England, in an amazing league."

Chelsea were ten points clear with 12 matches to play. They are next at West Ham where they were beaten in the EFL Cup. "It will be a tough game," said Conte. "We will know the other results of the other teams and it will be pressure, positive or negative. But we are ready to play this game and try to do better than our last game there."

Slaven Bilic felt Chelsea could yet slip up. "I'm surprised how good they have been. I was expecting him to have a strong impact because he had it at Juventus. I watched Juve quite a lot and I was studying his game. I didn't know (how he'd get on) because no one knows. I expected him to do great long term and it is a surprise they are ten points clear. Conte is a great manager, he did it at Juve, he did it with Italy. A brilliant manager, of course. It (the title race) is still very open. If they slip up, which you can in every game, other teams need to be ready."

SATURDAY, 4 MARCH 2017

John Terry revealed the most significant change that Conte introduced during his time at Chelsea - "proper running".

Conte's decision to force his players to run for miles in pre-season came as a shock to his experienced squad when the Italian took charge. Speaking to BT Sport, Terry said: "In all my years' playing, I've had Jose Mourinho, Carlo Ancelotti, Robbie di Matteo, I've never done the kind of running, you know like proper running. Everything's been with the ball. So in the past, under Mourinho, from day one pre-season, you get the balls out. But Conte has come in and from the start of pre-season we have done running. This is a group that hasn't done that for seven, eight, nine years. A shock? Yeah, it was a little bit yeah but after two, three weeks of doing it the lads were going, 'Physically we feel much better'."

Conte also has more emphasis on tactics than any of the other former Chelsea managers, which has been a massive eye-opener for the veteran defender as he takes his coaching badges. The team was transformed since Conte changed to a 3-4-3 formation. "We do a lot more tactically now. If I would have said to you I'm going to stop playing last year, and hadn't had this experience with Conte, I would have gone into my management with the mindset of 'I'm not running my players, not too many tactics because the players don't enjoy it too much' but that's the exact opposite. I have seen a completely different side of it."

SUNDAY, 5 MARCH 2017

Chelsea were "almost unstoppable" and Manchester City had to win every game to stay in the title race, argued Pep Guardiola.

City beat Sunderland 2-0 to move within eight points of the Blues, third in the table, but could move above second-placed Tottenham if they won their game in hand at Stoke on Wednesday.

"It's a pity that the distance between Chelsea is so big." said Guardiola. "But that's true. We are there behind, of course, Chelsea because they are almost unstoppable. I feel we are playing quite well and that's why we are getting results, but now, of course, we are in a position when you arrive in March and April, every game if you win, you stay; if you lose, you are out. In the Premier League, in the cup, in the Champions League. The players know, we know, the club knows, if we are not able to win the next game we will be out."

Pochettino, however, still believed Spurs can catch Chelsea after beating Everton 3-2 at White Hart Lane. "The most important thing is to show the belief on the pitch and today I think we showed that." Pochettino said. "More than talk and more than speak outside, it is better the team show their performance because I think (regarding) belief the answer is very easy. We need to be there, it's not up to us of course, but it's up to us to be ready if they fail."

The Tottenham players were in the unusual position of supporting the club's fierce rivals West Ham. "We want West Ham to win against Chelsea." Harry Kane admitted. "We don't normally say that here." Spurs set a club record by securing their ninth successive home victory in the Premier League in what is expected to be their final season at White Hart Lane.

Conte and his players were missing Champions League football. Conte was used to Champions League football after managing Juventus and was looking forward to bringing Chelsea back into the competition next season. "Yes, yes (we miss it). For me and my players, yes." he said at a news conference at Cobham Training Centre. "The Champions League, I think, must be an appointment for us every year. It must be our house, the Champions League. For this reason, we are putting our strength into playing in the Champions League next season. It's a great competition for every single player, club and manager, and we want to stay there and try to fight to win it. I watched the Manchester City game against Monaco live because I wanted to breathe it in, the right atmosphere, and feel this type of game. In the future, also, I hope to sit and watch games live. I saw a great game, a great game. To see eight goals is not simple, and not usual to find this."

The competition for Champions League places had become especially fierce with Chelsea, Liverpool and Manchester United all missing out on qualification last season. Conte added, "We started our season trying to fight until the end to win the title, and to try and fight until the end to be in the right position to go into next season's Champions League. This was our target. Our target. But for sure, it wasn't easy to start the season and know that six strong teams fight for the title and the Champions League. Don't forget, in these six teams, two won't play in the Champions League next season. They have to go into the Europa League, which is a bit different to the Champions League. But now this league is very, very difficult. To win the title and also find a place to play the Champions League is not easy."

Former Chelsea players, Kerry Dixon and Paul Canoville previewed the Blues' clash at the London Stadium in a live Facebook chat with Goal's Nizaar Kinsella. Chelsea can stretch their lead to ten points with a win. "Everyone is together at the moment, on and off the field and that is the difference." Dixon said at the launch of his new documentary film, by Legend Lives at the Sanctum Soho Hotel. "The two real stars are Costa and Hazard. They are the two real stars. Hazard can unlock a defence and make it happen. No disrespect to any other player, they are all playing their part. There are many unsung heroes in that team. It takes not just eleven but around 16 (players)." Canoville added: "Everyone is fighting. Under Conte it has been unbelievable. He is enjoying it, he looks like a young guy. This is great for ex-players. I am loving that Chelsea are winning and they have to be favourites for the league, but we can't say that it is over until it is over."

MONDAY, 6 MARCH 2017
West Ham United 1-2 Chelsea
Premier League

Conte went to address the away fans as they sang "We're gonna win the league". Two clenched fists from the Italian; ecstatic as he jogged to the tunnel. But he warned his players to "keep their feet on the ground".

Conte said: "We must think we have to take 26 points. We go step by step. We must think every opponent will want to beat us from now until the end. To dream is good, but it's important to keep our feet on the ground."

Chelsea were the seventh side to accrue 66-plus points from their first 27 games of a Premier League season, having done it themselves twice before (69 in 2005/06 and 68 in 2004/05). All six previous sides have gone on to win the title.

The instant reaction, though, told a different story. Phil Neville, former Manchester United defender, on Radio 5 live observed: "I think what we have seen tonight is the new Premier League champions. There is no team playing with this quality, organisation. There is no one who can get close to them."

Alan Shearer tweeted that N'Golo Kante could win Players' Player and Football Writers' Player of the Year after the France international played 50 passes, completing 45 of them, and ran 12.4km - only Fabregas (12.7km) ran further.

Diego Costa and Eden Hazard scored as Chelsea extended their lead to ten points with their 21st victory of the league season and another big step towards the title.

The Italian was once again spot on with his tactics - nullifying the predictable aerial threat of 6ft 4in frontman Andy Carroll early in the match, then in the 25th minute mounting a devastating counter-attack. Kante intercepted a pass from Hammers' Robert Snodgrass deep inside the Chelsea half on the left and played the ball to Hazard. The Belgian drove forward, played a one-two with Pedro and then shifted the ball past Darren Randolph before slotting home. Chelsea had scored the opening goal for the 21st time this season in the Premier League, four more times than any other side.

The Blues doubled their lead after the break when Hazard's corner from the left was turned in with his thigh by Costa for his 17th league goal of the season.

Sofiane Feghouli's low drive was brilliantly saved by Courtois and Alonso blocked Manuel Lanzini's half-volley with his arm moments later - but referee Andre Marriner deemed it to be accidental. West Ham finally scored in stoppage time. Carroll robbed Fabregas and fed Andre Ayew, who squared for Lanzini to fire in.

Chelsea had now enjoyed 118 Premier League London derby wins, more than any other side (one more than Arsenal).

Conte told Sky Sports: "I think we played a good game. We controlled the game. It's a pity for the goal we conceded at the end. To give away a clean sheet at the end is not good. We must improve in this situation. But I'm pleased. We showed great concentration and commitment and will to win. N'Golo Kante has great stamina. He covered a lot of the ground. He's improving a lot. We must continue. It's important to rest really well and prepare for the FA Cup game against Manchester United."

Eden Hazard also on Sky Sports: "It's easier for me to play more inside now and link up. Last season I was more out wide and there I am sometimes alone, against two guys. Antonio Conte is a great character and he helps us a lot. We want to win the trophy as soon as possible and bring it back to Stamford Bridge."

Hazard sent Twitter users into a frenzy on Monday night following his audacious 'back' pass - he had fashioned a pass literally off his back, flicking the ball on to Kante while facing in a different direction. And, as if it to show it no fluke, it was footage from his time at Lille that emerged on Twitter, with @HazardStuff_ (who else?) sharing a clip of a similar move a few seasons ago. One Twitter user noted that it was "phenomenal" while another said: "Hazard's first touch off his back in the lead-up is a better first touch than I'll ever produce in my life."

"It was something natural" he later explained. "I did it once before, in France, it's for the fans." It was the best way for him to execute "a good pass" rather than showboating, he insisted. "Because if we had lost the ball and conceded a goal then I would have been in trouble with Antonio."

"I think sometimes when I'm on the pitch I see him twice, one on the left, one on the right. I think he plays with a twin." Hazard joked on Kante.

In the main media debriefing Conte made it clear he had "trust" in his players to finish the job. "I must have confidence in my players. Until now, we have deserved to stay on top of the table. For sure, it won't be easy to stay there because Tottenham and City, also Liverpool, are there. To see Arsenal drop three points and Manchester United drop two points (this weekend) was very important because the games are starting to be fewer, but this league will still be really tough until the end. I listen to the other coaches of the other teams, and they trust (themselves) to win. And it's right to have this ambition. It's important for us to know the others have this ambition so that we keep our own anger and will to fight and stay on top of the league. I trust my players to do this because they are showing me great commitment not only in games but during the week in every training session, great will to work and improve, to improve our work. I trust them. Absolutely!"

Slaven Bilic observed: "There are enough points available if they slip, and every game will be difficult for them. It will not be an easy ride, but they are not going to become casual. That's 100%. They look very, very serious. I think I can see them staying on top with the quality they have, but also with how solid they are and how concentrated they are. They look in good shape. There are many good teams in the Premier League with attacking football, flair and individual class. But from all these teams, Chelsea look the most solid. They always defend with numbers. They always defend with five and two holding midfielders, minimum. So seven players. And, because they are really fit, they make that offensive transition their main offensive weapon. They're ten points clear at the top. This is why."

Conte was impressed with his players' response to seeing City and Spurs claim victories on Sunday, despite still being unhappy about a lack of ruthlessness in the final third. "We must be more clinical to finish the game because, when you are 1-0 or 2-0 up, in England anything can happen. You can see that, had West Ham scored after 85 minutes rather than 92, we'd have been in trouble. For this reason, we have to be more clinical when we create chances and score, score, score. But I'm pleased for my players. Today was not easy, to play after your opponents and know they have won, so if you drop points you give hope to your opponents in the chase. But we played under good pressure today, and our answer was very good. I'm very pleased for my players. We controlled the game and conceded not a lot. Our central defenders played very well against these long balls for Carroll. I'm pleased with the commitment and the focus."

Chelsea's plans for their new £500m stadium on the site of Stamford Bridge were approved by the Mayor of London. The 60,000-capacity venue was approved at a Hammersmith & Fulham Council meeting in January, but still required the approval of city mayor and Liverpool supporter Sadiq Khan. They duly received approval with Khan praising the "high-quality and spectacular design". Chelsea aimed to be playing in their new stadium by the start of the 2021/22 season, with three years in exile from the summer of 2018. Wembley being a likely temporary venue.

Once Chelsea have left for their temporary home, the old stadium itself will be demolished and earth removed to enable the new pitch to be sunken below ground level. The rebuilt Stamford Bridge was being designed by Herzog & de Meuron, the team behind the iconic Bird's Nest Stadium in Beijing and Bayern Munich's Allianz Arena. The new stadium will include the construction of an elevated walkway over the nearby District Line, linking the stadium to Fulham Broadway station.

The club statement read: "Following a review by Mayor of London Sadiq Khan, we are delighted he has chosen to support the council's decision. This is the latest significant step toward redevelopment of the stadium and the delivery of the extensive local community programme. Further steps lie ahead, both during and after the planning process, before construction work can commence. We continue to collaborate with all stakeholders and will keep you informed of progress made. We would like to acknowledge all residents, businesses and other parties locally who are engaging with us during the process."

Khan said: "London is one of the world's greatest sporting cities and I'm delighted that we will soon add Chelsea's new stadium to the already fantastic array of sporting arenas in the capital. Having taken a balanced view of the application, I'm satisfied this is a high-quality and spectacular design which will significantly increase capacity within the existing site, as well as ensuring fans can have easy access from nearby transport connections. I'm confident this new stadium will be a jewel in London's sporting crown and will attract visitors and football fans from around the world."

The club's application includes an investment of £12m in community activities, such as employment and skills training, as well as a contribution of £3.75m towards affordable housing in the borough.

TUESDAY, 7 MARCH 2017

Diego Costa reiterated that his training ground bust-up with Conte was "nothing", blaming the fall-out on people in England's tendency to "make up a lot of stuff."

He was keen to play down the significance of his row with Conte. "It was nothing." Costa told ESPN

Brasil. "People here (in England) make up a lot of stuff. Things happen, but I'm showing now that there's nothing to it. I'm playing and scoring goals, and that's the important thing. Everyone knows that anything I say has bigger repercussions than what it was."

Having netted in each of his last three appearances, Costa said the squad was focused on securing their second league title in three seasons. "The manager is someone who works us really hard in training. He's got his personality just like I've got mine and others have theirs, but the important thing is to show your personality in a way that benefits the team. There's still a long way to go. We do have a good advantage but we have to keep doing what we're doing. We just have to try and keep winning and take it one step at a time."

WEDNESDAY, 8 MARCH 2017

Marcos Alonso had jumped at the chance to join Chelsea despite holding talks with Barcelona over a potential move. The 26-year-old has been a revelation as a left wing-back for Conte since signing from Serie A side Fiorentina.

He told IBTimes UK that despite offers from some other big clubs he had no hesitations over moving to the Premier League side. "There were some great teams interested in me in the summer but I decided to join Chelsea because they are a team that I had always liked." said Alonso. "I saw a possibility of succeeding here. I had some other offers from other teams from Italy and Spain but when Chelsea came to get me I did not think twice. Chelsea are a club that had always attracted me. From my early years at Bolton I knew that Chelsea were a great club and the truth is that I was right to come here."

It's fair to say that eyebrows were raised when the club paid £23m to bring Alonso back to England after underwhelming spells at both Bolton and Sunderland. He explained: "Things are going well but I have to continue this way because I think I still can give much more. Now with the tranquility of not having to prove anything I have to keep improving."

Alonso addressed the specific reports that Barcelona were keen on him. "Well, I think there were some conversations (with Barcelona) but the truth is that at that point it was not in my plans to leave Fiorentina. It was only when the interest from Chelsea arrived in the summer when I started to consider to make a change."

Cesc Fabregas posted a mischievous picture of the Blues' victorious Spaniards celebrating their win after defeating their Brazilian teammates in the final at their Cobham training ground. Fabregas and Alonso were joined by Pedro, Azpilicueta and honorary Spaniards Courtois and Matic in claiming victory. Costa was born in Brazil but has represented Spain at international level before deciding he was Brazilian again for the kick about.

On his Instagram account, Fabregas posted: "Spanish team wins again!

Back to back wins, undefeated! Thanks to our new coach Julio Tous for the tactics. Easy win in the semis against England and entertaining final against Brazil."

Replying to the post Alonso posted a cheeky dig at Costa, commenting with grinning emojis: "@diego.costa traidor" - (traitor).

THURSDAY, 9 MARCH 2017

The last time Jose Mourinho's Manchester United side visited Stamford Bridge, back in October's Premier League clash, they were stunned by a 4-0 thrashing. Now, with an FA Cup quarter-final tie looming, Chelsea appeared to strike first with the Mourinho-like mind games.

On the official website was the following statement: "The current record of 12 consecutive wins was first set between 19 May and 21 November 2009 and matched with results from 24 September to 10 January 2015, the second of those runs while Mourinho was at the tiller."

"To arrive at this stage of the FA Cup, his current side saw off Championship clubs Reading, Wigan and Blackburn, with a solitary goal against. The Blues took on League One Peterborough, and the second tier sides Brentford and Wolves, likewise conceding only once."

"In form Pedro's goal in each round to date (four in total) means he can still emulate English 'Peter' – the peerless Osgood – who hit the net in every round of the 1969/70 competition, including the replayed final."

"Pedro's superb finish at Molineux last month was unsurprisingly the 5ft 6in Spaniard's first header in the competition, whereas five of the eight scored by 6ft 1in Ossie 47 years ago were nodded in."

"Monday's cup opponents are enjoying a long unbeaten run in the league stretching back to October. **It has lifted them all the way from sixth to sixth.** That last defeat was, of course, the one they endured at the Bridge. Pedro's 29.6 seconds opener in that 4-0 triumph remains the fastest goal in the league this season."

© Chelsea FC.

FRIDAY, 10 MARCH 2017

Conte refused to even consider toning down his touchline celebrations. Jose Mourinho had been upset by Conte's euphoric reaction to the fourth goal when his team were thrashed in the league.

Mourinho claimed it was an attempt at "humiliating" his team. They had not spoken since but Conte said: "It's not important. We have nothing to clarify with him. I've shown at Chelsea and with every team I've managed that I live the game with great passion. Sometimes I want to share my enthusiasm with my players, my staff and also the fans. It is normal."

United had lost only twice in 31 games in all competitions since; two inconsequential defeats which did not halt their progress in the Europa League and the EFL Cup. Chelsea, meanwhile, were ten points clear at the top and targeting the Premier League and FA Cup Double they won back in 2010.

"For us, now, it is better." said Conte. "In October, we didn't know our future. In March we are top, we have a good identity and a good team. We are showing good football but it will be a really tough game against United. With Manchester City, they have the best squad in the league with a lot of great players, with great talent and great experience. We want to get into the next round. Until now, we didn't win anything."

Mourinho pointed out Chelsea's comfortable week of preparation in contrast to United, who did not return from a game against Rostov in Russia until 3.30am on Friday morning. "The most difficult thing to have is time to work, and they (Chelsea) have time to work." Mourinho said. "I know that he (Conte) said a couple of weeks ago that it's not his fault that they are not in the European competitions - it's my fault and the players' fault. But the reality is that he's got in his hands a situation where they have time to work, time to rest, time to relax, times to disconnect, time to travel, time to have holidays, time to go to America and enjoy America for a couple of days. They have time for all these things so they are in a position of privilege, the same privilege that Liverpool had a couple of years ago and they almost won the Premier League. But I don't want to say that they don't deserve credit for it."

"My players and I are focused on the game on the pitch." reported Conte. "The most important thing is to prepare the team in the right way, with good organisation; to think about my team, try through work to improve my players. These are the most important things for me and for every coach. The mind games, they're strange, no. The mind games don't bring you the win."

Jose was looking forward to returning to his former club but for different reasons than people expected. "Yeah (it's special) but probably in the opposite way to what people think. I'm not looking for revenge or anything wrong or bad. If you say something special, maybe one thing is to have Gary Staker (Chelsea's player liaison officer) in the tunnel before and after the match - a close friend. Another thing is going to Spurs and I don't know the man in the tunnel. If it's different, it's different in a positive way, not a negative way."

Mourinho said this culture of success - as well as his own achievements at previous clubs - created high expectations that his current side cannot currently match. "The hard part is the expectation." he told the BBC. "The club is guilty of it because of the history. I'm also a bit guilty of it because I'm used to winning trophies in every club and the relationship between our true potential and the expectations we create, there is a gap and that's the most difficult thing."

"It looks like, this season, that to be phenomenal defensively and good in counter-attack is art." the Manchester United boss added, without directly referencing Chelsea. "They choose a certain style of play that I think is very adapted to the qualities of these players. They defend a lot and well, and they counter-attack and kill opponents similar to my Chelsea. But the difference is they play with five at the back and I played four at the back, but the same criteria - a very strong team to defend and a team that kills on the counter-attack. They are doing very, very well and that is why they are going to be champions easily."

Conte responded to Jose's suggestion that Chelsea will go on to win the Premier League by playing defensive football insisting he has never prepared for counter-attacking football. "I have to tell you one thing. Not only here (at Chelsea) but I never, ever train for the counter-attack. Never prepare for the counter-attack. I think the counter-attack is an option, above all, if you have this type of player, players who are very, very fast. Also Costa is a counter-attacking man, and Willian and Pedro. It's normal to have this situation with space, so they know what they can do. It's important to train the other aspects - when we have the ball, when we stay almost always in our opponents' half, to prepare when we are attacking. It's very difficult to train counter-attacking but it's not my priority."

SATURDAY, 11 MARCH 2017

As a player Conte was occasionally told to stop running so much in training and even sent to the changing room to rest by Juventus manager Giovanni Trapattoni; a source of irritation for the then-midfielder. Now, more than two decades on, Conte claims that N'Golo Kante is a better version of himself from his playing career. Whilst he never stopped running for Juve, neither does Chelsea's contender for PFA Player of the Year. Not even at their Cobham training ground. "I don't want to stop him." Conte said. "In my career, I remember Trapattoni tried to stop me from running during training, telling me to go into the changing room because I had to run during the game. I wasn't happy about this. I wanted to stay with my teammates. N'Golo is a great player and he always puts 100 per cent in the game, but also in training."

Has he tried to send Kante inside at Cobham? "No, never." Conte continued. "I never tried to do this. I like this type of player a lot. I was this type of player. And I always appreciated this type of player, with great generosity, great ability to work for the team."

Chelsea's killer on the pitch, or "assassino" to his Italian coach, was aiming to win a second successive title after Leicester City's famous 5,000-1 triumph. Kante is one of Chelsea's quieter players at Cobham, though he is constantly wearing a grin. So can he be called their smiling assassin? "Ah, assassino." Conte said. "No, no. It's a good smile. Not an assassin's smile. It's the smile of a good guy, and he is a really good guy. You try to talk with him and he's always smiling. During training sessions he works a lot, but always with a smile. To see this, it's great for the other players, the staff, for me, the people who work at Chelsea."

So, Kante meets Paul Pogba in midfield at Stamford Bridge. Conte knows Pogba very well, having coached him at Juventus where they won two Serie A titles together. Chelsea's manager is mindful of the £89m footballer. "We are talking about a top, top player." Conte confirmed. "A top player in all situations. We are studying Manchester United to try to find the right solution. Paul is a really good player and we must pay great attention to him, above all when he arrives in the box. We must think about the whole Manchester United team. They're very strong."

Having coached them both, it was only natural that Conte was asked for a comparison and, naturally, a tactful reply was given. "It's very difficult to try to compare Paul with N'Golo. Two players with different characteristics. Two great players, but different."

Kante can still improve. "He played very well in the past, last season, with Leicester. He's playing very well also this season with us. We are working on some aspects to try to improve him, to make him a more complete player."

If Conte and Kante are so similar, were we watching Conte version 2.0? Conte: "No. He is stronger than me. There is no contest."

Eden Hazard offered an insight as to how Conte works. "Even if English is not his first language, he talks a lot, to give confidence to the players. If you do something different from what he wants, and you do something bad, he will tell you off… (so) if you do something different, do it well!"

Former Chelsea manager Glenn Hoddle hoped Conte will stay longer than others. "The people at the top have to leave him alone. It's no good if he loses a couple of games and he's put under pressure or there is interference." says Hoddle. "If they allow him to run the team and strengthen at the right times, as Sir Alex Ferguson did at United, they will have him for five very successful years. I saw Chelsea lose 3-0 at Arsenal in September and they were all over the place. Late on, he changed to three at the back and they looked like a team. They're living proof that managers and systems do make a difference."

SUNDAY, 12 MARCH 2017

Conte wants to match Mourinho's trophy haul at Stamford Bridge as he hoped to knock the former Blues' manager out at the quarter-final stage of the world famous cup competition and win the Double.

However, he had some way to go to match Mourinho's seven major trophies during his two spells as Chelsea manager. But Conte was hopeful of emulating his achievements. "His history with Chelsea was great." he said ahead of the game. "I know very well he's in the heart of Chelsea's fans. It's great this because he deserves it. For sure, I hope in the future to emulate his wins here. Jose Mourinho wrote a good part of the history of Chelsea. He won a lot with the players. He did a great job here in Chelsea. It's important, always, not to forget this. I have great respect for him because he's a winner. I like his mentality. He has a winning mentality. For sure, he's one of the best in the world and, here, he did a great job. I think every single fan must respect him."

Eden Hazard picked up the February award for Premier League Goal of the Month after his brilliant run and finish put Arsenal to the sword in the 3-1 win at Stamford Bridge. It was a popular selection chosen from the combined votes of a panel of experts and the public, seeing off competition from Leicester City's Danny Drinkwater and Burnley new boy Robbie Brady to scoop his second prize of the year (following the October 2016 Premier League Player of the Month award). "It is one of the best Premier League goals I have scored for sure." Hazard confirmed. "I was not thinking about scoring but step by step I came close to the goal and in the last ten metres I was alone. When the ball went in I felt that I created something special so I was happy."

With three young sons - the eldest is six - Hazard is fiercely protective of family life. "Football is good but family, close friends, my brothers, I have family everywhere, is the most important thing." he says. "If you told me to choose between family and football then it is no choice. I take family, of course, like everyone. But I prefer to keep it private and that's it. I just focus on the football. When the game is finished, it's completely finished. I'm with my kids. Sometimes people say to me 'Oh, did you see the game?' and I say 'No, I didn't see the game'. I watch if my friends are playing or my brothers. But not always. No, my kids now, the big one is six, another one four, they start to play so I am with them and they want to play if I start to watch TV. They tell me: 'Come on, play in the garden.' They watch more football than me. And they play everywhere, even inside the house, like I did as a kid."

Hazard and Kante, key players for Chelsea, both targeted a league and cup double. Kante told Chelsea TV: "We're going to try to win everything. It's not going to be easy, but we're going to train and work hard to win these two things."

Hazard added: "We are at a club where every year you have to win something. We can win both the cup and the league. We will give everything. We have eleven games to play in the league. We hope we can win as soon as possible the league. And the cup is a bonus, but it's a good bonus."

Hazard believed his form was nearing the standards of two seasons ago when, under Mourinho, Chelsea won the League Cup and Premier League title. Hazard, who struggled last season with a niggling hip injury and poor form, added: "When you see last season it's completely different. I reach almost the same level as two years ago. Two years ago we won the League Cup, the championship. I want the same. I want to win trophies. I give everything to win trophies. This is the target for Chelsea."

Hazard and Kante - with his first Chelsea goal — were both on target in Chelsea's 4-0 Premier League win over Manchester United last October. Hazard said: "It's my job. Doesn't matter the team we play against - Man United, Arsenal, Burnley - I try to score every game. If I want to be considered a big player, you need to score in big games."

After the win at West Ham Hazard had joked that it felt at times like there were two Kantes on the pitch and that the France midfielder had a twin. Kante said: "Thank you for the compliment. I'm single, but we work together for a win. Me and all the team, we have to defend together. I give my best for the team."

Hazard added: "We have to work, even if he's one of the best players in his position. We have to defend, because the manager wants that. (But) it's true sometimes we say 'I don't defend now, because N'Golo is there'. If we have to do a marathon - he will win for sure. He can run ten hours. I can run ten metres, then I'm tired."

Chelsea were determined to win the Double to get over the trauma of the last campaign. "We are

Chelsea." Hazard explained in an in-depth Daily Telegraph interview. "We have to be at the top... talk on the pitch, walk on the pitch. And win games." He was cited more than most as the reason for the instant decline and Mourinho's dismissal. "We all have something to prove."

Hazard recalls Leicester City in December 2015. He walked off the pitch, to Mourinho's disgust, and was unable to carry on. His hip was causing him too much discomfort. "I started last season with pain. I remember the game at Leicester. It was so painful." He was accused of not trying. "When you play a bad game, we lost the game and the manager (Mourinho) was sacked, so everyone was talking in a bad way. But you have to deal with it. I deal with it this season, so I am happy."

He was eventually allowed to recover, had a good Euros and then returned free of discomfort. "We started the season well and when the whole team is on fire they give a lot of confidence."

Chelsea had suffered two bad defeats this season, the second by Arsenal. "You start thinking, 'Oh no, I don't want to do the same as last season'." Hazard admits. "You know the manager, though, would not let that happen. No. Not like that. He wanted to change something; he changed something. We talked together, and yeah, we said: 'We don't want to do the same as last season'."

Conte changed the system and altered Hazard's role. "I am more central now. I like it when I am in the middle, I am closer to the ball. The manager wants me to pass, to make assists, create chances and I do more because I think the position is more central and I don't ask all the time for the ball at my feet. To come back after last season - this is completely different. We are back to fighting for the title with more motivation because you don't want to be the same as last season. You want to be better and you know you are a better player, so you know you have to do better. The whole team - it's not just about my situation - but everyone was in a bad moment. Yes, we all have something to prove."

Conte had made a difference. "Fantastic manager. He gives the spirit to the team. Of course, we have worked a lot and hard. But if that's the key to winning games, we will work hard. For me, it is a privilege to play with this manager, and I hope we can achieve something together. Sometimes in the dressing room he says some words just to you, personally, and then you think 'Yes, it's true'. So you have to do something in the game. Like, for example, against West Ham I missed two (training) sessions during the week, and he told me: 'OK, this week you didn't run, but on the pitch, do something.' And I scored, so he was happy. Sometimes some words can make the difference."

As for Conte's touchline behaviour? "I saw a lot - but not in the moment of the game. It is incredible. Sometimes on the pitch you don't see the manager. You hear him - for sure! Of course. When my family came to one of the games, I think my dad looked at him more than on the pitch. Because it's funny. But his attitude is like this - he was a great player, now he is a manager, he has the same spirit. That's him, that's Antonio Conte."

Chelsea were ten points clear with eleven games to go. "But you saw what happened in the Camp Nou, Barcelona." Hazard reflected, recalling the amazing Champions League reversal when Paris Saint-Germain surrendered a four-goal lead. "I think if we don't win the title this season it's something like PSG; the same feeling. Because, you know, you win 4-0 at home and then you think that you can go through. If we don't win the title this season it will be something of the same feeling because we have the opportunity to win so we have to. But don't think too early about the title, think game after game."

The Double? "One month ago I told people that I thought United will be the best team in the second half of the season, because they started slow, and then they have great players, a great manager, and they know what to do. OK, sometimes at home, they have lost some games or drawn, but they are in a good form. They had a long trip (to Rostov in Russia in the Europa League). I expect a good game from them. They want revenge because we won at home 4-0 (in the league, in October)."

The FA Cup? "I never won it so I want to win it. It's the oldest cup so I know for the fans it's really important, for the players also because in the last ten years Chelsea have won it four times. So now it's in the minds of the fans that something can happen. So we have to win this cup."

In the wake of Claudio Ranieri's sacking Jose Mourinho rebuked Leicester's players for their drop off in performance compared with the previous season when they won the title. Mourinho's remarks appeared to double as a thinly-veiled dig at Chelsea's players, who had done something similar under his watch, but he insisted he did not want any credit for their achievements this term. "I am not asking for any credit." he said. "I know the work I did there, I know what I did but I am the kind of guy that moves (on) and have no regrets and I am not looking for bad feelings at all. Am I sadder to lose against Chelsea than another team? No. For me it's just a game that comes in the wrong moment for us because the Europa League is a competition that can give us a Champions League spot and the FA Cup, it doesn't, so the Europa League is more important than the FA Cup for us."

Mourinho, though, couldn't resist his latest dig at Conte. "I'm surprised with the way that they play, I'm surprised. I thought they were demanding a different kind of football, because I think Chelsea is phenomenal, but Chelsea is an amazing defensive team." he told BBC Football Focus.

Michael Carrick believed Chelsea deserve United's respect. He was full of praise for Conte's side but United were in a better place now than earlier in the season. "You can't say we have got a score to settle." he said. "There is plenty that has happened over the years so it is just a new game and a chance for us to go further in the competition and they will say the same. We have lost only one in 28 games now since that Chelsea defeat so we have had a good run of form. They have gone on a great run so you have got to respect what they have done. It is not easy in this league to go on such a run. We have gone on a good run ourselves but we have just had too many draws at home and that has killed us. We feel that we are getting closer but you have got to respect them, they are a good team, they are well drilled."

MONDAY, 13 MARCH 2017
Chelsea 1-0 Manchester United
FA Cup, Sixth Round

Chelsea were on course for the Double as N'Golo Kante's second-half winner settled it. Jose Mourinho was involved in touchline clashes with Conte and was verbally abused by Chelsea fans at the scene of many of his triumphs, including three titles.

This was a game-changer; the day the Chelsea fans fell out of love and expressed their unflinching affection for "Antonio".

Mourinho, though, insisted he was still the No.1 at the Bridge, if no longer 'The Special One' in the eyes of the fans who had a new darling and someone else's name to chant.

The home fans repeatedly chanting "Antonio, Antonio, Antonio" was chastening for Mourinho, and they also turned on their once 'Loved One'.

Mourinho responded to four-letter abuse from Chelsea fans behind his technical area by raising three fingers to signify the Premier League titles he won at Stamford Bridge. He was taunted with chants of "Judas" - even though he was sacked!

Mourinho retorted: "They can call me what they want. I am a professional. I defend my club. Until the moment they have a manager that wins four Premier Leagues for them, I'm the No.1. When they have somebody who wins four Premier Leagues for them, I'll be No.2. For this moment, Judas is No.1."

Cardiff City boss Neil Warnock later defended the 'Special One', claiming he was the one who put the Blues on the map - and they must not forget it. "You get a few morons everywhere." Warnock told talkSPORT. "Some of them just come to do that, and I'm afraid there's not much you can do about them. The majority of their fans know what he has done. Where were they before he came? I can't remember Chelsea being anywhere. He put them on the map. It is disappointing."

Mourinho was furious when Ander Herrera was sent off ten minutes before half-time after a second yellow for an innocuous foul on Eden Hazard, and the managers were kept apart moments later after Alonso was brought down. It was United's third red card of the season, with two of those shown to Herrera.

Kante's low 51st-minute drive finally beat the defiant David de Gea, who had saved superbly from Hazard and Cahill before the break to keep Mourinho's side in contention before Chelsea made the breakthrough.

With Ibrahimovic suspended, Rooney and Martial injured, Marcus Rashford came off his sick bed to play and he created United's best chance for himself after an error from Luiz but Courtois saved with his feet.

Mourinho's first return to the Bridge since having been sacked as Chelsea manager had ended in the humiliating 4-0 defeat and this time he was pacing his technical area from the first whistle, applauding, imploring and cajoling his team, and clearly fired-up. It seemed evitable he would clash with his passionate and animated successor. The flashpoint came seconds after Herrera's sending-off. Mourinho, still simmering, felt Alonso had dived, exploding in fury. Moments later he confronted Conte head-to-head and ended with the pair being separated by fourth official Mike Jones.

It was always going to be a riveting encounter both on the pitch and by the touch line. Such was the anticipation, the match, shown live on BBC One and online, had a peak audience of 7.7m - the highest of the season in the FA Cup. A further 1.1m watched online.

With tensions still high, Conte reacted angrily in the second half when Mourinho kicked the ball along the touchline apparently too close to the Chelsea manager. The players, too, engaged in their own clashes, with Marcos Rojo booked for stamping on closely-marked man Hazard.

In the absence of Ibrahimovic, Mourinho needed £89m world-record buy Pogba to step it up, but he was overshadowed by Man of the Match Kante, who crowned a magnificent performance with the winning goal. All three of Kante's goals in English football had been scored at home, with two of them coming in the games against United this season.

Chelsea's fans revelled in Pogba's struggles as they chanted "what a waste of money". Kante looked a £30m bargain, by comparison, as Chelsea were now unbeaten in 12 games against United in all competitions (W7, D5) since a 3-2 home defeat back in October 2012. Only twice in their history have United had a longer winless run against one opponent (13 vs Liverpool in 1927 and 13 against Leeds in 1972). United had just 28% possession in the match, their lowest figure in a match this season.

A happy Conte commented: "It was a good performance against a strong team with good players. United has the best squad in the league. We must be pleased to go into the next round." But he accused United of targeting Hazard. "In 20, 25 minutes for Hazard, it was impossible for him to play football. I see only that he got a lot of kicks. I don't think that I'm crazy and I see only him in this situation. He started receiving kicks and finished receiving kicks. No one person can say this did not happen."

Conte had not seen the incident in which Rojo appeared to tread on a falling Hazard late in the game but he added "This tactic, to play by going to kick the opponent, does not exist. It's not football for me. I don't think this can be a tactic. I think sometimes when you play against players with great talent you try and intimidate these players. I think the referee must protect this type of player."

Conte said Hazard had shown "great character" in a "very difficult and dangerous" situation. He added: "We go to play football and my players want to play football."

Mourinho avoided confrontation later by saying: "I don't speak (about the red card). I just want to say that I'm really proud of my players and Manchester United fans. Everybody can analyse from different perspectives but we all watch the match until the red card and after the red card. So we can compare the decisions of the two yellow cards, in this case with others which were not given. I don't want to go in that direction. Michael Oliver is a referee with fantastic potential but in four matches he has given three penalties and a red card. I cannot change that. I shook his hand and said many congratulations."

But the lingering anger and frustration at his second sacking finally surfaced with another rant about how much rest and preparation time Chelsea have had without European commitments. "We spoke about the fact we are playing in Europe and our opponents aren't. You know, our opponents could (have been playing in Europe). I left the club last season in the Champions League, winning the Champions League group, in the knockout phase playing the second leg at home. If they won the Champions League last year, they'd be playing in Europe this season. It's not my fault. It's the ones that stayed here and didn't win the Champions League. What I share with them is that we didn't have a good Premier League, and I share responsibility with that."

N'Golo Kante had become the defining signing to change the old Mourinho team into the new Conte 'Special One's' version. Kante is the "best central midfielder in the world" was the view of Frank Lampard soon afterwards.

Alan Shearer, reporting from Stamford Bridge for BBC Sport, said: "I think you are looking at the Football Writers' Player of the Year and the players' Player of the Year" after previously suggesting that he "could" win the accolades.

Lampard described Kante as a "driving force". Former Red Devils defender Phil Neville, who was working alongside Shearer and Lampard, described him as the "most effective midfielder in Europe at the moment". He added: "I don't see anyone with the influence he has on a team. He's a number six, an eight and a ten. He breaks up play and then sometimes he finishes it off too."

On naming Kante as his Man of the Match, BBC summariser and former Arsenal defender Martin Keown said: "Man of the match? It's men of the match. He was everywhere."

"Kante was perpetual motion, starting attacks, breaking up moves and crowning another magnificent performance with the winning goal, emphatically drilled past De Gea. Pogba simply could not get into the game." Phil McNulty, BBC Sport's chief football writer, said in his match report. "Chelsea's fans revelled in Pogba's struggles as they chanted 'what a waste of money' - no such charges will be levelled at Kante, who looks a £30m bargain."

Kante had 91 touches, only bettered by Azpilicueta and Hazard, and made more tackles and clearances (four of each) than any other Chelsea player. He won more 50-50 duels with an opponent (78.6%) than any other outfield player.

Captain Cahill commented: "N'Golo has been fantastic. His performance level is right up there. You saw what he did last season but he has kicked on again this season. He is a humble guy off the pitch and works hard. He is so important, especially to us at the back. He's been a tremendous addition to the squad."

Praise for Kante was all over social media:

Gary Lineker: "Bloody hell, if @nglkante starts scoring goals as well he'll become the best midfield player ever."

Alan Shearer: "The energy he has is staggering. He has stood above everybody else this season."

Marcel Desailly: "71% of the earth is covered by water. The remaining 29% is covered by N'Golo Kante @ChelseaFC Hahahahahahha"

There were now three London teams in the FA Cup semi-finals for the first time since 2002 (Arsenal, Chelsea and Fulham). Chelsea had reached their 22nd FA Cup semi-final, the fifth highest in the competition's history beind Arsenal 29, Man Utd 28, Everton 26 and Liverpool 24, and waited for the draw...

Chelsea and Tottenham Hotspur were drawn against each other, leaving Arsenal to face Manchester City.

"Tottenham have given Chelsea problems this season and it is a London derby too so gives it an edge." noted Frank Lampard, speaking as a BBC Match of the Day pundit after the Blues' quarter-final win. "They are two very form teams but I think Chelsea are slight favourites as it stands."

Former England striker Alan Shearer added: "When the big boys joined in the FA Cup it got off to a slow start with teams resting players. But now there are four big hitters left and they are two semi-finals to look forward to."

TUESDAY, 14 MARCH 2017

Diego Costa was feeling as good now as he had during his time at Atletico Madrid. Speaking to Spanish radio station Cope, the 28-year-old said: "At Atleti I lived a great moment, and this year I'm feeling very good. There was a lot of talk about going to China, but you see, here I am."

Costa, however, threw a certain amount of doubt over Courtois and Hazard, with big-money moves to Real Madrid. He said: "We know Courtois loves Spain, his family lives there, he's a great goalkeeper and (Real) Madrid needs people like that." Barcelona as well as Real wanted Hazard; eleven goals in 30 appearances this season. He added: "It will be bad news for Chelsea if Real Madrid sign Hazard and Courtois. Eden is the best, he's top. Barcelona and Real Madrid will have their eye (on him) and if a team like these knock on the door you have to think about it. It is normal that they love him but hopefully he will not leave."

Pedro had scored seven and created seven but despite his current form it's almost forgotten that he had endured a rocky start to life in England after arriving from Barcelona in the summer of 2015. At the time the Blues were struggling under Mourinho but with Conte he could see Chelsea flourishing. "The last year was very difficult for us and the team." Pedro told BBC Sport. "It was a difficult situation for the team, the players and the club. With Antonio it's difficult because it's a big challenge for him to come here and prepare the team, make us strong and compact and go game-by-game. Now it's a very good moment for the team."

Asked whether he believed Chelsea would win the Double, Pedro replied: "Yeah, it's a dream for me. It's very difficult to win this title. The Premier League, for me, is the best league in the world. It has the best competitiveness. It's a dream for my career (to win the title)."

Meanwhile, N'Golo Kante couldn't resist a return to his former side, Leicester City, to witness his old teammates record another stunning chapter in the club's history, beating Seville to qualify for the Champions League quarter-finals.

WEDNESDAY, 15 MARCH 2017

Conte defended Mourinho's decision to sell Romelu Lukaku and Kevin De Bruyne. The Belgian duo had both left Stamford Bridge in 2014 on permanent deals and had gone on to forge successful careers.

De Bruyne starred for Wolfsburg in his only full season at the Bundesliga club before joining Manchester City in August 2015. Lukaku joined Everton and has become the Toffees' leading goalscorer in Premier League history in recent weeks.

Asked whether Mourinho made the wrong decisions, Conte refused to criticise. "It's very difficult to take always the best decision and sometimes you think one thing and in the future it happens differently. Football is not simple to give always a correct evaluation for all players. Sometimes it happens that one player didn't play well one or two seasons ago, but then had a fantastic season."

Lukaku was linked with a return to Stamford Bridge after telling Everton he wouldn't be signing the new £130,000-a-week contract on offer.

THURSDAY, 16 MARCH 2017

Conte hailed the "fantasy" that Cesc Fabregas has brought to his team in pursuit of the title.

After, perhaps surprisingly, been used as a substitute on many occasions, he has frequently appeared off the bench to change some of Chelsea's more difficult games following his manager's preference for the physicality of Kante and Matic. He started the last two league fixtures but even with Hazard, Kante and Costa playing so well, Conte was adamant it was Fabregas who should not be overlooked. Hazard's creativity and Pedro's movement forged an impressive attack, but Fabregas has become an impact substitute, somewhat similar to how Ole Gunnar Solskjaer was used by Sir Alex Ferguson's dominant Manchester United, as Conte said: "Cesc gives you great quality, great fantasy and assists. It's important to manage the situation and understand when it's right, for example, to play with Cesc or with Matic. We are talking about two great players, with different characteristics. Nema (Matic) is more physical, more technical, less fantasy than Cesc; Cesc has more fantasy but is less physical than Nema. He has always had a great impact, whether he starts a game or comes on. He always has a great impact. He's technically very good, and can put the ball where he wants. He's a great player. Often he's decisive with the pass, with the assist, and also to score a goal. This season, he has improved a lot in all aspects and, for me, he is a really, really important player."

Last season was Fabregas's worst in English football, when Chelsea surrendered the title and Mourinho was sacked, but Conte's team were closing in on a return to the Champions League, which would likely lead to him playing more. "Cesc, this season, is showing to be a great professional but, above all, a great player. I'm very pleased to see that in him; his commitment and work-rate. This season he has faced a new situation. Cesc, in the past, has always played every single game. It's not easy to change. But, for sure, Cesc showed me that he is not only a great player but a great person."

David Luiz opened up on his transfer, knowing he had made the right decision. "I enjoy it a lot, I feel at home here. I was missing it a lot." He confirmed. "Sometimes you cannot choose everything, sometimes cycles end, sometimes they start again. I am happy to be here. I am working hard, because I have some business to finish. I hope so (to win the league), we need to work hard. I want to have this feeling."

FRIDAY, 17 MARCH 2017

Jamie Carragher in his Daily Mail column argued: "We were obsessed last summer. Before the season began we couldn't stop talking about Pep Guardiola's arrival, the return of Jose Mourinho and the charismatic Jurgen Klopp. The Premier League had become the centre of the world in terms of football managers and those three figures dominated nearly every conversation, even though another new face was joining the argument. We allowed Antonio Conte to slip under the radar."

"Conte had an outstanding record in Italy with Juventus, taking them from seventh place in the table to winning Serie A three years in row. He went on to lead Italy at Euro 2016, where his standout results came against Belgium and Spain as they reached the quarter-finals. But he had no special pedigree in the Champions League, the competition we fixate on in England. So without that on his CV we allowed him to come into our game unheralded. It was our mistake."

"Back in August, in just my third column of the season, I argued that it would be foolish to write off Chelsea completely, despite their dreadful defence of the title in 2015/16. But did I expect them to be running away with the title in mid-March? No. This was supposed to be a shootout between Guardiola and Mourinho. Both men had more time to prepare their teams and both spent more than £100m to try to keep their rivals in the shadows. Chelsea shelled out money too, on N'Golo Kante, Marcos Alonso, David Luiz and Michy Batshuayi, but I don't think Conte secured all the players he wanted. Luiz was the prime example, given Chelsea failed with bids for Leonardo Bonucci and Kalidou Koulibaly, two defenders Conte knew well from Serie A."

"If I was a Chelsea supporter, I'd have been worried in the opening weeks of his reign, particularly after those back-to-back defeats by Liverpool and Arsenal in September. The team were not functioning, Conte was dour in interviews and he looked permanently downcast. Would there have been a point in those early months when a section of the Chelsea support hankered for Mourinho still being their manager? You always felt after Mourinho left the first time, in September 2007, that Stamford Bridge yearned for him to come back. When he returned with Inter Milan in March 2010 and knocked Carlo Ancelotti's Chelsea out of the Champions League, they pined for him even more. The hankering continued last season even after Mourinho was sacked, as the crowd turned on Chelsea's players."

"Now the yearning is over. Monday night was the line in the sand. Mourinho had tested Conte before, goading him and sniping at him. It all started on the afternoon Chelsea dismantled Manchester United 4-0 in October, when Mourinho shouted down the Italian's ear at the end of the game and accused him of lacking respect. There were other issues, not least on February 11 when Mourinho said: 'Chelsea are a very good defensive team and defended well with lots of players.' There was another dig last week, when Mourinho said he was 'surprised by the way Chelsea play'. It is nonsense to say Chelsea are defensive. Only Liverpool have scored more goals so far in the Premier League, but they have played an extra game. There is a huge difference between being a defensive team and being very good defensively. Conte's Chelsea are the latter. Mourinho should know that better than anyone. He had to contend with the same arguments when he arrived at Chelsea in 2004/05, and they won eleven of their 38 games 1-0, conceding just 15 goals en route to the title."

"Conte has not allowed himself to be bullied and it felt like a huge moment on Monday when he stood up to Mourinho on the touchline as Chelsea knocked United out of the FA Cup. In many ways, it could be the moment Conte cemented his place in the affections of Chelsea's fans. What Conte has proved in the last six months is that it was naive to think he would play second fiddle to the battle for supremacy between Guardiola and Mourinho. This, make no mistake, is one of the finest managers in the business. Every question that has been asked of him, Conte has responded positively."

"His three big signings have all become mainstays in the team: Kante has been remarkable and should win the PFA Player of the Year, Alonso is vital to making the 3-4-3 formation work - that system shows Conte's tactical acumen - and Luiz has been outstanding. Another thing you want a manager to do is improve players - and look at Victor Moses. I never expected him to have a future at Chelsea, given he had been out on loan so much, and the levels he has shown have taken me by complete surprise. He has been excellent in his new role of right wing back. Then there is the way Conte has rejuvenated men such as Eden Hazard, Thibaut Courtois, Nemanja Matic and Pedro, all of whom looked to be drifting 12 months ago. His tough stance with Diego Costa, when a bid from China arrived in February, was also impressive."

"Being absent from Europe and getting knocked out of the EFL Cup in the third round have clearly benefited Conte. He has used the free time to improve Chelsea's fitness - they do two intense sessions of running each week - and help them understand his methods. The extra down time has also enabled him to pick a settled team. It will be fascinating to see how they cope with Europe next season and the demands of squad rotation. To highlight how settled Chelsea have been, Conte has made just 24 changes to his starting line-up so far. Mourinho made 78 changes in his first year, Ancelotti 107."

"Chelsea's last Italian manager won the Double in his first year, but that success - along with all the rest between Mourinho's first spell ending and his second starting - felt like it had something to do with the Portuguese. The spine of that team was his team. Now, though, Chelsea are moving into a different era and never did change feel more in the air than when the Stamford Bridge fans had a go at Mourinho during the FA Cup quarter-final. This feels like Conte's Chelsea now. Not only has he shown himself to be a special manager but he has banished the ghost of Mourinho."

Looking ahead in the league, Michael Owen thought victory for Chelsea will all but seal the title. But Stoke had not lost at home in eight league games, a run stretching back to November. "If Chelsea win at Stoke I think they will have at least one hand on the PL title." Owen wrote on BetVictor.com "But the Blues have only won two of their last seven in the Potteries and I expect to see a tight, close encounter with little goalmouth action." Owen recommended punters bet on there being under 2.5 goals in the game.

Stoke manager Mark Hughes had held talks with out-of-favour Chelsea captain John Terry about the possibility of giving him regular football. The 36-year-old was in his final season at Chelsea but had struggled for game time under Conte, with his last Premier League appearance coming back in November. Terry had been limited to only ten outings in all competitions this season, with a back three of Azpilicueta, Luiz and Cahill. "I played with John when he was just starting off and it was a conversation after the Chelsea game (late December) in terms of what he's going to do." Hughes told the Mirror. "You'd imagine he's looking to have one or two seasons where he's playing regularly. So you look for opportunities that will give him that." Hughes implied Stoke would not renew their interest in the summer.

Conte had two injury doubts but would not reveal his two concerns. "Victor Moses trained well (on Friday)." he said. "I think he's available but it's important to check a couple of situations and then make the best decisions (for selection on Saturday). I'd prefer to keep those to me."

SATURDAY, 18 MARCH 2017
Stoke City 1-2 Chelsea
Premier League

Gary Cahill made up for conceding a penalty by scoring a late winner and at the final whistle Conte was the chief cheerleader swinging his arms round and round in front of the travelling fans, leaping onto the top of the dugout.

"We're gonna win the league, we're gonna win the league and now you're gonna believe us..." they sang.

Even the absence of Eden Hazard, with a muscle problem, did not thwart Chelsea, whose relentless consistency has been extraordinary. Hazard's absence, only confirmed an hour before kick-off, was the major surprise as Conte's side sought a fifth successive win. Pedro proved a willing deputy, but it was two players who scored against Stoke in the reverse fixture at Stamford Bridge who provided the goals. Willian, who struck twice in a 4-2 win over Hughes' side on New Year's Eve, caught out Lee Grant with a marvellous piece of quick thinking to whip his first-half free-kick inside the near post. Cahill's winner, only three minutes from time, came after a decent five-minute spell of Stoke pressure as the game opened up in the closing stages. The decisive goal was a tribute to the work ethic Conte instilled in his players - coming from a corner won after substitute Loftus-Cheek harassed Erik Pieters into over-hitting a back pass.

Chelsea had now won 20 of their past 23 matches in all competitions, and looked unstoppable as they moved thirteen points clear of Tottenham, although Spurs had a game in hand.

Diego Costa was involved in a running battle with Stoke's defenders, booked and involved in incidents that saw Bruno Martins Indi and Phil Bardsley cautioned. And, the home side were reduced to ten men in added time when Bardsley was sent off for a second bookable offence.

Willian gave Chelsea a first-half lead with an inswinging free-kick from the left that caught out keeper Lee Grant at his near post. Eight of Willian's past 19 goals for Chelsea have been from direct free-kicks. His sixth in the Premier League was his best tally in a single campaign in the competition. Martins Indi then had a goal ruled out for a push by Saido Berahino on Azpilicueta. But the home side drew level when Cahill pushed Jonathan Walters, who blasted in the resulting penalty.

The visitors had nearly all the chances, with Alonso firing a free-kick against the bar and Pedro denied by a fine save from Grant.

Mark Hughes had spoken in the past of his admiration for Costa - a striker of undoubted talent who plays on the edge. Hughes, a fearsome centre-forward in his own playing days, suggested he saw a bit of his own playing style in Costa's game. Costa roughed up Stoke's defenders, and seemed in danger of getting sent off himself after he was booked with only a quarter-of-an-hour gone. His tussles with Martins Indi, in particular, were a feature of the game, and referee Anthony Taylor had to speak to both players following an early off-the-ball tangle.

Costa, though, drew the Stoke defenders into the battle and then concentrated more on his football after half-time to keep himself out of trouble. He made sure not to retaliate when Bardsley clattered him shortly before the break, and then forced Martins Indi into a challenge for which he was booked. No goal for Costa - chasing his 50th in the Premier League - but Stoke lost their discipline.

Conte rolled the dice with a formation tweak demonstarting he was not content to leave the bet365 Stadium with just a draw. Starting the weekend with a 10-point lead, he was on course for a point but unwilling to settle for such an outcome, even with their huge advantage at the top, he brought on Fabregas with 20 minutes to go - replacing Moses and altering his 3-4-3 system to a back four so he could accommodate his substitute in a central role. "During the game, when you want to take more risks, when you want to try and take three points and not only one, you try to change. But, when you change, for sure there is a greater possibility to score the goal but also to concede a goal. You must know this and then sometimes I prefer to decide to risk it to try to take three points. In other situations I prefer to keep the result."

"This win is important, honestly. We played two games away, West Ham and Stoke, and to win both games is very important in this part of the season. There are ten games to go. I like to think that now we need to take 21 points to be sure to win the league. But today it is important against a strong team and in a stadium with a great atmosphere."

Conte confirmed Hazard was left out of the matchday 18 after sustaining a calf injury during a training session. "In the last training he felt a bit of a problem in his calf, for this reason I decided not to risk him. That is why he didn't play."

Asked if it's Chelsea's title to lose, he added: "To have a ten points gap, 13 at the moment, but I like to think our opponents will win tomorrow. We have to look at ourselves. We are happy. We must be ready to fight, today we were ready."

Hughes commented: "We are desperately disappointed we did not get anything out of the game. The ball dropped kindly for them and they got the winner. It was an evenly matched game and they had late opportunities when we went for a goal. It is Chelsea's title now and you could see from their celebrations we ran them close. We kept on going, kept on moving the ball but there was a suggestion for a red card for our penalty. It was a little bit feisty, we gave everything and I cannot criticise our players. We had a goal disallowed and the player made a meal of the slight push. He was not affecting Bruno Martins Indi getting to the ball. We have given a good account against the champions-elect. Diego Costa draws fouls and tries to make most of contact - when they are not fouls. He is adept at the dark arts and everyone in football recognises that. He has many elements and factors, you have to put up with them."

Referee Anthony Taylor's patience wore thin as early as the 16th minute when he cautioned Costa for dissent as the striker flew into a rage when not awarded a free-kick despite a blatant dive. Costa subsequently showed more restraint to avoid further punishment. He had almost as many bookings - ten - as goals - 16 - last term, but he has so far found the net on 18 occasions already, and Courtois commented: "They were very physical and it was hard to find our usual game. They tried to put our players out of the game by doing that. They know Diego doesn't like it and he maybe starts to fight with people. Maybe they do this to get him a red card or something. In some moments maybe Diego exaggerates a bit as well, but I think most of the time they were hitting him quite well. After four or five 50-50 moments where the referee can whistle or not whistle, he gets a bit angry and gets a yellow card. So it's important for him to stay calm and he's developed that a lot this season. When they kicked him, he remained calm and that's very good for us because in the worst case, he would have got a second yellow card and been out of the game. It's a good job he remained calm and dealt with what happened to him and moved on. Diego is the type of guy who has a lot of energy and goes for every ball and he gets kicked as well. People know how he is as well and a lot of Stoke players got a yellow card for fouls on him. He was always calm and he does well for us."

Azpilicueta made his 150th Premier League appearance for Chelsea, becoming the first Spaniard to reach the milestone for the Blues. Cahill was the first Chelsea player to score a goal and concede a penalty in the same Premier League game since Salomon Kalou did so against West Ham in April 2009.

Cahill remarked: "The manager told us to keep playing our football and wins are all that matter at this stage. We only had two Premier League games in this month. We managed to get the results and now we can sit back and watch tomorrow's games. There will be pressure. I have played in that situation where a team has won and you have to go out and get a result."

"How we got the win wasn't important, it was just getting that win." Cahill later confirmed with Chelsea TV. "It could be vital at the end of the season. The manager said at half-time it was important to not get brought into a scrap with them. We just had to keep patient and try to play our football, which is what we did. We got the break and we're just delighted to have got the win. At the end of the game, and even in the dressing room, everyone was absolutely buzzing because we know how important it was. Next month is a very important month for us so we needed to put ourselves in a healthy position. Now we need to keep doing what we've been doing and try to get the job done."

His goal was his fourth in the Premier League, sixth in all competitions.

"It just fell and it would have been harder to miss I think. My eyes lit up when I saw that chance and I was delighted to stick it away. I was disappointed in myself that I was involved in their goal, in terms of the penalty. I haven't seen it back, I thought it was soft at the time so when something like that goes against you, I was thinking there's only one way I can get myself out of this, and that was the way, so I was delighted."

"It is still a long way to win the title." David Luiz told the club's official website. "Nobody makes it easy. It is always difficult to play at Stoke. They are a strong and physical team. It was a typical Premier League game, we are happy with the victory. We played a good game, kept calm and had the opportunity to score the second goal. We had to believe."

Luiz was determined to keep improving. "I try to improve every day. This is my goal. Everybody can see my football, the team is doing very well. The results are coming. As a defender they do not talk about the good things you do, they talk about the mistakes, so I am trying to play the best football I can to help my team. Sometimes you have to give them more security, defend to get a positive result. It is important to understand my role in the team (but) it is not just me, it is Diego Costa, Eden Hazard, everybody. Everybody understands what they need to do."

It was the first time since August his team had needed to wait so long to clinch a win, when Costa scored in the final minutes against West Ham United and Watford. "This must be Chelsea's mentality." insisted Conte. "It is a great team and we must play always to win. In this game we showed from the start until the end the will to win the game, not to come here for only one point. I think when you want to win the league, it's important not to drop points when you play against teams that are medium or at the bottom. It's important to keep a continuity in the results. This is a winning mentality."

"This win is really important and I wanted to share my joy with my players and our fans after a very tough game. My players are understanding my idea of football and they are adapting to my system, my philosophy of football. For sure I think we are building something important. I have to thank all my players because they are working hard and they trust in our football, our idea. They are showing me in every game a great commitment, a great will to fight and to show we can win the league. But I think you can improve everything and for sure we must improve. We have to take 21 points to take the title, otherwise we risk to lose. We have to think positively and take it game by game."

"Now there is an international break and a bit of rest for some of the players, and then we come back to Cobham and it's important to be focused because we have two games at home against Crystal Palace and Manchester City."

Cahill had scored six. "Gary can play also as a centre-forward." joked the manager. "He has good quality, acrobatic qualities, and he's very good, very strong during the corners and set-pieces. I'm pleased for him because we conceded a penalty after the referee saw a little push by Gary and then he found the solution to score the second goal to win."

Dion Dublin, former Leicester City and Manchester United forward, on BBC Final Score remarked "The passion from Chelsea boss Antonio Conte is outstanding. It transmits down to the players. That's what makes you champions."

SUNDAY, 19 MARCH 2017

Jan Vertonghen believed Tottenham were missing the best player in the Premier League while Harry Kane was out injured. Kane was set to spend four to six weeks on the sidelines after damaging ligaments in his right ankle during last weekend's win over Millwall. Kane, though, had a chance of making the FA Cup semi-final against Chelsea in five weeks, as well as a north London derby against Arsenal eight days later.

With ten games left Spurs were the closest to runaway leaders Chelsea and in the process of completing their best ever Premier League season, after scrapping to a 2-1 home win over Southampton without Kane. Later in the day Manchester City dropped two points at home to Liverpool to severely damage any hope they might have had of catching the leaders. Vertonghen said: "Obviously Chelsea are the favourites at the moment for the title but we won't give up until they lift the trophy and I think we are doing well and we have to aim for the highest thing possible and at this moment we are in second place, but we will push for first."

MONDAY, 20 MARCH 2017

Belgium international manager Roberto Martinez expected a 10-15 day injury absence after Eden Hazard pulled out of his country's games against Greece and Russia. Hazard was due to captain Belgium in their World Cup qualifier against Greece. "Eden has suffered an injury before the match against Stoke, it does not look so serious." Martinez told his press conference. "But he will not play against Greece. We are going to follow the injury. It is a big disappointment for Eden that he cannot lead the team. If you want to be a good team, you have to absorb everything. This is a good test for us. I see enough players who can take over his role."

Martinez later announced that his absence could last even longer, putting a return in time for Chelsea's resumption of their title charge in doubt.

Hazard returned to London to be assessed further by the Blues' medical staff. Fortunately the injury was considered minor, and Conte hoped Hazard would be fit to face Crystal Palace at Stamford Bridge before Manchester City visited four days later.

However, Chelsea would take no risks with the final 10-game run-in in the Premier League and an FA Cup semi-final against Tottenham.

TUESDAY, 21 MARCH 2017

Conte was determined not to relax and urged his players to maintain their focus as they attempted to see out the season, and emphasised the need of a further 21 points.

Harry Redknapp claimed in a Daily Telegraph article that he, Glenn Hoddle and Stuart Pearce would have been a managerial dream team for England. Speaking in his capacity as a pundit for BT Sport, Redknapp said: "I love Glenn. Glenn's fantastic. If Glenn had kept the job when he had it at that time, I think we'd have gone on and done good things. Because he had a way of playing. You would've had a style."

England would have played three at the back. "I've played three at the back at West Ham when we finished fifth a long, long time ago. I went to Portsmouth and in my first year when we won the Championship, we played three at the back all season. I think it is a great way to play. Glenn would have played that way, I would play that way, I love the system. Now, every week, there are more teams playing three at the back. Go through the teams that have changed this year. But why does it take Conte to play three at the back for everybody to say, 'That's a good idea! We'll all follow'."

Redknapp suggested that his England team would feature Dele Alli and Ross Barkley and no holding midfielder. "Too often, we're too (wedded to the idea that) we've got to have a holding midfielder, we've got to have a defensive midfielder. Okay, I know Chelsea have got the boy who sits in. But why can't Barkley play? Barkley's six-foot tall, incredible build; Dele Alli's six foot, one inch, whatever. We're not talking about tiny little kids who can't defend or can't tackle or have no strength. They're good players. Play your good players. Find a way of playing them. Why can't they play together? The pair of them can run all day, can tackle, they head it; they've got everything."

WEDNESDAY, 22 MARCH 2017

During an international break, and with little domestic football to occupy thoughts and back pages, mischievous headlines can emerge, and this one was no exception:

Diego Costa: "Hice todo para volver al Atletico de Madrid" - which translates as "I did everything to return to Atletico Madrid"

Costa disclosed "he did everything" to return to former club Atletico Madrid but ended up staying at Stamford Bridge, with the striker insisting he is now not so keen to force a move back to the Spanish capital, having spoken to Conte to patch things up. "Atletico knows I have a special feeling for the team. I lived the best moment of my career there." he told Spanish radio station El Larguero. "El Cholo (Diego Simeone) knows it wasn't impossible for me to come back to Atletico. The relationship with Conte didn't start well because when he arrived I told him I wanted to go to Atletico. Chelsea's fans love me a lot, even more than in Atletico, imagine! I've done everything to come to Atletico but it did not happen. I've done everything to return to Atletico Madrid but I would not fight like that to return (in the future). When Atletico had to wait I did not wait." Costa was away with the Spanish squad, who faced a World Cup qualifier against Israel before a friendly in France.

Whilst appearing happy at Stamford Bridge, at least for now, Costa also stated "In life, everything can happen, I do not rule out anyone, China or Atletico? Atletico, imagine!" and despite having a "good relationship" with Sergio Ramos, at Real Madrid, he added "It is almost impossible that I go to Real Madrid, by the relation that I have with Atletico."

Real Madrid were, though, interested in signing Alonso, but the Blues are not willing to sell.

Thibaut Courtois then dismissed talk of a potential move to Real Madrid: "I don't see myself anywhere else. I won't be at Real Madrid next season. They're a club where the demand is very high, like at Chelsea, in Manchester or any big club in Europe. I'm very calm because since my first year (at Chelsea), I've heard things like that (interest from Real Madrid). Here at Chelsea, we're fighting for the League and the FA Cup and I'm happy."

"I have two more years of my contract left. In London, everything is going well for me and I'm happy. Would I like to be offered a renewal? Certainly! I'm very happy at Chelsea and if they want me to stay, great. We're working very well under Conte and there's a long-term project to win trophies on a European level. Until now, we haven't talked about my renewal. At the moment, we're focused on winning the league, although we're ten points clear. Both the club and the coach want peace of mind right now, so we're not thinking about renewals. We'll see if, when the season finishes, they offer me something, but at the moment there isn't one."

THURSDAY, 23 MARCH 2017

The rumour mill was in overdrive: Hazard and Courtois to Real Madrid. Hazard to be offered yet another new contract. Conte to have turned down the chance to sign Neymar, despite Roman Abramovich agreeing a world record fee with Barcelona.

Well, you takes your choice, but it was all pure speculation.

In particular, who in their right mind would reject the chance to coach Neymar? But, according to Turin-based newspaper Tuttosport, the Chelsea owner had reached a verbal agreement with the La Liga giants to sign the 25-year-old for an estimated £155.5m. But Conte would prefer to trim his squad down first before bringing in any new recruits, and doesn't believe Neymar would suit his style of play. It sounded like transparent propaganda as Inter were chasing Conte, and if Chelsea won't buy Neymar, then Inter will. Far-fetched indeed... probably.

FRIDAY, 24 MARCH 2017

Eden Hazard's representatives held "positive talks" about a potential switch to Real Madrid, according to reports in Spain.

Marca claimed he was lined up for a move to the Santiago Bernabeu, with Real president Florentino Perez already suggesting he is willing to splash out on at least one new 'Galactico' purchase for his club this summer - and Hazard appears to be top of the list.

In a presidential year at Real, and with the club having gone the best part of two years without making a headline signing, pursuing the Chelsea talisman would be a major statement in the transfer market.

Marca claim Hazard's current Blues' salary to be around £8million net per year, putting him on a level with Madrid's top earners, Cristiano Ronaldo and Gareth Bale. The Spanish paper say Real were interested in Hazard last summer but the player was not willing to contemplate a move. Conte's interest in Colombian forward James Rodriguez, currently on the books at the Bernabeu, could swing Madrid's move for Hazard in the La Liga club's favour.

SATURDAY, 25 MARCH 2017

Diego Costa invited more transfer speculation by complimenting Marseille and failing to rule out a move to France. In fact, Ligue 1 trio of Marseille, PSG and Monaco, are all showing an interest in Costa and the striker has now ensured that fans of all three clubs will be keeping an eye on him.

"It's true that Marseille has a great project and is growing up." Costa told French football programme, Telefoot. "I'm very happy with Chelsea, but in football everything can happen, and if we have to change, France is a place where I've never been to I never played, so why not."

When quizzed about PSG and Monaco, he said: "Everyone knows that (PSG) is a respected team in Europe. Monaco also has a great project and great players."

Would he be at the Bridge next season? "Anything can happen. Why not? You never know." he said recently after being asked about a move away. "Now I'm happy at Chelsea but if tomorrow the Chinese come and Chelsea tell me I have to go, I will no longer want to stay with them."

MONDAY, 27 MARCH 2017

Ruben Loftus-Cheek reflected with satisfaction after seizing a rare chance to shine by scoring twice in England Under-21s' 4-0 friendly victory in Denmark. The 21-year-old continued to struggle for game time at Chelsea and has made only four starts for Conte's side this season. However, he showed no signs of rustiness with two well-taken strikes which help England Under-21s win for the first time since Aidy Boothroyd was appointed full-time manager.

Loftus-Cheek told BT Sport: "I really enjoyed it. I haven't played much for my club so it is important for me to work hard and try to get my sharpness when I come away with England."

He opened the scoring with a cool finish after ten minutes and wrapped up victory with a powerful effort in the second half. Boothroyd said: "He was excellent, he was terrific, but the only reason he was terrific was because he had ten other players on the pitch that worked really hard for him and got him the ball. He made some really good decisions and overall I think it was a terrific performance. He has still got bits to do in certain aspects of his performance, but they all have. They are not end products yet."

TUESDAY, 28 MARCH 2017

Conte earmarked Alexis Sanchez as one of his summer transfer targets. Real's James Rodriguez and Everton's Romelu Lukaku were also among their targets, as is another Madrid man, Alvaro Morata.

A couple of days later in his media briefing ahead of the next game, when specifically asked about his interest in Sanchez, Conte said "I think it's very disrespectful of players from other teams (to talk about this), but for sure, he's a top player. I can say this. But I don't like to talk about players from other teams because it's disrespectful for the players of other teams, other clubs and my own players. For us the most important thing is for us to try and finish this league and try to win. Then, once this season is finished, with the club together we will talk about the right way to try and improve our team and our squad. That will be very important, but I don't see any problems about this. This club has great ambitions. It was so in the past, and it will be so in the future. I'm very happy to be coach of this club."

However, Conte had already discussed summer transfers with the Stamford Bridge hierarchy and the club, particularly director Marina Granovskaia and technical director Michael Emenalo, were well aware that Arsenal would be reluctant to sell to another Premier league club, let alone to a fierce rival.

Sanchez's agent, Fernando Felicevich, was fully aware of Chelsea's interest. The Chilean striker was demanding an increase in salary from his current £130,000-a-week to £250,000-a-week. Wenger stated that contract talks with Sanchez are on hold until the end of the season, with his future in north London largely dependent upon whether they qualify for the Champions League. In addition, Inter's new Chinese owners, Suning, were keen to make a statement in the transfer market in an effort to challenge Italian champions-elect Juventus and Sanchez would fit the bill. Conte clearly needed to make a statement of his own, especially if he lost Hazard to Real.

Chelsea would not be able to stop Hazard from joining Real, according to former club president Ramon Calderon, who signed Arjen Robben and Ruud van Nistelrooy during his time at the Bernabeu. "Chelsea aren't a selling club, so it wouldn't be easy, but as always it would depend on the wishes of the player." Calderon predicted to talkSPORT. "If he wants to leave, he will leave - that's always the point. Chelsea will ask for a lot of money, I think that's what the situation will be at the end of the season."

Chelsea obviously had no intention of selling at any price, but if a deal was to be agreed then it would surely be in excess of £100m, making Hazard the most expensive player in the world - and Calderon does not see money being an issue for Real as they look to sign another 'Galactico'.

"Chelsea knows quite well how much has been paid in the market over the last few years, with Ronaldo, Bale and Pogba - £100m is now the bar." he added. "That bar has been set by those transfers, so I think that's how much a club like Chelsea would be asking for and the economy at Real Madrid is healthy - I don't think that would be a problem for them. But it's all about the player. The player must say, 'I want to leave and go to Real Madrid', and that will be the moment they start negotiating."

Chelsea were ready to open talks over a new deal for Hazard, determined to keep him for Champions League football. Hazard's pay would head towards £300,000 per week with built-in bonuses. He was currently paid £200,000 after signing a five-and-a-half-year deal as recently as February 2015.

Hazard was currently happy in west London and not itching to leave. And, in response to a Q&A on the club's official website he hinted that he and his children would be perfectly happy to remain in London. Asked where he sees himself living when he retires, Hazard said: "Maybe I will live in Belgium, to be close to the family, or else I could go somewhere with nice weather. My kids are very settled in London so it could be here, that's a long way off yet so we will see."

Ray Wilkins believed his old club should do everything in their power to stop Hazard moving to Real Madrid and that he's not worth selling for any amount of money. The former Blues' assistant manager, who spent six years with the club as a player, is convinced the Belgian is "one of the five best players on the planet."

In fact, he would give up his season ticket if Abramovich sold Hazard. "It looks a very good front page, but that's about as far as it goes." he told Sky Sports. "For Chelsea to lose Hazard, who is one of the five best players on the planet, they would have to replace this guy and he is irreplaceable at this moment in time. He's a wonderfully gifted footballer and why would Chelsea want to give him up? I don't see there's any money out there… Roman Abramovich has an enormous amount of money himself. I couldn't give a monkey's what they offer. Chelsea wish to be the best club on the planet and they're heading in the right direction. What they've done over the past 10-12 years has been nothing short of phenomenal, so if you want to be the best why sell the best? They'll never get there if they sell Eden Hazard, who has been absolutely brilliant. I would imagine Mr. Abramovich would not even consider any offer that comes in. You cannot replace him. If they sell him I'll give up my season ticket. He's that important."

WEDNESDAY, 28 MARCH 2017

On opposing sides on Tuesday night but N'Golo Kante, Diego Costa, Pedro and Cesar Azpilicueta put international rivalries to one side as they travelled back to London together. Kante and Pedro were the only Blues players to get game-time at the Stade de France as Spain beat their hosts 2-0. Unused substitute Costa had played and scored in the win over Israel but Azpilicueta watched both games from the bench without making an appearance. Kante got through 180 minutes for France over the international break - beating Luxembourg before losing to the 2010 world champions.

Azpilicueta wasn't getting carried away by the praise coming his way and told French TV station, Canal+: "It's always nice to hear nice things about yourself, but you have to step back, there's still a lot of work. When I'm in France, I see the careers and the prize list of my teammates, I think that I have not done anything in football, and there is no reason to take it for someone else."

The Police decided to drop their investigation into the alleged homophobic chants made by Manchester United supporters during the club's 1-0 defeat by Chelsea in the FA Cup earlier in the month. A complaint was made the following day after supporters sang the alleged homophobic chant "Chelsea rent boys" when the two sides met on 13 March. Officers concluded that the matter did not meet the threshold for further investigation and legally the matter was closed. Inspector John Childs of Hammersmith and Fulham Police said: "The Met takes all allegations of homophobic chanting or behaviour very seriously and we investigate all matters brought to our attention. We routinely work very closely with football clubs, national football associations and partner agencies to monitor behaviour to ensure public confidence and safety."

The incident, however, remained under an FA investigation and Manchester United may yet face action. United pledged to use the club's Official Sanctions Policy to deal with the guilty parties. Under section two and clause (h) of the club's policy, "homophobic or discriminatory language" would trigger a punishment that could range from anywhere between "a 3-match ban" and an "indefinite ban". A United statement read: "The Club aims to work closely with Chelsea to identify anyone believed to have engaged in discriminatory behaviour at the game and will follow the terms of our Official Sanctions Policy if necessary. In addition, we will liaise with Chelsea to determine any activity to discourage such behaviour before the next fixture."

THURSDAY, 29 MARCH 2017

Hazard and Courtois both returned to training following injury. Conte threw himself into the session and was pictured closing down his own players as they attempted to make a pass. Chelsea entered this weekend's fixtures with a sizeable 10-point lead at the top.

Conte had made his side formidable with his 3-4-3 system. "He's widened the vocabulary of English football, tactically." former Arsenal defender Martin Keown told the Daily Mail. "Conte played three at the back in the summer with Italy but has managed to vary it up slightly at Chelsea and still managed to get the right balance between attack and defence. That has been key to them dominating the Premier League like they have."

BBC pundit Phil Neville believed N'Golo Kante "is the one who has knitted this Chelsea team together." as BBC Radio 5 produced a special programme. "I thought he was a number six like former Chelsea player Claude Makelele. But he plays absolutely everywhere, three different positions." he said. "I played with one of the greatest at Manchester United in Roy Keane. He got the ball off the back four, played passes, joined up with the frontman, and I think Kante is the most complete midfielder in the Premier League at the moment."

Joey Barton - who had a season on loan at Marseille when Kante was still at Boulogne – offered a word of caution, as he recently told French newspaper Le Journal du Dimanche: "At the moment, everyone swears by N'Golo Kante. It's fashionable. For pundits, he's the best midfielder in the world. That's not the case - he's very good, but I played against him three weeks ago. He's a phenomenal destroyer who played in a phenomenal team, but he's not a creator. And it's impossible to be so definitive with a player who has not played in the Champions League."

Neville agreed that the question about lack of Champions League experience was valid.

Conte knows Kante can be improved. "We are working on some aspects to try to improve him, to make him a more complete player. In the pass, yes. I think he has a lot of room to improve in the pass, and to look to make his first pass a forward pass. He can improve on these aspects, definitely."

'Dave' Azpilicueta concedes that having no European football has been an advantage but points to the early signing of Kante and the rapid adaptation of Conte, as just as important in the title charge. "Kante was a vital piece of the puzzle and the club did fantastic work in signing him. And, what is more, it was early too." he told the Daily Mail. "He had time to train with the team and adapt and that was very important. He started well and he has kept getting better. People forget this is only his second season in England. You have to admire what he achieved last season and what he is doing this season. His work-rate is incredible not just in games but in every single training session."

"It's not so easy." he says when asked why City and United's league campaigns had not lived up to expectations. "People think you can win the league before it's even begun. They are two great clubs with two great coaches and with big money invested on great squads. They are great rivals and I'm sure they will fight to the end but it's hard to win this league. Every season I've been here teams have got better, the type of players that have come in from abroad has taken the level up, and the English have improved hugely. You have to fight hard in every single game. Every point is hard to win."

The new manager could keep up with some of the players. "It's true that he still goes for a run every day." Azpilicueta says. "He still has that competitive streak from having been a player. He likes to keep himself very fit. At no time has he had any sort of demands; he has always helped the club. It's difficult to adapt as quickly as he has but he pushed himself from the beginning with speaking English, with getting to know all the players, with everything."

Asked if Conte, who is now Azpilicueta's fifth manager in as many years, tapped in to the Premier League know-how around him he said: "He is intelligent. As the manager he makes the decisions, but he likes to get other opinions."

Azpilicueta is somewhat of a mouthful. Fans call him Dave. "Some fans still call me Dave and the team bus driver is called Dave, so we're two Daves, but teammates call me Cesar now." The nickname comes from the BBC comedy Only Fools and Horses, the running joke of Trigger calling Rodney 'Dave'.

Conte made a season-defining decision when switching to 3-4-3. Azpilicueta was the square peg that found a round hole suited him. He commented in the Mail article: "At the start of the season things were a bit 50-50. We were winning but not convincing. I don't think he (Conte) was completely satisfied, the team didn't have the identity that he wanted, but since the change of system we've put a lot of work and got the results. The manager asked me about the possibility of me playing in a three. I had no worries about doing it because I knew that he would work with us on it, in training to the maximum. Antonio is a coach who is very keen on working on the tactical order in every session, with the emphasis always on being very together on the pitch. This change of system has helped get the best out of every individual."

Of the back-three with Gary Cahill and David Luiz he said: "We complement each other. One does one thing with greater ease than the other two and that gives us confidence as a unit."

Barcelona switched to a back three adding to speculation he might be one of their summer targets. "Right now I am only thinking about Chelsea and I feel loved here. Of course it's flattering because it means you are playing well, I was not hearing those stories last season. It comes from us being top but my objective here has always been to grow as a player and a person. I feel very well adapted to the city, to the country; I am comfortable with the language, my family is very happy here and my only objective is to continue with Chelsea. This is the first year since I signed for Marseille (in 2010) that I have not been in the Champions League and it's hard. A bad season last season has left us out of it and so there is nothing we can do but when I'm watching it at home, I want to be there and involved. Last season we found ourselves in a position that Chelsea should not be in. We knew we had to first of all come back in the Premier League. We are now in a good position although we know there are still ten games to go. Palace is the first and we know it is not over. We have this gap at the top because we deserve to have it, but we have to go on fighting to finish the job. From there the next step is to get back into European competition and do as well as possible but maintaining the same level in the Premier League."

FRIDAY, 30 MARCH 2017

Mauricio Pochettino was talking about Eric Dier's development at Spurs and his role in the team, including within a three-man defensive system which he had adopted before Conte. "We provided all the tools (for Dier) to be a Premier League player. My first game in charge against West Ham, he (Dier) started as a centre-back, next to Kaboul. Kyle Naughton got a red card, he moved to full-back and scored. That season, he played like a full-back, like a centre-back but never as a midfielder. Then in the summer we were looking for a midfielder and we had plenty of options (to buy one), but I decided to play Eric in midfield. I created a system that he felt comfortable in. He played like a midfielder without the ball, but with the ball he was a third centre-back. You can see in possession he dropped in between the centre-backs or between the full back and the centre-back, and always we play with three. People say now Chelsea changed the system, but no, we played always the three in possession. Out of possession, Eric moved in front and without the ball he tried to press and play like a midfielder. Then we signed Wanyama and played both, but we had some injuries like Toby and Jan, and Eric was the perfect player to play as a centre-back. That is a good thing for the player, the possibility to play in different positions and do well in every one."

Arsene Wenger wryly taunted Chelsea over their interest in Alexis Sanchez, saying: "There's only one team in London."

Sanchez had seemingly opened the door to a move across the capital during an interview in his homeland this week, saying: "I want to stay in a city but in a team that wins, that has a winning mentality." Wenger confessed: "It is true (we have sold players to rivals) when we were in positions where, financially, we had to sell our best players. That's not the case any more. Sanchez has one-and-a-half years left on his contract. I don't think it's an immediate concern to Arsenal Football Club."

On being asked how he had interpreted the Sanchez interview, Wenger, tongue-in-cheek, said: "In a very positive way. There is only one team in London, so he is happy!"

Conte refused to be drawn on Wenger's claim that "there's only one team in London" by insisting he has respect for all the clubs in the capital. Conte arguably took the moral high ground during his pre-match press conference. When asked if there is in fact just the one team in London, he said: "I didn't know this, but I think in London there are many teams. Tomorrow, for example, it's a derby against Crystal Palace. I like to listen to the other coaches but, for me, I prefer always to have great respect for all the players from all the clubs."

The visit of London club, Crystal Palace, meant the meeting of an old acquaintance in Sam Allardyce, who had welcomed Conte to West Ham's training ground during his spell in east London. "It's a pity Big Sam took charge of England for just one game." Conte said, but identified that the Eagles now had "a top coach". He added: "I knew him from my travels in England, and I stayed with him for two days at West Ham's training ground. I had the opportunity to speak with him and I think he's a top coach. It's a pity for him being sacked by the national team after only one game. I know the importance of being the coach of your country, for the national team. It's great. But it's a great pleasure tomorrow to see him and chat with him before the game, then after the game."

Pressed over the future of Eden Hazard, Conte was not outwardly concerned about an explosion of speculation and, in particular, the tried and tested unsettling tactics of Real, who have long coveted Hazard. "I think it is positive. This is part of the game to put these rumours out there and put a bit of difficulty in the mind of the players. But we have great experience of this situation. And so do my players. Eden is a Chelsea player, our player, we are happy with him and he is happy with us. I don't see problems about him. When other top teams want your players, it means we are doing a great job. So I'm happy. That's great. We must be proud of this. It means we have, in our team, good players who are doing a good job. But he is already in a great club with great ambition. The will of all is to be a great team. There is a great will to do great things in the future, but I hope to do great things in the present."

Conte believed Hazard can realise his career ambitions with Chelsea: "Now it's a great challenge to win the Premier League, more difficult a challenge for a player or a coach than other leagues. I think this league is really top in all aspects. Even if this club calls itself Real Madrid. We are in a great club. We have started to build something good for the future, and the ambitions of this club are the same as mine and my players. We stay in the right place if you want to be competitive in the game, be competitive in the future. I hope to play in the Champions League next season. I'm sure about this, that you'd be staying in the right place, in a great club with great ambition. I can tell this with 100 per cent. I think it's very important to stay, to feel that you stay in the right place with ambition. I think, I repeat, we are building something important together. Now we are putting the foundations in. If we are able to win the League this season, I repeat, I think we will be doing an incredible path, an incredible thing, because we are at the moment a club in transition."

Looking ahead, Conte added: "We hope to finish this season with a great success for us and our fans. We need 21 points to be champions. This will be a very difficult game for us, for many reasons. We have to pay great attention. It is not easy after the international break. This week we are faced with a lot of problems. It is a game of fundamental importance for us. Football is strange, it's full of surprises. In my experience as a footballer, I won a lot, but I also think I lost more. For this reason, I want to keep our feet on the ground."

Hazard was in fact an injury doubt and asked about his chances of facing the Eagles, Conte said: "I'm confident not only to play, but to play really good."

Chelsea had a reasonably favourable run-in. OK, they had the two Manchester clubs, but their final two home games were against Middlesbrough and Sunderland. Conte said: "I think we deserve to win (the league). But there are ten games to go. For sure our opponents don't want to accept that Chelsea is champions."

Sam Allardyce commented: "You've got to give huge credit to Conte. He's gone back to what system he knows best and instilled confidence in the Chelsea players. Conte's one of the top coaches. We have nearly all the top coaches in our country now. I always like pitting my wits against the best and this is the best league in the world. I'm not taking anything away from Antonio Conte and his team, but by not being in Europe, the same players have been fitter longer and he has had better time in training to get his points across."

Conte wanted "continuity" at Stamford Bridge, his agent confirmed. He had already enhanced his reputation as one of the best managers in world football and, with substantial backing from the Chelsea board, looked set to enjoy several productive seasons in west London. But his agent, Federico Pastorello, as if to avoid any complacency indicated that his client could still be tempted to leave depending on the circumstances.

"Will Conte stay at Chelsea? If he wins a title and begins the cycle the objective is one of continuity." Pastorello told journalist, Gianluca Di Marzio. "But if offers from clubs arrive, new opportunities may arise, especially at historical clubs."

Conte had been linked with Serie A giants Inter Milan, but he was quick to pour cold water over the reports. He affirmed: "My situation is very clear. I have a contract with Chelsea. We are trying to do something important with the club, for the present, for the future. Every coach, when you start work with a new club, you hope to stay many, many years, because it means you are working very well. You have the possibility to improve your players, to improve your team and to grow together."

Conte hinted at his desire to stay at Chelsea for a prolonged period when discussing Hazard's future at the club. Conte outlined that he wanted to build "something important" at Chelsea and that Hazard was a key part of his plans. "They (the players) are doing a good job, but I repeat, I think now we are already at a great club with a great ambition." Conte said at today's press conference. "We want to build something important for the present and the future, and I think we've just started our path."

Premier League Table, Top 6, end of March 2017:

		P	W	D	L	F	A	GD	Pts
1	Chelsea	28	22	3	3	59	21	+38	69
2	Tottenham Hotspur	28	17	8	3	55	21	+34	59
3	Manchester City	28	17	6	5	54	30	+24	57
4	Liverpool	29	16	8	5	61	36	+25	56
5	Manchester United	27	14	10	3	42	23	+19	52
6	Arsenal	27	15	5	7	56	34	+22	50

CHAPTER THIRTEEN

APRIL 2017

Two defeats and the gap at the top narrows.
Through to the FA Cup final. Conte is an "animal".

SATURDAY, 1 APRIL 2017
Chelsea 1-2 Crystal Palace
Premier League

No, it wasn't an April Fools' Day joke. Although it may have looked like one.

Chelsea's lead was cut to seven points after they suffered a shock home defeat and Tottenham maintained their threat not to give up the fight to the bitter end by beating Burnley. The title race was back on and Conte described it as "more interesting".

"For you, it's a good result." Conte said with a smile in his post-match press conference. "It makes it more interesting, the championship. But I always said that the league finishes when it is mathematically sure you have won. Otherwise you must play every game to try to win because, I repeat, in England easy games do not exist. Every game will be very tough from now until the end whether the team is Manchester City or a side fighting in the relegation zone. I think, today, we deserved at least to draw. I don't want to say win, but at least a draw. We created many chances. We dominated the game against a team, very strong with really good players. Yes, it's a pity but today wasn't our day. Yes, we have to play on Wednesday against Manchester City and we all know the strength of this team. But, now, the most important thing is to recover very well and rest."

Pochettino, conversely, was enthused by the double turn around in results, as he and his players still believed they could catch Chelsea following a much deserved 2-0 win at Burnley. "It's an important, a massive three points for us, to still believe we can fight for the title." said the Argentine. "We showed great belief and character and faith. That makes us proud."

Prior to Palace's visit, Chelsea had not lost in any competition since a 2-0 defeat at White Hart Lane on 4 January.

The Eagles, having looked in real danger of going down earlier this season, were now four points

14 July 2016, Antonio Conte poses before his first press conference at Stamford Bridge.

15 August 2016, Conte celebrates Costa's late winner against West Ham...

...and then races down the touchline - it was to become a familiar sight.

24 September 2016,
Conte deep in thought
during the pivotal
3-0 defeat at Arsenal...
possibly considering
three at the back.

23 October 2016,
Jose Mourinho claims
he was "humiliated"
by Conte following
United's 4-0 defeat
at Stamford Bridge.

The Conte Costa relationship was, at times, a tempestuous affair.

Home comforts... Conte on one of his regular visits to Santa Maria restaurant in Chelsea with Head Chef Emanuele Tagliarina (left) and General Manager Claudio Bruno.

Artist Massimo Guerra (from Foggia, Puglia) holding his painting of Antonio at the Gola restaurant in the Fulham Road, where Conte often goes for his favourite Italian food.

12 May 2017, Michy Batshuayi scores
the title-winning goal at The Hawthorns.

12 May 2017, Conte and players celebrate
in front of the Chelsea fans at The Hawthorns
following clinching the Premier League title.

15 May 2017,
the Champions enjoy a
ticker-tape celebration after
the 4-3 win over Watford.

HOME OF THE CHAMPIONS

21 May 2017, John Terry departs the Stamford Bridge pitch, as a player for the final time, to a guard of honour...

...and later, makes an emotional farewell speech.

21 May 2017, Chelsea are crowned 2016/17 Premier League champions.

21 May 2017, family man Conte celebrates with wife Elisabetta Muscarello and daughter Vittoria.

22 May 2017, Conte receives The Sir Alex Ferguson Trophy for the LMA Manager of the Year, sponsored by Everest, having already won the Premier League Manager of the Year Award.

27 May 2017, Cup final defeat to Arsenal at Wembley but Conte was already planning for next season.

clear of the relegation zone. "Nobody expected it." Sam Allardyce admitted, who has never been relegated from the Premier League as a manager. "It's an absolutely outstanding victory for us, particularly in the position we're in."

Conte's side had won their past ten league games at Stamford Bridge and had not lost there in any competition since 16 September 2016, but saw that run ended by the battling Eagles.

It had all started so well as the Blues struck first when Cesc Fabregas turned home Eden Hazard's cross after only five minutes. However, within six minutes they were behind: Wilfried Zaha produced a fine solo finish to turn and fire in from the edge of the box, and then only 91 seconds later set up Christian Benteke to put Palace ahead with a delicate dinked effort.

Chelsea had conceded two goals in the opening eleven minutes of a Premier League home game for the first time since October 1995 (vs Manchester United). The international break may have disrupted their rhythm but that did not seem a problem when Hazard, back from a calf injury, and Fabregas combined early on.

Although Fabregas had scored in his 43rd Premier League game this was the first time he had been on the losing side.

After falling behind Chelsea proceeded to pile on the pressure and had 24 shots, their second-highest total in 29 league games, but Wayne Hennessey made eleven saves to ensure his side won a fourth successive game.

Putting Pedro in as right wing-back in place of the absent Victor Moses did not seem to cause the leaders too many issues either, as many of their best attacks came down that flank.

A drop in energy levels might have played a part. N'Golo Kante, who played 90 minutes for France against Spain in midweek, was noticeably below par.

More than ten minutes of stoppage time gave Chelsea extra hope but by then they did not appear any more likely to score and were reduced to hopeful balls into the box as Hazard's influence faded.

Conte's side remained in a strong position at the top but, if tiredness was an issue, it could affect them again in the next few days.

Chelsea's lack of European involvement meant they were not used to playing in midweek, and only 13 different players have started 22 league games for them since 1 October. And, with two games in the next seven days coming up, at home to Manchester City and away at Bournemouth, the strength in depth of the squad would be tested for the first time.

Despite their lack of sparkle, Chelsea's defeat was not down to a lack of chances - 24 attempts on goal in fact. But, when they did break down Palace's determined defence they found Hennessey in inspired form, although sometimes his goal led a charmed life. His best save was an instinctive stop on the line from Diego Costa in the first half. Hennessey had to move quickly to keep out Marcos Alonso's dangerous cross-shot, dashing from his line to prevent Costa from stretching to poke the ball home, and was tested from distance by Nemanja Matic.

Hennessey was helped enormously by his defenders when dealing with the sheer number of crosses from the home side - 35 in total, 12 more than Chelsea have previously made in any league game under Conte - but superbly marshalled a back-line that changed twice during the game because of injuries to James Tomkins and then Scott Dann.

"I think this defeat is totally different." Conte said. "If you compare this defeat with the other defeats we are another team. I think we are a strong team. Today for sure it wasn't our day because we created a lot of chances to score a goal. We dominated the game. When you lose this type of game in your mind you try to apply a lot of questions. But it's very difficult to find a reply to this result today."

Conte turned to one of his coaches, Carlo Cudicini, and searched for the phrase in English. "There are times when things go your way and times when they don't." offered the former Chelsea goalkeeper.

Palace remained four points clear of the relegation zone, with a game in hand on third-bottom Hull, and a vastly superior goal difference. Allardyce was the first manager to win a Premier League game against Chelsea with four different clubs. Benteke had now scored in his past three Premier League appearances at Stamford Bridge, each with a different club (Aston Villa, Liverpool and Crystal Palace).

"I think we deserved at least a draw. We created many chances." Conte added. "But this is football. We must accept this result. We scored our goal after five minutes and then we conceded two in a few minutes. When you concede goals in that way you must understand the situation and improve on those mistakes. In every game in England, anything can happen. The league is so strong. We faced a team today with strong players. I think they showed they were a good team."

"There are nine games to play and we have to think step by step. At the end (of the season), if we deserve to win the title, we will be very happy. They (Manchester City) have a really strong squad but I think it's right to think about ourselves, to go game by game. In England, every game is very tough, whether the name of your opponent is City or another team."

"I think that this league was not finished before this game and it's not finished now. I repeat, at the end, if we deserve to win the title we will be very happy. If someone else deserves to win the title it means that they have played better than us."

When asked by Belgian journalist Claude Atcheba whether he'd still be in the Premier League next season, Hazard hinted that he would, initially offering: "There is nothing to say. I take it game by game. I try to play as much as possible. That's it." Pressed by Atcheba whether he would 'fancy' going to Spain, he replied: "Why do you want to put me in s***? No, I'm very well here. I have stuff to finish this year. I have a contract until 2020. Voila, for now I'm here."

Chelsea next had a big chance to make immediate amends on home turf when they host Manchester City. Despite holding a seven-point lead over Tottenham Conte acknowledged they cannot afford to slip up again. "Now we have to think about the next game. If we had won we would have been happy but now it is important to focus on Manchester City. It will be a tough game, but every game from here on will be tough."

Martin Keown on Match of the Day commented: "I don't think it can be done. But Tottenham have been brilliant since the turn of the year. They're the two best teams and let's see what they can do."

MONDAY, 3 APRIL 2017

Totally focused as always, Conte worked after Saturday's loss. There was a dinner with his wife, Elisabetta, daughter, Vittoria, and his brother Gianluca (an assistant first team coach), but he also reviewed the match. "I have to go through what happened, and then to restart." Conte admitted.

Jamie Redknapp in his Daily Mail column commented: "The title race is back on - especially if Chelsea lose to Manchester City on Wednesday. Doubts are bound to creep in after the defeat by Crystal Palace. This is Antonio Conte's biggest test since switching to a back three. Tottenham will be the side Conte fears most. Gone are the days of 'tippy tappy Tottenham'. This is a team packed with aggressive, young players who will have learned from their collapse at the end of the last campaign. You look at the likes of Toby Alderweireld, Victor Wanyama and Dele Alli and see leaders all over the pitch. Chelsea manager Antonio Conte knows his side must respond against Manchester City. Burnley had the Premier League's sixth-best home record before Saturday's game. To go to Turf Moor and win 2-0 is no mean feat without Harry Kane and wing backs Danny Rose and Kyle Walker. When I was playing, people used to see Tottenham as a stepping stone. Under Mauricio Pochettino, they believe they can win the league. Chelsea must focus on the fact that they can put the title to bed with victory over Pep Guardiola's side. If they don't, Tottenham are ready to pounce."

Alan Shearer commented on the BBC web site: "When you are chasing the title and you lose at home, like Chelsea did on Saturday, then you want the chance to respond straight away and prove it was a blip. Antonio Conte will want a reaction from his side when they play Manchester City on Wednesday and there is probably no better opposition for them to go out and show everyone that they are back on track. It is a huge game for City as well, but not in terms of them catching the leaders - I would be amazed if Pep Guardiola's side won the title now. I don't think City's top-four place is in serious danger despite three successive draws but, because of how much they have spent and who their manager is, they simply have to qualify for next season's Champions League. They cannot really afford to lose. Despite Saturday's defeat by Crystal Palace, I still think Chelsea will end up as champions. I don't see any twists in the title race. Every top team has those days where, whatever you try, it doesn't work and you come up against a brick wall. Palace's defending was just brilliant and their whole team played to their maximum."

"That result meant City could have cut Chelsea's lead at the top to nine points if they had beaten Arsenal on Sunday, and reduced it to six with a win at Stamford Bridge. City could only draw at the Emirates but, even if they had won, I don't think it would have made any difference to their title chances. Like Tottenham, they would still have been left needing to win all their remaining games just to have any chance of overhauling Chelsea. I just don't see City doing that because defensively they are poor, and they give too many goals away."

"Like Guardiola, this is Conte's first season in England, and the Chelsea boss looks set to start by winning the league. It is a great achievement but not being in Europe has definitely helped Conte, and he has been fortunate with injuries too. Chelsea have played fewer games than all of their title rivals, and have not had to test the depth of their squad. Guardiola has not had that luxury, but I think he will still be desperately disappointed if he finishes his first season at City empty-handed, which is why the FA Cup has become very important for City now."

Pochettino urged his players to seize on the belief that they can be within one point of Chelsea by lunchtime on Saturday.

In a remarkable twist the difference between first and second could be reduced from ten points as of last Saturday to just one in the space of eight days. Should Spurs beat Swansea on Wednesday and Chelsea continue to choke and lose against Manchester City, then Pochettino will be able to pile the pressure on their rivals when Spurs face Watford in the early kick-off on Saturday, with Chelsea not playing until 5.30pm at Bournemouth.

Pochettino said: "That's a good lesson for all - belief is the most important thing in football - not only quality, running or being strong. Belief, faith and fight. Nothing is impossible in football and that is our idea, our philosophy. We need to keep going in that direction and it's true the Premier League is tough to play in, and to win every game and compete. It's so competitive. But if it can happen? Yes, of course it can happen and our mind must be positive to try to imagine and dream and believe and give our best. If we are focused only on the next game and nothing around and nothing after, and if we are positive, I think we can get the three points but first of all we need to play, we need to be better than Swansea and it's sure we will need to fight a lot against them."

Thibaut Courtois split from his pregnant girlfriend and the mother of his child. The Sun said rumours persisted that Courtois was looking for a move to Spain, keen to live back with Marta Dominguez, who was expecting their second child. The couple already had a daughter, Adriana, who was coming up to her second birthday. But according to Belgian news-site Nieuwsblad, Courtois was back on the dating scene. It reported Courtois as saying: "In September we decided to split up, on amicable terms. We still love each other and we get along very well, but we don't have a romantic relationship anymore."

TUESDAY, 4 APRIL 2017

On this day a year ago, Chelsea announced Conte would become the club's first team head coach in the summer on a three-year contract. It had been an incredible first season so far, with more twists and turns predicted in an unpredictable run-in. "The time flies.' Conte said. "It's good. For me this is a fantastic experience and good experience for me, for my family also. It's great to stay here, above all to talk about to win the league. It wasn't sure one year ago."

Conte was asked what he had been saying to his players after defeat at home to Palace: "If we win, lose or draw the training session doesn't change. Our philosophy doesn't change. This part of the season is very important for many teams. For the teams fighting for the title and the relegation zone. But we have to continue in the same way and work very hard to prepare in the right way for every game. At this point I'm pleased for my players because I'm always seeing a great commitment which is very important. You can lose a game but we didn't deserve to lose against Crystal Palace. Tomorrow we have another game. Anything can happen in the league. For sure we need 21 points to win the league mathematically. We are in a really good position that nobody thought that Chelsea could fight this season for the title, but we stay there and we want to keep this position. We know there are many teams that want to win the league but this is normal. Whoever wins the league will deserve to win the league."

Conte claimed Manchester City had more quality players in their squad, which was normal when they are playing in Europe and Chelsea were not. "When you have to face the Champions League and Europa League like Man City, Man Utd, Arsenal and Spurs, it's normal that you must have a squad with 22 or 23 very strong players. Chelsea this season is not playing in Europe and for sure in our squad we have less players, but we have good, young players that are growing very well."

Guardiola had never been beaten by the same team twice in one season. Conte was hoping to put an end to that, but wasn't worrying too much about records. "It's good for him. Guardiola and me won't be thinking about that. Tomorrow is a game that we want to win and also Manchester City want to win. It's important tomorrow to play a game. It won't be easy because Manchester City are a good team."

Sergio Aguero's challenge on David Luiz at the Etihad back in early December had caused ructions. Aguero and Fernandinho were sent off in the 96th and 97th minute respectively and Conte was quizzed how Luiz felt facing Aguero again.

"We must understand that when there is a game, if someone is losing the game it can happen.

I have great respect for Aguero, he is a really good player. David Luiz's knee is better than before but for sure he needs to have good treatment."

Conte wasn't sure if Victor Moses was available, or at least he wasn't giving anything away. "I don't know if he will be available tomorrow but we have another day to check the situation in the right way. There are a couple of situations we have to check."

Conte was asked if he or anyone at Chelsea were given any indication that Alexis Sanchez expressed a desire to move to Stamford Bridge. Conte was giving nothing away out of 'respect' for both sets of players. "I don't like to speak about the other players of the other clubs. It's not the right moment to speak about this."

Costa insisted it was vital the Blues didn't panic. "Now is not the time to let ourselves down. We should keep our heads up and think ahead for the next game since it will be very important. A derby (against a big team) will always be an important game. After a loss at home and with a rival closing the gap this importance only grows. We know this game against Manchester City will be a six-point affair since if we win the game they will (practically) be out of the title race while we keep the advantage. It also depends on the match between Tottenham and Swansea. In any case, we will do our best. We hope that the next game the ball will go in, and that we do a better job at handling these counter-attacking plays so we do not suffer from early goals again, and thus avoid what happened (against Palace)."

Pep Guardiola had recently anointed Chelsea champions - something then laughed off as mind games by Conte, who denied the title race was over.

"It's normal with 27 points available that anything can happen in the league." Conte added. "We need 21 points to win the league mathematically. I think we are in a really good position. Nobody thought that Chelsea could fight this season for the title, but we stay there. We stay there and we want to keep this position."

The defeat to Crystal Palace had not unduly concerned Conte. "It's an important part of the season, but we have to continue in the same way, to work, to work very, very hard. To prepare in the right way every single game. To keep concentration. I'm pleased for my players. I'm always seeing great commitment of my players. It can happen. You can lose a game, but I think we didn't deserve to lose the game against Crystal Palace. Football is wonderful also for this type of result. Tomorrow we have another game."

Conte was mildly dismissive of Spurs. "I think the difference between Chelsea and Tottenham is this: if you stay in Chelsea and win it's normal. If you stay in Tottenham, if you win it's great, great, but if you lose… it's not a disaster, no? Not a disaster, because you find a lot of situations to explain a good season. But, I repeat, in this season, us and Tottenham stay in the same level. Chelsea were underdogs at the start of the season, but now we are top and we want to keep this position."

Conte included Guardiola's side in, what he claimed, were the three clubs still fighting it out for the title. "I think you have to put also Manchester City in this run." he said when asked whether, with the lead reduced to seven points by Spurs, it came down to a battle between his team and Mauricio Pochettino's side even if City were a further four points in arrears. "It's important to see the result tomorrow, but this run must give you enjoyment. It must make you proud to be in this run. Also because, I repeat, don't forget nobody thought Chelsea, in this season, would fight for the title."

That late collapse at Juve when Conte was the captain was back on the agenda. "Yes, it's true."

he again confirmed. "When you play in these teams, it's normal to have good experiences, positive experiences, but also negative experiences. I won one Champions League final and lost three. You think that's not the same? It is. It's the same. It's not easy to accept the defeats. But defeat is part of our job, part of our culture. You must accept it, but also try in the future to evolve away from defeats. I know only one way: work and work."

Conte may be the best according to Guardiola who "learned a lot" from teams managed by him.

Both were in their debut season in English football and Conte was eleven points ahead of fourth placed City. "My opinion about my colleague Conte is that he's superb." said the Catalan. "He was able to make Italy play beautiful football - Juventus too - in a culture where it's so defensive. He's an excellent manager. I learn a lot when I see his teams - Juventus, Italy and now. I like to do that because you see what they want to do. Their teams control a lot of aspects. Maybe he's the best."

Guardiola was always realistic about what he could achieve with City during this campaign. "In my case I had to win the treble and change English football. Expectations were quite high, that's why I'm going to fall short definitely. I cannot have success this season. In Barcelona we won the three titles in a row, we played all the competitions, we played the Champions League every three days and we were able to play almost immediately. Sometimes you need more time."

City's performances against the top teams gave Guardiola belief his side were moving in the right direction; draws against Tottenham, Liverpool and Arsenal this year, beating Arsenal in December. Chelsea had won 3-1 at City after coming back from a goal down. "We finished the game against Chelsea four points behind them. Believe me, I saw the game many times. We were much, much better. I'm sorry Antonio but we were. We deserved to win."

Yes, Chelsea had suffered a shock defeat by Crystal Palace but Guardiola was convinced it wouldn't affect their confidence. "They will be more focused. When you win 10, 11 or 12 games in a row, the danger is to be relaxed. You are winning and have a points advantage. But when you lose a game, after that the warnings are there."

Kevin De Bruyne believed his former club could still throw away the title under pressure from the chasing pack by suffering back-to-back defeats at Stamford Bridge. Victory would move City to within eight points of the leaders with eight matches to play and De Bruyne was refusing to concede the race. "They're still a lot of points ahead but obviously they will try to win the game against us because if they lose and Tottenham win then maybe they have a little bit of pressure that they haven't had throughout the whole season until now." said De Bruyne, who left Chelsea for Wolfsburg three years ago before his £55m move to The Etihad. In the end you don't want the pressure that you've not had all season. I don't think they will be shaken (by the Palace defeat). They are professionals who know how to cope with a loss. But even if it's very difficult (to win the title this season) it's still possible mathematically. As long as nothing is given away it's still possible. We just have to try to win our games and in the end we will see what happens. It doesn't mean we're going to get the title but if Chelsea make a mistake and we can do something afterwards we will see."

Cesc Fabregas was besotted with his newborn son Leonardo as he shared a photo with his Instagram followers holding his child in his arms with a heartfelt message of thanks to his wife Daniella Semaan. He wrote: "Tuesday night we welcomed our gorgeous boy, Leonardo Fabregas Semaan to the world. A special Thank You to @daniellasemaan my love, for everything you have given me and being the bravest women on earth. I love you so much. Both mummy and baby are doing amazing."

Leonardo was Fabregas's third child with his wife but his first son who will join sisters, Lia and Capri. Semaan also has a son and daughter from a previous marriage with millionaire businessman Elie Taktouk.

WEDNESDAY, 5 APRIL 2017
Chelsea 2-1 Manchester City
Premier League

Chelsea maintained a seven-point advantage over Tottenham with a hard-fought victory over Manchester City.

Conte, who was more nervous and jumpy on the touchline than normal, at the final whistle, pumped his fists in the direction of Chelsea's fans. He confirmed to Match of the Day: "My look is tired because I feel like I played it tonight with my players. I suffered with them. But we must be pleased because we beat a strong team - the best team in the league. I think they have a great coach - the best in the world. To win this type of game at this time of the season is great."

Conte admitted he can be short of motivational words. "In Italy for me, honestly, (it) was easier to find the right words to motivate my players. Here I am studying English but I am not at a great level to give a great motivation. But I try. I try to push sometimes with the words, sometimes wave my hands. Six wins. It wasn't easy, but when you play against City, it's normal to suffer in some part of the game. But I think we suffered as a team in the right way. It was a good win for us, above all because when you play after a bad defeat against Crystal Palace, where I think we didn't deserve to lose. In this part of the season it's not easy, because the pressure is very high. To drop points in this moment is not good, because you give hope to your opponent."

Eden Hazard told BT Sport: "We are nearly there but there is a long way to go. We have some difficult games but we are ready for everything. We have eight games to play. We want to finish top. That's the target. I don't know if the way we played was beautiful but the most important thing is to win games. I think the way we played we can do better but after a defeat it's good to come back here and win three points."

So, Pep Guardiola had suffered league defeats home and away to the same opponents in a single league season for the first time in his managerial career as City finally ended all hope of the title and were left to fight for a top-four place. For Conte the three points was the importance of the occasion not inflicting a new unwanted record on Pep.

To be fair, Guardiola had come to the Premier League for the first time with the weight of expectancy of delivering the title for City, while for Conte relatively little had been expected at the start of this momentous season in his career.

Hazard, the catalyst all season for another title push, gave Chelsea a 10th-minute lead when his shot slightly deflected off returning City captain Vincent Kompany past keeper Willy Caballero, who leaned to his left as the shot flew past his right and should have done better. Hazard became the first Chelsea player to score home and away against City in the Premier League since Salomon Kalou in 2007/08. He now had ten Premier League goals at Stamford Bridge this season - more than any other player - the second time he'd reached double figures at home in the league, after netting ten in 2013/14.

In the other goal, Courtois was badly at fault when his poor clearance fell to David Silva, whose shot was saved but dropped straight to Aguero for an easy tap-in equaliser after 26 minutes.

However, in an exhilarating first half, Chelsea were back in front following the award of a penalty when Fernandinho tripped Pedro after being nutmegged just inside the area. Even though Caballero saved Hazard's spot-kick, the rebound fell kindly for Hazard to follow up from close range.

City had the better chances in a tense second period, with Kompany's header bouncing back off the bar and John Stones shooting over from six yards in injury time. But Chelsea held on for a win which was greeted by wild celebrations, even more vital as Tottenham had mounted a dramatic late comeback at Swansea City; one down for much of the game but scoring three very late goals.

As the BBC reported on the night: "In the final reckoning, Chelsea showed the bloody-minded defiance of champions - and this is the sort of result that could earn them that crown."

City's hope of a top-four finish was unexpectedly aided by Bournemouth (Chelsea's next opponents) who scored a late equaliser at Liverpool.

Guardiola commented: "It's an honour to have the amazing players I have. We come here to Stamford Bridge and play the way we have, with huge personality. I'm a lucky guy to manage these guys."

Guardiola, who felt City's performance was better than in Sunday's draw at Arsenal, said: "Absolutely (City were better than Chelsea). But it's not enough. They got six points. We got zero. Football is results. Today I'm happier than the Arsenal game when we got one point. We play for us. We compete against us. The opponent is there, but the performance is for ourselves. I don't like to be reactive. I like my teams to be proactive. I like to convince my players to play in that way. After that you can win, you can lose. The way we played, I'm so satisfied. I'm a lucky guy to be here with them. Today the Premier League is gone and in the last eight games, we have to think to qualify for the Champions League." While City were out of title contention, 14 points behind Chelsea, he still believed Tottenham "is there".

Guardiola, who had no complaints over the penalty award, reckoned City's season might have been different had they beaten Chelsea at home four months ago. "The game in Etihad against Chelsea was a key point in our season in the Premier League."

Conte targeted six more wins in their remaining eight games and called on Hazard and his teammates to make the season a memorable one.

Conte said: "Tottenham could win eight games. For this reason to win the title we need 18 points. I think this is the best way for us (to think). (Hazard) is an important player. Also he's growing in his mentality. I think he's playing a really good season. This season for all my players, for me, we will remember this season if we win. We must be focused and try to win six games and take three points (six times). If we are able to do this, we will win the title. Otherwise it will be a good season, but not a great season. We will remember this season if we win. Usually I like to say only who wins write the history."

At Swansea, Alli, Son Heung-min and Eriksen's goals in the 88th, 91st and 94th minutes came after Routledge's first-half opener as Pochettino proudly confirmed: "It happened because we believed, and never gave up."

Last season Spurs were champions Leicester's closest challengers before fading in the final weeks, eventually finishing third with Arsenal beating them to second on the final day. Pochettino felt his side learned from that bitter experience. "It's important to show that we've learned from last season and that is a good thing." Pochettino said. "Maybe that is a game we would have lost last season."

Asked if he believed if Spurs could still catch Chelsea, Pochettino replied: "I believe that we can win every game if we play like today - and then we'll see. It's important to go game by game and be focusing on our opponent, and on ourselves. Today was another example that football is a collective matter. It was a massive moment (when Son scored to put Spurs 2-1 ahead) because how we turned it around was unbelievable. We're still pushing, believing, pressuring the opponent (Chelsea). It means a lot. We realised the three points would be fantastic for us. From the touchline, you must translate confidence, trust and belief. We allowed them to believe because we conceded a goal, but the most important thing for us was to show collective faith and spirit."

Conte was busy directing his team from the touchline during Spurs' win but footage emerged which suggested that he was also keeping an eye on events at the Liberty Stadium, a game which had kicked off 15 minutes earlier. Twitter user @Kejal1 posted a short clip showing Conte appearing to ask coaches Steve Holland and Carlo Cudicini a question after walking back towards the home dugout. Cudicini answers 'three to one' - the final score in south Wales. Conte looked less than impressed!

THURSDAY, 6 APRIL 2017

Conte was forced to reiterate that he intended to be at Chelsea next season, distancing himself from a suggestion by Italian agent Andrea Pastorello that he may be open to leaving. Pastorello, who is close to Conte and whose brother Federico has become an increasingly prominent figure at Chelsea since the 47-year-old's appointment last year, fuelled rumours of a possible move to Internazionale. Conte wasn't happy with Pastorello for talking on his behalf and stressed his intention to build on his superb first season that could still end with a League and FA Cup double. "I don't like it when others speak for me." said Conte. "Pastorello is a friend, I know him well but I don't like when others speak for me. If someone wants to know something about me, then they must ask me. We're fighting for the title and we want to achieve this goal, then we'll try to build something important together."

Asked whether that meant he will be at Chelsea next season, Conte confirmed: "Yes, for the next season."

Cesc Fabregas admitted the leaders were feeling the pressure but had the character to finish with a flourish. "It was a massive game and thankfully we won," Fabregas told Chelsea TV. "The result on Saturday put a lot of pressure on us. We know we still have a good advantage, but this is the Premier League and you don't want to be giving points away, especially at home. We have character. We can bounce back at anything that comes in front of us. It wasn't the most pretty game from us, but it was a very consistent performance. We knew what we were doing, we had a game plan and I think it worked perfectly."

Conte was assuming that Tottenham would win all of their eight remaining games and Fabregas added: "We've been saying it since the beginning of the season: it's one game at a time. We have to worry about ourselves, not what the others are doing. As long as we keep winning then we don't have to worry."

Hazard was linked with a £100m move to Real Madrid but Courtois told the London Evening Standard: "Eden is not affected by it. They are just rumours. He is just calm. He knows that he is important to Chelsea, like I do. We are both very happy to be here. This was my 100th game for Chelsea and I hope for many more. Eden is one of the best players in the world. Chelsea have ambitions to win the Champions League again and always look to play for the title. If you want to do that, you need the biggest players and he is obviously a big part of that."

There were suggestions that Diego Costa may face disciplinary action for an alleged off-the-ball confrontation with Kompany but both Conte and Pep Guardiola played down the incident. "Did I see it? No but during the game is very difficult." said Conte. "You see this type of contact but it is impossible to tell and judge this type of contact."

John Terry, despite being an unused substitute again, posted a photo of Hazard on Instagram and wrote: "Big nights at the Bridge require big players, and there is no bigger than this man right here @hazardeden_10. The boys were immense last night. Unbelievable support from our supporters."

Both Manchester City and Chelsea had made contact over Antoine Griezmann's situation at Atletico Madrid.

The £86million-rated striker had long been a target for rivals Manchester United while Real Madrid and Barcelona asked to be kept informed of any developments. The 26-year-old France international stressed in recent weeks he was considering postponing any departure for a year to stay with coach Diego Simeone as the club made its transition to their new stadium. City and Chelsea had alternative lists though, Lukaku for Chelsea, while City were admirers of Borussia Dortmund's Pierre-Emerick Aubameyang.

Eric Olhats, one of Griezmann's advisers confirmed to France's RMC Sport: "Nothing concrete, but Manchester United, Manchester City, Chelsea, Barcelona and Real have inquired."

FRIDAY, 7 APRIL 2017

Details of the tunnel bust-up at Stamford Bridge emerged. Coaching staff from both teams clashed continually during the game with Guardiola complaining to the fourth official on several occasions. It was not the first time that the behaviour of Conte and his staff had upset their rivals. Mourinho had accused the Italian of trying to "humiliate" United with his enthusiastic goal celebrations.

The tunnel incident was sparked by an obscene comment made by Chelsea fitness coach Paolo Bertelli towards Manchester City masseur Mark Sertori. Bertelli and Sertori traded insults from their positions in the dugout during the game, and it escalated as they headed down the tunnel at full-time. Bertelli shouted "we f****d you up the a***", and there were allegations of obscene gestures. Sertori, who is half Italian, understood the comment and reacted furiously. Stewards and other members of staff stepped in, although the confrontation was not physical. Guardiola was in danger of becoming involved as he walked down the narrow tunnel and witnessed the incident, but neither boss was involved in the row. Conte had already gone down the tunnel to the home dressing room, where he gave a victory speech to his players, and missed the trouble.

A Chelsea spokesman, who was present during the argument, branded the accusation "utter nonsense" adding: "He said nothing of the sort." Guardiola also claimed that his team "are so polite in defeats" and tried to play down the incident. "The tunnel at Chelsea is so tight." he said. "Come on, it was nothing. We congratulate Chelsea for the victory - we are so polite in our defeats. And especially we are so polite when we win, especially that."

Chelsea sources told Sportsmail that Bertelli was surrounded by City staff, including Guardiola, and that a gang of them stood outside Chelsea's dressing room after the tempers had calmed down waiting for Bertelli to reconvene the dispute. Chelsea have CCTV footage from the tunnel and sources say that if it was made public City would come off very badly, although City sources told Sportsmail that they would welcome release of the footage.

Conte was asked about the events during his press conference. He was unaware of what occurred, saying: "If something strange happens, I try always to find the right solution to face the situation. It's important, always, to show great respect. I stayed in the changing room. I didn't see what happened. I saw, during the game, that there was one moment a bit of confrontation. Okay, but then it finished. Myself, I tried to calm the situation. But I think it's normal. It's normal because, when you are in this moment of the season and there are two great teams playing for the title, there are nerves. A bit of nerves from both sides. The most important thing is to show always great respect, the winners and the losers."

Conte once again dismissed constant speculation linking him with a return to Italy. Reports, this time quoting agent Federico Pastorello (brother of Andrea), suggested he was considering a move, with Inter Milan the most likely destination. "I'm very happy to stay." Conte said. "I read this interview about Pastorello. I don't know him and I don't know why this person has spoken about me. I worked in Italy. They want to come back for me in Italy. It's normal. I have two more years of contract with Chelsea. This is the truth. This is the most important thing. I don't like when I listen to other persons talking about me."

He addressed speculation linking him with New York City's Andrea Pirlo, who played under him at Juventus. Ray Wilkins, a former Chelsea player and assistant manager, told talkSPORT he had seen the 37-year-old at Stamford Bridge "on a number of occasions this year."

"He's the one that Antonio Conte would like to come in and replace assistant manager Steve Holland." he added. Holland was leaving to join Gareth Southgate as England coach.

But Conte said: "Andrea Pirlo is playing and he wants to continue to play. I don't know why someone wants to put this type of situation for me."

Claudio Ranieri visited the training ground. He had been without a club since Leicester controversially sacked him. The 65-year-old enjoyed nearly four seasons as manager of Chelsea at the turn of the millennium and he briefly spoke with Under-18 boss Jody Morris before watching on from the sidelines as Conte put his squad through their paces with a number of training drills and a seven-a-side match. They then shared a quick chat as Chelsea's players continued their training session in sunny conditions.

Earlier in the season Conte had criticised Leicester's decision to sack Ranieri and accused the Foxes of showing a "lack of respect".

He was now on course to replicate Ranieri's achievement of winning the Premier League but next opponents, Bournemouth, were unbeaten in five matches.

Conte was sure that Diego Costa would emerge from his goal draught. Costa had 17 goals in the Premier League but had only found the net three times in 2017, still looking for his 50th Chelsea strike.

"Goals are very important for the forwards." Conte said. "But I think he knows that, for us, he's an important player if he is scoring or if he doesn't score. He must continue with his commitment and then I'm sure he'll score. He's playing good football and doing what I want. I'm not concerned about this I speak with all my players if I'm not happy with someone's commitment or behaviour, but not if he's not scoring. It can happen. In a lot of circumstances he was unlucky. But a player like Diego Costa can score in every game and I'm sure he can do this. The quality is his experience. His character. His personality. That's very important for us and the team. Also, Diego won in the past and he has good experience."

Costa himself still appeared full of confidence. "I want to play - playing right now is great." Costa told the official Chelsea website. "We are playing to win a championship. During the previous season I was out a lot of the time, either because of a suspension or an injury or for another reason. So this year I really want to play the remaining matches and enjoy myself here in Chelsea. The team is more compact, we feel more confident. The formation Antonio has introduced has been really good for us. It has been impressive because there are players who had never played in the positions they are playing now and they are actually doing really well. I always enjoy playing, always try to give the best of me. Whatever the formation I always try to play well and score in order to help the team."

SATURDAY, 8 APRIL 2017
Bournemouth 1-3 Chelsea
Premier League

Chelsea maintained their seven-point lead under extreme pressure as Spurs earlier in the day had thrashed Watford to narrow the gap to only four points - the closest it had been since December.

Chelsea looked to be cruising after two goals in three first-half minutes, but Bournemouth, who had already hit the post, got back into the contest through Joshua King's long-range deflected effort. But, the Blues gradually regained control to secure the points through Marcos Alonso's impeccable free-kick.

Chelsea's first goal was quite bizarre as Diego Costa's superb control and turn ended with a horribly scuffed shot that fortuitously went in off the head of grounded defender Adam Smith.

N'Golo Kante then produced an incredible cross-field pass to find Eden Hazard who killed the ball with his impeccable touch, ran on goal and sent the keeper the wrong way with a wicked body swerve. Hazard had now scored four times in his last three Premier League appearances against Bournemouth and his haul of 14 Premier League goals was his joint-best-ever return in a season in the competition (also 14 in 13/14 and 14/15).

Kante provided his first ever Premier League assist for Chelsea in his 30th appearance. Conte, whose demand for improvement is ceaseless, stressed that Kante's assist underlined how even the likely Footballer of the Year can still improve. "N'Golo has to improve." said Conte. "If he is able to improve this situation, he is a top, top player. Every good coach, their real function is not only to win, but improve his players and to find the right way to work with them to improve physical and tactical aspects."

Alonso's curling, dipping free-kick killed the contest, scoring his fifth Premier League of the season. Of the Premier League defenders only James Milner (7) and Gareth McAuley (6) had more. Alonso said: "We have seven finals left, every game is going to be massive, we are going to have to play each game as the last one."

It was in fact third time lucky for Alonso, scoring with a free-kick, after striking the woodwork with set pieces at Crystal Palace and Stoke. "Everyone was saying to me, 'Please, one inch lower'. The goal gave us the peace to relax."

For Bournemouth, Benik Afobe was unfortunate to hit the woodwork when arriving late to meet Charlie Daniels' cross and King lashed in his 13th of the season from outside the box, via a touch off Luiz, with Chelsea complaining of a Smith handball in the build-up.

The only concern for Conte was that Diego Costa had now gone five domestic games without a goal. Former Blues boss Glenn Hoddle claimed he would've failed a trial if he'd played like that in front of him. Hoddle told BT Sport after the match: "It was a strange game for him. How that's ended up in the back of the net? He has got that in his locker, I've seen him play a bit like this, it seemed like his timing was off in everything he wanted to do. If it was a trial and he'd come for a game you'd ask 'who brought him for a game? Get him off!'"

Conte insisted that Costa had actually put in a good performance and that his focus was on the team rather than individual goal statistics. When asked whether Costa had a bad game, he replied: "Yeah but I think the first goal Diego provoked it. He played a good game, good commitment, he fought a lot for the team. It's important for the team, the team won. It's important now to rest and prepare the game for United. I am happy for his performance. In this moment Diego is not scoring, but is totally involved in the team."

Eddie Howe observed: "I thought it was a tight game and we were well in it. It doesn't help going 2-0 down and it took a 'worldie' free-kick to win the game. I have to compliment Chelsea, they're an outstanding team and their system works very well for them. But I compliment my boys as well because they played very well. In the end Chelsea were too strong."

Conte commented: "I'm very satisfied because it wasn't easy to play this game after the win for Tottenham but our answer was very good. When you play after your opponent and you see your opponent very close, it can bring a bit of pressure. I'm very happy to face this type of situation, to play with only four points in front of our opponent. I like the pressure, I live off pressure. I don't see pressure, I put (on) pressure. I think pressure gives you the best of yourself. It's normal to have a pressure. We started the game very well with great attention and focus. Then we conceded the goal and we lost a bit of confidence. In the second half we managed the game and scored another goal, then the free-kick from Marcos Alonso. When you have this type of opponent, Tottenham, who is in good form and wants to catch you, it is important to have a good answer. This is a good answer. There are six games to go and in England it is not easy, there is a lot of pressure. We have to stay focused and concentrated because it's sure Tottenham has great desire to win the title. Don't forget that last season Tottenham fought for the title until the end. That means they are a really good team. And Tottenham is stronger than last season. It's important to understand this. There are seven games to go. Our schedule is not easy. We know this but it's important to go game by game. After the result against Crystal Palace where we didn't deserve to lose, we could have dropped points against City and then against Bournemouth. Instead we won both games. We have to continue this way."

Even before kick-off Hazard felt he would score and in targeting his best-ever league goals return he revealed that he expected to score against certain sides, but aimed to score against every opponent. "You have teams that you know before the game that you can score, or that it's your team." said Hazard. "I remember in France I always scored against the same teams, but if you want to be a top player, you have to score against every team. It was a good goal, I like to score against them. I scored two goals against them here last season." Last April, Hazard broke a Premier League scoring duck of 355 days with a brace in Chelsea's 4-1 win at Bournemouth, with stand-in boss Guus Hiddink sure he would return to top form.

Hazard insisted Chelsea would not wilt under pressure from Tottenham and that the players were also coping with the challenge.

Quizzed on his own current form, Hazard replied: "Fantastic. Like the whole team. It's a massive win for us, especially as we knew what Tottenham had done. Maybe before the game we felt pressure but once the game kicks off we just think about winning, after that we didn't think about the Tottenham result. We know if we want to be champions we've got to go to win every game. We scored two very beautiful goals in the second half."

Bournemouth next faced Tottenham at White Hart Lane, with Howe expecting another stern encounter. "Now it will be a normal week in preparation for Tottenham. I watched them against Watford and it will be another tough test."

Wing backs Alonso and Moses were lavished with praise for their "fantastic" performances.

Harry Redknapp was effusive, speaking as a pundit on BT Sport, he said: "He (Alonso) played here three or four years ago, he was at Bolton. He's a lovely footballer, absolute quality, he has got a great left foot. His delivery is top class, he always looks very composed, he suits the system. Moses was going nowhere in his career, suddenly in this system he has blossomed, he has been fantastic."

Fellow pundit Hoddle was equally impressed, saying Alonso had proved the doubters wrong, after his big money move from Fiorentina was initially greeted by scepticism. Hoddle said: "Him and Moses, at the beginning of the season people weren't too sure about the wing backs, but they have proved themselves. Alonso has that lovely left foot balance. The number of times they change the play, he is out there all the time. The diagonal pass is always in play."

From the comments emerging from the Spurs camp, it was clear why Chelsea had to respond in such a positive manner. "We are talking about building a winning mentality." said Pochettino. "This is a good opportunity to see how we can win trophies in the future. It is about keeping going and respecting how we play. We want to keep pushing. How Chelsea do is their problem but our job is done. It's up to them to win Premier League. The message for us is to win games. We have to be focused on next game, if not, you're not spending time in reality. This has happened in nearly three years. The chairman and all the staff believe it's important to get this winning mentality, to believe it's possible to win the Premier League. We have been working a lot since day one and the job is starting to reward us. We still have lots of work to do but we are excited."

Pochettino hailed the return of talismanic striker Harry Kane. The England international played the last 30 minutes against Watford following a four-week injury lay-off. And Pochettino added: "We are stronger with him and he is ready to fight for the team. But football is about the collective."

Kieran Trippier, who was named Man of the Match as he stood in for Kyle Walker, underlined the belief within the squad that Tottenham can still win the title. He said: "We believe in ourselves and as a team. We just have to keep performing. We want to take it game by game, we can't affect Chelsea but we have to focus and see where it takes us."

Chelsea's title battle would continue with yet another reunion with old boss Jose Mourinho, this time at Old Trafford; arguably their sternest of the six league fixtures remaining and a game that was sure to reignite old wounds.

Asked how much respect he had for Mourinho's past history at Chelsea, Conte swerved the question neatly. "I have already replied to this question before the FA Cup game." he said.

"The most important thing is on the pitch. For us, it's always important to control our emotion because we are playing and fighting to win the title. For sure, this game will be a tough game but we are ready to play. I think United for sure will have good motivation, because they are playing against Chelsea. Every team will want to beat us."

Having won 24 out of 31 Premier League matches, Conte was adamant that, yes, of course his team will go to Manchester United with the purpose of emerging victorious rather than simply avoiding defeat. "For sure." said Conte. "It's important now in every game to try and take three points, including at Old Trafford. We know this game will be very tough but we are in good form and the players have the right confidence."

Chelsea had previously handled the knowledge of Tottenham's 4-0 win against Watford without difficulty. "If you compare these two games - we face United away and Tottenham face Bournemouth at home - I think that it's easier for Tottenham to take points in their home stadium." said Conte. "I think Manchester United for sure will have good motivation because they are playing against Chelsea. Every team wants to beat the top of the table. We know our schedule is not easy. We are having a good season but we want it to become a great season. To become a great season and to write history you must win."

SUNDAY, 9 APRIL 2017

Diego Costa insisted he was "very happy" at the club despite the decline in his form; scoring only three times since 22 January. But, with speculation that he might leave having not subsided Costa only served to fuel the rumours about his future by saying he is not necessarily happy in London. "I have another two years on my contract. I am always very honest with those close to me. I tell them that I am very happy at Chelsea." Costa told SFR Sport. "The club gives me a lot, the fans, the teammates. I am in a team that is winning and that motivates me even more. Last season was not the best, not just for me but for other players and for Chelsea. This year I hope will be different, that we win titles. If you are in a team that is winning, you always want to stay for the allotted amount of time. I am happy at Chelsea, I am not necessarily saying that I am happy with my life in London, but that is something completely different. It has nothing to do with it."

Frank Lampard heaped praise upon Eden Hazard. "He's the best player in the league for me at the moment." Lampard told Goals on Sunday, "The composure, the ability there to take it round him, he's just playing with ease and confidence at the minute."

Hazard had emerged as a leader in the dressing room and Lampard was impressed with his improved attitude under Conte. "For me there's a new maturity about him this year." Lampard added. "Not just on the pitch, but off the pitch. He's doing more interviews, he's speaking English. These things are important for me when you become a player at the level he's at - he's captained Belgium a couple of times. There were times last year where he was so confident in his ability that he'd beat someone twice. Now there's a real directness to his play. He's more efficient. He's getting in areas to make goals and score goals."

Conte remained on course to claim silverware in his first season at Stamford Bridge and Lampard was impressed with his immediate impact in west London. "It's an incredible turnaround." Lampard said. "To come in, from where they were last year - they had a very difficult season. What's really impressive about the way they are playing is that everybody knows their job. Every player on that pitch in that system, and other teams are now emulating that system throughout the Premier League with three at the back. But I think Chelsea are the one team that do it brilliantly in every position."

MONDAY, 10 APRIL 2017

Eden Hazard wanted to avoid getting stick from Spurs' Belgian contingent when they all link up with the national team at the end of the season. "That is why we want to win the trophy because if we go to the national team they will speak too much!" Hazard told Chelsea TV. "So we need the trophy for Chelsea." And, addressing Dembele, Vertonghen and Alderweireld, Hazard warned that Chelsea were "ready for everything."

"When we see Tottenham, everything is not done. It is one step closer but we have seven games left to play and we have to be ready for everything."

Spurs' 4-0 win over Watford had helped inspire the 3-1 victory at Bournemouth. Hazard explained that regaining their seven-point lead over their nearest challengers provided extra motivation to collect all three points. "We passed the test." he told BT Sport. "We know the result of Tottenham before the game. We wanted to stay seven points ahead. We scored three goals, we deserved to win. It's more easy to control the game when you score first. But at the end of the first half we went a bit down. But we controlled it in the second half. We have to believe in everything. We have seven games to play. We are ready for them."

Claudio Ranieri believed Leicester shouldn't have sold Kante to Chelsea and that the Foxes could have achieved something special in the Champions League had he stayed. While Leicester were set to face Atletico Madrid in the quarter-finals of the Champions League, Ranieri insisted they would have had a better chance of winning it with Kante. He told Sky Sports: "I didn't want to sell him (Kante), the same I didn't want to sell Vardy and Mahrez. I felt these players were the heart of the team. I wanted to make a fairytale, I believed those players could do things in the Champions League."

MONDAY, 10 APRIL 2017

Ranieri admitted to being hugely impressed by the impact his fellow Italian was having at Chelsea. Speaking on Sky Sports' Monday Night Football, Ranieri said: "The character is the same. In Italy, he was very passionate. It was normal. He changed some things. He adapted his character to the Premier League players and the ambience. It is harder in England."

TUESDAY, 11 APRIL 2017

Former Chelsea favourite Marcel Desailly believed Alonso, Kante and Moses were key to helping Chelsea have an amazing first season under Conte. "I'm very pleased (with Chelsea)." Desailly told Sky Sports News HQ. "When you look at last season where it was very difficult with Mourinho in charge, a whole lot of controversy and the tactics were not working, this year you change it and have three new players: Kante, Alonso and Moses and you just change a little bit of the tactics, it's just an amazing season for Chelsea."

Arsenal hero Thierry Henry lavished praise on Conte, describing him as an example to his fellow coaches. "As a coach, Conte has done exactly what you're supposed to do. He arrived at Chelsea, assessed the situation and didn't do what he wanted right from the start." he explained to Sky Sports. "He did what a good coach should do, in that, when it's not working he changes it. And it worked because his system has helped every single player to do better."

Conte's mediocre start was turned around after he "reached a compromise" with his star players, according to former Blue Hernan Crespo. Conte oversaw two losses in his first six outings, but Chelsea's imperious run which followed makes it hard to envisage Spurs catching them. Crespo credits Conte for his change of approach and rallying call to his top players for the marked turnaround. "There was great expectation on Conte and a lot of curiosity to see whether he could apply his football vision in the Premier League, where there are many big players." Crespo told Omnisport. "That was a big challenge for Conte and it wasn't easy - he struggled at the beginning.

Then, Conte and his players found a middle-ground solution and came to a compromise. Conte made sure that the defensive group was solid and reliable, then organised the midfield tactically. It proved to be successful. It allowed more freedom to offensive players to express their talent and making that move was key to Chelsea's success this season. Conte deserves much credit for Chelsea's success. He is proving that once again managers from the Coverciano school (Italian FA headquarters and training centre) are the best tactically, without a shadow of a doubt."

Crespo believed Conte was replicating "what he had already done with his previous teams" at Chelsea - including the Italy national team. Three top flight titles, as he had achieved with Serie A giants Juventus, would be nice at the Bridge!

Graeme Souness believed Jose Mourinho was wound-up "big-time" by Conte's instant success. Souness said. "They won the league the year before and then for whatever reason, the players downed tools. That shows you the power of the modern day dressing room. One of the biggest names in management in world football and they got him out of the door." Sky Sports pundit Souness believed Mourinho had reignited the belief at United but the pressure was on to secure Champions League qualification.

Souness added: "He has got a trophy and United supporters are encouraged by the football they are playing. For me they have the player of the year there in Zlatan Ibrahimovic. United are the third biggest team in the world; only behind the two big Spanish clubs and on a par with Bayern Munich in terms of size and stature. It would be very disappointing for them not to get in the Champions League. I think they will through the Europa League."

Chris Sutton, Match of the Day pundit and former Chelsea striker, commented online: "There is pride as well as points at stake at Old Trafford on Sunday because Manchester United manager Jose Mourinho will not take it well if Antonio Conte beats him in his own backyard. Conte has not just won both their previous meetings this season, his Chelsea side are 18 points above United and closing in on the Premier League title. I did not expect the gap between the two teams to be so big but nobody could have foreseen how well Conte would do in what is a highly competitive league - I certainly didn't."

"If you are looking for a comparison, you could say his impact in his first season in the Premier League has been Mourinho-esque, the same as when Jose first came to England in 2004 and blew everyone away. In many ways, Conte is the new Mourinho - he has only been in England for eight months but has already taken over his mantle. By that, I mean the way Conte has been the outstanding manager this season with his results and how he has implemented his style of play to build a team that is exciting to watch and a threat going forward. Just as with Mourinho, you would not exactly say that everyone loves him, but most people admire the job he has done at Chelsea. Mourinho may see a bit of himself in Conte and I would understand if he is a bit envious of the success the Italian has had. He has stolen his thunder with what is essentially Mourinho's team, and got so much more out of the group of players he was left with after Mourinho's second spell at the club."

"I was one of those who thought Mourinho would quickly transform United in a similar way, but they simply have not made the same transition since he took charge. Yes, there are signs of improvement from the Louis van Gaal era but I still think United will finish outside the top four, which is pretty unacceptable when you consider how much money they have spent."

"Mourinho has already clashed with Conte on the touchline this season, and he will be absolutely desperate to beat him this time. I don't think United can play an open game against Chelsea on Sunday because, if they try to go toe-to-toe with them, the way Conte's team counter-attack will really cause them problems. So I am expecting a cagey affair. If you asked me to pick a winner I would go with the Blues but I just have a feeling Zlatan Ibrahimovic will play a big part in the outcome. I would not put it past him to do something special to decide the game - but even if United do come out on top at Old Trafford, they face a huge task to break into the top four now. You cannot rule United out of winning all of those games, simply because of who they are and the quality they have in their team. But, on this season's form, I just cannot see it. United are unbeaten for 21 league games, going back to their 4-0 defeat at Stamford Bridge in October, but it is their inability to score goals that has been the determining factor in where they are in the table, because they have not beaten a lot of teams you would expect them to run riot against."

WEDNESDAY, 12 APRIL 2017

David Luiz was "unrecognisable" during his second spell with Chelsea and had featured on the winning side an impressive 21 times in the Premier League.

Garth Crooks reckoned Conte deserved special credit for being bold enough to bring him back. He told BBC Sport: "As the season draws to a close and Chelsea put a date in the diary for a trip to the Premier League engravers, I would like to commend manager Antonio Conte and technical director Michael Emenalo for having the foresight and courage to bring Luiz back to Stamford Bridge. The Brazil international is unrecognisable from the irrational player we saw during his first period at the club. Since his return, he has played some glorious football and been a unifying figure in a new era at the Bridge."

Jose Mourinho was the reason Diego Costa chose to leave Atletico Madrid to join the Blues. "In all honesty I always tell people I am grateful to Mourinho because he helped me a lot." Costa told Sky Sports in an interview with Thierry Henry prior to the crunch clash with Manchester United. "As a player when you want to improve you always look for the best coach and Mourinho is one of the best. I wanted to come to Chelsea because of Mourinho. When I considered Chelsea I thought about the fact that Mourinho was here. He is a coach that demands a lot from his players, he wants the maximum." Costa touched on the troubles Chelsea endured last season but failed to go into any detail, simply saying "He helped me a lot and then what happened is that the following season didn't go well, these things that happen, but the truth is that Mourinho helped me a lot to improve as a player."

THURSDAY, 13 APRIL 2017

Jose Mourinho would field a strong side against Chelsea despite United facing Anderlecht in Belgium before taking on the Premier League leaders and then the second leg of the Europa League quarter-final at Old Trafford all within a week. Previously, Mourinho had hinted that winning in Europe to qualify for the Champions League was now his priority, casting doubts on the strength of the team he would pick for a league match in between the two Europa League ties. United were fifth, four points behind fourth-placed City with a game in hand, needing to finish in the top four or win the Europa League to qualify for next season's Champions League. "When it is still mathematically possible to finish in the top four I think if we play against Chelsea with our second team you would kill me. The football country would kill me. There is no reason not to try while it's mathematically possible. If on a certain moment of the season we have no chances to get top four and we are still in the Europa League then nobody can criticise. I hope we have no more injuries, no more suspensions and I hope the players keep showing amazing character to keep going and going. Until it's not possible we are going to fight for the top four."

Football agent Silvio Pagliari spoke to CalcioMercato.com about Inter, focusing on the summer ahead for the Nerazzurri: "Surely Inter can invest in big names now, because if they want to reduce the gap with Juventus they need more important players. Juve gets stronger every year and all the title contenders must do more because the gap with Juventus is huge. I hope that in the summer Roma, Inter and Milan can help and make Serie A the most entertaining league next season."

Interestingly, when quizzed about Conte he said: "The return of Antonio Conte? I think it's unrealistic, I do not think that Chelsea's goals can be matched by Italian clubs."

Real Madrid's Alvaro Morata confirmed he'd had calls from Chelsea and felt "indebted" to Conte, who brought him to Juventus before departing to manage the national team. "Conte is the manager who most 'bet' on me, without even ever having had me in his team." Morata said in an interview with the Guardian. "He bet on me for Juventus but left before I arrived, then he wanted me at Chelsea come what may. He knows me better than I could imagine, I'm sure, and that's important: it motivates you to work hard, train well."

Tantatisingly, he suggested it was only a matter of time before he played for a team under Conte again. "I feel indebted to him because he's the coach that most trusted in me, most wanted me, who made me feel I could perform at the highest level, and yet I've never had the fortune to actually work with him. I'm sure sooner or later I will. The future excites me, whether that's Madrid or somewhere else. I still have to learn, improve. I can do a lot but I need to play more and for someone to really back me." Morata made his return to the Spanish capital after Madrid exercised their buy-back option in the contract the striker signed with Juventus.

Morata had conversations with Chelsea and Tottenham. "'Various Premier League coaches called to tell me to play for them. I said yeah, I'd like to, that if I had to leave I would almost certainly go to London, but that I didn't know what Madrid would do. I knew they'd bring me back but I didn't know if it was to keep me or sell me. I spoke directly to Mauricio Pochettino and Antonio Conte, although the norm is clubs call my dad or agent. Madrid said they didn't want to sell, so here I am "

Pochettino clarified: "It is a special thing because I know Morata from when I started my (managerial) career at Espanyol. The reality is that he sent a text to me when I was manager at Espanyol, he contacted me for some advice and then we kept the relationship. He is a great kid and a very good player but it is not realistic to think Morata (will play) for us because it is one thing to maintain a good relationship between him and me but another to think about bringing him here. There is no sense to it."

N'Golo Kante and Eden Hazard's efforts in the title race were, unsurprisingly, recognised with nominations for the Professional Footballers' Association Player of the Year award. Kante, who was shortlisted last year for his part in Leicester's remarkable season but did not make the top three, was the bookmakers' favourite for the 2016/17 accolade, with Alexis Sanchez, Zlatan Ibrahimovic, Romelu Lukaku and Harry Kane also on the six-man shortlist. There was no place for Dele Alli, despite the young England international's stunning season, although he led the nominations for the Young Player of the Year prize.

Conte, naturally, refused to choose between Hazard and Kante as his pick for PFA Player of the Year. "I think it's great, for them, it's a great achievement to receive this nomination. I hope for them to be the best player of the year and also I want them to win the league. Awards are important but the most important thing is if you match the two. But I don't like to make a choice between two of my players. It's not right. They deserve the best because they are having a good season, but I think all my players are having a great season. I'm pleased because it's a fight between two of my players and four other players from other teams. I want to see who is the winner."

"With or without the ball, Eden is working very well for the team." Conte continued. "When we are in possession or not. Eden is becoming a complete player, which is great for him." Asked about rebuilding the player's confidence, Conte said: "I think it's very important to speak with your players. I think it's also very important to find the right moment to speak with them. It's crucial at the start of the season but also during the season when you understand there is less hunger, less concentration. After you've had a good result, it's normal that the focus and concentration is a bit less than before."

Jose Mourinho insisted he felt no emotion over United's forthcoming clash with Chelsea despite two explosive meetings with his old club already. Asked on Thursday night if his third meeting of the season with Chelsea would be just as emotional, Mourinho replied: "You say that word emotion. For me, it is just a game. One more game. No difference for me, not at all." Mourinho once again pointed out that Chelsea's title challenge was helped by lack of involvement in Europe. Sunday's game was United's 53rd of the season compared to 39 for Chelsea. But he acknowledged that his old club had become very hard to beat under Conte.

"First of all, some guys are fresh, some guys are tired - that's very important in football. But, for some reason, they are top of the league. It's not just because they are fresh. It's also because they have individual quality and they have collective quality. They have a certain style of play, they stick to it, they do it very well. Not every team defends with eleven players, and they defend with eleven players. Not every team is so objective in their counter-attacks. They are very objective in the counter-attack and they have individual players out of the context of the game that can also resolve the problems. So they are a very strong team."

Mourinho was trying to balance his team selection. "If we arrive into a situation in the Premier League where mathematically the top four is not possible, then it's an easy decision: rest them and go with them in the Europa League if we're still in. But at this moment we are in a position where we have two matches in hand. If we win both matches we are in the top four. We have to fight for every game."

FRIDAY, 14 APRIL 2017

Conte smiled at the Good Friday question.

"Yes, I go to church today. I go to an Italian church in Chelsea. I don't pray for winning the Premier League title but I do like to pray every day. I pray before breakfast, before lunch and before dinner to say thanks. But usually I like to pray for the safety of my family, and also of my players and my team."

His prayers were certainly answered by numerous key players, certainly David Luiz and Eden Hazard, who were alienated by the managerial methods of Jose Mourinho but now flourishing under Conte.

"When you arrive at a new team," Conte said in his press conference, "you must love this team, love the shirt, love the players, love the fans."

As for Luiz, "I heard a lot of bad things said about David when he arrived at the club again and I heard people wondering why he was coming back to Chelsea. I heard that he had performed badly and that he was 'not a defender' and that we were spending a lot of money on him. This was a great challenge for him, but also for me. But when we decided to buy him, to take him back, we were sure. We were sure we were buying a really good player and put him as one of the best defenders in Europe and, I hope, in the world. You can see that David is a really strong defender, and I have always repeated to him that it's very important to have the right concentration. His role is crucial for us and I think he has performed very well. He is strong, he has good technique, he can start our possession, and he has the personality to do this. The position is fantastic for him."

The same was true for Hazard, one of the contenders for the PFA Player of the Year award along with Kante. "I'm very pleased they have been nominated." said Conte. "Because this is my task - to put every single player in the best situation, physically, tactically and mentally, so they can give the best of themselves. We are doing a great job with the players. During the game you can see their commitment, and I think that's great."

He would like the unsung defenders on the PFA nomination list; perhaps Luiz, Cahill or Azpilicueta. "It's more difficult for defenders, no? For this reason Paolo Maldini never won the best player in the world award. The defenders are a bit penalised, aren't they."

Conte diplomatically played down his rivalry with Mourinho, insisting there's not a problem between the two of them. "I don't see the problem, it is a sporting competition. He wants to win with his team, me with mine. It is only a sporting conflict. He won a lot with this (Chelsea) team, this club has always shown him great respect for his past, if you remember I thought the same and it doesn't change. I have great respect for his history of this club."

Conte was avoiding any emotion and simply being realistic ahead of this next encounter with Mourinho. "This game is a game like any other. For us, the most important thing is the three points. We will face a really strong team because Manchester United are a really good team, really strong physically and technically. Also, because United want to find a place in the Champions League and arrive in the top four. They have all the possibilities to do this. But we are fighting for the title and we'll fight for the title until the end. This was our target at the start of the season. Now we are in a good position to fight until the end. The road is long and there are other teams who want to win the title. For this reason, this race will be until the end of the season."

Conte aimed a dig at Klopp's title challenge as a response to criticism that his own team benefitted from not playing in Europe. When questioned whether his team had been at a big advantage to other sides chasing the title, Conte pointed at Liverpool's flimsy title challenge. Klopp's side were 12 points behind the Blues, having played one more game, and saw their trophy hopes disintegrate during a disappointing start to 2017. Conte believed his men deserved more credit. "I listen to this story (of not playing in Europe as an advantage) from when I was the coach in Juventus in my first season but I can tell you why Liverpool is the same. For sure, we had more time to work with the team and this is my first season with a new club but I think if this is the only reason you stay on top of the table it's a great mistake. We are doing a great job and we hope in the future to play in the great competition of the Champions League - I prefer this."

Conte was put in a potentially awkward situation during his press conference when asked if any United players would get into his Chelsea side. "No, no, no, no, no!" he said, before laughing.

"No, no, no, no, no. It's not a good question because I think… I think my players are the best in the world. For sure at Manchester United there are a lot of great players, top players, but they are United players. I would keep my players and be very happy to do this."

Conte, though, believed Zlatan Ibrahimovic was playing the best football of his career at United. Conte hung up his boots just as Ibrahimovic arrived at Juventus. "Zlatan is in the top of his form in his career. He is a great player now, a top player. Not only a finisher, but he plays for the team. It is good to have this type of player because it's very good to play for the team. For me, he's one of the best players in the world, Zlatan."

Ibrahimovic had scored 28 goals in all competitions in his first season in English football and Conte explained: "We must have good defensive organisation and we must pay attention because, when he attacks the box, he is very dangerous. Also when he receives the ball, he's dangerous. He's a dangerous player. For this reason, I think my players must pay great attention and great concentration tomorrow to stop him, and not only one player, but the team."

Conte knew United would target Eden Hazard, who was singled out for rough treatment by United when the teams met in the FA Cup. But it had backfired as Herrera was sent off for fouling Hazard and United went on to lose 1-0 at Stamford Bridge. Conte had been angered by that approach but, ahead of Chelsea's trip to Old Trafford, he had not made any preparations for more of the same. "No, it's very difficult to prepare for this type of situation. We are preparing the tactical aspect of the game and trying to find the best solutions offensively and defensively. This game will be very tough but I didn't prepare anything for this situation. The coach has to work on the tactical aspect, the physical aspect, the psychological aspect. In this type of game it's important to prepare your team to face every situation - tactical, physical or mental - to be ready. My expectations are for a tough game. I think when I talk about a tough game I invoke the tactical, physical and mental aspects. It's not right to tell only one of these aspects. There are many great players but technicality is not enough. You must have good impact physically and with the right mentality."

Conte would visit United for the first time as a manager, although he had fond memories of a goal he scored for Juventus at Old Trafford in the first leg of the Champions League semi-final in 1999. "We drew 1-1 and I scored." he recalled. "I remember because I didn't score a lot in my career. It was a great goal, and then Ryan Giggs equalised in the last minute. It was a great atmosphere, a great stadium and a great team. Then, in the second leg, we were winning 2-0 after 25 minutes and lost 3-2. I remember Manchester United won the Champions League in that year."

"No, no injuries." he added. "We have one or two situations to check but no injuries. The situation is good but we have another day to make the best decision for the team. I want to wait."

Didier Drogba stated recently that Romelu Lukaku, sold by Chelsea to Everton for £28m in 2014, had a point to prove at "the house he knows" but Conte refused to be drawn on this. "I think it's not the right time to talk about this. I have great respect for Drogba, a legend for Chelsea, but I can't talk about this. It's not right to talk about players from other teams, we must have respect for players and other clubs."

Interestingly, Conte's team score and concede at roughly the same rate as they did in Mourinho's title-winning season of 2014/15. However, Conte's team were running and intercepting more, tackling less, playing more directly.

"A lot of players have the will to win, but sometimes if winning becomes a habit, the hunger might drop and you will lose some games." Thibaut Courtois observed. "But it's always nice to have a manager who keeps the players at the level they need to have, who keeps our focus and doesn't allow us to drop our guard."

Courtois urged his side not become apprehensive as they edged ever closer to the finish line. "To win the title, we just have to do the same as we have done over the last few months. We have to stay calm, whatever happens. We just have to keep our winning mentality and fight until the end." Tottenham set their sights on "bigger things" than finishing above Arsenal.

Spurs were now 14 points clear of the Gunners, having played a game more, while Arsenal had won only one of their last five league matches. Tottenham had not been this far ahead of their north London rivals in the table since May 1963 but Pochettino was more concerned about catching Chelsea. "I think we're playing and fighting for bigger things." Pochettino said. "If we look at the bigger picture it's to try to reduce the gap with Chelsea. I think today it's not important the gap we have with Arsenal. The most important thing is to do our job, try to win games and try to reduce the gap with Chelsea."

Tottenham again had the chance to cut Chelsea's lead to four points, before the Blues faced the tricky trip to United. They were boosted by the return to fitness of Harry Kane, who came off the bench against Watford last weekend, and was likely to make his first start in almost five weeks at White Hart Lane. Kane had been nominated for PFA Player of the Year with 24 goals in all competitions but Pochettino says his star striker can still reach 30.

SATURDAY, 15 APRIL 2017

Tottenham made it seven wins in succession for the first time since 1967 and continued their unerring pursuit of Chelsea with a dominant victory over Bournemouth.

The game was essentially won in a three-minute period in the first half in which Moussa Dembele fired Spurs ahead from close range following a corner, before Son Heung-min doubled the lead with a darting run and neat finish. Kane, making his first start in a month, made sure of the three points with a low finish just minutes into the second half, making him the fourth player to score 20 Premier League goals in three consecutive seasons after Alan Shearer, Ruud van Nistelrooy and Thierry Henry. Vincent Janssen scored just his second Premier League goal in injury time, soon after coming on as a substitute.

Pochettino's side were now just four points behind Chelsea, as Bournemouth managed only one shot on target. Tottenham had surpassed the 70 points that had given them third place in 2015/16, during which they challenged for the Premier League trophy until their 36th fixture - a 2-2 draw at Chelsea.

A more clinical Tottenham side than 12 months ago was illustrated perfectly in this faultless performance. Spurs had scored the joint-most goals in the division, conceded the fewest, hitting peak form at the right time, making White Hart Lane a fortress with their 12th victory in succession. It was their longest-ever winning streak on home soil in a single top-flight season and they were doing everything to capitalise on any potential Chelsea slip-up.

Pochettino, speaking to BBC Sport, remarked: "I am proud of our players after that performance. We have to wait to see what happens. Harry Kane is a fantastic player - he is one of the best in England and it is fantastic he is fit again to help the team. Son is brilliant - he needed time to adapt his game but he is now fit and healthy and he is feeling really comfortable. I was happy for Vincent Janssen because I knew it was his only chance to score and it's important he feels the happiness when you score. At the end of the season when everyone is tired, we need everyone to have the right mental attitude and happiness helps. We now need everyone to rest and get ready for the next few games. The three points are very important to keep our dream."

Pochettino insisted his side had "improved a lot" from 12 months ago and were ready for the scrutiny and pressure of a closely fought title run-in. "That was a very bad period at the end of last season. We expended a lot of energy fighting against Leicester, against Chelsea, against the media. We fought against everyone. But now we are focusing on fighting our opponents when we play. From the beginning of the season that was our chance to improve our mentality, our belief, and I think you can see the group and the team have improved. It was important for us to get the three points and we got the three points. Now the pressure is on Chelsea to win at Old Trafford. Tomorrow will be a very tough game for them but there are still lots of games to play. It will be fantastic if after the game tomorrow the gap is still four points. The gap is still four points which is a lot. If they drop points tomorrow it will be fantastic but they are still the favourites to win the Premier League. We are fighting for ourselves to be there. To be fighting for the top four for the second consecutive season is great for the players and fantastic for the club."

"If you analyse where we came from, it's a fantastic time for Tottenham. The way you build your project is important to analyse. Tottenham is not building now in an artificial way. It is not about putting in money, money, money, and building a fantastic stadium and fantastic team. Tottenham is very genuine, it is a very natural process and it is so exciting because it is unique in the world." Concluded Pochettino.

"Tottenham are so good because they keep the ball so well. They make it difficult for you to build. It's a nice mix they have. They are the team we aspire to be but they are certainly a level above us at the moment."

"That could be an understatement." Bournemouth coach Eddie Howe added when asked if it had been a difficult day. "Tottenham were everything we expected them to be but we're disappointed with the manner of the goals we conceded. We contributed to our own downfall."

Tottenham's impressive form made Chelsea nervous, according to Frank Lampard. "Chelsea are very aware that Spurs are there and it'll be a tough game for them tomorrow." Lampard told BBC Sport. "There will be some nervousness but so there should be."

In his Mail on Sunday column, former Chelsea manager Glenn Hoddle observed: "Antonio Conte does what Mourinho used to do so well. There is no team in the Premier League better balanced than Chelsea. There was a moment in the game against Manchester City recently, just before half-time, where they looked to be on the back foot and seemed as though they were really struggling. City were flying forward, with loads of space for David Silva and Kevin De Bruyne. I was watching it thinking, 'this is going to be hard for Chelsea'. Conte took a look at that, takes off Kurt Zouma for Nemanja Matic, puts Cesar Azpilicueta back in defence and releases Cesc Fabregas forward. The wing-backs pulled back a bit and stopped flying up the pitch to tuck into deeper positions. It was a very shrewd move to get through the game, shore it up and ultimately seal a victory that could prove decisive in the title race. I do not think Pep Guardiola would have done that in a million years. He would probably deem it negative. But it was exactly what was needed. Chelsea have the match-winners in their team but Conte is smart enough to use his tactical awareness to good effect. That is the balance you need. And that is why they are going to win the Premier League this season."

SUNDAY, 16 APRIL 2017
Manchester United 2-0 Chelsea
Premier League

Chelsea's lead now stood at only four points and the title race was wide open again after they were well beaten at Old Trafford.

Conte took the blame in his 'flash' interview immediately after the game on Sky Sports: "They deserved to win, because they showed more desire than us, more motivation. In this case, the fault is the coach. It is mine. In this case I wasn't able to do the right motivation. To play this type of game from now and until the end we must have great enthusiasm, great motivation to try to reach the target. This for us is a fantastic target. I have concern because we have to work together and find quickly the right ambition to win this title - if someone thinks it's normal for Chelsea to win the title, we started as underdogs after 10th place last season. Tottenham is in good form and playing with enthusiasm, we must find the same."

Marcus Rashford was paired with Jesse Lingard up front while a jaded Zlatan Ibrahimovic was rested. The teenager, Rashford, finished coolly after seven minutes and Ander Herrera - detailed to do a brilliant man-marking job on Eden Hazard - saw his shot deflected in off Zouma past an already falling reserve keeper for the home side's crucial second goal only four minutes after the break.

The Mourinho masterstroke was to deploy Herrera as Hazard's shadow; the Hazard menace being completely snuffed out.

Kurt Zouma was a late replacement for Marcos Alonso, who pulled out in the warm-up, with Nathan Ake moving into the matchday squad.

Courtois was ruled out with an injury, with Sky Sports reporting the problem was sustained during "filming for an NBA commercial", but Conte declined to discuss the reasons. "It's not important to understand the way he had this injury." he said. "During the week he had an ankle injury and he didn't recover for this game. I hope only this game (he misses)." He was replaced by Asmir Begovic.

Courtois had played in 31 Premier League games, keeping 13 clean sheets, and pundits Frank Lampard and Graeme Souness suggested the way he picked up his injury could leave Conte seeing red. Souness said on Sky Sports: "As a manager you aren't going to be too happy with that. They have commercial responsibilities. You're tearing you're hair out with something like that." Lampard added: "Someone is getting it in the neck. If it's a club thing it's different, but if he has done that off his own back..."

On the handball by Herrera in the build up to United's opening goal Conte commented: "Last game against Bournemouth we conceded a goal in a same situation, against Palace a clear handball, against Stoke a penalty with great doubt. This is not important. It is important to find the right solution, but the decision of the referee wasn't good for us. We were unlucky."

Herrera naturally disagreed: "I didn't want to touch the ball with the hand. I was running with my hand next to my body. If your hand is in a natural position it is not a handball. There are always some things to improve, but it was almost perfect. They didn't have any chances. I have been looking for a goal for a long time. Today I was a bit lucky, but I think we deserved this."

So, Tottenham were four points behind with six games to go and had the superior goal difference. Chelsea had looked to be strolling to the title until that sudden stumble, a home defeat to Palace and now defeat at United. It was matched by an irresistible surge from Spurs to bring the run-in to a knife-edge. However, five wins from the six remaining games would see Chelsea home. They only had to face one other side in the top six whereas Spurs faced a much tougher run-in; four of their remaining six matches were away, including a trip to reigning champions Leicester and their final two games at the Lane were against Arsenal and Manchester United.

Conte speaking to Match of the Day: "This league is not closed. Tottenham are on great form and playing with great enthusiasm, but we are playing a great season and we must try to reach this target."

Asmir Begovic, speaking to BBC Sport: "I think the defeat is down to a combination of things. United were more aggressive, they won second balls and probably wanted it more. They got a great start and then went on from there. We need to be better going forward. We have a lot of match-winners, it was not just a case of Eden Hazard being man-marked and taken out the game. We weren't at it today but we have a lot of character and can bounce back. We have a four-point advantage and at the start of the season we would have taken it at this stage. If we win our games it doesn't matter what Spurs do."

Jose Mourinho marched down the touchline towards the Stretford End pointing at his United badge after a win that was as much his as his players as he produced tactical masterstrokes, using the pace of Rashford and Lingard, utilising Herrera to man-mark Hazard, and recorded a win that will be celebrated in parts of north London as much as Old Trafford. United were, in fact, dominant in all areas.

Mourinho speaking to Match of the Day commented: "Maybe we didn't 'rest' players ahead of Thursday, we just chose the team we thought was the best team. We went to Stamford Bridge in the cup with same tactics, the game was totally controlled with eleven players, only the decision that made us play with ten men for the second half and ten minutes in the first half, gave Chelsea a chance to be dominant. We knew that playing this way would be very difficult for them. Marcus Rashford played fantastically well. He had a very good game at Stamford Bridge in the cup, exactly the same chance to score, because he is faster than their defenders. Today he scored and it gave the team more confidence, more stability. Chelsea are the best counter-attacking team in the country and we controlled them very well. I'm really happy with the boys. I'm happy - not because it's Chelsea, it's because we need these three points. I don't feel extra joy at beating Chelsea - we beat the leader. It doesn't matter if the leader is Chelsea or another - we beat them convincingly. Nobody can doubt our credit to win the game. I want to say I was convinced even before the cup that controlling the two players that played behind Diego. Sometimes Hazard, sometimes Hazard and Pedro, controlling the position of these two players, and controlling the full-backs because they go really deep with two wide men would create them lots of problems. And I repeat the same: They are phenomenal in counter-attack, and when they have the ball it's more difficult for them and when they have the ball we are compact and when they try to play counter-attack we were always in control of these link positions. Diego is very dangerous but the two link positions are the two positions we have to control. We did that at Stamford Bridge when we played with eleven, with ten it was more difficult and today we control."

Marcus Rashford on Sky Sports: "Today took a lot of discipline to carry out the game plan and actions. It's not so much stepping up to the plate in Ibrahimovic's absence, everyone is together and we grafted to put the work in to get the result. It was a clever pass from Herrera, we made eye contact and he put the ball exactly where I want it. It's something we need in this team."

So, Chelsea had lost two of their last three Premier League fixtures, and failed to register a shot on target in a league encounter for the first time since September 2007. It was only the fifth league defeat of the season, but all the big names 'didn't turn up'. Diego Costa fell back into bad old ways, distracted by a running battle with Marcos Rojo and Eric Bailly rather than pose any sort of threat up front. Another worry for Conte is that Chelsea had gone ten Premier League games without keeping a clean sheet for the first time since December 1996 (13 games).

Gary Cahill refused to concede his decision to help Lingard back up to his feet in the build-up to United's second goal was a costly mistake. Lingard was indirectly involved in Herrera's second and

Cahill admitted he looked "silly in hindsight" for his decision not to focus on his defending while the ball was still in play, but he did not believe it played a significant part in the goal.

Ashley Young's whipped delivery from the left was partially cleared by David Luiz. Lingard fell to the ground inside the box and Cahill was preoccupied with the winger as Herrera's shot cannoned in off Zouma. He told Sky Sports: "I don't see how it could have cost me (picking up the player from the ground). My instinct was I was nervous it could have been a penalty, the sooner I get him on his feet I can stop the ref thinking otherwise, maybe it looks silly in hindsight. We spoke before the game and said we expected them to start fast and they did. The most disappointing thing is we were below the standards we have been setting. We have to react in the right way, we didn't deserve to win, we dust ourselves off and go again. We need to realise it is not over and we need to dig in now."

Sky Sports pundit Graeme Souness agreed that Cahill's decision to check on his England international teammate Lingard was a mistake, believing he ought to have been getting his defence to push out. Souness pointed out: "Watch Cahill in the middle of the box, he's picking Lingard up, he should be out. And shout to everyone around you, 'let's get out!' Play them offside, instead he is being Mr. Nice Guy and ultimately it has cost a goal because if you are further out the goalkeeper might get a better look at it."

Gary Neville questioned the fragility of the Chelsea side as Alonso's absence unbalanced the team. In his punditry role for Sky Sports Neville said: "If they'd have lost Hazard and Costa and came here and lost I'd say fair enough. But they've lost Alonso. Are they that finely-tuned that they lose a left-back, he's a decent left back but he's not Roberto Carlos, and we're saying that basically they can just fall apart? It did unbalance them without the left-foot of Alonso, there is no doubt about that. A little bit worrying that it does though, one injury to your outfield player, that was the perfect Chelsea team apart from one player."

Neville cited losses suffered by other top teams, with Chelsea's charmed life on the injury front in comparison. "United had six or seven players missing, Liverpool had Lallana, Henderson, Mane out so every team misses players. So to think that one player missing would have that level of disturbance..."

Fragility exposed by Alonso's absence highlighted a need to strengthen in the summer transfer window. "It is disturbing moving forward, it is a glimpse moving forward for Chelsea if they are going to drop so far with one or two injuries, they do need to strengthen that squad."

He then turned on Conte. "Chelsea didn't turn up and where was Conte today? You talk about the players, but the manager has been so active on the touchline all season and you expected him to get them going, raging up and down the touchline. He seemed a little subdued today, like he lacked belief. For me, Chelsea didn't turn up."

Chelsea's next game was against their title rivals Tottenham, in the FA Cup semi-final, with the next Premier League game on the following Tuesday, at home to Southampton. It couldn't have been a more important stage of the season.

Was Conte now genuinely worried or playing mind games? He claimed the title race had become a 50-50 tussle. "We lost two games. The two games were totally different - we didn't deserve to lose against Palace - today we deserved to lose. There are six finals until now and the end. The league is open. We have a 50 per cent probability of winning the league. The pressure is normal - I prefer to have the pressure rather than not fight for the title and to stay calm. We are lucky to have the pressure - last season Chelsea had no pressure as they were 10th place. Something important is happening this season. We are doing a quick job, a miracle this season considering the problems last season."

"I am concerned, we have to work together and find quickly the right desire and ambition to win this title. For us it is a fantastic target. For me if we were able to reach this target it would be a miracle. We must understand this and find the right motivation. We stay in a great position, but Tottenham are in good form and playing very well and with enthusiasm. We must have the same."

"I think that the impact was very tough today, but when you play at Old Trafford it is normal to have this type of impact against a really strong team as United."

"We will be good to finish on top of the table and it means we deserve this. Otherwise we deserve another thing. I think Tottenham now are the best team, they are in good form and have a lot of enthusiasm. They are feeling the possibility to write history."

MONDAY, 17 APRIL 2017

"Title race blown wide open. Conte claims Chelsea only have a 50 per cent chance of winning Premier League crown after defeat at Old Trafford." - Daily Telegraph.

"It's All My Fault. Conte tries to take heat off Blues as title race ignites." - Daily Express.

A MailOnline graphic dramatically depicted the story of how Spurs had cut a lead of 13 points to four in a matter of only four weeks.

Gary Cahill's late winner at Stoke on 18 March had put Chelsea 13 points clear, but Spurs had a game in hand and beat Southampton the next day, so technically it was ten points. Nevertheless the graph neatly showed the trend of the narrowing of the gap at the top.

"No, no, no never was, not 13 points." So Conte said in the press conference. Whether it was 13 points or really ten, the fact is that it was now only four!

Captain Gary Cahill was angry at Chelsea's performance, expecting an immediate response. Cahill hoped it was a bad day at the office rather than the start of a slump. "We didn't click." he told chelseafc.com "It's disappointing. We tried to work hard in the second half, tried to push and create, but we were below the standards we've set. We weren't at the races and it makes us a bit angry. Let's hope it's an off day and it doesn't cost us too much. We expected them to start fast and we had to try and control that, and we never did."

Ruud Gullit, on Football Focus, wasn't unduly worried stating there would be "No panic over Chelsea's Old Trafford defeat" and that "Manchester United were prepared unbelievably for the game last weekend. Mourinho had lost at Chelsea and again to them in the FA Cup and he certainly didn't want to lose that game. He prepared the team mentally to be physical, especially on Hazard. It can happen, you can lose against Man United."

Chelsea and Spurs last met in the FA Cup semi-finals in 2012 and it was Chelsea who ran out comfortable 5-1 winners. Gary Cahill, who came off the bench for Roberto Di Matteo's side that afternoon, wanted a reaction. "We have to react in the right way. We have to dust ourselves off and prepare for a huge semi-final, and then we go again with some important home games coming up."

Cahill wanted a similar answer to the Palace set-back as a fifth Premier League crown was not simply waiting for Chelsea at the end of the season. "We reacted after Palace, we bounced back with two wins so it's a similar thing. We have to go again. We are still in a great position. There are only six games left, and we are still in a good position. We need to realise it's not over, we need to realise there are points to play for, and we have to dig in. No one is going to give us this league, we have to work for it like we have done for the majority of this season."

"That defeat has given us all a kick up the backside." Cahill admitted to Standard Sport. "We know the league is not over, that it will be difficult, but we know we are more than capable of doing it. I certainly think we can win our last six league games. We can't let things get too twisted. Saturday will have nothing to do with the league. It is purely a cup game. Regardless of the opposition, we want to win it. We want to win the match because we want to pick up the FA Cup, it's one of our goals. Anything else is irrelevant in my eyes. There are two aspects to the current situation and what we do. The first is a positive: we are still in a great position and have six games left to play. The negative is: no one will give us this league. We are not going to get the trophy just because we have done well for the majority of the season. We need to work hard in training and go again. But we must also remember we are still in a strong position."

Asmir Begovic insisted: "It's not getting nervy. We are an experienced group of players who have been there and done this before. We have to just focus on getting better for the next game."

Ex-England, Queens Park Rangers and Manchester City star thought it was all over though as he took to Twitter:

@RodneyMarsh10 - "Loads saying title race is ON!!! Wrong, title race has been over for weeks!"

@RodneyMarsh10 - "Spurs are not going to be perfect & Chelsea won't lose more than two games....#QED"

Meanwhile, Spurs legend, Ossie Ardiles was more focused on the FA Cup:

@osvaldooardiles - "Next Saturday game is getting more and more important. By the hour. We have to play our football. We are better than them. COYS"

Chelsea captain John Terry and the club jointly announced he would leave Stamford Bridge at the end of the season.

The 36-year-old centre-back had made 713 appearances since his debut in 1998, scoring 66 goals. He captained Chelsea 578 times - a club record - but had made only four Premier League starts this season. "I feel I still have plenty to offer on the pitch but understand that opportunities here at Chelsea will be limited for me." Terry said.

Terry is the club's most decorated individual and the third highest all-time appearance maker, behind Ron Harris and Peter Bonetti.

"I will, of course, always be a Blue and am desperate to end my final season as a Chelsea player with more silverware. I've always been conscious that I depart at the right time, in the right way, and I feel that the end of this season is the right time for the club and I. After 22 years there is so much to say and so many people to thank at this great football club. From coaches, teammates and staff to the fans who have given me so much support down the years, I can't thank you enough. There will be opportunities for me to speak further about this over the coming weeks. I will decide on my future in due course, but for now I am committed to helping the team achieve success this season. The club and I have always had a fantastic relationship, which will continue beyond my playing days. We had some really positive talks but with everything taken into careful consideration I have decided it's the right time for me to leave. Finally, words cannot describe the love I have for our football club and our amazing Chelsea fans. I would like to thank each and every one of you from the bottom of my heart for the unbelievable support you've shown me over the years. You mean the world to me and every trophy we've won during my time at the club we've won together. I will never forget the incredible journey we've been on. Thank you so much for everything."

Chelsea Football Club stated: "Everybody at Stamford Bridge would like to express our enormous gratitude to John and wish him the very best of luck for the future. John has given us more than two decades of dedicated and exceptional service. In that time he has displayed the utmost pride at wearing the Chelsea shirt, something he has done on 713 occasions since his debut in 1998, scoring 66 goals. He is the club's third highest all-time appearance-maker and has captained Chelsea a record 578 times. This season he has featured less on the field but remained an influential and inspirational member of the squad which, under Antonio Conte's guidance, sits top of the Premier League. Throughout his career 'JT' has contributed immensely to us achieving consistent success unequalled in the club's history. He has won the Champions League, four Premier League titles, the Europa League, five FA Cups and three League Cups. His 14 major honours make him our most decorated individual of all time."

Speaking on Sky Sports, Gary Neville and Jamie Carragher, who both played with Terry for England, questioned who benefited from the news coming out now. Neville said: "The timing for me is really strange, I don't understand the timing at all. I can't think why that suits Chelsea or the dressing room at all. Maybe John, but I'm sure John would sacrifice himself if they said: 'look give me a couple of weeks'. Maybe it was something pre-agreed before the game that they would do it. Maybe he has signed a pre-agreement with somebody and they couldn't keep it quiet any longer. I'm not sure who it suits and what the importance of doing it today is."

Carragher added: 'It could be a time for his actual experience, that you need there, that leadership because it's something that they lacked (on Sunday). They weren't their normal selves. With John Terry I still think he has a lot offer as a player in the Premier League."

Neville continued: "Chelsea haven't kept a clean sheet in quite a bit now. I think he could be useful for them. They're going to wobble, they're already wobbling a little bit, they're going to wobble a little bit more in these next few weeks, you'd better get him in the team to get you over the line. He has got the experience and the resilience, that sort of toughness that would get his teammates over the line and drag them by the scruff of the neck. He might be Chelsea's most important player in these next few weeks."

Carragher ended his career a one-club man. Terry's is not technically in the same position but he said "I'm not sure he's a one-club man, I think he went on loan to Nottingham Forest but you associate him as a one-club man really. I think it's sad when a player of that stature at a club puts on a shirt for someone else."

TUESDAY, 18 APRIL 2017

Thibaut Courtois would recover in time for the FA Cup semi-final after twisting an ankle during a photo-shoot for an NBA basketball promotion last Tuesday. Together with teammates Nemanja Matic, Asmir Begovic, Nathan Ake and Marcos Alonso he was involved in the event which had been organised by Chelsea at the club's training ground in Cobham.

It also emerged that Conte's preparations were interrupted in midweek by illness. Alonso had pulled out of the starting line-up in the warm-up as he was suffering with a virus, and Diego Costa and Victor Moses also felt under the weather.

The bookmakers were still very much with Chelsea though. The Blues at 1/7, Tottenham 5/1. But as last season proved, they don't always get it right as Leicester were famously 5,000-1.

Didier Drogba would have relished the chance to play in a team managed by Conte. "I would have loved (to play for Conte). I think I would have scored a few goals." Drogba told Soccer AM. "The way the team is playing everything is set up for the strikers. I've spoken to him many times and played against him when he was at Juventus. What a team - character, attitude, desire to win games and hard work. He's really doing a good job there."

WEDNESDAY, 19 APRIL 2017

Here we go again… Inter will offer Conte £41.8m, according to reports about his future that resurfaced in Italy.

La Gazzetta dello Sport reported that Conte, along with Atletico Madrid boss Diego Simeone, were on Inter's radar to replace Stefano Pioli. It is understood that Inter believed Simeone would be easier to acquire but that they would offer Conte a five-year contract worth just over £8.3m a season.

Chinese Super League side Tianjin Quanjian FC were "still working" on a deal to sign Costa. They had not lost their interest, and billionaire owner Shu Yuhui insisted a deal was still in the pipeline. "I can only say that we are still working on the deal (to sign Costa). And we have already made contacts with several players." he told Chinese digital sports media platform, Sina Sports. "We have high standards (in buying foreign players) and those players prefer top clubs such as Bayern Munich and Real Madrid. It's safe to say that we have the same transfer targets as those illustrious clubs. We may have to pay a bigger price because our club is now competing with Real Madrid and Bayern Munich."

Costa's form had certainly dipped in 2017 since he was linked with a move and Conte was planning for life without the striker, with Romelu Lukaku and Alexis Sanchez on his wish list.

Eden Hazard was moved to once more deny a falling-out between himself and Jose Mourinho. "With Jose I had a super rapport." he explained to TF1's Telefoot. "The year before, I was the Player of the Season and maybe he expected more from me. I was not so good and it was complicated. I was always close with him and with Antonio Conte it's the same."

Asked to describe how Conte differs from his predecessor, he stated. "They have different methods Conte works a great deal on tactics but Mourinho let it be. For me, I had great moments with Mourinho for two years and this year with Conte everything is going very well. I always take the positive from coaches. The two are different managers. They have always won, here and in the past. Many people said I didn't listen to Mourinho, but that's not the case. It's not at all the case. I've always had a lot of respect for him."

Hazard had never won the FA Cup and wanted to complete his haul of English silverware. "The FA Cup is a massive competition in England, it's the oldest cup in the world." Hazard told the official semi-final match programme. "Since I came here, I have reached the semi-final but I've never had the chance to play the final. So I hope this can be my first year to reach the final and, why not, to win the competition. Wembley is a massive stadium to play at - it's one of the best in the world and this stadium is all about the big games. We need to shine when we come to play here."

THURSDAY, 10 APRIL 2017

Conte reacted to defeat at Manchester United by shaking up training, trying new combinations.

John Terry was under consideration after Gary Cahill was taken ill. Cahill was admitted to hospital on Tuesday and released on Thursday after a bug hit Stamford Bridge. Conte had to decide whether to risk Cahill or recall Terry, who was now officially in his last season with the club.

Cahill's illness - he was treated for gastroenteritis - was not connected with the bug which hit Conte's squad prior to the defeat against United.

"He arrived on the training ground with a bit of a fever and our doctor preferred to take him hospital to check his condition," added Conte. "Now he's getting better. If you ask me for tomorrow my answer is it will be very difficult." said Conte on Cahill's chances.

Although Terry had managed only 366 minutes in the Premier League this season he had made three starts in the FA Cup. Kurt Zouma, who replaced Alonso in the line-up against Manchester United, was also an option. "It's impossible." said Conte when asked if Cahill might feature. "It is not a serious problem, he is getting better but this period has not been lucky for us. Ake deserves this chance. He has shown me great commitment and worked very hard. His behaviour has been great. Don't forget he was playing every game with Bournemouth and he wanted to come and work with us and help us fight for the title. He is a good player and he is ready for this opportunity. I trust him."

Conte would consider Terry for the role in the centre of his back-three where David Luiz plays, and confessed he was disappointed to learn he would be losing his club captain at the end of the season. "John has been very important for me." said Conte. "The problem is that John wants to play regularly and we have to respect his decision. I was a footballer and I know when you arrive at this point in your career and your mind and body tell you that you want to play regularly it is right to continue. Because when you finish you finish."

Bookmakers William Hill had a "massive gamble" on John Terry joining Arsenal as the odds were slashed from 33-1 to 5-1, with 90 per cent of the bets coming from the Reading area and a large number placed by new accounts. William Hill spokesman Joe Crilly said: "The figures would not have been massive but they were massive for a novelty market."

Diego Costa had lost form at a vital time of the campaign but according to his manager "He is keeping the goals for the finale of the season. It is the right moment to score." smiled Conte. He added: "You're restarting this about Diego to China. The most important thing for us is to be focused. Has he lost his focus? No, no!"

Costa was the toughest forward Toby Alderweireld had faced. He first came across him when he joined Atletico Madrid in the summer of 2013 from Ajax. During their time together at Atletico, Alderweireld marked Costa in training. "Was he (Costa) the toughest forward I marked? Yes, he's a winner." Alderweireld told the London Evening Standard. "He is talented, strong, clinical in front of goal and he has a good technique. He is one of the best in the world. I was at Ajax as a young kid and then I went to Atletico, playing with the big boys. It helps so much to train with people like Costa."

Chelsea and Tottenham each had four of their players named in the PFA Premier League team of the year. Cahill, Luiz, Kante and Hazard were Chelsea's representatives. Tottenham's quartet were Walker, Rose, Alli and Kane, with De Gea, Mane and Lukaku making up the XI.

FRIDAY, 21 APRIL 2017

Pochettino moved the pressure onto Conte: "If there's a favourite it is Chelsea. They are more experienced. We are talking about a team who has won European competitions in the last five years.

They are top of the Premier League, with players who won the World Cup and a great manager who has won the title in Italy. Our players have won nothing - or maybe some titles - but we are in a good moment too. We are improving. We are hungry, and to challenge this team is important for Tottenham. We will see. It is important to enjoy the game. We must feel the happiness. It is a very important competition and we are fighting the best team in England. We are showing we learned from last season. If we only look at the data we improved a lot. With six to play, we have 71 points when last season we finished with 70. We have improved, that's a reality. The team is playing in a good way, exciting football, scoring goals, conceding not too much. Now is the moment to translate those statistics and that feeling and show if we've grown up and learned. If you are very close to winning the league or the FA Cup, that's the most difficult step to achieve. It's nice to say we are ready and we want to win. Nice words. But it's not an easy task. It's difficult to win trophies. We are in different part of the process with different momentum to Chelsea."

It is almost three years since Pochettino arrived from Southampton and, at the end of his first season, Spurs were beaten by Chelsea in the League Cup final. "When we signed it was all about how we can reduce the gap with the top four. Not only have we reduced the gap but we are fighting for the Premier League, to win titles. That's the position we wanted and we achieved that. For us, it is a big thing that people include Tottenham in that level of clubs like Chelsea, Man City, United, Liverpool and Arsenal. It means something important is growing here. That feeling is good, I like it. It means a lot. We are in a completely different project and it makes us proud."

Spurs had to banish the mental block they developed at Wembley. "I will tell you after." said Pochettino, when asked if Spurs might end the trend. "It's true we struggled a bit but we need to make Wembley our home, get that feeling, and this is a good opportunity. We were in a new competition for us, the Champions League and it came in a period when we struggled a little bit and you can see what Monaco have done since. We were competing with a very good team."

Conte, in reaction to Pochettino, rejected the theory that Tottenham were the underdogs as they had to win something soon. "Tottenham must be considered at the top. Tottenham now is a really great power in English football. They have been working for three years, I think it's the right moment to consider them, and not to consider them the underdog and have this excuse. They are a great team and for the second year are fighting for the title. Last year they missed this, this year they are trying again, and I think in the future they will fight every year for the title. They are full of strong players and they are building something important. There is a moment where you have to finish. I think this is the right moment."

Conte did not believe the result would impact on the title race. "I think these are two different competitions. The FA Cup is a great competition, with great tradition, the oldest competition in the world, and then there is the league. They are two different competitions. I don't think if one team wins or loses it can affect the other competition."

Conte wanted to emulate fellow Italian Carlo Ancelotti by winning the Double with Chelsea in his first season in English football, although their circumstances are different. "You must always hope and you must work to reach this target, but I think my situation, if you compare my situation with Ancelotti's situation it is totally different. We started our work to put the foundation and to build something important. I think in that moment, that was the foundation."

David Luiz spoke highly Tottenham, suggesting their players are "monsters".

"For me they are an amazing team with an amazing coach in Mauricio Pochettino." Luiz told the

London Evening Standard. "They are the best physical team in the league. All eleven players are monsters. I love that team. It will be a difficult game for us. We need to be ready to play against one of the best sides in this League. But it was always going to be hard when you reach a semi-final. Will we have to be monsters too? Yes. Chelsea also have some monsters and play like a monster like N'Golo Kante. We have different kinds of monsters. It will be a fantastic game; both clubs are in amazing shape. It will be a top-quality match to watch and you have to play top quality to win."

Chelsea were playing their first game at Wembley this season, while Tottenham had used the national stadium as their home ground for European ties, ahead of their expected move there next year while they rebuild White Hart Lane. Spurs had failed to make it feel like home though, winning only one of their four European fixtures there. Conte commented: "For sure, to play in your stadium is an advantage. It's the same for us. I think we play at Stamford Bridge it would be another thing, if you play at Wembley. And it's the same for Tottenham. This season it's very important to have your stadium and that is your stadium and you stay in your house and you feel this, and your opponent feels this when he comes to play against you."

Conte was not ready to give up his dream of a league and cup double without a fight: "We have a semi-final and then six games to go to try to write history. I think we must be focused about this and we must enjoy this moment and to stay together and to fight together. Then, if someone is better than us at the end of the season we must be honest and to clap them. The most important thing for us is to be focused. To continue to do what we are doing until now. To be focused on the present, to keep the concentration. We have to finish a good season for us and then we want to do something extraordinary for me, for the players, for the club."

Several ex-players were entering the debate in the lead-up to the semi-final tie, including:

"Chelsea will win league" predicted Glenn Hoddle, the former Chelsea and Tottenham manager on 5 live. "I don't think this tie will have an effect on the title race. If Chelsea and Tottenham were going to play one another again in the league this season then maybe. This semi-final is a one-off game. The league will take care of itself. Those last four fixtures Chelsea have got are relatively easy and that's why I think Chelsea will win the league." He also added: "I have a sneaky feeling Tottenham are coming into good form. Chelsea are having a slight wobble. I've got a feeling Tottenham might edge it."

"Tottenham do need to win a trophy" according to Martin Keown, the former Arsenal defender on Football Focus, suggesting the pressure was on Spurs now. "This Tottenham team is purring. Other sides look with envy at what Tottenham are about and what they might accomplish. In particular, with players like Dele Alli getting all the plaudits, Spurs have such a strong midfield. But Tottenham do need to win a trophy, because that is the natural next step and it will allow the club to keep all their top players."

Remembering Ugo Ehiogu

Tributes poured in for Ugo Ehiogu. The former England defender died at the age of 44 after suffering a cardiac arrest yesterday. England manager Gareth Southgate, who was Ehiogu's centre-back partner at Aston Villa and Middlesbrough, described him as "colossal" on the pitch and a "gentle giant" off it. Pochettino said: "A big loss for us, a big loss for all the Tottenham family. We need to adapt in our life to live with that pain in our heart. All we can do is give all our support to his family."

"It is very difficult to comprehend" said a shocked Gary Mabbutt on Football Focus. "As you can imagine there is a very sombre atmosphere at Tottenham. The whole football world was shocked and saddened. I was at the training ground with him laughing saying he looked fitter and younger than when he was playing. Most people remember Ugo's performances for Aston Villa, Middlesbrough and England and won't know that in the last few years he has been instrumental in putting Tottenham where they are today. He has been nurturing, mentoring and coaching all of those players. He has done a fantastic job and will be difficult to replace. He was a friend, a family man and a gentleman of the game."

Martin Keown added: "Ugo Ehiogu was a mountain of a man, very strong but very unassuming away from the football pitch. He was everybody's friend, loved a chat, loved football. It's such a shame and for Tottenham, I think this could have an effect on the players. I know the Spurs medical team worked to keep him alive and it's just so tragic."

SATURDAY, 22 APRIL 2017
Chelsea 4-2 Tottenham Hotspur
FA Cup, Semi-Final

The team news caused much debate and comment.

No Hazard. No Costa. Conte 'will not hear the last of it if it goes wrong' was the general reaction from the media. What would the media say, though, if they get it wrong and Conte gets it right? Nothing, usually!

Dean Saunders, ex-Liverpool and Wales striker speaking on Final Score: "Would Tottenham have rested Dele Alli and Harry Kane for today's game? Of course not. It's a shocking decision by Antonio Conte. I had thought Chelsea would win this, but looking at the line-ups I now fancy Spurs. If I was one of the best players in the world, a Diego Costa or Eden Hazard, I would be devastated to not be playing in the semi-final of the FA Cup at Wembley."

Frank Lampard on the BBC: "Conte must have thought long and hard about it. We will see, it will either be a genius move or, if they lose, people will be looking at it."

Danny Murphy, former England midfielder on BBC One: "A couple of surprises, but still a fascinating game and so many battles all over the pitch. The absence of Diego Costa and Eden Hazard was a surprise, but that's a compliment to Tottenham. Defensively Antonio Conte wants everyone on board, sometimes you don't get that with Hazard."

Chris Waddle, ex-Spurs and England winger at Wembley for 5 live Sport: "I think Diego Costa is out of form and I can understand him being left out. But I do not understand not selecting Eden Hazard. Antonio Conte must have in his mind two upcoming games back-to-back in the league. Of course, he can always bring either or both on from the bench. Tottenham will be delighted that Eden Hazard is not playing, but I'm of the opinion that Willian is a top player. Nevertheless, I think when comparing the two line-ups it's advantage Spurs. Tottenham are a big side, and they are especially dangerous from set-pieces. It's one way they've scored plenty of goals this season."

Leon Osman, ex-Everton midfielder on Final Score: "In the semi-finals of the FA Cup, not to play your strongest team is a big surprise. Chelsea have some breathing space in the league, so I don't understand the logic of resting players."

Conte explained "I took this decision about our starting XI. At this moment it is part of the season whenever we play any game it is important to have a player in your mind and make a decision. You risk in the same way if you start with Diego or Eden or they come on. I try to make the best decision."

As it transpired, Eden Hazard came off the bench to make the decisive contribution in a classic Wembley semi-final.

Conte had taken one of the biggest gambles leaving Hazard and Diego Costa on the bench against a Spurs side high on confidence after closing to within four points in the title race. Conte raised eyebrows with a team selection that also saw outcast Michy Batshuayi given a rare outing on this huge occasion, leading to suggestions Conte was prioritising the title race. But Hazard emerged as substitute to help settle an enthralling encounter.

Conte summarised: "I am proud for this achievement. It is great for the players for me. This is my first season in England and it is great to fight for the title and reach the final of the FA Cup, a great competition. I am pleased for my players and for our fans. Today they were great from the start until the end. Now we have to continue, on Tuesday we have another tough game, I hope our fans push us a lot."

"During the season there is a moment as a coach you must take a strong decision. You have to take a risk. If you win the plan worked, if you don't the responsibility is on you. I think today our plan worked very well."

Willian, in for Hazard, gave Chelsea the lead with a fine free-kick after only five minutes. Harry Kane levelled with an unorthodox stooping header. Willian put Conte's side back in front from the penalty spot just before the break after Son Heung-min stupidly went to ground fouling Victor Moses. Conte was forced to interfere as Michy Batshuayi attempted to take the penalty with the match finely poised at 1-1. Batshuayi stepped up and grabbed the ball but Conte could be heard shouting "Willian" from the touchline and Azpilicueta intervened by grabbing the ball off the Belgian striker and handing it to Willian. The Brazilian sent Lloris the wrong way to give Chelsea the lead going into the break.

Spurs then gained the momentum after Dele Alli converted Christian Eriksen's brilliant pass seven minutes after half-time before Hazard was introduced along with Costa on the hour. Hazard shot powerfully past Hugo Lloris after 75 minutes and Nemanja Matic set up an appearance alongside either Arsenal or Manchester City in the FA Cup Final with a spectacular drive five minutes later.

Conte used Hazard and Costa at a crucial point, on the hour mark, with Spurs the more assertive team after having equalised for the second time. Hazard, who had previously scored the goal that ended Spurs title chances last season, was involved in what turned out to be the defining moment 15 minutes after coming on with a low drive that gave Chelsea a lead they would not surrender for a third time.

To emphasis that Chelsea's squad was far stronger in depth than Tottenham's, they were also able to bring on Cesc Fabregas to help change the game.

Since beating Chelsea 2-1 to lift the Carling Cup in 2008, Spurs had now played at Wembley nine times, winning once, losing seven and drawing one. This was their third FA Cup semi-final loss in that time, which also included a 2-0 defeat to Portsmouth in 2010 and a 5-1 thrashing by Chelsea two years later. They also lost League Cup finals to Manchester United in 2009 and Chelsea in 2015.

This emphatic response from Conte's side re-asserted themselves over their closest rivals with a win they hoped would have sufficient psychological impact to give them that extra push towards the league title.

Hazard remarked: "It's always good to win this kind of game - a semi against a London team - so for the fans it's good. It's my first final in five years at Chelsea so it's good." And, on starting the match on the bench he conceded: "When you play football you want to play every game, but the manager did a great choice - he put in Willian and he scored two goals."

Scorer of the stunning fourth goal, Matic at pitch-side on 5 live Sport commented: "It was a nice goal! But first of all I want to say I am very happy for the team that we're going to play in the final. Today was hard against a very good team. Congratulations to Spurs, who didn't give up. I am happy for my goal, it was a great goal, but it's not the best I've ever scored. I scored a harder one in a Benfica vs Porto derby (fans immediately scrambling onto YouTube to find that goal)... this is perhaps my second best ever! It's great when you have a chance to play in this stadium. For our supporters, you can see this is something special. To have a chance to win this trophy is significant for us as players. This result gives us more confidence of course - it's always good to win. Now we have to recover quickly for the next game on Tuesday."

Pochettino added: "Congratulations to Chelsea. We dominated the game but they were more clinical than us. I feel proud, we were fantastic in the way we played and in our philosophy. They had five shots and scored four goals and we score only two. The penalty for me was a soft penalty or was not a penalty. To go into the changing room 2-1 down was difficult and again we played well in the second half and scored but then they came back. Only now we can look forward. We are four points behind them and we will try to win our next game. I am not worried. The team is strong, we are focused. We were competing today with one of the best teams in Europe. Did we deserve more? Sure, but that is football. Now we will try to be calm, watch the game again and try to improve. We have another difficult game coming up against Crystal Palace. It is a tough league to play but we are OK."

Conte then challenged his players and fans to use this victory as a springboard to win the Premier League but complained that his club were being unfairly treated by being forced to play again against Southampton on Tuesday night due to TV scheduling, while Tottenham had an extra day's rest before their fixture against Crystal Palace. "We have to try to exploit the momentum because, for sure, the win is very important against a team that is fighting you for the title. We must exploit this. Also, we have to know that on Tuesday, we have a really tough game against Southampton with technical players who want to come to Stamford Bridge and play a really good game. For this reason, I want our fans to be there to help the players on the pitch. It is a really important moment for us and we need our fans in the same way today they pushed us a lot. It's very important."

Conte elaborated on his annoyance that TV demands meant Chelsea had one day's less recovery than Tottenham, with Sky Sports showing both games. "It is not easy to understand why. I don't understand that we get one day less against Southampton, a team that has rested for ten days. And Tottenham have to play on Wednesday. One day more to rest against Palace, who have to play tomorrow (Sunday). It is very difficult to understand this dynamic. At the end of the season, you must try to have balance to understand the situation and put the teams in the same situation to fight. We have to have the best answer on the pitch. But it's not easy."

Conte had rested Costa and Hazard but had brought them on with the game at 2-2 on the hour. "It is not easy to decide to start the game without two really important players like Eden and Diego but you must take this responsibility and involve your players in your plan and then to take this risk. Our plan was this and I tried also to tell my players to stay in the game because, if we passed more time, it was better for us. Then I decided in the last thirty minutes to put on Eden and Diego, and Cesc, who don't forget, he was very important for us."

Looking ahead now, Fabregas was fully focused on the target. "(We have) six games where every single one of them we need three points, because I don't believe Spurs will drop too many."

He admitted that Chelsea's absence from European competition was beneficial as the leaders faced a crucial period of fixtures. "It's the first time Chelsea have not been in Europe for a very long time. Maybe it has been a little bit of an advantage because we didn't have to rotate as much." Conte did, of course, rotate at Wembley and Fabregas added: "To have these kind of players and then when we are struggling at 2-2 in the second half we can bring these type of players it's fantastic and it worked very well."

Chelsea's lead had been seven points before the Easter Sunday loss at Mourinho's United and Fabregas praised this response. "The good thing this season is that every time we had a defeat or draw we bounced back very quickly. We didn't have time to let ourselves feel sorry. That's a good quality. There's always moments for every team to, not collapse, but to drop points. It happened to us in the last four games. We just have to make sure it doesn't happen again. There are winners in this team and we have to keep it up. It's these little details that make you champions or not."

The reaction of the bench behind Conte was striking. John Terry and Costa hugged as Willian curled in a free-kick and Kurt Zouma wailed in disbelief and fell into the arms of Nathaniel Chalobah as Matic fired the fourth into the top corner. The video clip went viral. "Everyone was together and celebrating." said Fabregas, who won the FA Cup with Arsenal. "We are full of winners and I'm proud to be here. The strength, that's what you need to win titles. And that's what we will need to do in every single game until the end of the season if we really want to win something. You never want to accept it as a player, whoever you are. When you are used to playing all the time you feel a bit down. What I like is that we scored the first goal and everyone on the bench was together and celebrating. The togetherness we had on the bench, scoring the goals and then coming on and not with the feeling like 'Oh, I was on the bench', but coming on to make a difference and show character and hunger to win. It means the whole squad is ready to go. Whoever plays is ready to step up. It's good to see."

Hazard was back showing his ability to influence big games. "Eden can be whatever he wants to be." Fabregas added. "Ability-wise, there is only one player above him and we all know who he is - Lionel Messi. He's up there with the best. For me, he has to be more selfish as all the top players are and have that killer instinct to score more goals. I've told him many times. Sometimes when we have a counter-attack and he passes the ball, I tell him: 'You have the capability to score by yourself, do it'. I'm sure he will improve in the future. And then he will be unstoppable. We have to help him to achieve that."

Immediately thoughts were on the preparation for Southampton and their bid to close out the first half of a possible double before returning to Wembley at the end of May. "Southampton didn't play for ten days and it will be a very tough game." Fabregas said. "It's one of the most important games of the season. To achieve the Double would be something special, especially in England. Sometimes you need a bit of luck and definitely we need to be very, very consistent until the end of the season."

Conte believed finishing with two trophies would be a bigger achievement than that of Carlo Ancelotti, who inherited a team of Petr Cech, Ashley Cole, John Terry, Frank Lampard and Didier Drogba at their peak. "I think that now at Chelsea we are in a period of transition. In this season, we have lost Ivanovic, Mikel and next season we lose John Terry. We are talking about players who wrote the history of this club. They won a lot. Now we have to find the right substitutes for these players and then work to put these players at the same level. I think that in the period with Carlo - and Carlo is the best Italian coach, I have great respect for him - he arrived at Chelsea when they had a really strong squad. Now we are building. We are building something important. We need time. It's not easy when you lose these types of players, but we need to show patience to build the foundations and then improve every season. If you ask me last season, after our 10th place, and this season you stay on top of the table and you reach the FA Cup final, but you didn't change a lot, I think it's great. But we must continue to work and improve."

Conte argued that Chelsea were actually behind Tottenham in their development. "If you compare our team with Tottenham's, Mauricio Pochettino has worked for three years. I started to work only seven or eight months ago. If we are able to take the right players to improve this squad and to continue to work with these players, we can improve for sure."

Alan Shearer on BBC One said: "Tottenham had a big chance today. There was no Cahill, Costa or Hazard in the starting line-up. I think it will damage Spurs. It was a brilliant game of football. Chelsea deserved it. They were dogged and determined. We talked about the decision to leave, in particular, Hazard out but Conte had the firepower to come on off the bench. You could have had two or three goalkeepers in goal for Matic's strike and they wouldn't have saved it. Conte's game plan worked perfectly. The guys he left out gave a reaction and the guy he brought in scored two goals."

Jermaine Jenas speaking at Wembley: "Spurs didn't deserve to lose the game in the way they did. They were the better team throughout the game - they dominated possession. But granted, Chelsea were much more potent in front of goal. Spurs have dominated that game. Chelsea were on the back foot for the majority of it - hanging on."

Chris Waddle also at Wembley for 5 live Sport: "For long periods Tottenham were the better side but the game turned when Eden Hazard came on. Chelsea used all their experience and were well organised. Credit Tottenham who gave everything they had but it just wasn't to be. We didn't predict the game would be as enjoyable as it was. You can see now on the pitch how much respect there is between the two teams. As for Matic's strike, there are times when you hit the ball and you can't believe how clean a strike it was. When it happens, and when it flies into the top corner in off the crossbar, then you know it's your day. There's not a lot between these teams. Tottenham dominated for long periods, but the difference? When Chelsea created chances they took them. Eden Hazard has changed this game. As soon as he came on he's made a difference. Yes, Tottenham have tired slightly but the impact Hazard has had cannot be debated. Antonio Conte's decision to bench Hazard? Well, he got it spot on."

Robbie Savage, later on BBC 6-0-6, added: "Spurs had more possession but if you don't do anything with the ball you don't win. The substitutions won the game for Chelsea, so well done Antonio Conte. Mauricio Pochettino is a very good manager but why did he play Son as a left wing-back? And of course it was Son who conceded the penalty. Antonio Conte got his tactics spot on. He left out Diego Costa and Eden Hazard and was able to bring them on late. When the team was announced I expect the Tottenham players thought today might well be their day. But fair play to Chelsea's manager, who once again has been proven right - his substitutions won the game."

SUNDAY, 23 APRIL 2017

Alan Shearer, reflecting on the BBC online, said: "The way Chelsea beat Tottenham in Saturday's FA Cup semi-final showed why they are going to win the Premier League title too. As usual, Antonio Conte's side were dogged and resilient - and the manager's game plan worked perfectly. They were content to soak up Spurs' pressure and possession and, when they went up the other end, they took their chances brilliantly. The Blues scored four goals against the team with the best defensive record in the top flight, so you cannot say they did not deserve their victory. And anyone who doubted Chelsea after their defeats against Manchester United and Crystal Palace just had to watch them at Wembley to see how good they are. This was a superb display that won a brilliant cup tie and, psychologically, could and probably should pull them across the line in the title race too. They know they beat their closest rivals despite not having three key players for the majority of the game - Gary Cahill, who was out injured, and Eden Hazard and Diego Costa, who came off the bench with less than half an hour to play. Conte's decision to leave Costa and, in particular, Hazard out of his starting line-up was a huge call, but it worked. The guy he brought in for Hazard - Willian - scored twice. Then, when he brought Hazard on in the second half, he changed the game. Hazard scored Chelsea's vital third goal and he also rolled the ball into Nemanja Matic for his fantastic strike to make it 4-2. When you make big decisions, you want them to work in your favour, and things could not really have worked out any better for Conte on Saturday. He has not got very much wrong in his first season in the Premier League, especially since switching to his favoured formation of three at the back at the end of September. The Double is definitely on, which would be an incredible achievement. Kenny Dalglish (with Liverpool in 1986) and Carlo Ancelotti (with Chelsea in 2010) are the only other managers to have done it in their first season in England, and now Conte has a fantastic chance of doing the same."

Harry Kane and his teammates wanted to win the Premier League for Ugo Ehiogu. "Ugo was a great character around the training ground." said Kane. "The last couple of days have been tough. It was just shocking news. Of course we'll do everything we can to win the league for him - we wanted to win (on Saturday) for him and for ourselves as well. There are still six tough games left in the Premier League. We can't control what Chelsea do now."

Tottenham now go to Crystal Palace on Wednesday. "A lot of people will be looking at us and waiting to see what will happen." Kane added. "Are we strong enough to bounce back? I think we are. We were the better team but for one reason or another we didn't get over the finish line. It's not easy but we will fight until the end. We can't control what Chelsea do. They will obviously be buzzing from this game but it doesn't always mean you're going to win every other game you play."

Alexis Sanchez's scrambled extra-time winner secured Arsenal an FA Cup final showdown date with Chelsea and ensured Pep Guardiola would end a season without a trophy for the first time in his coaching career.

Sanchez settled a contentious semi-final eleven minutes into the extra period after City failed to clear Ozil's free-kick. Arsenal showed great resilience to come from behind and eased the pressure on Arsene Wenger, after Sergio Aguero raced clear of Nacho Monreal to put City ahead in the 62nd minute. Monreal made amends with the equaliser eleven minutes later as he volleyed in Alex Oxlade-Chamberlain's cross at the far post. However, City were left nursing a serious sense of injustices as they had a goal wrongly ruled out in the first half when Leroy Sane's cross was adjudged to have gone out of play before Aguero and Raheem Sterling combined to turn it into the net, while Yaya Toure and Fernandinho both hit the woodwork after the break. Wenger was now aiming for a record seventh FA Cup triumph.

Thirty-nine-year-old Chelsea legend, Didier Drogba, who had scored 16 goals in as many appearances against Arsenal, took to Twitter and teased Gooners that he would be making a comeback for the final:

"Dear @PHXRisingFC I'll be off on loan with @ChelseaFC for two days 26/27th of May, just to make it 17/17 against #afc #IswearIBeBack #banter"

N'Golo Kante won the PFA Player of the Year during the ceremony at the Grosvenor Hotel in London and Dele Alli won the young player prize for the second successive year.

@nglkante - "So proud for such an honour! So amazing. As I always said, it's a team work: thx to my teammates, @ChelseaFC members and all the fans."

After the award Kante said: "It's a huge honour to be chosen by the other players. It's the biggest honour to get this award. My first two seasons were very beautiful. Last season was very beautiful. This season so far, we have had a good season but we have to finish well."

Kante could become first player to win successive titles with different clubs if Chelsea can stay ahead of Spurs. He had now played every minute in the league this season apart from the Boxing Day game against Bournemouth, when he was suspended, and the final eleven minutes against Tottenham on 4 January.

BBC pundit and former England midfielder, Danny Murphy, speaking on Match of the Day 2, described Kante as irreplaceable in the Chelsea line-up. "He's the one you can't replace. If Eden Hazard wasn't there, you could put Willian in. Kante is the best midfielder in the Premier League, if not Europe."

Matthew Upson, the former England defender, added on the same programme: "It's 100% deserved. He is the most valuable player in the Premier League with his contribution. He might not be the most creative player, or have the biggest sudden impact, but over the course of the season he is the most valuable player in the Premier League. He's been outstanding."

Speaking earlier this season, BBC pundit Phil Neville described Kante as "the one who has knitted this Chelsea team together" adding that "He will redefine what we are looking for from a midfield player."

Kante's total of 110 tackles in the Premier League this season was second only to Everton midfielder Idrissa Gueye (127), while 72 interceptions was bettered only by Ander Herrera of Manchester United.

Watford captain Troy Deeney recently spoke about what it is like to play against Kante - an insight that perhaps explains why his peers voted him the best of their number. "Whenever we broke on them last season, I always had the fear factor that Kante was coming back and I knew we didn't have much time before he got there. Even if I actually did have time, I always thought he might be there, so I would rush things a bit."

Also during the evening David Beckham received the PFA's merit award for his achievements for club and country, and discussing the impression Kante had made on him he said: "He's a special talent. What I like about him - actually what I love about him - (is) he plays the game in such a humble way. He works hard, he can pass the ball, he can tackle, he can score goals. To have won the Premier League the way he did last season with Leicester was special, and the position Chelsea are in at the moment - if they go on to win the title it'll be a special couple of years for him. We'll see what happens towards the end of the season, but he's a special talent, and to be the man mountain that he is, and the size he is, says a lot about him."

MONDAY, 24 APRIL 2017

Interestingly, Chelsea had spent around £110m on their squad last summer but recouped over half, £60m, on Oscar alone in January and Conte was keen to talk about his thoughts and plans on spending money in the transfer market. "I think this season it's very important to understand that it's not always about who spends more money who wins." said Conte. "Otherwise, in this league, this season the name of the team wasn't Chelsea or Tottenham or Arsenal or Liverpool. You understand? I think in every situation it's important to find the right balance. If you have to spend money, try and spend that money in the right way to take players with the right characteristics for your idea of football."

Conte wants to make significant additions to his squad. Asked if he expected City and United to spend more again, he replied: "Yes, like every year. You've seen the past. You can see that every season they spend a lot of money. I don't want to go into the situation of the other teams, other clubs, other managers. Every single club decides their own strategy. But, if you ask me, this season isn't the only season the Manchester clubs have spent a lot of money. Look at the past. It's normal for them. It's right for them to do this, to reinforce their teams, if they think this is the right way to win the title. But, for us I repeat, this season is very important because we are trying to build something important for the present, to put the foundations down and be strong, stronger for the future. And to build, also, slowly slowly to become a real power. A real power in the future."

Manchester United spent £89m on Pogba alone, while Chelsea signed Kante for a relative bargain price of £30m. "N'Golo was a target, our target and we were very pleased to reach this target in our transfer market." said Conte. "I think we spent this money in the right way. Sometimes you can see players with great talent, with great talent to score goals, these players are important. But if you trust in an idea of football and you trust in the team, it's important to have a squad with good balance, with talent, but also with people like N'Golo - very strong to win the ball, to fight and work hard for the team. You must be pleased with this."

Conte believed this was a crucial week in the title race, with forthcoming games against Southampton and Everton. On winning the title in his first season in English football, would it be his finest achievement? "Yes, for sure. For sure. For me, for the players, for the club. I think, now, to win the title in England is a great achievement. A top achievement for the coach, the players and the club. To win in England these days is not easy. To win this league is difficult. I repeat, we must be proud in our work. We must know that now it's a good season. It will remain a good season. But we want it to become a great season, a fantastic season. To become a great or fantastic season, there is only one way - to try and win."

Conte rejected Fabregas's call for Hazard to be more selfish, saying it is "not my idea of football". Fabregas said Hazard could reach the level of Messi if he was "selfish" and showed greater "killer instinct". In direct contrast Conte said: "In my team, I don't want selfish players. I prefer to lose a game than to have a selfish player. For me, it's sad to listen to this. The first target for every great champion is to play for the team and to put your talent into the team. The best players in the world don't exist without a team. I will never understand this. Never, never. I don't want this and I can't accept this. I don't want my club to buy me a selfish player one day. Never. No."

Hazard insisted there was nothing to report on the contract front. He told Sky Sports: "There is no sign of a new contract for the moment. I am focused on the last month, and we will talk later. It's not in my mind now. I have two or three years left. I just want to finish the season well and we will see afterwards."

After beating Spurs a pleased Conte confirmed: "It's great to know that we have a final to play a week after the championship finishes." And, with Cahill back in training: "I have in my mind the starting XI but tomorrow I want to check the physical condition of every player. But we have trained very well this season and we have a lot of energy to face this type of situation. It is important for us to win and look at ourselves, but we all know that tomorrow it won't be easy because Southampton is a very good team with a good coach and good players."

Chelsea had won only three of their last eight Premier League matches against Southampton at Stamford Bridge, losing last season's fixture 3-1. Saints had been a tough nut to crack in the past and now Chelsea had lost two of their last four league games, twice as many as in the previous 22 matches. The stakes couldn't be much higher and Conte warned that their Italian striker Manolo Gabbiadini has one of the best left foots in the world.

Marcos Alonso declared himself ready having finally overcome the effects of a sickness bug that had ruled him out of the clash at Old Trafford. In fact, he admitted that he was so ill before the game that he missed the second half after falling asleep on the team bus. "I was throwing up the night before and wasn't feeling very good. I tried to do the warm-up the following day but I was about to faint on the pitch. I did not want to ask for a substitution after five minutes, so I pulled out. I watched the first half in the directors' box but I had to go to the team coach to have a lie down on my own. I fell asleep (and missed the second half) as I was feeling so bad."

Despite playing the full 90 minutes against Spurs, he was still feeling the effects of the illness on his match fitness. "I took a couple of days off and did not eat a lot. But I felt good against Spurs. I was a little bit tired in the first part of the game because it had been two weeks since I'd last played, but I'm ready for Tuesday."

Antoine Griezmann's advisor confirmed that there was interest from United, City and Chelsea. Eric Olhats, the scout who helped to discover the Atletico Madrid forward, said: "We're at the stage of gathering information from clubs who have a concrete interest." Talking to French TV station Telefoot, he said: "There is an unavoidable €100m (£85m) clause so that restricts the number of candidates. You have United, City, Chelsea, Barcelona and Real Madrid. United were the first to come and see us and the most concrete in their wishes."

TUESDAY, 25 APRIL 2017
Chelsea 4-2 Southampton
Premier League

The home crowd were celebrating silverware ahead of the kick-off as fans were able to acknowledge Kante as the PFA Player of the Year. The midfielder was presented to the crowd, with the stadium announcer hailing it as the club's "first trophy of the year".

Fortunately the match didn't turn out to be an anti-climax as Chelsea restored their lead at the top to seven points even after a very nervy and uncertain period for much of the first half.

A delighted Conte said: "We passed a big step - a big psychological step - after the defeat against Manchester United. We lost three points, then we had to prepare a semi-final against Tottenham, then another tough game here. Mentally we have had a really important test. Our answer was very good. We must be pleased. But we must think this race is open. We reached the final in the FA Cup, which is a great incentive for us. But the other competition, the league, is totally open. But I think we are ready to fight until the end. But now it's normal. It's normal that we have to try to push until the end to keep this position."

Eden Hazard and Diego Costa were back in the starting line-up and the two combined brilliantly after only five minutes to put the title favourites into the lead. Costa cleverly pulled the ball back on a break for Hazard to strike first time low and with pin point accuracy into the far corner. It was now his 15th league goal, his best return in a single campaign in the competition. He managed 14 in both 2013/14 and 2014/15 but this is now his most prolific season since he scored 20 Ligue 1 goals for Lille in 2011/12.

Former Chelsea midfielder Oriol Romeu bundled in an equaliser from a well-rehearsed corner and it felt like it would be one of those nervy frustrating nights; in fact a rare game under lights now there was no European football. But Cahill's determined header restored the narrow advantage with virtually the last action of the first half to give Conte a vastly different dressing room to address than might have been.

Cahill had now scored 26 Premier League goals - excluding penalties - the second most of any defender in the competition (after John Terry with 40). Most of his teammates immediately ran to celebrate with the captain whereas David Luiz, famed for his eccentricity, chose to swing from the crossbar in front of the Shed End.

On whether he was distracted by Costa attempting an overhead kick, Cahill told Sky Sports: "He tried to claim it after I think as well! I saw Marcos was going to win that and he popped a nice ball back across. It's one of them for a defender or any striker when the ball has been lofted over like that - it's dying to be attacked. It was great timing for the second goal. We went in at half-time with our tails up and it was a big boost for us and I'm sure it deflated them."

Costa stamped Chelsea's supremacy with a header early in the second half. It was his 50th goal in the Premier League in his 85th game - only seven strikers had reached the milestone faster: Andy Cole (65), Alan Shearer (66), Ruud van Nistelrooy (68), Fernando Torres (72), Sergio Aguero (81), Thierry Henry (83) and Kevin Phillips (83). He was too strong for Ryan Bertrand when he arrived on the end of Fabregas's cross to score the decisive third. The assist by Fabregas was his 103rd in the Premier League - second only to Manchester United legend Ryan Giggs (162). Despite Fabregas having had limited first team opportunities this season his assist now put him ahead of Frank Lampard, who was at the Bridge alongside his father Frank Snr.

Costa then scored his second after a move of enormous close control and intricacy around the box with a couple of one-twos and a neat exchange with Pedro. The superb finish was very much the Costa of old and finally put the result beyond doubt against a Saints side that had played superbly well.

So, Costa had ended his seven-game goal drought with a brace to ensure the Blues took a major step towards the league title. The last time Costa had endured such a run was back in 2012/13, when he went six La Liga matches without a goal for Atletico Madrid.

On Costa's return to goal-scoring form, Conte said: "It's normal for the strikers, for the forwards, that it is important to score. The goals are their life. But, for me, I've always said I've been pleased with his commitment, his work for the team. He always worked for the team. Sometimes he was unlucky in different circumstances, but I was always confident about him."

On the constant speculation, he added: "I continue to repeat this concept and it's important that we focus on the moment. The moment is important for all of us. In this period I'm reading a lot of speculation about everyone at Chelsea (but) it's right to be focused and I'm sure for my players that they are focused on our target. It's normal at this part of the season to also have someone that wants to put problems into our team, to create disorder but we must be stronger than this speculation. We must be compact and to think that our target is more important than the other things."

Conte applauded all four sides of the ground as the clock ticked down on a vital night in the title race but former Chelsea player, Bertrand, was on target with a header in the dying seconds when outjumping Cahill. At that stage, though, the victory was already assured to put intense pressure on Spurs at in-form Crystal Palace. However, Conte was far from happy that Chelsea had failed to keep a clean sheet in their past eleven Premier League games, the worst run since December 1996. Hull City were the last team to draw a blank against Conte's side back in January.

Conte was again credited for his team selection as Hazard and Costa, both starting on this occasion, made decisive contributions. Before the kick-off he defended his decision to drop Willian after he had scored twice in the previous match against Tottenham. Conte highlighted the importance of having options off the bench as one of the reasons why he named Willian as a substitute along with Pedro. "We have already played with those players in the starting eleven. I think Cesc is a player who can play in different positions. He has great personality and great quality in this part of the season. He is very important to us. On the bench Willian and Pedro give me an option during the game. It's of fundamental importance now."

So, once again the manager was proved right on all accounts as Stamford Bridge ended the game in celebratory mood and with Chelsea's momentum at the top restored.

"It's always good to play before and put pressure on them." said Hazard. "It's always good to score and create a lot of chances. We scored four beautiful goals. We will see tomorrow. We can stay at home tomorrow to watch the game and we will see."

Cahill called the win a "massive step", adding, "It's the first time for a long time we've played before Tottenham."

The pressure was now on Spurs, having to respond to the Blues' win that had restored their seven-point lead, as well as the disappointment of losing the FA Cup semi-final to their London rivals. Tottenham had reeled off seven straight league wins - their best sequence since 1967 - but Sam Allardyce's rejuvenated side had beaten Chelsea, Arsenal and Liverpool in recent weeks.

It was turning into a defining period of the season with a huge weekend also ahead as Chelsea travelled to Everton, in arguably their toughest assignment in the run-in, while Spurs would face Arsenal in the north London derby the next day - Chelsea again having the potential advantage of playing first.

WEDNESDAY, 26 APRIL 2017

"COSTA BRAVO - Diego's double helps Blues restore seven-point lead in title race" - Metro Sport

"CATCH US IF BLUE CAN" - Sun Sport

Fair play to Tottenham as they kept up the pressure on Chelsea; Christian Eriksen's superb long-range strike secured a hard-fought victory at Palace.

Spurs struggled to break down Palace for much of the game and it looked like they would have to settle for a point. But Eriksen fired into the bottom corner from 30 yards with only twelve minutes remaining to keep Spurs within four points of Chelsea with five games to go.

Palace, who lost influential Mamadou Sakho to injury in the second half, rarely threatened. Tottenham moved to 74 points, surpassing their previous best ever Premier League total of 72 - set in 2012/13 - when they finished fifth. And, should they beat rivals Arsenal in their next game it would ensure they finished above the Gunners in the table for the first time since the 1994/95 season.

Pochettino commented: "It was good to get the three points and be alive in the race for the title. The challenge is to keep going. It is always better to win but it is true (the Arsenal game) is a big derby, perhaps the last at White Hart Lane and I think it will be an exciting game. It's not a motivation or a distraction. Our challenge now is to try and reduce the gap to Chelsea again and think about bigger things than only to be above Arsenal. For one day, to win big trophies and achieve big things, your mentality must be bigger. You must think about bigger dreams. Big dreams. It's important to have them."

After winning eight consecutive league games and a club-record tally of points in the Premier League era, he added: "It was a great opportunity to show we are focusing on us, spending energy trying to improve our game and trying to fight with our opponents. We are showing that we learned a lot from last season. That is so important because last season was a big challenge. Last season the team were fantastic, playing well, and it was a massive challenge to improve. But we have improved a lot this season and one area that was key for us to improve was in our mental attitude. The team are now showing we are ready. We are ready this season to fight and, next season, we'll be even better."

With an eye on the future as well as tradition, Conte congratulated Chelsea's U18's after they won the FA Youth Cup.

Chelsea's Academy had in fact won their third consecutive FA Youth Cup and their sixth in eight years. The Blues defeated Manchester City 5-1 (6-2 agg) at Stamford Bridge with Conte watching the final alongside Roman Abramovich, as well as club legends John Terry and Frank Lampard.

Conte visited the youth team and Academy coach Jody Morris in the dressing room to congratulate them on their win. After side-stepping Trevoh Chalobah's (younger brother of Nathaniel) victory dance, he put the victory in the context of Chelsea's traditions and expectations. "Congratulations. You played a very good game. I think you deserved the trophy. It is very important to win for us and is a great tradition for the club. I hope you continue this way. Well done, good job."

Pep Guardiola responded to Conte's 'it's all about the money' jibe as he was quick to point out that Chelsea had also spent heavily in the past. "I agree with you. I played with Barcelona and won the Champions League with eight guys growing from the academy. Zero cost to win the Champions League, that's happened. But all the clubs are going to spend a lot of money and you cannot forget all the players that Chelsea have that cost a lot of money. People think that just City spend money, but all the clubs around the world, in Spain, Germany, England and Italy, they spend a lot of money. This summer it is going to happen again."

THURSDAY, 27 APRIL 2017

"Eriksen keeps title race alive" - The Times Sport

After missing the semi-final clash with Spurs Gary Cahill disclosed that he'd had to deal with a painful gallbladder problem throughout his career.

"I was in (hospital) for one night. I had a viral infection, a problem with my gallbladder. It was causing me a lot of pain and that's why we went to check it all out. They kept me overnight to keep an eye on everything. Thankfully I got rid of the pain and everything, and recovered, but it was just too late (to make the semi-final). I'd not trained one minute, I'd not eaten anything and I'd lost a bit of weight. It was obviously not ideal me going into the game. I was disappointed with that, but I'm happy I'm over that now and am back out on the pitch. It's something I've had since I was small. I have been aware of it and it is just a matter of keeping an eye on it. The worst thing at the time was if they had to take it out, or whatever, and that would have obviously set me back for the season. I was happy that wasn't the case. It's just a matter of keeping an eye on it and monitoring it. There have been times when I knew it was going to come on and I'd take some strong painkillers for it. If you get it in midweek, it tends to be okay. But a night before a game is not ideal because you can be up all night and that's not great. But it was this on top of the viral infection, so when I was in there they tested my blood and wanted to keep me in."

In an interview with Italian TV show Emigratis (Football Italia), Conte admitted he would not remain at Chelsea forever. Asked if he would return to Serie A, Conte said: "Yes. My heart is always in Italy." But no club in Italy can afford his wages? To which Conte replied: "Haven't the new owners come in now?" It was a reference to Inter Milan and AC Milan, who both had new Chinese owners. Inter sold up late last year (2016) and Suning Group promised a £127m spending spree on the squad. But the show was filmed back in January ahead of Chelsea's clash with Hull, so why it was brought up now was a mystery. He admitted that he had struggled to initially adapt to live in London. "It took me six months to get the English to appreciate me." he joked. Asked if he was happy living in London, Conte replied. "Well…"

But, Conte has no plans to leave Chelsea this summer, according to Massimo Carrera, the Italian's former assistant at Juventus. Carrera, who was wanted by Conte as part of his coaching staff at Chelsea last summer, insisted Conte was staying. "Antonio is the best in the world because his players follow him and when they go on the pitch they know everything about their opponents, absolutely everything. Every single strength or weakness is known down to the slightest detail." Carrera told Calciomercato.com.

"We speak often. Antonio is very happy and I think he wants to play the Champions League with Chelsea, with a team he has built. Working with, and learning from Conte was great. He spends hours talking to his players, he's very demanding, he wants to prepare them for anything. And he does the same with the staff. If they lose, he gets very angry… he only accepts defeat if his players have left it all on the pitch."

FRIDAY, 27 APRIL 2017

Conte addressed the media as usual and started his news conference by confirming that all his players were fit for Everton. Were the Toffees the toughest side the leaders had left to play? "I don't know, but Everton are a really good team, a strong team, with great players in their squad and a physical team. They have a good coach, a good manager. They play organised football. It will be a very tough game for us, for sure, but at the end of the season, every game becomes tough for many different reasons. For us, it's very important to look at ourselves, prepare very well and arrive to play this game with great physical condition, good organisation, to know our tasks defensively and offensively."

As a five-time Serie A and Champions League winner as a player, plus three-time Serie A winner as a manager, where would winning the Premier League title rank in his career? "For me, this is the first season in England and to arrive here, in a different country, with a different language and to bring my philosophy and idea of football, it's not easy in the first season. To fight for the title and the FA Cup, for me, is a great achievement but I hope, always, to stay in the future and have always this type of situation. And to try to win with my players. With the club. With the fans, together."

A draw or a win at Everton would guarantee Champions League football - "a good achievement" according to Conte, but the Premier League title was clearly his main focus. "When we started this season, our first target was to play in the Champions League next season. It's an important target for the club, for the fans, for the players. But, for sure now, we stay in a position to try also to win the league. Obviously, with six teams between Chelsea, Tottenham, City, Arsenal, United, Liverpool, two strong teams won't play next season in the Champions League."

The fighting spirit of Conte's team emerged in recent weeks and now it was a crucial week in the title race. "For sure, after the United defeat, I think it wasn't easy to face this type of moment. Above all, because after the United defeat and you saw you only had four points, and then you had to play a semi-final against Tottenham, your opponents in the League. After this game, you then had to play two-and-a-half days later against Southampton, a team who had rested for ten days. I think that it was a good test, for our mental condition. I always thought that this week would be very important for us. I considered this week crucial for us, to get to the FA Cup final and also for the league. I thought we had to be good to keep these points with Tottenham and at the same time you had to face Tottenham to reach the final, then Southampton, then Everton away. I think in the team we have a lot of warriors. I work every day to bring them to be warriors. I think it's great to have talent. But I like a lot when you are a warrior during the game and, above all, if players with talent work hard during the game. This is an incredible experience for me, but not only for me." reflected Conte of his time in England. "For every coach, to work in this country. It's great, it's great every day to discover different situations and then have to try and adapt yourself."

Some aspects of English football were a first for Conte. "I always said, for me, it was very strange the first time to arrive and to listen to the music in high volume in the dressing room. I always thought that, before the game, you must be focused, no? I thought the silence helped to find the focus."

He then added in deadpan fashion: "I would like to listen to disco music before the game, or pop music, but it's impossible for me to bring my favourite music to the changing room. The sounds I like depend on different moments. When I stay relaxed, I prefer Italian music - we have a lot of great singers - but when I am excited, I prefer pop music."

It brought up the subject of him dancing. "Not in the dressing room, no. In the dressing room, no, no, no. I keep the self-control."

Conte's compatriot Andrea Bocelli had performed Nessun Dorma and Time To Say Goodbye at the King Power Stadium as Claudio Ranieri celebrated his title triumph a year ago. Conte added: "Bocelli is a great singer and I watched during the celebrations when Claudio Ranieri invited him to sing for Leicester. Who would I invite? We have to win first."

More seriously, does he dance to the tune of Costa or Lukaku?

"Lukaku is scoring a lot of goals this season, but not only this season. We must pay great attention to him. In my team? As I said before, for me my players are the best in the world. I don't change my players with other players."

He elaborated: "Lukaku is a good guy but for us Diego is very important and, in this part of the season, he will be decisive for us. We are talking about two great strikers. But you know that Diego, for me, is the best striker in the world. I think it's great to have talent. But I like a lot when you are a warrior during the game and above all if players with talent show they work hard during the game."

Conte was now braced for an approach for Hazard from Real Madrid in excess of the £89m world record Manchester United paid for Paul Pogba. Asked if he could offer any guarantee about Hazard staying, Conte said: "It's impossible for me to take this responsibility, not only for Eden but for every single player. I can say my opinion, but the club has the final word. I don't think that this idea is in the mind of the club. We have to improve the team, to reinforce the team. But in football there is also the will of the player. I think Eden is very happy to stay at Chelsea, to stay with us and work with us. I can tell this. But I haven't got a crystal ball. You must understand that there are different wills to compare, and then to take the decision."

He added: "He's a great player. This season, he has improved a lot, not only on the pitch but also he's becoming mentally stronger. At this level it's very important to try to have this step because it brings you up to the best players in the world. Eden is starting to take this step."

Did he agree with N'Golo Kante being awarded PFA Player of the Year? "In this case, I prefer to have 23 votes and to vote for every one of my players." Ever the diplomat.

Conte called on the Premier League to change their fixtures, as it was unfair that Tottenham and Chelsea played at different times during the run-in, only playing at the same time on the final day. He wanted the final three fixtures at the same time. "For sure, at the end of the season, I think that when you have two teams in the race, in contention for the title, I think you must have a good balance to try to put the fixtures in the same hour, on the same days, and don't give advantage to one team or another. When you arrive at the last three games, when you see there are two or three teams very close to fight for the title, you have to find a solution not to give advantage for one team or another. Try and keep it the same hour, the same days to rest. I think, at this part of the season, every game is very tough for many reasons. You have a lot of pressure. You know you have to win. When you have to play with this target, yes, it's not simple. It's not easy. But not only for us, also for Tottenham. But we are ready, I repeat· we've worked a lot to arrive at this point fighting for the title. For this reason, we want to reach our target with all our strength. We have to do our job with the right pressure but, at the same time, to enjoy this moment."

Conte was clearly concerned and annoyed at Chelsea's failure to keep a clean sheet in eleven games. "It's important to know that I don't like it. Sometimes the stats are not true, above all for possession. You can have good possession and lose the game. It's not so important, some stats. But about the clean sheets, I think it's an important stat. It's eleven games that we are not able to keep a clean sheet and, for this reason, it's important to improve, to work on the situations we're conceding the goals. But I'm not concerned about this. But, at the same time, we are working."

Pochettino urged his Tottenham players and fans to put aside the emotion of the north London derby. "My challenge and my aim is not to be above Arsenal. My challenge, my aim and my dream is to be above 19 teams and be on the top. With respect, I don't care what happens with Arsenal. What I care is what happens with us. That's our big, big challenge at Tottenham. We are so close, only four points. Only, but it is massive with only five games to play. I will be very disappointed if we don't win the title but I won't think: what is Arsenal's position?"

Nemanja Matic warned Tottenham that Chelsea will fight to the "very last minute".

"Of course we have experience from winning the league two years ago. We have to stay considered until the last minute of the season. Not the last game, the very last minute. I'm sure we're on our best and I think the next game will be crucial for us. I can say it's difficult to focus game by game, but we have to do that. If you want to win the title, you have to be ready for everything. You have to know the Premier League is like this. This is football, it's the Premier League, so we are focused. We always work very hard, and we will do that until the end of the season. In every moment, we have to be ready for everything. It's really important for us to play in the final, because the FA Cup is very important for every football player in England." Matic told Chelsea's website. "I'm very happy. It's going to be an interesting game and one I'm looking forward to. We're in a good way. We have four more points than Spurs so we'll try to give our best to win the title. And of course the last game of the season will be the final. We'll try our best. You never know what will happen, but we're confident. You cannot win all your games. Sometimes you lose, but after that the reaction is important. We lost against Crystal Palace but after that we won against Manchester City and Bournemouth. The most important thing is the reaction. We lost against Manchester United, but after that we beat Tottenham and Southampton. So I hope that we can continue this now, and Sunday I think is a crucial game for us."

SATURDAY, 29 APRIL 2017

Conte and his Chelsea stars took up residence at the Titanic Hotel in Liverpool in preparation for the Goodison Park encounter. The Titanic! Really? Clearly, not superstitious then!

He was plotting a big change, Pedro for Fabregas. Hoping his decision wouldn't sink without trace, no doubt!

Somehow, when the club announced its team on their official social media channel, Petr Cech was named instead of Courtois. The error was quickly rectified shortly afterwards, possibly to the relief of both goalkeepers.

SUNDAY, 30 APRIL 2017
Everton 0-3 Chelsea
Premier League

Chelsea took a significant step towards the title with three second-half goals.

Pedro's 25-yard stunner, Gary Cahill's close-range rebound and Willian's tap-in after an inch perfect pull back from Cesc Fabregas temporarily placed Conte's side seven points clear of second-placed Tottenham, who responded brilliantly later in the day to beat Arsenal 2-0 in the north London derby at the Lane.

So, Chelsea now had the luxury of being able to drop three points in their remaining four games and still claim their second title in three years, even if Spurs won all of their remaining fixtures.

However, Spurs would play first in the next round of games at the Olympic Stadium on the Friday night where they could move to only one point behind with Chelsea not playing until the following Monday, albeit with a relatively easier game at home to relegation threatened Middlesbrough.

Chelsea had to be patient at Goodison, with Pedro's left-footed, long-range strike not coming until the 66th minute. Cahill sealed the win when Maarten Stekelenburg parried Hazard's free-kick onto the onrushing defender, before Willian slotted home from Fabregas's cutback. Cahill had now scored more Premier League goals against Everton than against any other opponent (four).

This was Tottenham's strongest hope of Chelsea surrendering points in their run-in, with Everton placed higher than any of their four remaining opponents, and with three home games left. Win three more and they would be champions for the sixth time. The celebrations from Conte and his players at the final whistle suggested they felt they would get over the line.

Ronald Koeman faced the league leaders with an outside chance of still creeping into the top four and sneaking a Champions League spot, but they failed on a day when both City and United dropped points. Koeman knew if they had any chance of coming out with anything he had to nullify Hazard. Idrissa Gueye, a former teammate of Hazard's at Lille, man-marked him and for the second time in as many games Chelsea's best player was quiet and eventually replaced; two of Conte's substitutions combining instantly for the third and final goal.

Romelu Lukaku and Diego Costa had scored 43 times between them with Costa five shy of Lukaku's 24 in the league, but Chelsea would have been 15 points worse off without his tally of 19. Costa was involved in the build-up to the final goal, while Lukaku looked unlikely to score for the first time in six appearances against his former club.

Koeman's two heaviest league defeats in charge of Everton have now both come against Chelsea this term (5-0 and 3-0). Koeman on Sky Sports: "We did well, until 1-0 maybe. After that we had more problems but that was all about their quality, before that we played well and made it tough for them. Maybe we didn't create a lot of chances, but I was happy. Idrissa Gueye played a fantastic game; Hazard was not the player he can be because of the man-marking. It is really tough to beat Chelsea. They showed their belief and their quality. They will be champions. We need to find the motivation to finish the season strongly."

Even by his usual exuberant standards Conte surpassed himself as he jumped onto Courtois' back pumped the air with his fists and then joined his players in their celebrations with the travelling fans.

Conte admitted he is an "animal" during games. "There are two Antonios. Two different people. During the game, I know I am an animal. After the game, I must be relaxed when we win but I think it's very good to celebrate this win with the players, staff and fans. I live for this. I think we must continue this way - to play game by game and take three points in every game. We know every win in this part of the season is very important. The road is long so we need to rest and prepare in the right way. We must be pleased because we played a game with the head and, at this part of this season, it is important to use our head, then your heart and then your legs."

Asked how close the title now was, he said. "I don't know. It is a great win but at this part of the season every win is a great win for us. For this reason we must celebrate in the right way, with my players, with the staff, with our fans. We have to have great enthusiasm and great patience because I think we are having a great season but to become a fantastic season we must win. Now it is important for us to prepare the right way the next game. If we don't win against Middlesbrough then you lose this great win. It is very important after this crucial week for us because we played against Tottenham in the FA Cup and then on Tuesday against Southampton and now against Everton. I think we finished a crucial week very well. We all know there is this part of the season that is more important."

Chelsea now had 81 points from 34 games; their highest at this stage of a campaign since 2005/06 (85) when they won the title. The Toffees had failed to score in a Premier League game at Goodison Park for the first time in 2017, having averaged 3.7 goals per game prior to this defeat. Chelsea kept their first clean sheet in the Premier League since January (vs Hull), ending an eleven-game run without one; pleasing Conte no end.

Conte hailed the impact of Fabregas following his display as a substitute, delivering a wonderful assist for Willian. He labelled the Spaniard as "decisive" in whatever role he deploys him, from the start or as a creative impact player. "I think Cesc is a player, in this part of the season, who is showing to be decisive in every moment. If he starts the game (or if) he came on during the game. Also Willy (Willian), I know very well that it's not easy for a player who is used to playing every game and to come on during the game."

211

Conte singled out Nathan Ake who came on for an injured David Luiz in the 81st minute to make just his fourth appearance since his loan spell at Bournemouth was cut short in January. Despite his lack of chances, Conte's been impressed and said the Dutchman performed like a "veteran" on Merseyside. "I am very pleased with Ake's impact. He came on and he looked like a veteran. He is only a young player. He is showing great commitment, work-rate and concentration when I ask him to play. It's not easy to be used to playing every game for Bournemouth and then arrive at Chelsea and be on the bench or sometimes in the stands. But he understands I trust him. I put him in the semi-final against Tottenham, and I put him today in a moment very important for us. I'm also pleased for this because to play a young player is a great thing for us."

In fact, Conte was overjoyed with his entire squad. "I must be pleased with them because they are showing me to be great men and fantastic players."

Pochettino, speaking to BBC Sport: "The race for the title is down to four points and we will see what will happen. In Italy and Spain, when you are playing for the title, the teams play at the same time. Here in England it is different with the fans wanting to watch the teams live. We understand that. To be above Arsenal for the first time in 22 years is fantastic for our fans. It is fantastic for us too, but we want to win the title. To win against Arsenal in the last derby at White Hart Lane, it was emotional for everyone. We tried to pay the supporters back for the energy they gave us. But the most important thing was to keep the gap with Chelsea. We have to keep focusing on our game and now we can say that we are more mature than last season. Today was another chance to see the team learning and improving. I can understand our fans being excited about finishing above Arsenal, but I don't feel the same because for me it is about trying to win the title. It is so important now to try and win trophies, that is our aim. We have another big game against West Ham on Friday, another difficult derby. That could be a chance to put psychological pressure on Chelsea. We play before them and, if we win, we will see what happens."

Cahill summed up the euphoria at Goodison Park. "We have made a massive stride, there's no getting away from that. We knew how big the three points would be. There's still time to go but it's a huge step."

Although Chelsea couldn't shake off Spurs Cahill stressed that the Chelsea camp had expected this. "We have been saying we expect Spurs to win every game and it's down to us because winning the title is in our hands."

We would, of course, find out in May…

Premier League Table, Top 6, end of April 2017:

		P	W	D	L	F	A	GD	Pts
1	Chelsea	34	26	3	5	72	29	+43	81
2	Tottenham Hotspur	34	23	8	3	71	22	+49	77
3	Liverpool	34	19	9	6	70	42	+28	66
4	Manchester City	34	19	9	6	65	37	+28	66
5	Manchester United	34	17	14	3	51	25	+26	65
6	Arsenal	33	18	6	9	64	42	+22	60

CHAPTER FOURTEEN

MAY 2017

Chelsea are crowned Premier League champions! JT says farewell. FA Cup final defeat but, overall, an excellent season.

MONDAY, 1 MAY 2017

In the latest of the continuing saga Conte's agent expected him to stay at Chelsea despite reports claiming that he has received a major offer from Inter. "I prefer not to say anything because it is Conte who has to decide and must talk about his future." Federico Pastorello told Sky Sports. "Chelsea believes he is happy to stay and indeed I think Antonio assumes that he will stay. He has two more years of his contract."

Slaven Bilic believed Tottenham were the best team. They had lost only three league games but remained four points behind high-flyers Chelsea. After losing five straight games earlier in the year, West Ham were unbeaten since early April and were looking to guarantee their top-flight status with a positive result against Spurs. Bilic said his West Ham side were up against the best team in the league when they welcome Tottenham to the London Stadium on Friday night. "That game is always big, it's a derby, and it can't be just an ordinary game. Then, if you add to that that they need points to stay in the race and we need points to climb or to make us safe. We're going to approach it in a very positive way, knowing we are playing, for me, against the best team in the league. Hopefully, I'm going to enjoy it, but it's going to be a very nervous game. We will have to be on top of our game. But we did it last year, beating them at home when they were also on fire and everything."

Conte had told his squad to "keep calm and stay in the game" at half-time at Everton with the contest poised at 0-0. Chelsea could ill-afford to hand a window of opportunity to Tottenham ahead of their clash with Arsenal. Conte, though, spoke calmly to his players at the interval and later confirmed that the win was morale-boosting. "Everton are a strong team and they prepared the game well, so we must be pleased." said Conte. "We had a lot of patience for the right moment to hit, and we deserved the win. In this type of game it's easy to lose your head, lose your balance. For this reason at half-time I told them to be calm and to stay in the game. We scored an amazing goal with Pedro, then the second and third, but it was not so easy. This gives us lots of confidence. Now it is important to prepare the final rush. If in the next game against Middlesbrough you don't win you lose this victory. We must look step by step."

He gave an insight into the relationship with his players when asked what he said to them in the dressing room. "After the game the message was not with words, only hugs to show great enthusiasm. I think it is important to win but also to have great enthusiasm. It is very important to stay together in this moment because we must feel this season could become fantastic."

David Luiz provided a promising update after he had limped off with eight minutes remaining at Goodison Park, appearing to tear a muscle. Luiz did not appear overly concerned, taking to social media to reassure Chelsea fans of his condition. In his Instagram post, which was accompanied with wink and fist emojis, he was lying on a treatment bed but crucially waggling his left leg. When asked about Luiz, Conte said: "I didn't speak with the doctor about his injury but I don't think it is a serious injury for him. I hope in the next game that David Luiz is available to play. Also now in this part of the season it is important sometimes to try to play if you are not 100 per cent with your condition. He is showing us great commitment in this season. Don't forget his injury in the knee after the game against City - but I am very pleased for the impact of Ake in the Everton game."

Rio Ferdinand praised Conte for masterminding Chelsea's demolition of Everton. "Antonio Conte is on fire." Ferdinand said in a video on his YouTube channel. "He is just churning out results. Chelsea travelling to Everton at Goodison Park. Everybody thought they'd slip up (against) their bogey team. Conte sent them out and Chelsea dismantled Everton at Goodison Park. I can't see them slipping up."

Alan Pardew explained why Conte would be his choice for manager of the season. "Conte, without a doubt for me, has been manager of the season." Pardew told Sky Sports' Monday Night Football. "To go and make that tactical change at a big club from going to a four to a back three and making such a success of it… he has had some fantastic wins against the top teams. He was new to the Premier League. He didn't really know it. He has changed the training regime there. He has made it much tougher. For a foreign manager coming in, he has been as good as anybody."

TUESDAY, 2 MAY 2017

David Luiz described his quest to win the title as "an obsession" as he praised Conte's "meticulous" approach. Luiz, who won the Champions League and Europa League during his first spell from January 2011 to June 2014, told FourFourTwo: "I had already won several titles with Chelsea, played my part in a beautiful period in the club's history and made so many friends. I thought it was time to move on, so I had no regrets. But things change quickly in football. Winning the Premier League has always been an obsession of mine. This is one of the toughest competitions in the world. We've worked hard to make this dream come true."

On his manager, he added: "He's extremely meticulous. There isn't a tiny detail he isn't aware of. He's the type of guy who sees things most people wouldn't. In training he creates situations that he thinks could occur during the upcoming games - and it makes all the difference. He also knows how to motivate us and gives confidence to the whole squad. We all know that he trusts in our ability and one of his best qualities is that he treats everyone equally."

When asked by Sky Sports if he had matured this season, Luiz replied: "You have to, and also as a person. I think the experience gives you many things, and yes, as a person and a footballer, you have to if you want to learn. If you are open every day. I read more of the game now, I can understand more of the game, it is a different pressure now with the big games. Many, many things. I think if you want to improve, you need to think you are a better player than you were. I've worked with six, seven, eight coaches, they have improved my game, different leagues and different countries."

WEDNESDAY, 3 MAY 2017

As Ajax tore Lyon apart in the first of the two Europa League semi-finals, Bertrand Traore, on loan at the Amsterdam Arena, was named as Man of the Match. He fired in two goals against the Ligue 1 side to put the Dutch giants in control of the last-four tie. Watching Traore's performance, Chelsea fans were very keen for Conte to bring him back to Stamford Bridge as soon as possible.

THURSDAY, 4 MAY 2017

Conte disclosed that low expectations spurred him and his team on. "The expectation for Chelsea at the start of the season wasn't high. I think the expectation was to try to fight and to arrive in the

Champions League. I think this situation pushed me a lot - the players and I - to try to change the opinion of the press, of the people who look at the football every week."

He admitted that while the motivation was there, he didn't expect his start at Chelsea to be quite so successful. "For sure (I've exceeded my own expectations). This is my first season. It is very good for me because for me this is a great experience. This is the first time to work in another country as coach; different language, different habit. I think that I am satisfied for my impact in this league. But for sure now I want to arrive at the end and try to win with my players with the club and with our fans. After a really good season like this it's important to become a fantastic season and there is only one way to become a fantastic season - to win."

Chelsea would continue their pursuit of the title at home against Middlesbrough on Monday. If Tottenham won against West Ham the gap would be just one point. "Every game in this part of the season is a single test and is a tough test for us." Conte told Sky Sports. "Because in this part of the season is very difficult if you make mistakes. It's very difficult then to recover. For this reason it's very important to keep right concentration and be focused. To play game by game. So in this case Middlesbrough for us must be a final."

"I have nothing but praise for them. When I watch them I wonder how Chelsea made that gap, but they had two periods without Harry Kane. Spurs are in form, but they've been in form for two months. We are positive, four unbeaten and three clean sheets in four games. Yes, they are electric, with confidence, pace, passing and changing positions and everything, but our form also improved. Spurs are very versatile. Sometimes you know where the ball is going but you can't stop it because of the quality." That's how Bilic, in his media conference, set the scene for the derby showdown that would determine Spurs' title challenge, and maybe his own future as manager. "This is a big match anyway. It is a derby, whether you need the points or not, it's a derby game against Spurs at our stadium. They need points, we need points, so it is massive game for us and a massive game for them. We will try to get the points that will mathematically secure our status. You don't need extra motivation when you play against Tottenham. Last season's game at Upton Park, when we beat them 1-0, was one of the most electrifying atmospheres. It is a big game for us, a big game for the supporters, it is under the lights which is always a special one, and we are ready for it."

Tottenham might have won nine consecutive league games but West Ham will remember that they were only minutes away from doing what no team has managed this season - beating Spurs at White Hart Lane. However, Tottenham fought back from 2-1 down in stoppage time, with two Harry Kane goals, to claim a 3-2 win in November.

"We keep going, it's hard to do anything else. We can't control what Chelsea do, we just have to keep winning our games." said Kane. "We have another London derby on Friday night and hopefully we can win that, drop it down to one point and see what happens. We're playing as well as we ever have done in the Premier League."

Nemanja Matic had offered to buy Bilic dinner if West Ham beat Spurs. Bilic confirmed to eastern European sports channel Sportklub that Matic promised in a text message: "If you stop Tottenham, I'll take you out to dinner."

Bilic added: "Matic is a wonderful guy, a great player. I will accept that offer with pleasure."

FRIDAY, 5 MAY 2027

Conte confessed that he would not be tuning into the West Ham game, instead he would spend time with his family. "I have my wife and daughter and it is a chance to have a dinner together in

London." Instead he was worrying about his preparation for Monday night. "This week we are struggling with two situations, about David Luiz and N'Golo." He confessed to the media. Courtois was fit and had trained, but Luiz and Kante had problems, though he said there was still time for both of them to recover.

Conte added: "We must play a great game and try to take three points. With only four games to go it's important to win. It won't be easy. Our plan is to continue to work very hard and prepare for the final four games and then the FA Cup final. Pressure at this stage of the season is normal. You must cope with this. Everyone at the club has experience to face it. Middlesbrough have to win, and for us it's the same."

The big, and frankly tedious, transfer rumour again linked Diego Costa with a big money move to China. Conte said he did not know about the rumours and had not discussed the issue with Costa. "I don't know about this, I have not discussed the future with Costa. It is important for every single player and person to work for Chelsea, to focus on the present, it is important for us, more important than the future. We have to be focused and concentrated to prepare in the right way for these games from now until the end."

Asked if he expected Costa to remain at the club, he referred back to his comment on Eden Hazard the previous week when he implied the "will of the player" had to be taken into account. "I repeat the same concept about Diego and every single player. But I'm not worried (about his focus). I see my players every day and I can see the right concentration, the right focus, about my players. I think in this part of the season you arrive with four games to go and have the possibility to reach a fantastic target for us - don't forget we started this season with a lot of problems and now we have a fantastic possibility to reach a great target and win the Premier League and also to play the FA Cup final, another great competition... these two big targets for us are very, very important. They are the most important things for us. Speculation or news, for me, is not important. Now it's very important for every single player and person who works for Chelsea to be focused on the present, because the present is more important for us than the future. But I'm not worried about this. I see my players every day and I see the right concentration and focus in them."

He was irritated by a suggestion that some senior players who were reduced to cameo roles may be unhappy. "I'd like to underline a concept: that's it not about keeping the players happy. We must win. You speak about people being happy but I speak about winning and working hard. Players are not always happy to work hard but my target is to put in the mind of the players a winning mentality. And that winning mentality doesn't have to keep the players happy. It's very difficult to keep 20 players happy, above all because I don't actually want to. I don't want this. I want players ready to fight and to try to put themselves in the team, to try to win together. If you are happy or unhappy, I don't care. It's important to stress this concept, you understand? Anyway, if you are unhappy in a season when you are fighting for the title and to win the FA Cup... I don't like this."

As for Cesc Fabregas specifically, he pointed to his "great commitment, great work-rate and great behaviour all season".

During the evening I was at the Sanctum Soho Hotel, behind the Cafe Royal, for a momentous night... if you're a Spurs fan that is. It was the night of the Ossie Ardiles film premiere in the company of the Argentine Ambassador and his lovely wife, Ossie and Ricky Villa and their wives, and Glenn Hoddle, with the glittering FA Cup on show. After the screening, the match from the London Stadium was live in the cinema for those who wanted to watch it. While the film was a huge success, Spurs were certainly not against the Hammers, as history repeated itself. West Ham have a habit of upsetting the applecart, and they did so in spectacular fashion - although not so for the Chelsea and West Ham fans present at the Sanctum!

Spurs could have narrowed the gap to a point but were well below par as the Hammers helped Chelsea toward the title. Adrian made a string of first-half saves from Harry Kane and Eric Dier before Manuel Lanzini smashed in a loose-ball winner leaving Chelsea needing just two wins from their final four games to be crowned champions. Chelsea had home games against three sides in the bottom seven. Conte's side could now secure the title on Friday, 12 May if they beat both Middlesbrough and West Bromwich Albion.

"It was already going to be hard, so now it is going to be even harder." said Dier. "We are still fighting." said Pochettino. "We must wait but it is now more difficult. I feel calm. But I'm disappointed, of course, that we missed the opportunity to reduce the gap."

Conte's team now had the chance to open up a seven-point gap if they beat Boro in three days' time. "Seven points will be difficult with three games to play, but in football you have to try your best. It is true it will be difficult." Said a disappointed Pochettino. "When you have the chance to reduce the gap to one point and you lose it's hard to find the positives."

"This season is not over yet." insisted a resigned Hugo Lloris. "We've got to secure the second place, that is the most important thing. My feeling hasn't changed after this game. It's the same as before this game: we must stay focused on ourselves and try to finish the job in the best way. There are three games left and we must try to win all of them and finish second. This would be a success for Tottenham, even though we wanted more."

Chelsea were not yet champions. "It is not tonight because they must finish the job on the pitch obviously. It demands so much force to try to catch Chelsea." continued Lloris. "It's been a while now that they've been first and at one moment they were 10, 11, 12, 13 points over us. So we tried to push as much as possible. We must not forget everything we've done before tonight, especially in the way we've played football. Against West Ham we slipped collectively. We were not able to increase the level and it was not enough. Our collective performance was not enough to expect a better result. So we need to stay positive especially because we have a lot of young players, very talented, who represent the future of the England national team too. They have the mentality of winners. But when in front of us there is a machine that is difficult to beat and because they haven't played European games this season that has been something positive to them."

SATURDAY, 6 MAY 2017

Rachel Riley received hideous personal abuse after apparently criticising Tottenham's defeat at West Ham. Riley, who was presenting the match live on Sky Sports, described Spurs' failure to close the gap as a "proper bottle job", comments which were rather well received by supporters of Tottenham's title rivals, but the Countdown presenter received abuse from Spurs fans on social media. Riley quickly clarified her comments, claiming she was highlighting that Spurs' fixture against West Ham was a test of nerve and she wanted a closer title run-in.

The Football Writers' Association (FWA) would announce their Footballer of the Year on Monday and Conte believed one of his players would be a deserved choice. The prestigious FWA accolade was first presented in 1948 to Stanley Matthews and is decided from a vote of the association's now 340-strong membership. Conte commented: "I think this is a great achievement for N'Golo and also for Eden (to be among the contenders), because I think they are having a really good season, but I also believe there are many (Chelsea) players who deserve to be in this group who try to win the best footballer of the year."

Boro head coach Steve Agnew was in no doubt of the qualities Kante brings to Chelsea. "Kante has been absolutely top class. He is the one player who knits it all together - he did it for Leicester last season. He has had an excellent season - well, Kante has had two seasons where he has been different class."

SUNDAY, 7 MAY 2017

Conte reiterated that Tottenham "have an advantage" because Pochettino had been in charge at White Hart Lane since 2014.

"I must be honest about this topic. I think Tottenham have an advantage, if you compare Tottenham to Chelsea. This is my first season and I found a lot of situations, a lot of players. Mauricio Pochettino has been working there for three years and has changed a lot of players and is working very well. For me, Tottenham are a really strong team and it's normal to see them fighting for the title."

Spurs, who were Leicester's main challengers last season before fading to finish third, would have easily won the Premier League this season if it were not for Chelsea's impressive season. "In this season, if Chelsea had not performed in this way, Tottenham would win the title without difficulty. Only this great season from us is pushing them to fight and, maybe, to win or not to win the title. But, I repeat, Tottenham's position for me is more advanced if you compare Tottenham's to Chelsea."

The media were queuing up to pour accolades in Conte's direction as Chelsea were now proclaimed as champions-elect.

The Mail on Sunday pointed out that before the UEFA A licence, Italians required their coaches to complete 900 hours or course work and a dissertation to work in football. Conte's was entitled 'Considerations on 4-3-1-2 and the didactic use of video.'

Conte commented on the recent power of Italian coaches in English football. "Honestly, I don't know. Every coach is different. For sure, in England, I looked at the past and saw many Italian managers won the title in England. I think it's great for us, it's great for our school. But I think it's not important, the country where you arrive. In England now there are top managers from different countries, and also I think we have really good English managers here."

He was immensely proud of his compatriots' achievements. "I think it's logical to be proud, no, for this? Last season I supported Claudio Ranieri a lot to win the title. In Italy we celebrated this win in a great way. I think Claudio deserved this for his career."

He acknowledged that the Premier League provides challenges. "I think in Italy there is a good school. But, honestly, when you arrive and you face this league, you must change your mind on a lot of things to adapt very well and very quickly to this league."

The next big challenge looming was the Champions League and Conte believes it is difficult for English clubs to succeed in the Champions League simply because of the strength of the Premier League.

In the past six years, five English clubs reached the quarter-finals, compared to 17 from Spain and ten in Germany. Conte observed: "This league is very difficult. Every single game you must fight a lot and, I think, also for this reason it's not easy to arrive at the end of a European competition. It is so clear here, every season will be tougher and tougher to qualify for the Champions League."

Asked specifically about the benefits of not playing European competitions this season, which saw Spurs face eight extra games, Conte replied: "I don't know. But don't forget that Tottenham dropped out at the first group stage of the Champions League, and then dropped out in the first game in the Europa League. If you consider our games and their games, there is a difference of what, eight games? But if you consider the squads, the numbers in each squad, you can see the difference: one team prepared to play the Champions League with 25 or 26 players, and another who prepared to play the league, the FA Cup and the League Cup." Conte clearly making the point that Chelsea dominated the domestic game with the smallest group of players of any team in the division. He had relied on the same nucleus of starters, with seven making at least 30 league starts and three with at least 25.

So, Conte had excelled in his first campaign in English football. "I think no one person thought this season that Chelsea could fight to win the title *and* could fight to be in the final of the FA Cup." He claimed.

Asked whether new signings were under consideration, he replied: "Yes, for sure. But I think every team risks losing big players. My expectation was a great challenge in this league against City, United, Tottenham, Arsenal and Liverpool. Next season for us it will be the same. But we have one year to work and then the possibility to go into the market and choose the right players on my idea of football. For sure, we are in a moment of transition. We are losing a lot of top players who have written the story, the history, of this club. This season we lost Ivanovic, we lost Mikel and, next season, we'll have lost John - three players. Don't forget Oscar, who went in the transfer market when we sold him."

MONDAY, 8 MAY 2017
Chelsea 3-0 Middlesbrough
Premier League

Chelsea moved to within one win of the title and Conte pronounced his players as worthy winners.

The Blues were now one win away from securing their fifth league trophy, as Conte told BBC Match of the Day: "This is my first season in England in a tough championship. I'm delighted for my players, they deserve this. We are showing that we deserve to win the league. Now, we have taken another step to the title. We have to rest well and prepare for West Brom. We must try in the next game to become champions. West Brom will want to play a good game against us, but we are ready."

Conte's side can now become champions with victory against Albion at The Hawthorns on Friday night while Middlesbrough were back in the Championship after they were swept aside with ease. However, even if they don't win, they still have two more opportunities to wrap up the title against Watford or Sunderland at home.

Chelsea created a succession of chances before Diego Costa turned in Man of the Match Cesc Fabregas's pass after 23 minutes. Alonso scored at the far post through the legs of Brad Guzan eleven minutes before the break. Fabregas created Chelsea's third which Nemanja Matic converted; a hat-trick of shots through the keeper's legs.

Fabregas was brought into the starting line-up after N'Golo Kante was ruled out through injury, providing the pass for Costa's opener and Matic's third, and has now claimed ten assists and four goals in 26 games. But there were doubts whether the first 'assist' would count as it touched a defender en route.

"It's been a difficult year for me. I'm used to playing a lot but I feel I have matured a lot." Fabregas told Sky Sports. "Many people told me I am not the type of player for Antonio Conte and I should leave but I like challenges. I hadn't played every game but I think I have played in the last 20 games. When I have been on the pitch maybe my contribution is better than a full season."

Former Chelsea and Middlesbrough goalkeeper Mark Schwarzer said on Match of the Day: "His interview just shows the calibre of the player. He wants to play week in, week out. He has got so much in the locker, his ability on the ball, how he is able to pick out players from anywhere on the pitch is outstanding. He may be lacking pace but his reading of the game is still world class. Every time Chelsea want an option or need an outlet, they go to Fabregas. He has been the ultimate professional and a huge weapon for Chelsea."

Baggies' manager Tony Pulis was watching from the stands and will have gone away with a plan to stop Chelsea being champions on his patch, aware that Conte's team are quick starters; Guzan had turned Alonso's shot on to the bar in the opening minutes as Chelsea played with the swagger and menace of champions-elect.

Fabregas became the first player to record ten Premier League assists in six different seasons. Costa became the third player to score 20+ goals in a Premier League season for Chelsea on two occasions (Jimmy Floyd Hasselbaink in 2000/01 & 2001/02 and Didier Drogba in 2006/07 & 2009/10), and he had now scored the opening goal of a Premier League game on seven occasions - no other player has done so more times.

Conte commented: "We must be pleased. It was a great performance, my players showed commitment and work-rate for three important points. At this stage it was important to win and exploit Tottenham's defeat. Now, another step to the title. We have to rest well and prepare for West Brom."

Not a great day out for Boro, though. They were delayed in the London rush hour on the way to the Bridge as the team bus had a minor bump in traffic, arriving 20 minutes later than originally scheduled.

It was a who's who of ex-Chelsea in the crowd: Carlo Ancelotti fresh from winning the Bundesliga with Bayern Munich. Jimmy Floyd Hasselbaink, who scored 88 goals in 177 games before moving to Middlesbrough in 2004. Andriy Shevchenko, scorer of 22 goals during his relatively unsuccessful time at Chelsea. And, stars such as Ron 'Chopper' Harris, the original 'Captain, Leader, Legend', were paraded on the pitch at half-time. They all witnessed Chelsea's 300th home win in the Premier League - becoming only the third club to notch up that feat behind Manchester United (347) and Arsenal (306).

John Terry was set to take his final bow and one supporter, in particular, of the skipper had made a 1,500-mile journey to witness him in action. Before the game he held up a banner reading: 'John Terry... I came all the way from Algeria to say thank you. More than 700 matches... 14 trophies... you deserve the best." The Blues' skipper eventually made an appearance as an 84th-minute substitute for David Luiz.

It was a day which also saw N'Golo Kante voted the 2017 Footballer of the Year by the Football Writers' Association. The official ceremony would be held later in the month.

Kante pipped his Chelsea teammate Eden Hazard to the award, despite the Belgian playmaker's outstanding season, on the 70th Anniversary of the FWA. Between them, Kante and Hazard had polled more than 65 per cent of the votes.

A proud Kante said: "It is a fantastic honour to win this award. With so many great players in this Chelsea squad and in the Premier League, for the Football Writers' Association to name me their Footballer of the Year is a very proud moment in my career."

TUESDAY, 9 MAY 2017

Inter Milan sacked their coach Stefano Pioli but refused to comment on reports that they were planning to offer Conte a deal as a replacement.

Pioli was sacked after only six months as head coach. With three matches of the season remaining, Inter were seventh in Serie A, three points adrift of AC Milan and the final qualifying spot for the Europa League, and winless in seven league games. Pioli was Inter's ninth manager since Jose Mourinho left in 2010.

But later in the week at his news conference Conte confirmed, "I have a contract with Chelsea for also two more years. But it's logical that, when you start the work in a new club, the will is to continue to work and improve your work for many years. For sure, this is my will. But now the most important thing is to reach our target. To arrive at this moment, in this position, to have this great opportunity... we worked very hard for the whole season. Now it's important to be ready and to try to do this step, to win and then to celebrate together."

When asked whether he was prepared to finally end the rumours, Conte added: "I repeat what I said before: I have a contract for another two years with Chelsea, but also I like to repeat in this moment, for me and my players, the important thing is to be focused on the moment. The moment is very important. It's not important the single person, me, or the future for the players. Now we must be focused on the next few games and try to reach this fantastic target. I think it's right. It's normal to have a lot of speculation around my players and the coaches, different coaches, so it's important not to lose the concentration and be focused. The moment is fantastic for us, and I want to transfer this message."

Conte had in the past admitted to finding life "hard" in the capital, away from his wife and daughter, who have stayed in Turin. But home comforts at restaurants in the Chelsea Harbour area, where he lives, have helped him to settle into local life. In particular, Claudio Bruno, manager of the Santa Maria pizza restaurant on Waterford Road, a favourite of Conte's, confirmed, "He came here with his wife and daughter just a week after he moved here. He loved our tiramisu (head chef, Emanuele Tagliarina, deserves a mention). I said it was homemade and he begged me for the recipe. We reminded him of his home. He was fantastic and very friendly."

Another favourite haunt is Italian restaurant Gola near Stamford Bridge and Aaron Rutigliano, who runs the restaurant, said Conte loved the Puglian food (head chef, Angelo Prezio, deserves a mention too) that reminds him of his hometown Lecce. "He comes back so often. He is a nice, simple relaxed guy. He comes in by himself to eat dinner or sometimes just to watch football, or sometimes with a friend or his lovely wife and daughter. He's incredible with the customers, very polite. He has hundreds of people asking him for a picture and he never says no. Never, ever. Jose Mourinho wouldn't do that. But Antonio Conte is always standing up and smiling in every picture."

He noted that Antonio now seemed more settled. "At the beginning it was not easy for him, he had never worked outside of Italy before and London is a huge city. He needed to discover the city and the people, so I told him 'it takes eight months to fall in love with London'. It's not easy for anyone to come here but his mood has improved. I think now he is enjoying living in London."

He added that Conte asked him to check what his players eat. "Many times I have to send him a picture of the player and what they are eating. He is very hands-on but the players all love him."

Conte is also often spotted at his local Tesco Express - which he cleared out of Prosecco as a Christmas gift for his backroom staff.

Interestingly, Elisabetta, 41, and Vittoria looked set to join him permanently in London this summer, a good reason to believe he was staying at the Bridge. They had remained in Italy because of Vittoria's schooling and for her mother to finish a university course, although do arrive in the capital for a few days every week. Conte blew kisses to his wife and daughter in the crowd when Chelsea beat Middlesbrough. He first met his wife, whose family lived near his, when he was 21 and they married in 2013. Soon afterwards Conte, a former altar boy, had an audience with the Pope at the Vatican.

Victor Moses appreciated Conte's part in his elevation to a regular in the starting line-up. "I have always believed in the ability that I have got. I have always known that I've got the ability to play in a big club like Chelsea. I have proved that, and we have got a manager here that is willing to give everybody an opportunity. It was at Hull (in October) that it all started. I really enjoyed it and I took everything in. I kept watching the video of myself after the Hull game, to make sure I was in the right place, and after that I took it in and kept on improving. It's a big position. You need a lot of stamina to be able to play there, and it's a responsibility. I have been learning a lot defensively as well, the manager has been teaching me. As he played as a winger he could understand what wingers are going to do before they try and go past me. The more games I play, the better I get. He didn't say to me: 'Do you fancy playing wing-back?' He just put me in there, and constantly he was talking to me in training to make sure I was improving in it, talking me through it. I took that in and I didn't look back."

Not everyone liked Conte's style though. Arsene Wenger warned English football not to risk its mass appeal by following trends to play without the ball like, presumably, Chelsea and Leicester. He explained, "In the last two seasons, teams who do not have big possession have won the league. Football is about balance. We had games this season with 70 per cent possession like West Brom where lost 3-1 and Crystal Palace where we lost 3-0 and that means our balance was not right. But you cannot say to youth teams we do not want the ball. You cannot buy big players and say we do not want the ball. Big players want the ball. Sport has to encourage initiative. If it rewards too much teams who don't take initiative we have to rethink the whole process because people will not come forever to watch teams who do not want to take the initiative."

Wenger claimed the success of Chelsea and Leicester supports the theory that it is becoming physically impossible to compete effectively both at home in the domestic competitions as well as in Europe. "Teams who were not involved in Europe at all won the league, because the league is so physically difficult maybe it is very difficult to cope with both. We will see how Chelsea responds next season."

Ricardo Carvalho had some sympathy for Jose Mourinho and suggested that Chelsea's impressive season is more down to the players rather than Conte. Carvalho, who won three league titles under Mourinho at Stamford Bridge, explained that his former manager had already laid the foundations for Conte. "The truth is that Chelsea have great players too. They were champions with Mourinho." he told Omnisport. "The next year things did not go well, but the players are there. The players, who have been champions, most are there. And so, of course, Conte has merit too because he changed the team's strategy a bit, but most of the players who were champions with Mourinho were there. So quality and talent were there. And this (season), fortunately, they are playing well and will manage to win again, at least they are well on the way."

Thibaut Courtois believed last season's nightmare 10th-place finish would make winning the league even more special than in 2014/15. "This year it will be even more special, even more nice because last year was very bad. We had a lot of criticism and a new manager (Conte) came in." Courtois told talkSPORT. "We also lost a few games near the start and again there were a lot of critics, but we bounced back as a group very hard. We have played very well, so from that point of view it will be great to lift the trophy very soon."

Chelsea now needed only one more win as Courtois warned his teammates against celebrating too early. "We hope to do it at the first attempt. We know West Brom are a hard team to play against, we had a very tough game here. Every opponent who goes there has a hard game, they are eighth in the League and have had a very good year."

WEDNESDAY, 10 MAY 2017

Black Market tickets for Chelsea's potential title party at The Hawthorns were being offered for £1,800 with a face value of £30. Touts were cashing in as the away section was officially sold out but second-hand online sellers were touting tickets in this the first season of the Premier League's £30 price cap policy on away tickets. The cheapest away ticket on Ticketbis was £540 with the most expensive at £1,789.

FootballTicketTrade, another website, had tickets at £950. When Leicester City won the title, touts demanded as much as £8,000 a ticket from fans who wanted to be at their final game at the King Power Stadium. Albion still had some home tickets for sale but only for fans with a history of going to matches at the Hawthorns.

There was to be no trophy presentation at The Hawthorns even if Chelsea were confirmed as champions. They would have to wait until their final game of the season at Stamford Bridge for such a ceremony. It is the Premier League's preference to hold a presentation on the final day of the season, regardless of when the title is won.

Gary Neville told Sky Sports that he had not expected Chelsea to win the title. "The feeling I had at the beginning of the year was that they wouldn't win the league. I think we thought it would be one of the Manchester clubs. But (Conte) was picking up an experienced Chelsea squad and thinking about his Juventus teams and Italian teams, they were always experienced. I don't remember seeing many young players in those squads."

Pedro won the April Goal of the Month with his opener against Everton in a win that was a key milestone in the title race, beating off competition from Dele Alli, Roberto Firmino, Xherdan Shaqiri, Leroy Sane, Sam Clucas, Philippe Coutinho and teammate Diego Costa (Chelsea vs Southampton). Pedro's 12 goals from 39 games was one of the reasons for the team's success and he expressed his satisfaction in Spanish, with the translation: "Very happy with the April Goal of the Month Award. Thanks for voting #ComeOnBlues @chelseafc." His strike in the 2-1 victory over Tottenham back in November had also won a Goal of the Month award.

N'Golo Kante spoke of how his teammates showed their delight when they first saw him after he had won the PFA award. "They gave me a round of applause and that's very important because without them I couldn't receive this award. We are having a good season and I hope we can achieve something bigger than this award because I think football is about sticking together. I feel good on the pitch because of my teammates and they helped me a lot to get this award. We are playing very well together, we want to win and we want to give our best to win trophies for the club and for the fans."

THURSDAY, 11 MAY 2107

Tony Pulis, speaking on the eve of the game at his 9am media conference, commented: "We have three great games, three very competitive games left to come this season: Chelsea, Manchester City and Swansea on the last day. We're doing our damnedest to make it a competitive game and a good game. I don't think Antonio Conte will expect anything different. You've got to give Antonio and the players great credit for having a chance of lifting the Double. They deserve to be where they are. They've been the most consistent team in the league this year and they come to our place with a chance of winning it. We'll give it our best. We're still chasing a points tally that will keep us in eighth position, so we have a lot to play for."

Pulis was amused by Conte "going mad" during games, saying, "It's funny how things spin around. Seven or eight years ago Arsene Wenger was an absolute genius - he was a teacher and a prophet. He sat there and never got involved in the game and just worked things out from his seat. Now, however, Conte is an absolute genius going mad and bouncing up and down on the touchline."

Later in the day it was Conte's media conference and he stressed how tough it had been in his first season. "This season has not been easy. We faced a lot of problems but I want to thank the club, the players and the staff for working so hard to change things. I want the job to become a great one, because there are two opportunities to finish the season in the right way. This is another big step for me, because I like big challenges in my life. It's a good season and we want it to become a great season and then a fantastic season."

Conte revealed that it was a nice after dinner surprise to learn that Spurs had lost at West Ham. Asked what he did that Friday evening: "I had dinner, yes, with my family, with my wife and my daughter. I didn't watch the game. But after the dinner the surprise was great."

Back in 2013, his Juve players threw him in a cold bath to celebrate the victory in Italy, and asked if he was worried that his current players would do it again, he said: "Worried? I hope (they do). I think after one season where you work a lot and you suffer also, if you are able to win and to reach your target the celebration moment must be fantastic. Now is not right to think about this because we have to take three points, but after this I am sure my players want to celebrate in the right way, and I am the same."

Conte's press conference went as follows:

Injury news?

"No, I have all my players available for the game"

Are you finally excited?

"For sure this moment is a really good moment for us as we are so close to reaching a fantastic target for us. We mustn't forget we have to take three points in these three games. Tomorrow we have the first chance, but we must know to play against West Brom is not easy. They are a strong team, a good coach and the atmosphere will be very hot. It is important to enjoy this moment and this part of the season. We worked a lot and very hard. I like to repeat this is a good season, we want to make it a great season and the only way is to take three points."

Nursing the nerves of the players?

"I think my players are totally focused on the moment, they are feeling this moment is important for the club and the fans. It is important to live this moment in the right way, with the right pressure. We are in a good position, but we mustn't forget we must take three points to take this moment. I am seeing my players very focused and concentrated, and it is great for me to see this in the training session."

Better to do it at Stamford Bridge?

"Honestly, I prefer to try to win as soon as possible. It is not important where, but to win. Then you celebrate where you win. For this reason we must go game by game, tomorrow's game is the most important for us. It is our final and we are always thinking in this way, we must think this for a long time. It won't be easy because West Brom are a really strong team. We have a lot of respect for them. They played a great match against us at Stamford Bridge and we must pay great attention, but want to try to get three points."

Curse of Premier League-winning managers being sacked, will you be there next season?

"I have a contract with Chelsea, for two years. It is logical when you start the work in a new club, the will is to continue to work, you work, for many years. For sure this is my will. Now the most important thing is to reach our target, because to arrive at this moment, in this position and have a great opportunity, we have worked very hard. Now we need to be ready and do this step and to win and then to celebrate together."

New contract afterwards?

"When you reach a type of level the money could be important, but it is not all. When you stay at this level the money only explains your value, it is not important. If you work in football before as a footballer, stay at the top level for many years, then the same when you become a coach I don't think money is as important, it is important to win and to write the history of the club where you work. Money is important, but not all."

Why stop and watch a freestyler?

"I was finding a new player for next season [he joked]. I found this person with a ball that was doing incredible things. I stopped to watch him because it was very funny."

Secret to success?

"First of all I like to underline that this season at the start it wasn't easy because we faced a lot of problems. We had to solve a lot of problems. When you arrive tenth in the league, it means the problem is not only one, but there are a lot of problems, not only one person. You must divide the fault of this, for this reason we started this season to solve problems and to find the right solution to change the situation that was created in the last season. I have to say thanks to my club, players and staff to work very hard to change this. I have to say thanks to my players because it is not easy to adapt to a new method, philosophy and to work very hard to change totally the work if you compare the work of this season to the past. We are doing a really good job, but I want it to become great and fantastic. We have two very big opportunities in this season to make this happen."

How big an achievement?

"My biggest achievement was with the players to give me the ability to work hard on the physical and tactical aspect, for the set pieces and lots of situation, if you compare this season with the past. When you have this type of change it is not easy, you must be finding good men and then good players. I must be happy for this."

Where does it rank?

"This is another big step for me. I like to have a big challenge in my life, and now I only take this type of situation. When I started in my career, and then going to the national team maybe in our worst period, then Chelsea at a place where this could be another big, big step for me. In my career I enjoy to have this type of big challenge, I need to have this type of situation, where you arrive and have to work a lot and transform the situation in the right way."

N'Golo Kante?

"I can tell only positive things about N'Golo. He is a really good guy always have a smile in his face, he is working hard and always smiling, it is fantastic. N'Golo is having a great season for us, I am pleased for him and to receive the best player award in the league is great because in this league we have a lot of fantastic players. The most important thing is to have in his mind this desire to improve, this will to improve every day, because I think he can improve a lot and be stronger than now. (He's story) Is incredible, in my life I saw another situation like this. In Juventus (Moreno) Torricelli, who played with non-professional players and then played with Juventus and the national team and won a lot. It is great when you have this type of story, because this story gives people a lot of confidence that don't play professional. In football we always give this type of situation."

Inter Milan rumours?

"I repeat what I said before, I have a contract, two years with Chelsea, but also I like to repeat in this moment for me and my players the most important thing is to be focused in the moment, the moment is very important. It is not important the single person now, me or the future of the players, we must be focused on the next game. In this moment it is normal to have a lot of speculation, on me, the players, the coaches, we can't lose the focus, now the moment is very important for us."

Did you watch Spurs?

"I had dinner with my family, with my wife and daughter, I didn't watch the match but afterwards the surprise was great, honestly."

Rate the season?

"So far it has been great, when you arrive in a new country, new language, different habits and culture, bringing your idea of football it is not easy. For myself this season was a great challenge for me and also for my family, but I am enjoying it a lot. Honestly, you are arriving at the end of the season, it is normal to feel this season a bit. We are arriving now and you have to enjoy and live this moment with your players, and the club and every single person that works at Chelsea. In this season, every single person that works for Chelsea is deserving to enjoy this moment. It is very important to take these three points. After this I will be more relaxed, before this I am enjoying the moment but want to be more relaxed."

Resting players after tomorrow?

"The most important thing is to win, take the three points and prepare for the future. I am not worried about the physical condition, I am not worried for our shape, we worked a lot and the shape is good. It is important to take the three points to win the title, then we have the possibility to face the right solution before playing the final of the FA Cup."

What will the Chelsea players do to you if you win?

"Worried? (they throw him in the bath) I hope. I think after one season where you work a lot and you suffer also, if you are able to win and to reach your target the celebration moment must be fantastic. Now is not right to think about this because we have to take three points, but after this I am sure my players want to celebrate in the right way, and I am the same."

Conte reiterated how much he suffered in the early part of the season, and that he didn't see a moment when he thought he'd win the title. "It's impossible to win without suffering. When you work very hard, it's normal to suffer. I've never seen a player who, during hard work, doesn't suffer. I think that when you suffer, you become stronger and then you are ready to face every situation - above all, problematic situations during games. We started this season with three wins, but honestly I wasn't calm. I didn't see what I was wanting to see. But after a bad defeat against Arsenal… after that defeat I understood we had to change something in the tactical aspect and find the right solution, also to improve our work, our tactical work. Then I saw my team improving game by game and increasing confidence, increasing confidence in the work. In what we were doing. If you ask me a proper moment (when I knew we'd win the title), I don't see one. I don't see a moment."

West Brom had only lost at home to Chelsea for the first time in five games in the corresponding fixture last season. However, Chelsea's only defeat in the last eight Premier League meetings came at The Hawthorns in May 2015, a 3-0 loss after they had already won the title. Chelsea were out to complete the double over Albion for the first time in six seasons. There had not been a goalless draw between the two teams in 89 top-flight encounters since March 1924. West Brom had lost 1-0 in each of their last three games at The Hawthorns and could equal the club's Premier League record of failing to score in four consecutive home matches, set from November 2004 to January 2005. Albion had the worst record in the division since the start of April, earning just two points from six matches, so the scene was surely set for a title celebration…

FRIDAY, 12 MAY 2017
West Bromwich Albion 0-1 Chelsea
Premier League

THE DAY CONTE LANDED THE PREMIER LEAGUE TITLE

Conte would become only the fourth manager to lift the Premier League trophy in his first season in England, emulating Jose Mourinho in 2004/05, Carlo Ancelotti in 2009/10 and Manuel Pellegrini in 2013/14. He led his players on a walk through a rain-soaked Birmingham city centre in the morning on the way to the neighbouring Black Country. Eden Hazard, Thibaut Courtois and N'Golo Kante protected themselves from the elements with hoods up while their team bus, stopped on double yellow lines, had a parking ticket slapped on it.

John Terry would become the first non-Manchester United player to win the Premier League five times.

Meanwhile, back in north London, Pochettino would be watching on television, he confirmed at his mid-afternoon media conference. "I will watch because I love football, there is no reason for not watching - football is my passion. The season so far has been good, but when you don't win you feel disappointed as that is our ambition. It was difficult from Monday to Wednesday at training and it was difficult to be happy but then we have only been focused on Manchester United. We are looking forward to playing and the last game at White Hart Lane so there are many reasons to be focused. We have three games to play, we still feel disappointed from last week and it is difficult to take off this feeling. We missed a good opportunity to put pressure on Chelsea and to fight nearly to the end. Now it is in their hands to win the Premier League and it is so difficult for us to win. Before the game we thought anything was possible, but afterwards it was a big disappointment and it was difficult to lift everyone."

The Evening Standard had an interview with the captain in which Gary Cahill revealed how the players vowed to make amends for a diabolically bad defence of the title, as he said: "It's a motivation we have had - tasting disappointment last year and not wanting to be anywhere near that again. I wanted it so badly this year, along with everybody else. It's been largely the same group of players and we have had a real determination about what we wanted to achieve this season and getting back to the levels we want to be at. The quality has always been there, just with the right attitude and work ethic in training, day in and day out, we have produced this season. We didn't want the feeling we had last year. We wanted the feeling I have had the majority of the time I have been here."

He was determined to finish off Spurs' pursuit at West Brom. "Obviously we can see it now, it's a matter of one game. We want to get it done as soon as we can. There is calmness but there is excitement. We have been playing under a lot of pressure for the last few weeks. The way the games have gone and the way Tottenham have fought until the end means we have been under pressure. It's been enjoyable to get the results but it has been intense. Against Middlesbrough we played relaxed, in a good way. I hope that continues and we can produce the same tonight. We have put ourselves in a fantastic position and we should enjoy the moment and keep focused on one more game to seal a great season."

Eden Hazard still has ambitions to be voted as winner of the Ballon d'Or, the award for the world's best player and doesn't have to leave Chelsea to achieve it as he said on Sky Sports: "Could I win it? If I play next season, we win the League and Champions League and maybe I win the World Cup with Belgium, why not? You never know. In the last ten years, some of the Ballon D'Or winners play in Spain, but it's not automatic. If a player is better in England, he will win it."

Like Cahill, Hazard would rather secure first place this evening than rely on the home games to come against Watford or Sunderland. "We want to celebrate tonight, then come back to Stamford Bridge and celebrate with the fans. You never know what happens in football. When you can win a trophy you just have to win. We all know if we win we will be champions, so maybe we have a lot of pressure, but we are almost there."

A supporter was waiting to turn £10 into £71,000 after placing an inspired football bet on six different league title winners; with now only Chelsea left to force bookmakers William Hill to lavishly pay out. The mystery man from Romford backed Chelsea to win the Premier League, Newcastle to win the Championship, Sheffield United to win League One, Portsmouth to triumph in League Two, Hibernian to lift the Scottish Championship and Livingston to win the Scottish League One division. The six-team champions' accumulator with William Hill was at odds of 7087/1.

"Given that this bet was placed so long ago and for such a small stake, no one can recall the customer." William Hill spokesman Joe Crilly told the Mirror. "However, should Chelsea get the three points they need, we expect the punter will be coming to collect his/her winnings very shortly."

Chelsea became champions of England for a sixth time - with two games to spare.

Chelsea now need to win the FA Cup to turn a "great season" into a "fantastic" one after clinching the Premier League title, concluded Conte.

Conte lives through each moment on the pitch with his players. "Every game I feel like I have played with my players! I show my passion and my will, my desire to stay with my players in every moment of the game. This is me, I am this. In the present, in the past, I stay with my players in positive and negative situations. We won this title together."

Michy Batshuayi was the unlikely hero, a bit part player who cost a small fortune, with a late winner after coming off the bench to break the stalemate. Conte embraced his technical staff and sprinted up and down the touchline and jumped around hitting himself in the face!

"For me to win in my first season in England, I am really proud of the achievement." Conte told BBC Sport. "My players showed me great professionalism, commitment, work-rate and will to try to win this league. We have two games to celebrate, then we try to make this season from great to fantastic."

Chelsea had been eighth, eight points behind leaders Manchester City after losing badly at the Emirates Stadium earlier in the season. It had prompted Conte to, now famously, switch tactics late in the game, after which, he continued with the three at the back to launch a 13-match winning streak. Referring back Conte said "It was very frustrating for me because at the end of the Arsenal game I didn't see anything from my work or my ideas on football. But in this moment I found the strength to change and take responsibility and find a system for the players. It was a key moment in the season because every single player found in this system the best for him. When you arrive after a bad season and the team has arrived at 10th in the league it means there are a lot of problems. To find the right solution quickly isn't easy and for this I want to thank my players because they trusted in the new work, my philosophy, video analysis to see mistakes and they showed the right attitude and behaviour."

Conte was delighted that Michy Batshuayi had paid him back by scoring. He brought the forward on for Hazard in the 76th minute and six minutes later the substitute delivered the match-winner from close range following Azpilicueta's cross. It was only Batshuayi's second goal in the Premier League and first since August in a season in which he had struggled to adapt to English football; and he needed the Belgium keeper to translate questions for him when interviewed on the pitch after his unexpected exploits.

"I must be pleased, above all, for him. We all know the season, the difficulty he found in this first season for him. It's not easy to play in this league." Conte said. "I think this league is very strong. This league is fantastic to play and be a manager in. For him, I'm pleased because he scored two goals this season. These goals were very important for him and for us. My substitutions were very good... Michy repaid me a lot for this choice. Willian was also very good. It means I trust in my squad. Hazard was a bit tired and also Pedro. I wanted to get more energy with Michy." Conte added to Sky Sports.

Having been soaked in the dressing room during the post-match celebrations, Conte arrived to field questions from the press decked in a tracksuit. He apologised after arriving late to his post-match news conference, explaining his players had showered him with beer and champagne and that "my suit is a disaster". He had cut his lip as he celebrated Batshuayi's winner, but that it was not the first time he had been injured in this way. "In these moments, anything can happen." he said. "I hurt my lip during the Euros as well and they had to put a stitch in it after we scored against Belgium. (Italy international) Simone Zaza gave me a header - I don't think it was on purpose. I'm not sure if this was a header or a punch but I am ready to repeat this."

Conte's meeting with the media was short-lived as Diego Costa and David Luiz invaded the press area. Costa shouted random English words, removed a fire extinguisher from the wall and aimed the nozzle at his manager. Fortunately Chelsea's director of communications, Steve Atkins, a former Foreign Office press aide, spotted the incident. "Diego!" he shouted, and Luiz reached over to rescue the fire extinguisher as Conte continued to take questions…"To repay the club is very important for me…" Conte managed before the two players noisily bundled their coach out of his post-match press conference; they were impatient for their manager to rejoin their post-victory party, virtually dragging him away.

Earlier in the changing rooms, footage showed Costa in his underpants simulating an act on a kitman and then trying to rinse away the champagne he had inadvertently poured in his eyes with orange Lucozade. Costa then looked towards his manager. "Diego is No.1!" he shouted. "Diego loves you!"

"Yes, Diego" the Chelsea manager said plaintively, "I love you too."

"I cannot describe how he was in the dressing room afterwards." said Willian of his manager, talking outside the dressing room. "How he is on the touchline, he's the same with us. After the game, if we win he comes in and he's crazy." Conte might be a non-stop bag of energy on the touchline but he is focused and concentrated once he enters the dressing room. "At half-time, he's different." continued Willian. "He's calm. He's easy, he tries to find the best solution for the team and communicate it to them."

However, Conte freed himself from his players and returned to finish the media briefing where he commented: "If you can continue with these players you can improve a lot." Conte said he and his squad had only "started to do our work" adding, "Now they know my idea, I know them, the characteristics of my players, and we can improve. The club want to fight to win every competition - we have the same ambition. For this reason we try to keep the best players. I think the club want to fight to win every competition. We have the same ambition. For this reason we try to keep the best players. We must enjoy and celebrate because when you work hard it is important to celebrate… and also to prepare for the final of the FA Cup, because we have the opportunity to win the Double."

Asked if he would be at Stamford Bridge next season, Conte said: "Yeah, yeah. And we have to improve next season. We are working only nine months together."

Thibaut Courtois was already targeting the Champions League with Chelsea. "Of course, I'm committed to Chelsea. Next season there is a new goal of the Champions League. I think a lot of players are hungry for winning that as well." At only 25-years old Courtois has now won four league titles: the Belgian League with Genk, La Liga with Atletico Madrid and two Premier League titles. Although ranked alongside David de Gea as a future Real Madrid keeper Courtois has two years left on his Chelsea contract and will be staying to challenge for the Champions League, where he finished as runners-up with Atletico in 2014. "I don't think now is the moment to speak about that but, of course, I'm committed to Chelsea. I think next season there is a new goal of the Champions League. It's been a few years since Chelsea won it and I missed out on one (title) in the last minute, so I think a lot of players are hungry for winning that as well. Obviously you need additions because you play on four different fronts, so I think that's important, but I guess the club and the manager know what they're doing. We already have a lot of quality, but maybe sometimes you need a bit more depth because this year we didn't have injuries and you never know what can happen next year. So obviously I guess they will do their work now and hopefully we can finish the season with an FA Cup win as well."

Courtois reiterated his commitment despite being on Real Madrid's wish-list, and is adamant that this team need to challenge in the Champions League. He said: "It's amazing, especially after last year, to bounce back in this way, to be champions, having been top for a long time. Obviously, last year we had a lot of critics, a lot of laughter at us. We had a moment when we were 15th, 16th in the league. People laugh and people get criticised - it's not nice after a season when you won the league. Some criticisms were deserved and others not and if you bounce back winning the title again, that's amazing. They said we didn't want to play any more, they said we were lazy, that kind of stuff, and it's not true. We tried to win our games, but last year was just an off year, especially for a team like Chelsea and the players that were here. Everybody is used to playing for trophies and last year that was not the case and everybody's pride was hurt. I think that is why we wanted to bounce back this season. After the Arsenal game when we lost 3-0 we were in a bad moment again, but we bounced back. And we had an amazing six, seven months. We're very proud about that."

Conte had now effectively won four successive domestic titles as a manager after his trio of titles at Juventus between 2012 and 2014 - he had, of course, managed the Italian national side following success in Serie A. He now looked to emulate his compatriot Carlo Ancelotti by securing the domestic Double. "It's amazing." Conte told Chelsea TV. "I want to say thanks to my players, my staff, the club, who always support me. Now it's important to rest and we want to try to win also the FA Cup and for this great season to become a fantastic season. I'm living great emotion at this moment."

Gary Cahill said the players always believed they could mount a title challenge despite finishing 10th last season and 31 points adrift of champions Leicester City. "We felt confident in the dressing room all season. We deserved it over the season. We worked very hard and have been the better team. It is fantastic to wrap it up with a couple of games to go. It is very difficult in this league."

David Luiz confirmed that the chance to land his first English title was one of the reasons he returned to the club. "When I decided to come back here I dreamed to win the Premier League. I am very happy because my dream came true. Conte works with passion every day. He deserves it because he is working hard every day."

Conte enjoyed a post-match drink with Albion boss Tony Pulis and Chelsea assistant coach Steve Holland. Pulis was typically gracious in defeat, congratulating the champions on being the best side in the division. "They're worthy champions, they take a lot of credit and could do the Double." he told BBC Sport. "They're a wonderful team and they've been the best. They had a poor start but recovered from that and have been the most consistent. We gave them a really tough game though. It's the decisions that players make and a little bit of quality that makes the difference, but I can't fault the players. Chelsea got the goal and they deserve to win the league."

Pulis was also full of praise for the way Conte had turned around Chelsea's season. "It's good working against the top managers, which Conte is. He's been fantastic. His enthusiasm and attitude but he's also very good tactically. I had a chat with him before the game and he recognised he had to change it earlier in the season, or he might have got changed himself. He's made it his team. Italian teams are tactically organised and well run. He changed their shape and they've been superb from that moment onwards."

Conte and his players engaged in mass celebrations in front of their jubilant away supporters. They partied like worthy champions on the pitch and knew they had deserved it. Conte was thrown high into the night air by his players and John Terry threw his boots into the crowd. Eden Hazard ended up wearing his shirt the wrong way round.

Speaking to Sky Sports, Cesc Fabregas declared: "Football is f****** unbelievable. I thought it was going to be one of those days. We had so many chances in the first half and then we got a bit nervous. The beauty of football, a player who didn't play a lot scores the winning goal for the championship. Football is f****** unbelievable."… Cue the obligatory apologies from the Sky interviewer for the "bad language you might have heard!" Yep, we all heard it.

Captain Cahill tried to keep his calm despite being attacked during his interview by the likes of David Luiz. He said: "These are times in football. These opportunities that you want to grasp with both hands. You just want to cherish them. Consistently I think we've been the best team in the league. There's no better feeling than this in football. People have written us off as a team and individually and this has shut them up. We are champions. It's another one in the cabinet."

John Terry, who had spent most of the season on the substitutes' bench, was still proud of the newly crowned champions. "These boys have been on the field doing it week in week out. It's been a delight to sit and watch; a different perspective. The togetherness was shown from day one."

Conte added: "I think this achievement is a great achievement for the players, my players. I want to show thanks for their commitment and their desire to do something this season. After this win I think we must be happy for this season."

The switch to 3-4-3 formation was key to the club's charge to the title. "That decision changed our season. We had to change and find a new suit for our team. In my mind there was this option to play a 3-4-3 because I knew I had the players to do that. We were not lucky, we did a great job. It's important to rest. It is a great season but now we can win the FA Cup. Every game I feel like I have played with my players! I show my passion and my will, my desire to stay with my players in every moment of the game. This is me, I am this. In the present, in the past, I stay with my players in positive and negative situations. We won this title together."

The Hawthorns was unfortunately marred by fighting between supporters, following concerns about illegal ticket touting. Supporters from both teams were among ten people arrested by West Midlands Police. The authorities confirmed that four fans were arrested for invading the pitch, with the rest detained for public order offences. Demand for tickets among Blues supporters far outstripped the 2,773 the visitors were allocated by the Midlands club. West Brom said in a statement on Wednesday that "the last thing we want is for the occasion to be soured by safety and security issues." During the second half, police and stewards had to intervene as clashes broke out between supporters in the home end. At the opposite end of the ground to where travelling supporters were housed, security staff spent minutes trying to contain the violence and break up fighting fans - some of whom were led from the ground while others spilled on to the pitch. Albion warned fans that those selling their tickets to Chelsea supporters would face a ban from The Hawthorns. It read: "We have no official ticket-selling partner and it is an offence for any home end tickets to be sold on. We will display zero tolerance with anyone who is found to have broken the law in this way. Any fans clearly identified as Chelsea supporters in the home sections will be ejected. This is for everyone's safety and security. We have the prospect of a dramatic and exciting night at The Hawthorns which we all want to enjoy."

Following the violence among supporters, Chief Inspector Nick Rowe from West Midlands Police commented: "Police arrested a total of ten people during last night's West Bromwich Albion vs Chelsea match at The Hawthorns. Four arrests were for pitch incursion and the rest for football related public order offences. Overall it was a great evening match with an intense atmosphere, with only minor issues dealt with by officers."

And as the celebrations continued social media went into #Chelsea overdrive.

@ChelseaFC - "CHAMPIONS!"

In fact, at one stage, #Chelsea was trending at #1 worldwide with 400k+ tweets!

Fernando Torres sparked anger among Liverpool fans by sending Chelsea a special message. Torres, who made the controversial £50m move from Liverpool to Stamford Bridge in January 2011, posted on Twitter: "Congrats Champions!!! Now let's fight for the FA Cup".

Thibaut Courtois streamed a Facebook Live video of Blues stars celebrating, and there was one big name tuning in that caught the eye - Romelu Lukaku. The Belgium international liked the video and commented, perhaps poking fun at his fellow countryman Batshuayi, "Aaah Michy" over an image of Chelsea goalkeeper Courtois and winger Pedro in the visitors' changing rooms.

Batshuayi seemed more concerned about getting his 'in-form' and 'one to watch' cards on the FIFA computer game:

@mbatshuayi - "If I don't get my IF card after that I might quit Fifa bro yall better buy this OTW real quick"

Premier League Table, Top 2, as it stood on 12 May 2017:

		P	W	D	L	F	A	GD	Pts
1	Chelsea	36	28	3	5	76	29	+47	87
2	Tottenham Hotspur	35	23	8	4	71	23	+48	77

SATURDAY, 13 MAY 2017

The Reaction

"Batman to the Rescue" - Daily Express

Conte's triumph received plenty of attention and headlines in his homeland. Italy's two biggest newspapers both devoted their front pages to Chelsea after they had mathematically secured the title.

Corriere dello Sport led with the headline "Special Conte" and praised him for winning the top-flight title at the first time of asking. "After Ranieri, another Italian." they wrote; referring to Claudio Ranieri who led Leicester City to their remarkable triumph last season.

Corriere journalist Ivan Zazzaroni noted: "Conte is different. In my opinion, he is the strongest coach in the world at the moment." he claimed. "On the field, on the bench and in the locker room he is a phenomenon."

La Gazzette dello Sport congratulated the man of the moment. Their front page read "Conte Oh Yes! Chelsea Campione in Premier League" with a picture of him being hoisted in the air by his players.

Inside, they continued to praise the remarkable transformation of the former Juve boss. Gazzetta's Stefano Cantalupi, who was at the match against West Brom, wrote that Conte was now "a hero in two worlds," as Blues fans revere him the same way Juventus supporters do. "Winning at his first attempt, like Mourinho and Ancelotti. He'll be pleased to have done so with two games to spare and after a year in which they had finished 10th. A sporting miracle."

Fabrizio Bocca of La Repubblica made a special mention of the calibre of impressive coaches – Wenger, Klopp, Mourinho, Pochettino and Guardiola – that Conte had triumphed over.

Also in La Repubblica, Andrea Sorrentino wrote "He came, he saw, he conquered." adding his praise for the "spirit, ferocity and tactical awareness that helped them overcome all the obstacles in their path."

Tuttosport on their front page described him as "King Conte".

Conte had continually been linked with a move away from Chelsea and according to Italian sports channel, Sportmediaset, the coach will now meet with Roman Abramovich, seeking assurances from the owner about investment in the squad. Having won three consecutive Serie A titles at Juventus, Conte had quit citing a lack of funds in the transfer market that he believed would prevent the Bianconeri ever truly competing in the Champions League.

Conte and his backroom team were later back at one of their favourite haunts to enjoy a rare, but obviously deserved night off. The Italian Gola restaurant on the Fulham Road in west London had soon proudly posted a video of Conte opening a celebratory bottle of champagne.

Michy Batshuayi had got straight back into work mode with a gym session on Saturday morning, taking to Instagram to share the moment with his fans. Posting a snap of himself hard at work in the gym, Batshuayi wrote: "Free day ? LOL #nodaysoff #dedication."

John Terry, posting a video to his 3.2m followers, could be seen sitting at home enjoying a quiet Saturday morning, before panning the camera across to reveal the gleaming Premier League trophy with a smile. Captioning the video, Terry wrote: "What an incredible feeling waking up and being CHAMPIONS."

Thibaut Courtois and Marcos Alonso uploaded images taken in the immediate aftermath of the game, celebrating both out on the pitch and in the dressing room. Courtois enjoying: "That feeling of being champion again! Incredible emotions."

Cesc Fabregas wished fans a wonderful day while elsewhere on social media Chelsea greats added their tributes. Frank Lampard shared an image of himself suited and booted on The Hawthorns turf, revealing his pride to be present and see his former teammates clinch the title.

Didier Drogba, now playing in America with Phoenix Rising FC, posted a video of the full-time celebrations. "Perfect way to go to bed for me and perfect way for the best fans in the world to wake up. Chelsea FC Championssssssss come on you bluuuueesss. What a season boys!!! Well done it's well deserved My People !!!!" wrote Drogba.

When asked if he thought Conte could go on to build a dynasty at Chelsea, Frank Lampard said: "I think so. If you're a Chelsea fan that's what you're hoping for now. The way he's held himself this year and the results have been different class. I think he's going to be backed, and he does need backing. It's a great squad of players they've got there. Maybe a freshen-up, don't lose your best players and add one or two at the top end." Chelsea were deserved champions but he warned they might find it tougher next term. Speaking to Sky Sports, Lampard added: "They are by far the strongest team this year. The consistency, the desire, the quality in the team - they deserve it, and they deserve that moment with their own fans. It will be a big test next year. The formation they play won't be a surprise for anybody and all the other teams behind them will be back stronger."

John Terry has now won five Premier League titles and Lampard suggested the 36-year-old's influence will be tough to replace. "If he's going to leave this is the year to do it. He hasn't played a huge part on the pitch, but the part he's played behind the scenes, I know for a fact, once he goes, everyone will appreciate him even more. Someone has to take the mantle now. He's such a big miss for them. Gary Cahill, maybe he'll step up even more now, but John Terry is so important for this club."

Conte had won the title with a relatively small squad, using 'only' 23 players so far, equal lowest with Liverpool, Spurs and West Brom. Chelsea used 30 players when they won titles in 2004/05 and 2009/10, and 25 in 2005/06 and 2014/15.

Despite the recent FA Youth Cup success former Chelsea and Scotland winger, Pat Nevin, is convinced it will be a busy summer for Chelsea: "I think there is a lot to do. There is no way you will get into the latter reaches of the Champions League and the Premier League with the current squad unless some of the kids step up unbelievably and that's a massive jump... too big. Will you keep everybody that's here? Antonio's probably got his eye on four or five and if he gets them there is no reason why he will not continue to be successful."

BBC analyst and former Tottenham and Newcastle United midfielder Jermaine Jenas believed Conte deserves the credit for turning the club around, highlighting his conversion of Moses from a fringe midfielder to first-choice wing-back. "They lost their way last season, they were unrecognisable. He has come in and reinvigorated them. What I like about Conte is he gave Moses a chance and trusted him. He has made him a better player and a Premier League champion. The West Brom win typified Chelsea. They were professional, performed well and when it mattered put in a big performance. At times they had to be resolute. Antonio Conte is a master tactician. He made one decision that changed their season and then in this game another to bring on Michy Batshuayi. They are the little nuggets he brings that make him so special. Tactically, individually, what Antonio Conte has done with these Chelsea players and to bring them together is sensational. Antonio Conte already had winners in his ranks."

Andy Townsend joined the Weekend Sports Breakfast and heaped praise on Conte. Former Blues midfielder Townsend told talkSPORT: "They have been outstanding, they've been the best team, they've been the best prepared, they've been well-drilled, they haven't panicked when they've had one or two bad moments and they've dug in again and regrouped. They're an amazing team and you can only see them getting stronger."

Townsend then spoke of the work the Blues players put in to adapt to the changes Conte has implemented. "I spoke to Thibaut Courtois right after the game last night, and he said people don't always appreciate the amount of effort we've all had to put in to buy into Antonio Conte, to take on board exactly the way he sees it and the way he believes it works. And again, we were interviewing Frank Lampard and Eidur Gudjohnsen after the game, and they said unless you buy into it, unless you believe it, unless you're prepared to really go with it when a new manager arrives, it's not going to happen, it won't work. We see someone like Antonio Conte walk through the door and you see him have a little bit of an awkward start and then he changes it and goes with what he feels he knows best. From that moment Chelsea became the champions-elect if you like, because then, automatically, everything dropped into place and all of a sudden they were one. Whereas at the start of the season I think he was having a look at one or two; he was trying to understand what perhaps Chelsea had done previously that had worked for them. Then all of a sudden, it was, 'right, listen, we're all going to do this my way.'"

Claudio Ranieri was proud to see Conte carrying the torch for Italian coaching. "I am so proud to hand over the reins of the Premier League to Conte - from one Italian to another Italian." Ranieri told Gazzetta dello Sport. "It's another award for our school (of coaching). After my story at Leicester, this wonderful adventure at Chelsea was not easy at the first attempt, but Conte has passed the test of English football with flying colours. Antonio was very good with all the aspects - team management, relations with the outside world, media relations - the fundamentals remain a coach's job."

Arsene Wenger offered praise, quickly diluted with caveats: "I congratulate Chelsea on what they've done, but you see as well when they play in Europe, it'll be a different story. I think we struggled a lot after what happened against Bayern, a big blow, but it was still possible at the moment we played Bayern to come back at Chelsea. They've done well but in the last two seasons the team that won the league hasn't played in Europe. It'll be a different season next year because they will have to play on Saturday-Wednesday-Saturday."

Conte's former Juventus teammate Alessandro Del Piero insisted he can build on the title win. Del Piero believes Conte can build an empire and legacy at Stamford Bridge, should he wish to stay in west London. He told talkSPORT: "There are a lot of rumours regarding Inter Milan and, honestly, I don't know. He's just arrived in England. I think he has the possibility to build an incredible story there. I don't know what is going on, first of all, in his heart and then what the prospects of the teams are. Let's see. By the way, it's not a bad choice." Del Piero, who helped Juventus win the Champions League in 1996 alongside Conte, praised his compatriot's achievements, which mirrored his first campaign as boss of the Old Lady in 2011/12. "I think he did amazing work. Chelsea were in the same condition as Juventus, who had finished seventh in the table, and then we won the title. This is what has happened again, its history repeating in a different country. He's a great guy, and an amazing coach. I'm happy that, straight away, in his first year he can show his best and keep Chelsea at the top of the league, and probably next year top of the Champions League."

Pat Nevin witnessed a moment that underlined the absolute respect Conte commands. He told BBC Sport: "The fun guys at the training ground, the daft ones, David Luiz and Diego Costa, are always having a laugh. Costa was sneaking up behind people and throwing big buckets of iced water over them. He was running up behind Antonio and he was going to do the ice bucket over the top and, even though you know Antonio is a good laugh and he was having a joke, he got all the way up then chickened out. The players kind of think you're one of them but they're not quite sure. As a manager you've nailed it then - and Conte has nailed it. I have also spent a couple of hours with him and interviewed him. We spoke before, just chatting, but he is the classic mix in that he can be great fun but then you see the steely eyes and think you wouldn't want to get on the wrong side of him. You judge a manager by whether he gets the most out of his players. If you are managing a company, a newspaper, a shop or a football team, your job is to get the best out of your staff. He has done that."

"You see he is going 3-4-3 and you know who the wide man in the four is. It is Cesar Azpilicueta - only it isn't. It's Victor Moses. I love it and it impresses me so much when managers do things you don't expect. It is also about the player who plays alongside him. Moses was often alongside the manager, who was shouting and telling him almost inch by inch where to be, and he also has Azpilicueta beside him who is as good as there is in the business at closing down, getting close to people and not letting crosses in."

The tactical change was seen as Conte returning to old ways but Nevin disagrees: "Looking historically at what he'd done before to what he does now, he's not a 3-4-3 man. 100 per cent not. That worked because he needed to try something else. I'd seen Juventus a lot. I think most people thought they were a 3-5-2, or a version of that, and sometimes a 3-4-3 as well. I looked because I wanted to prove to myself how often he played Andrea Barzagli, Giorgio Chiellini and Leonardo Bonucci together and quite often it was four at the back but very adaptable. If he needed it, he could utilise it. At heart he wants to play two centre-forwards but when Andrea Pirlo came in at Juve he couldn't play a 4-4-2. You can't do that with Fabregas either because you need two in there like Kante and Nemanja Matic, who can do all the dogged work as well. What has interested me is that when he changed to a 3-4-3, which I thought was really quite out there as I didn't see it coming, it worked. I then thought he would change that quite quickly - he didn't."

Nevin has an ominous warning for Chelsea's rivals, saying: "I actually think you have only seen 20 per cent of his tactical nous. I think you have seen something that has scratched the surface so far."

Italian journalist Stefano Boldrini, London correspondent for Italian daily Gazzetta dello Sport, told BBC Sport: "Conte is a person who lives football every hour, every minute of the day. Conte thinks about football 48 hours a day. He is always focused on his work, not only on the training ground or in his office. When he is at his house in Chelsea he watches football, speaks with his staff. His mind is always on his work. It was the same in Italy but this is a new experience. He has had to fight against Jose Mourinho's Manchester United, Pep Guardiola's Manchester City, Jurgen Klopp at Liverpool, Arsenal of Arsene Wenger, Mauricio Pochettino at Tottenham. He likes the sea and he likes good restaurants but his life is about good football. He is enjoying life in England but Conte does not go into London a lot. His life is Cobham and his house. He is very focused on his work. He is a very reserved person. For him it was not easy because in one year he has had to learn English, to learn about English football. I don't know about the future but he is really focused on his work now."

Conte's affection for English football was demonstrated when he applauded the Middlesbrough fans who continued to support their team even though they were relegated with defeat at Chelsea. Boldrini said: "I know he is a passionate man but it was fantastic when he went to the Middlesbrough fans to applaud them. It was class behaviour and this is Antonio Conte. He loves England. He was celebrating the civilisation of English football with what happened with the Boro fans. It was honest."

"He has been very important for Moses because he hadn't made an impact at Chelsea until Conte came. Conte discovered what Moses could do in pre-season and it was a success for Conte because he saw something other managers didn't see. He speaks with every player. Conte has a very good relationship with Cesc Fabregas, who has not played all the time, and he also has a very good relationship with Diego Costa. He has spoken to him a lot of times about his behaviour, to be more focused on the game and not his opponent."

Has his success surprised his countrymen in Italy? "Maybe we didn't think he would win in his first year but we were sure he would be a success." answered Boldrini. "We knew of his focus and passion and had faith. In Italy, the pressure is outside the pitch. In England, the pressure is on the pitch because you play against Manchester United, Manchester City, Arsenal, Tottenham, Everton, Liverpool - the pressure is the football and this is the pressure he enjoys and is the big difference between Italy and England."

Chelsea were first up on the Match of the Day schedule. Former England and Arsenal striker Ian Wright commented: "The way he has got players playing, Victor Moses, Willian etc is incredible - he's kept the whole squad happy. There's been no red cards, discipline has been very good, and the amount of consistency through not changing players so often has kept the players together. Conte has also got that assured calmness - not so much on the pitch but behind the scenes."

Former England and Newcastle striker Alan Shearer added: "Antonio Conte's passion and enthusiasm has filtered down to all his players all season. The big change was the shift in the system after they lost to Liverpool and were beaten 3-0 by Arsenal at the Emirates. They were playing four at the back and it wasn't working at all so he had to do something. They went to a back three, changed a couple of players, and then won 13 games on the spin, which was an incredible turnaround for a team that had struggled. They've certainly benefited without being in Europe so they've used that to their advantage. There is a case for mentioning all their players but I've got to pick out Cesar Azpilicueta, who has played every minute of every league game and turned in an eight or nine out of ten performance every time."

Glenn Hoddle in his Mail on Sunday column summed up: "It has been an amazing season for Antonio Conte, adapting to English football in what has been one of the most competitive seasons ever in the Premier League. But it has been a great campaign to underline the importance of tactics to the game. No one would dispute that the turning point in this title race came when Conte switched to a back three after the 3-0 defeat at Arsenal. Watching that game, he switched to the system in the second half and the team looked a lot more solid and got a grip of possession. I remember speculating on the TV as to whether he would stick with the system after the game and that I thought he would."

"Antonio Conte has flourished in the most competitive Premier League season we have seen. Of course, I've always been a big advocate of that particular way of playing. I feel it gives you numbers in midfield and strength at the back with the flexibility of the full backs. And it is almost the full backs that have most impressed me this season. When Conte first started using the system, it was almost as if he didn't care whether he had the players that fitted the system; he was going to make it work whatever. Marcos Alonso and Victor Moses looked like the weak link but actually they have both turned out to be excellent. I've been particularly taken with Moses and the way he has adapted to his defensive responsibilities. But the other player who has shone recently is one who initially looked as if he might be the odd man out under Conte - Cesc Fabregas has been immense of late. He is a wonderful player and quite some player to have coming off the bench."

"The Italian's tactical switch at the Emirates was a clear turning point in Chelsea's season. If you are winning the game he is so good at keeping possession, which is exactly what you need to keep control of the match. And if you are losing, he is the man who can produce a game-changing assist. He showed that again against Middlesbrough on Monday night. Conte has managed so many situations well, from Fabregas to dealing with Diego Costa's apparent unrest in January to responding to his shaky start."

"In a league in which the likes of Pep Guardiola, Jose Mourinho and Jurgen Klopp were all expected to make the big impact, he has created a team with by far the best balance. They are best both in possession of the ball and without the ball. The hours and hours he has spent on the training ground, walking players through their positions, often without a ball and even without any opponents, simply to install the right shape into his team, will never make headlines or catch the eye but it is the unseen work of the coach which shines through on match day and that is what Conte has done this season. He deserves massive credit, as do his team. They have been by far the best. Let's hope that next season they can do something about the below-par performances of Premier League clubs in the Champions League."

The Arsenal defeat is universally seen at the big turning point. "It was very bad." reflected Courtois. "Maybe Michy had one good chance, but for the rest we had a bad game. It was hard to switch to 3-4-3. It's not so easy that you just change and you win your games. A lot of teams try to do it and find it not so easy. We did it and picked it up very well. That was our work ethic combined with a hunger of not wanting another season like 2015/16."

"I found the strength to change." said Conte. "I took responsibility. And it was the key moment for us. Every single player found in themselves the best of themselves."

SUNDAY, 14 MAY 2017

Conte's mission was now to balance preparations for Wembley and keep his leading players sharp with rewarding those who have had less game time and to give them a chance of a Cup Final appearance.

It was clear that he was focused and would demand his players maintain momentum as he targeted the Double.

"He's a winner." said Fabregas. "At the beginning we saw many changes. Maybe some of us were not used to it but we know now exactly what he wants from us. This season has prepared us well for what will happen next season. We worked hard to improve but we can do better. So hopefully we will prepare well for the FA Cup final and rest well for next season."

"If I say I'm not thinking about winning the Double, I am a liar." David Luiz told chelseafc.com. "Of course we think about this, but we need to think day by day, rest well, keep ourselves very good in these next two games to have a top performance against Arsenal. It will be a difficult game against a fantastic team, so we need to be at a high level."

Conte was planning major new signings, so this was the final chance to impress before a major clear out as well.

"I'm sure we will strengthen." predicted Fabregas. "We've won but that doesn't mean the team cannot get better. Every team, even if they win, will try to improve and I'm sure Chelsea will try to do that. We definitely feel we can do something in the Champions League. It's a big target. Lately, you see the English teams are struggling in it because the Premier League is so tough. It's the best league in the world, maybe not the best players in the world but the most competitive and the most difficult league to win, for sure. Anyone can beat you. That's why next season with the Champions League we will have to be at the top of our game to compete. It will be tough but we feel we can be strong next season, not just in the Premier League, but in the Champions League as well. You will see that six teams can win the league easily. Any of them can do it. Then some of them will play Europa League, Champions League. Then on top of that you have the League Cup and the FA Cup. Other leagues don't have these extra games, extra trophies and extra difficult games. You go to Burnley and it's difficult. In Spain, you go to other places, relegation teams and it's not as difficult. It will be very tough to compete, but we feel we can be strong next season, not just in the Premier League but the Champions League as well."

Fabregas, who spent eight years at Arsenal and won the FA Cup in 2005, knows the Wembley showpiece will be a special occasion against his old club. He started the 2005 final against Manchester United, which the Gunners won on penalties. "It will be emotional. It is not an ordinary game for me. It's not as if I like playing against Arsenal. They are a club in my heart and always will be. I have to put those feelings aside. You have to be professional. Arsenal are playing well and playing a different system. Maybe they are not performing fantastic in this system but they are defensively better. They are winning and that's important for them. Their belief is higher. But our belief is high. Hopefully we can hurt them in the way we want."

Asked what completing the Double would mean, Fabregas replied: "Imagine that! It would be fantastic. It would be fantastic for the players. It would be fantastic for the manager. To do it in the first season after the problems we faced. We started with a system, then we changed, it started well, then it didn't go well. Then we had to adapt to another kind of system with 5-4-1, 3-4-3, it depends on the time of the game."

With two more years on his contract, enjoying life in London and in the form of his life, there were no thoughts of leaving. "I feel in great shape. I've been feeling like that since early December. At the beginning it was frustrating and if you don't get into the team then you don't really know what will happen. But through hard work and belief I made it happen. I've worked hard to get back into the team and I feel I'm getting the rewards and have made it happen."

Guus Hiddink, Conte's immediate predecessor, was sure the Italian would stay due to "perfect circumstances". Hiddink told BBC Radio 5 Live's Sportsweek programme: "There are always rumours coming up but the club is very stable. It's a huge club to work for, perfect circumstances and very ambitious people. I think it's more rumour than reality."

Hiddink did not wish to dwell on what happened under Jose Mourinho when he returned to Chelsea, but can see how Conte transformed a dysfunctional unit: "The dressing room was quiet, too quiet, people avoiding each other a bit. We managed to overcome the problems and I didn't want to go too deep into what were the problems. (Now) I see a very, very stable team and a team enjoying playing football. Now it's a confirmation of his attitude, his professionalism, plus, of course, his energy, which he's putting in the team. He has also a very strong management team, with his coaches and Steve Holland. It's nice to see his development of the club."

Conte's current deal is reported to be worth £6.5m-a-year; less than Pep Guardiola, Jose Mourinho, Arsene Wenger and Jurgen Klopp. Mourinho's last contract at Chelsea earned him £7.5m p.a. Inter Milan are rumoured to have offered Conte a massive £12.5m-a-year deal but Abramovich would be prepared to offer the biggest salary for a manager in Chelsea's history, leapfrogging Klopp and Wenger.

"Retaining the trophy next year has to be the goal." said Gary Cahill. "I really hope we have learnt the lessons from what happened the last time we tried to do that. People talk about the hangover after success. Leicester felt a bit of that this season and we did last year. The fact no one has done it for so long shows how very difficult it is to do. It's nothing to do with players' ability, it is to do with frame of mind. We have proved that. History has proved it's very tough to win it back-to-back, but it has to be a target for us next year, 100 per cent. But we have to be right for that."

Conte was already planning a recruitment drive for the Champions League. "It's important." Cahill added. "People higher up in this club know a lot more about this than me and will make those decisions. I just think it's healthy, especially off the back of a good season. You have to keep that hunger and set yourself goals. When you talk about winning it again, you look at the great players over the years who have won championships time and time again, it's like an addiction. You want to have this feeling again and again. There is no better feeling than we had in the dressing room at West Brom, what we will have over the coming days. The worse things in football are complacency and not having anything to strive for. This football club enables you to fight for trophies but there are many others who won't, where if you finish in mid-table it is okay. I've been involved in both. At Chelsea you're always challenging for silverware and getting to the latter stages of competitions. To do that you need good players, you need competition. All the best players have to deal with that.

Look at John Terry and all the players he's had to compete with over the years and it keeps you right at the top of your game. People doubt you sometimes but all these things sit in your belly and make you produce your best football."

MONDAY, 13 MAY 2017
Chelsea 4-3 Watford
Premier League

It was celebration time. Off the pitch, on it, and just about everywhere around the Bridge it was party mood. But it turned out to be a hard-earned victory in an ill-tempered but thrilling encounter.

Conte and his players took the well-earned acclaim on a lap of honour following the final whistle after they were made to work hard for the win by a fired-up and physical Watford side. At the final whistle there was a fireworks display outside the stadium with a blue ticker tape tribute engulfing the pitch.

There was a sense of history and completion as John Terry returned as captain. With his departure imminent it was the end of an era and Terry celebrated his first league start since September by scoring Chelsea's 100th goal in all competitions this season and Chelsea's 1,000th in the Premier League since Roman Abramovich took over in the summer of 2003. It came after 22 minutes before he then gifted Etienne Capoue an instant equaliser with a poor header. Cesar Azpilicueta restored the lead with a sweetly struck half volley before half-time and it looked all over when Michy Batshuayi added a third just after the break to follow up on his goal that had clinched the title. It almost ended in tears, though, for the surprise goalscoring hero, when he confronted Sebastian Prodl; the defender had dived into a meaty tackle on Batshuayi, who reacted by jumping up and driving his head towards his offender. Prodl stayed on his feet, saving referee Lee Mason from having to make a big decision. Had he rolled around, the boy would have been red-carded.

The party was in danger of going somewhat flat, though, as first Daryl Janmaat pulled a goal back and then Stefano Okaka equalised in the 74th minute. However, Chelsea, as so often this season, found a way to win. Substitute Cesc Fabregas struck from the edge of the area with only two minutes left, while Prodl was sent off for a second yellow card in stoppage time.

Conte was loudly and emotionally cheered at Stamford Bridge within seconds of appearing in his technical area; his wife, Elisabetta Muscarello, in the stands was caught on camera shedding a tear of joy.

Conte gave his 'shadow squad' game time, resting Courtois and Matic, with Costa, Fabregas, Pedro, Cahill and Alonso all on the bench. In fact, he made nine changes to the starting eleven; according to Opta the most ever by a Chelsea manager in the Premier League. Only Hazard and Azpilicueta had kept their places. Claudio Ranieri had the famed nickname of Tinkerman whilst at Stamford Bridge but even he could not reach the levels of tinkering that Conte had achieved for this match.

John Terry led the team out with Nathan Ake and Nathaniel Chalobah getting a game, as Conte prepared for the FA Cup final. Terry enjoyed his first league start since the 2-2 draw at Swansea City on 11 September, and first start in any competition since the FA Cup fifth-round win at Wolves on 18 February. The 36-year-old's scrappy goal meant he had now scored in his 17th successive Premier League season. He scrambled in a mishit shot for his landmark goal but then made an uncharacteristic error to allow Capoue in for the equaliser.

Azpilicueta got himself on the scoresheet. It was just reward for a player whose outstanding consistency makes him a key component of this title-winning team, and who had played every minute of every league game so far.

Chelsea had now equalled the record of most wins in a single Premier League season (29, also achieved by the Blues in 04/05 and 05/06) and the unrelenting coach challenged his team to make it thirty.

Conte told BBC Sport: "It's a big night because we won the title. I made a decision to make nine changes and give the chance to start a lot of young players. I must be pleased because the answer was very good. We conceded three goals but we scored four and created many chances. The most important thing was we won. Now we have target to win 30 games. The most important thing is to win the league. Then if we have the possibility to improve these records, we must try. We can reach this target. The players and I want to reach this target."

Watford manager Walter Mazzarri had beaten Conte when manager of Napoli, and he told BBC Sport: "Congratulations to Antonio Conte because he's a great manager. They have great players. They deserve the title."

Chelsea now host Sunderland in their final league game as Terry admitted: "I've not ruled out Sunday being my last game and retiring from football." he told Sky Sports. "If the right offer comes along I will sit down and consider it with my family - whether that's here or abroad. Genuinely I haven't made any decisions yet and I'm evaluating all my options at the moment. It was great for me to get into the starting line-up and delighted to get on scoresheet. Then a couple of moments later I made the error and the boys dug me out. If in doubt, kick it out! It is a simple rule. People expected that, because we had won the league and they were safe, it would be a nothing game but it wasn't like that. There were some juicy tackles going in and a lot of passion. From our point of view the manager made it very clear in the dressing room beforehand that he wanted us to be the first Premier League team to earn 30 wins in a season. We got the win tonight, now hopefully it will give us the momentum to get the 30th against Sunderland."

On what could have been his Stamford Bridge farewell he added, "It was a tough day, it is always tough when you have been at a club for so long. Tonight was tough but on Sunday I'll be in bits. If I could have written my life, this is how it would have been - going out crowned champions - and in great hands with the owner, manager and players. Next week will be a sad day for me. But I'm delighted with the experiences I've had. We haven't come this far to lose in the FA Cup final. We can also be the first team to win 30 games in a Premier League season, that's the message from the manager and we want to do it."

Terry expected Conte to build a team to challenge for the Champions League as well as defend the title at home. "We'll have to add because other teams will do so. It's tough to retain the title."

An amazing career is coming to an end - Terry is the Blues' most decorated player, with this season's title earning him a fifth Premier League winners' medal to add to five FA Cups, three League Cups, the Champions League and the Europa League with 716 appearances since his debut in 1998 - 579 of them as captain.

Conte paid tribute to the player's influence to BBC Sport. "He is a great man. He helped me a lot in my first season. He had a fantastic role on and off the pitch. Against Watford he showed he can continue to play. I'm pleased for him, he scored a great goal. I'm looking forward to seeing him lift the cup on Sunday. He deserves this."

"Honest", just like Conte, is the sort of coach Terry wants to become. "He has been brilliant. Even with me, after leaving me out, which I imagine was a tough decision for him. He was honest, he brought me into his office and explained the situation. I have never really had that with a manger. His honesty and communication has been fantastic. That's what players want. He made it clear that I wouldn't get back in if the boys were performing; and obviously I was wanting them to win from the sidelines. He has been a great example for me in how I want to coach in the future. I never wanted to be that player hanging about, stopping the progress of a young player. The transition of being on the bench has given me a different point of view and that will serve me well if I want to go into management."

Terry will (hopefully) lift the Premier League trophy on Sunday. "I'm looking forward to seeing him lift the cup and I think the players want to see this too. It is the right finale for John." Conte wished.

Conte knew the loss that Terry would be but appreciated his decision. "He took his decision to (continue to) play regularly every game (elsewhere) and for this reason he preferred to leave Chelsea. I don't know where. For us it's a big loss because he helped me a lot off the pitch. He's always sending the right message to the other players. It's a pity for me but I must respect his decision. At the minute his heart, body and head tell him he wants to continue to play so it's right to allow him to. John wants to continue his career and I wish for him and his family all the best. Chelsea will always be his home. He's a great man and a legend for Chelsea."

Azpilicueta waved a huge Chelsea flag in the middle of the pitch. Batshuayi stood by it and gave a salute. Conte walked round the ground shaking hands and having his picture taken; a man very much in demand, and adored by the fans. A fan handed substitute Ola Aina a crown and, in turn, he ran over and placed it on the head of Conte. King Conte! Hmmh - Good title for a book, I thought! To be honest, I'd already thought of it some time ago!

Azpilicueta spoke to BBC Sport about their double hopes: "We are really focused on that. We know we have worked really hard to be in this position. We have to prepare for our final Premier League game well. Then we have a whole week to prepare for the FA Cup final. To do the Double would be amazing. We can enjoy it today because we have worked really hard. At the end we got the result we were looking for. Last season we were not in this position so we have to appreciate this. We conceded a lot of goals but we scored. It was our first game after being champions so we knew it could be tough. But we got the three points. We want to finish on a high on Sunday. We want to get as many points as we can. We have been first since game 12 so obviously we have showed consistency. Even when defeat arrived, we didn't panic and kept unity. Tottenham were doing well but we had it in our hands and we didn't let it go. It was a good moment to score my first Premier League goal this season after being champions. It was a special moment for me."

The party atmosphere came under threat just hours before kick-off when a section of the stadium was evacuated due to a fire alarm being activated in the hospitality section of the stadium; journalists in the media room were forced to leave their dinners and step outside for around ten minutes. Fortunately, it was a false alarm and staff were allowed to return just in time for the arrival of the team bus. It would have been a tragedy if the media nosh had gone up in smoke. It was so good, in fact, that Diego Costa later helped himself to some of it when he was bored sitting it out on the bench!

Conte joked that he was "very angry" Costa didn't get him a piece of chocolate cake during his half-time trip to the press room for a snack. When asked about the incident, Conte said: "Which type of food? It's very important this." After hearing it was chocolate cake he feigned anger, though not out of concern for his player's diet. "In this case I'm very angry with him because he must think to give me a bit of chocolate cake because I was suffering during the game."

TUESDAY, 16 MAY 2017

Eden Hazard would make the inevitable switch to Real Madrid, believed Danny Murphy. In fact, Hazard and Costa's futures both remained uncertain. When asked on Match of the Day who would be the biggest loss, Murphy replied: "Hazard for me. He is the game-changer, he's the superstar in that team. In all the big games I've watched he's been the difference between a draw and a win. Very hard to handle individually, fitness levels have been great this season and his end product has been really good as well. I don't expect to see him in a Chelsea shirt with everything we have heard. You hear what Madrid are saying, you hear what Hazard's saying - it seems inevitable there's a move in the offing. It seems like everybody has that desire to play for Barca or Madrid, when they come knocking you can't stop these players (from leaving). We will have to wait and see, it's going to be a difficult summer if they do go, two top players (Hazard and Costa)."

As one of their most influential players Hazard should to be scoring 20 plus goals according to Gary Neville. "Fifteen goals and five assists is a good season but I think he should be hitting 20, 25 and double figures for assists."

Fellow pundit Mark Schwarzer suggested Zinedine Zidane was a huge admirer of Hazard and Chelsea will have a tough task to keep Hazard him.

However, Pat Nevin disagreed entirely on BBC Radio 5 live: "I don't think Chelsea's squad, as good as they have been this season, is big enough to go that far in the Champions League next season and be competitive in the Premier League. They need three or four more players of a really top standard. They might get one or two back like Andreas Christensen from loan spells and they have youngsters like Nathan Ake. There's probably two or three big signings to come. They have the finances. They sold Oscar for about £60m and have not missed him at all. And they have to try to keep the players they've got. I don't think Eden Hazard will go anywhere."

Conte had benefited from Mourinho, according to Gary Neville. "I think ultimately Jose has built two great sides at Chelsea." Neville had told Sky Sports, ahead of Chelsea's match with Watford. "Ancelotti and Conte have profited - managed them brilliantly - but profited off the back of those two championship-winning teams."

Granted, Neville was impressed with Conte's impact at Stamford Bridge but expected his second season to be a much sterner test. "I think there are three big challenges moving forward for Conte and Chelsea next season. The first is a physical one. Those eight, ten, twelve matches less. Make no mistake about it, that's an incredibly big advantage when you play less football. You have more time to prepare, to recover. It's a big advantage against other teams that are in Europe. When you're not in the Champions League or Europa League you have a huge advantage, so the biggest challenge moving forward is physicality. (The) second challenge is mental. These players are the same players who have let Chelsea down before. They've climbed the mountain and can't get themselves up for next season. I can't imagine that they're going to drop to tenth next season but Antonio Conte's big job is re-motivating those players."

And, thirdly, Neville fears for the Blues, should they lose Costa. "Costa, for me, is an animal." said Neville. "When he's not scoring, he's contributing. The way Chelsea play, with a single striker, if he leaves it's a huge void to fill. Forget the fact that you might be able to get somebody who scored the goals he scored, which is a challenge in itself, but to replace that personality, that fire, (will be hard)."

Monday Night Football colleague Jamie Carragher stated, though, that Chelsea have a history of coping with high-profile departures. "Don't forget that spine that we felt, without them, they couldn't win - Cech, Terry, Lampard, Drogba. They've won two leagues without Frank Lampard and Didier Drogba, Petr Cech has moved on and they've won two without him. John Terry hasn't played this season. That's what I'm talking about - that winning mentality going through the club. Without Costa you would still back that club to find a way to win."

Shanghai SIPG star Oscar would be "delighted" if Costa joined him in China, having been heavily linked to Chinese Super League side Tianjin Quanjian. "It's hard for me to give specific advice to Costa. The only thing I can tell him is that I quite enjoy my life in China." Oscar informed China Central Television, Sports Channel, CCTV-5. "I don't have any problems so far. The culture here is obviously very different from that of my country, but we are getting used to it, bit by bit. Everyone has got to figure out the things he wants most. And I believe coming to China is the best choice for me. If Costa moves here, I will be delighted. He is pursuing happiness and I hope everyone has a happy life."

Victor Moses, Nemanja Matic and David Luiz all warming up ahead of the Watford game was a sure sign that there was no chance Conte would lose focus ahead of the FA Cup final. Asked if Conte had already picked his cup final team in his mind, Neville told Sky Sports: "He probably has. We just saw a shot there behind the scenes of Luiz, Matic and Moses doing some training on the pitch and that shows you straight away the focus is there. They are already preparing for next Sunday for the final. The reality of it is he is professional and he won't switch off too much. That detail of preparation is what I'd expect from a championship-winning team. You look at those three there, they're not involved tonight and the three of them they've still got to work and they've got to prepare. That's the key now for Antonio Conte in the next two weeks that they don't switch off or they don't over celebrate and it looks like he's got them back at it straight away."

N'Golo Kante's incredible season continued as he beat some of the world's best players to yet another award. Having won the Premier League with Leicester in 2016, he hasn't stopped, playing an integral role in helping Chelsea win the title and getting the team to the FA Cup final. At France's domestic football awards, the Trophees UNFP (National Union of Professional Football Players) du Football, he was voted the best French footballer playing abroad. On the shortlist he was up against Atletico Madrid striker and Manchester United target Antoine Griezmann, Real Madrid hitman Karim Benzema and Borussia Dortmund's brilliant youngster Ousmane Dembele. Kante was unable to attend the star-studded ceremony due to Chelsea's match with Watford. Edinson Cavani of PSG was named Ligue 1 Player of the Season and former Manchester United winger Memphis Depay won Goal of the Season for his long-range effort for Lyon.

WEDNESDAY, 17 MAY 2017

The BBC Sport online got together a group of eminent, former Chelsea luminaries to analyse Conte's new force within the game. First up was the question of whether he would stay:

Ruud Gullit: "From a football point of view, of course he will stay. His next challenge is to win the Champions League and he can do that with Chelsea. If he feels he has a team that can win it, why would he leave in order to start all over again somewhere else? It is different if it is a decision about his family. His personal life is important as well. If his family are not in London, it is a little bit odd because I think it is the best city in the world, so why are they not coming? It is understandable if people are very attached to their own customs, however. And, if his family want to be in Italy, then it is an easy choice for him to make."

Pat Nevin: "After spending a couple of hours talking to Antonio a few weeks ago, I would be stunned if he left. It would have to be an unbelievably spectacular offer to take him away from Chelsea and the only thing that usually means managers move on from positions like that is that they don't have the level of control they want. I don't think his own finances are a big deal for the guy and he told me he is enjoying London now. The other thing to consider is that when you stand at Stamford Bridge and you hear the fans singing 'Antonio, Antonio' then you realise the adoration he has got from everyone. That is hard to walk away from."

Chris Sutton: "The only way I see Conte leaving is if he does not get the players in he wants this summer. I don't think he will prioritise the Champions League because he will want to win everything, but I expect him to go really hard at it."

Champions League was the next big target for Conte:

Graeme Le Saux: "Any success going forward depends on the personnel and if they can retain the quality players they have got. Eden Hazard and N'Golo Kante are both 26, and they are young enough to make Chelsea a force going forwards. Diego Costa has been linked with a move to China, but it is important for Chelsea they keep this group of players together. If they do that, I think they will go into the next season as favourites to win the Premier League again."

Mark Schwarzer: "The potential is there for back-to-back titles, and Chelsea can win the Champions League too. Conte is very good at winning domestic competitions. Clubs like Chelsea, their number one priority is to win the Premier League and then look beyond that to try and win the big one, the Champions League. With the right additions, and a little bit of time, Chelsea can really challenge for that title but next season it is going to be a huge burden on them."

Nevin: "Conte has over-achieved domestically this season but, even so, the Champions League is a big jump - look at the lack of success by English teams in recent years. If he got Chelsea out of the group stage and into the latter stages that would be a success in his first season with the club in the Champions League. But that is predicated by one very important thing - who is he going to get in, and who will leave in the summer?"

New signings:

Nevin: "With the current group, he cannot do next year what he has done this season. There is just not enough numbers there."

Sutton: "Conte is clearly not big on rotation but he still had to change the make-up of his team around at times this season. He is fortunate he has got a lot of intelligent footballers who can play in numerous positions, but next season he will need more strength in depth and that means four or five really quality signings. Wing-backs would one of the areas where Conte will think he needs more cover and, whether Costa stays or goes, there is lots of talk about Everton striker Romelu Lukaku coming back to the club. Does Lukaku fit the Chelsea style? Absolutely. He likes to play between the two centre-halves and is not going to come deep to get the ball but, if he joins, I can see him being very successful playing that Costa role."

Gullit: "Even when you have success, you need to change little things to keep people on their toes - look at what happened to Jose Mourinho after winning the title in 2015 - all of a sudden they went from champions to nothing."

Nevin: "Conte will want a bit more strength and power in midfield - but if he can keep Hazard, Cesc Fabregas, Pedro and Willian then he does not need any more creativity. The biggest question is at centre-forward. I watched Michy Batshuayi when he was playing in France and he is a real player, a goalscorer - someone who will do very well. I don't know if it will be at Chelsea though. Considering I believe that Conte wants to play two up front, he might want to go for a different type of centre-forward. As well as Lukaku, Alvaro Morata has been talked about. What has impressed me most about Conte, though, is he does things you do not expect - those are the names we are thinking about, but he might know about someone completely different."

Costa is the continuing saga:

Gullit: "Even when Costa has not been scoring goals, he still does an important job for the team. He is an example of someone they have depended on too much - he is up there with Hazard as one of their most influential players. But if Costa feels he wants to leave because he wants a different challenge, then let him go. If that's his state of mind, it is better to sell him."

Youth - will young players finally break through under Conte:

Sutton: "Conte is not going to take his foot off the gas, if anything he will put his foot down harder. If any youth players get a game, it will not be down to him doing them a favour. Tammy Abraham has got something about him, and it will be interesting to see if he gets a chance. Ultimately, though, things have not changed since my day so it will be down to him - he will have to show what he can do in pre-season and hope it is enough."

Nevin: "Chelsea fans will tell you we have got these good young kids and they will come in and make it. Really? Hopefully they will, and it would be the perfect situation if they did but people make the mistake of thinking the jump from the under-21s to Chelsea's first team is one step - it's not, it is about 47 steps. Abraham is going to be a great player, and he is coming back to the club for next season, but I would be shocked if all Chelsea did was stick with what they have got, and drafted more youth players in."

Conte is credited with a change of system that turned the season:

Nevin: "I suspect Conte will be using different systems, systems that will suit Fabregas a bit better. You think of the way Conte's Juventus team played with Andrea Pirlo, and that would suit Fabregas absolutely. People said he was a 3-4-3 man when he arrived at Chelsea but that was never the case. If you look back, he often played with four at the back and very frequently with two up front. He has already started to show he can change things around, when he left Costa and Hazard on the bench for the FA Cup semi-final. So the sort of thing he will need to do next season is already happening now."

Sutton: "He seems an adaptable, pragmatic manager and I don't think he is frightened to change. You would not rule out him returning to four at the back if he sees fit. I don't think he is going to slacken off, though. Yes, he works the players hard in training but when you are successful it makes that treatment easier to accept."

The last time Chelsea were champions they finished 10th the following season. No team has retained their Premier League title since Manchester United won it in 2007/08 and 2008/09:

Le Saux: "The players clearly love playing for Conte and giving him everything as well. You would like to think all those values he is building at the club would hold the team in good stead going forward. I hope their success this year means there is some continuity there."

Pat Nevin: "Conte is young for a manager - he turns 48 in July. So the passion, the hunger that he has, it is natural - and he is still on the upward curve. I don't think we have seen 50% of his capabilities yet and I am dead keen to see him up against Pep Guardiola and Jose Mourinho, who will both be stronger next year."

Conte has transformed Cesar Azpilicueta from a solid player into a "world-class defender" according to Garth Crooks. "What a season this player has had. I remember him starting his career at Chelsea and having to play as a left-back." he told the BBC. "He coped brilliantly well considering he was naturally right-footed and while he solved the club's left-sided problem post Ashley Cole, he could not really show his true potential. Since the arrival of Antonio Conte, Cesar Azpilicueta has not merely shown his true potential but realised it. The versatile defender produced a world-class performance against West Brom at The Hawthorns and what a time to do it. He was imperious in defence and creative in attack. It was Azpilicueta's cross that provided the opening for Michy Batshuayi to slide the ball home. What he was doing so far up the field in open play tells you all you need to know about the commitment and desire of the Spain international. However, when you study his season, he has been ever present and quietly got on with his job. This was a brilliant performance by a player who has become a world-class defender under Conte.

Azpilicueta played the majority of the season on the right side of a back three, but had appeared as a right wing-back and left-back under Mourinho. "It's been a massive season for him." said Conte. "When you have this type of player it's great for the coach. If I ask him to go and put on the gloves and stay in goal he's ready. He's a model footballer and able to play in different roles."

Cesc Fabregas named Conte as the most tactical manager he's ever played under; and he played under Wenger, Guardiola and Mourinho. "Conte is something else." Fabregas told Cadena Ser. "We have run a lot this season, lots of gym work and sprints. We did very well, the team was phenomenal physically. There is a lot of pressure to go up and down (the pitch). He is the coach who worked the most tactically, more than with Mourinho and Guardiola. We have to take into account that this year we have not had to play in the Champions League, something that will not happen next season Conte is meticulous. Until everything is done, training is not finished."

THURSDAY, 18 MAY 2017

Westfields FC's chief executive Andy Morris had Conte to thank for showing him the way to Stamford Bridge to attend the Non-League Paper's National Game Awards ceremony where he was due to pick up a lifetime achievement award for his 50 years' service at the Hereford club. He had just got off the tube at Fulham Broadway and was struggling to find his way to the Bridge. He noticed Conte was walking into Pret a Manger with his wife, so asked him for directions. "I congratulated him on winning the title and showed him the invitation for the awards. I told him that I had never been to Chelsea before and asked him how to find it. He was in jeans and a T-shirt and he was kind enough to sign the invitation."

Writing in his column for Chelsea's official website, Pat Nevin discussed Conte's team selection for the cup final: "The real question is which team will Antonio pick? The bench will probably be harder to choose than ten members of the first team. The gaffer will make those calls but then what about the Pedro or Willian choice? That is a tough one though it pales when you consider how much time will be spent considering the relative merits of starting with Nemanja Matic or Cesc Fabregas. Arsenal's midfield wouldn't fancy winning against Kante and Matic in a battle, but it seems set up for Cesc considering the form he is in and that it is against his old club. The size of the pitch at Wembley would suit Cesc's passing, but might it be better to hold him in reserve for the second half to exploit tiring opponents? I suspect we have the right man making those decisions. Eden Hazard and Diego Costa on the bench in the semi and coming on to destroy Spurs. Michy coming on to win us the league at West Brom, and even Cesc rising from the bench to score the winner against Watford. Antonio's substitutions have been superb this season, but they appear to be getting even better as the big calls have to be made at the end of the season. I think I will stop second guessing and just trust in the gaffer."

John Terry apparently handed West Ham an extra incentive ahead of their match against Spurs, which virtually clinched the title for Chelsea. "John Terry texted me and Mark Noble saying 'If you boys beat Tottenham there's a dinner or a night out on the Chelsea boys', so that was nice." reported Hammers' defender James Collins to Betway. "But we wanted to beat Tottenham anyway. We're lucky we did in the end looking at the result we got after that (a 4-0 loss against Liverpool). It was a massive result, it put us safe and obviously to beat our closest rivals at home was massive."

John Terry now planned to lift the trophy with Gary Cahill, the on-pitch skipper.

"We will lift it together, of course." said Terry. "Me and Lamps (Frank Lampard) did that together for many years here. Gaz (Cahill) has been on the pitch week-in week-out, so it's him allowing me to go with him. He's been different class."

N'Golo Kante collected his Football Writers' Player of the Year award at the Landmark Hotel from FWA chairman Patrick Barclay talking up the possibility of an unprecedented quadruple. "Next season will be a new challenge because we are going to try to keep the title, to win the two cups and also we'll have the Champions League. For a club like Chelsea, we want to win everything, we're going to try and win everything. It's a new challenge for everyone."

Kante received the most votes in a poll taking in the FWA's 340 members, beating teammate Eden Hazard and Spurs' Dele Alli. He was in the running last season but lost out to then teammate Jamie Vardy, finishing third with Riyad Mahrez second. "It's special because I couldn't even say I'm the best player but it's very special and a great honour. It's not only me. I owe so much to my teammates because we have achieved so much together this season and we still have the FA Cup. It is very special, a few years ago I was playing in the French lower divisions. Five years ago I wasn't even professional so to receive this kind of award means I am the kind of player I cannot even imagine being here."

Five Chelsea players were nominated with Luiz, Costa and Azpilicueta also receiving votes. Kante collected more than 65 per cent of the journalists' votes, which were spread over a record number of 17 different players.

Kante believes Conte played a major role in converting the strugglers back into the Premier League's most formidable force. "He had a very clear idea of what he wanted from the team, and from me. Since I joined Chelsea he puts a winning mentality on everyone. The hard work, the important little details, he's a winner. He's a hard worker, he wants to work, work and repeat in every training session to win at the weekend."

Cesc Fabregas popped back to his native Barcelona on a day off for an event with Luis Suarez and Lionel Messi. He flew back home to the Catalan capital with his wife Daniella Semaan to attend the opening of a new boutique. He posted a photo on social media showing himself in the back of a cab with his old Nou Camp teammates. Suarez's wife Sofia Balbi and Messi's fiancee Antonella Roccuzzo helped open Argentinian footwear brand Sarkany's first store in Europe.

FRIDAY, 19 MAY 2017

Chelsea became the first Premier League club to have a dedicated Twitter emoji of their manager, which supporters could access by using the hashtag #ChelseaChampions.

That will, in turn, produce an emoji on the social media site of Conte holding up his arms in celebration - a much familiar sight this season. Speaking about the move to produce a bespoke emoji for Conte, Twitter UK Sports Partnerships head, Bruna Zanin, said "We're really excited about launching this emoji. Chelsea have long been incredibly innovative in their use of Twitter. Couple this with Conte being one of the highest regarded coaches in world football at present, and it seemed like a natural fit to get this special emoji live for fans ahead of Chelsea's crowning weekend."

Only a few days ago the Blues' Instagram stories' celebrations drew praise for capturing their fans' mood, mocking up a WhatsApp-style conversation which evoked the transition Chelsea had undergone in the space of only a year; written off but ending up winning the league.

This might be a first for Chelsea and for a manager but it's not new ground for Twitter, which had already created emojis for sports stars, including Paul Pogba. That saw the #Pogba hashtag appear on advertising boards around Old Trafford for United's game against Liverpool, and for El Clasico between Real Madrid and Barcelona.

Interestingly, the top five Chelsea moments on Twitter since August 2016 were:

1) Kante scores his first Chelsea goal in 4-0 win vs Manchester United
   - 31,000 Tweets per minute (TPM)

2) Chelsea confirmed as champions after West Brom win - 25k TPM

3) Hazard wonder goal vs Arsenal at Stamford Bridge - 23k TPM

4) Hazard makes it 3-1 to Chelsea vs Manchester City - 22k TPM

5) Final whistle at Etihad confirms Chelsea's comeback win - 22k TPM

Jurgen Klopp believed Conte's "outstanding managing skills" and passion were behind Chelsea's stunning campaign. He said "I love Antonio. What a fantastic guy. But I think even last year there was no doubt about the quality of Chelsea's players. They had a punch, and then they came back. Antonio has outstanding managing skills. He understands the game, so he saw what to do. Antonio's really passionate and smart, and that's a good combination, one you don't have too often."

Conte was in an upbeat mood, well, you would be wouldn't you?

He told the journalists in the media briefing that he wanted to keep it a surprise whether John Terry would start in the next, and final league game of the season. The long-standing captain has still got life in his legs and could continue his career elsewhere, and comparing his career with Francesco Totti, Paolo Maldini and Alessandro Del Piero, Conte said "I think this question is for John, not me. In this situation, above all when you are in this stage of your career it is important to take the best decision. It must be the decision of the player and not the club. John knows very well my thoughts about him. It is very difficult to find these players with this career. John is a legend for this club, his appearances and the way he played and victory with this club. He has won many titles. Totti played for Roma in all his career, Maldini also. I think John is a champion and deserves the best. For sure he has the possibility to continue his career, we know he is preferring to play regularly, so he is deciding to leave to play regularly every week. While he has the possibility to do this, he is still strong. When I call him to play he shows this. It is very important when you arrive at this point in your career you must feel if it is right to continue. He has all the characteristics."

Conte, though, has little time for sentiment and while Terry had led out the team in the penultimate game it would surely be Gary Cahill leading out the team this time, with Terry coming on and then lifting the trophy together with the vice-captain? "I think the situation is important to take your time to take the best solution for him. John deserves the best, for this reason on Sunday we will see what happens. It will be a surprise because it is to find the best solution for him. He is a legend of the club, very important to win the title. I must take my time to find the best solution for him. Gary Cahill is vice-captain this season and has the good prospect to be a captain, but we must think about now, not the future. He put the armband on every time John didn't play. He has a good prospect to be a captain, but we have to finish this season, and not think about next season."

Conte reflected on the achievement: "It's good. To win the league in first season, it wasn't easy. Half the squad won and half started to win. When you win you start to learn the right way to do and it's very important for Marcos, for Moses and also for Michy, but many guys that stay in the squad. To change was very important because we found the right suit for these players. I think it was very important. We continued to work very hard, but that is a simple word. When I speak and say hard work, it means hard work. Anyone can say it but in reality it doesn't happen. But it happened. I had players who wanted to improve and I think this was the secret. I want to say thanks to my players. Every single manager can have a good idea of football, but then there are players and if they don't go into the idea then it is very difficult."

And, looking ahead: "Every season is very difficult to win the title in England. To win the title this season was incredible because no one person trust in us to win the title. We did a great job this season and it's very important to have very clear the situation. We mustn't lose the reality. This year we won the league, but next year we must improve a lot. This is not just our thought, it is the club's. We have the Champions League and start as champions so it will be a difficult season. But if we work in the right way, then we can face it."

He confirmed there were no injury concerns and he "can't wait" to celebrate - again! "It is important to celebrate, it is a great win for me, the players, the club and the fans and we have to celebrate in the right way before we have to try to win the game. We want to be the first team to win 30 games in this league. It is an important chance for us, and to celebrate it is important. I can't wait to do this with my players and fans and celebrate John and Steve Holland. He is leaving after eight years. He is an important man in this club and won a lot, worked with many great coaches and I had the pleasure to work with him."

On the rumours of players leaving in the summer, he succinctly stated: "First of all the player must have pleasure to stay in Chelsea, this is very important. Every single player must have the pleasure to stay.

So, what about his own future - would he stay? Of course he was staying, but for now this is what he had to say: "It is important to repeat that I have two years to go. For me and the players it is very important to finish in this season and reach our target. We have reached an important target. On Sunday we have two targets, to win the 30 games in this league, which is unbelievable and also to help Thibaut win the Golden Gloves. Also to prepare for the FA Cup, then we have the time to discuss with our club. Now is important to be focused on these targets, the team is more important than individuals."

Asmir Begovic would receive a Premier League winners' medal but admitted he doesn't deserve one.

Premier League rules state that the club will receive 40 medals for the players, with everyone who appeared more than five times guaranteed a medal; Begovic played twice. Special dispensation for backup goalkeepers means that he will be handed a medal but he told Sky Sports News: "I think the rule should be changed, I don't know about the whole five appearances. Having been part of the group all year, we've all sacrificed, played our part in the team each and every day. But they really have to look at that rule again because I don't think five appearances should warrant a medal. It's the rule for now, thankfully I get one and obviously to have that in your career is great."

John Terry scraped past the five-game threshold, having made seven appearances and Oscar had made nine appearances before leaving in the January.

David Luiz spent over a million pounds to buy his teammates, Antonio Conte and Roman Abramovich unique, ultra-luxury souvenirs of their triumph. Luiz, now a first-time winner of the English title, bought 30 wrist-worn supercar keys that were handed out at the Cobham training base. The bespoke Senturion keys, which will be linked to unlock the champions' hoard of Bentleys, Ferraris and Bugattis, feature a fusion of precious metals and advanced blue carbon fibre composites with each one personally engraved. The most special 'thank you', for supplying the funds for the title campaign, was saved for Mr. Abramovich, whose 'key' was forged from a 4.9 billion-year-old meteorite, older than earth itself.

Senturion, who call their products "the most unique collectors' item in the world", normally only produce each series of their keys in limited editions of seven but made an exception for Luiz. Each key, which bears the appearance of a wristband, can be synchronised to a range of luxury cars with specialists hooking them up to vehicles' existing encrypted security systems thereby allowing them to be unlocked wirelessly.

Luiz personalised his key to be made with solid 18-carat handcrafted rose gold and 198 black diamonds and linked it to his Mercedes AMG G Wagon. On the inside its engraving reads: "God is Great, DL".

Prices for Senturion keys start at £38,000 but bespoke pieces, like those to be worn by Luiz and Abramovich, carry six-figure price tags. Senturion's Director of Communications, Ayla Varquin said: "It was very generous of David to commission special Senturion pieces for his teammates. While normally we produce editions of only seven pieces, in this case it was our pleasure to create a custom edition of 30 for his Chelsea teammates."

In 2012, Didier Drogba paid £800,000 for a set of exclusive rings to commemorate the Champions League victory; Luiz was a recipient then.

SATURDAY, 20 MAY 2017

Conte clarified his position on his future, planning to have his wife and young daughter alongside him in London ahead of the start of his second season. His first season in England was a huge personal challenge due to the separation from his family. "Honestly, for sure this season wasn't easy for me about my family because we decided, my wife and my daughter, they would stay in Italy to allow my daughter to finish school. But, for sure, next season our intention is to keep all the family in England and stay together. It will be a good opportunity, also, for my daughter to live in another country. To go to school in another country is a fantastic opportunity, and a great gift for her. We chose the school also last season, an Italian school, and this is the last problem. In England, and above all in London, there are wonderful schools for the kids."

However, he had yet to decide whether he would commit to a new long-term contract, with talks over a new deal scheduled after the Cup final.

Similarly, Arsene Wenger's future would be decided at a board meeting after the FA Cup final.

The 67-year-old Frenchman has been with the Gunners since 1996 and his contract had now come to an end. "There are many aspects to be discussed at a board meeting. One is what happens with the manager. Of course I will be there. At the moment we should focus on the short term on Sunday and then in the cup final." Wenger added: "We have to do our job, we are professionals and want to win. We are on a good run and all we can do is win our game on Sunday. After that what happens to me is less important. I am here to serve the club and the best way to do that is by winning the next game."

It was confirmed that Dennis Wise will kick-off the title celebrations when he takes the trophy out onto the Stamford Bridge pitch. The former Chelsea skipper will walk out with the trophy ahead of the post-match festivities. Wise was club captain when John Terry initially broke into the first team.

Wise will then hand over the trophy to Chelsea Foundation coach, Tom Horrigan, who will have the honour of presenting the trophy to Cahill and Terry.

The club nominated the 21-year-old coach as the Premier League Kicks Hero in recognition of his involvement with the social inclusion scheme. Horrigan has been involved with the club for a number of years, beginning his Premier League Kicks journey as a 12-year-old participant back in 2008. Since then, he has gained several coaching qualifications as a volunteer, before joining as a coach when he was old enough. His work had even been immortalised as a graphic novel, illustrated by Marvel Comics artist John McCrea. A delighted Horrigan said: "I'm made up to be named the Premier League Kicks Hero for Chelsea. It's a fantastic honour and I love the comic book that's been drawn to show my journey through Kicks. It shows a lot of the most important moments in my life. This is after Chelsea also nominated me to receive the Peter Osgood award this year for my community work. It's all a bit surreal! Presenting the Premier League trophy to Chelsea at Stamford Bridge is a dream come true for me. I can't thank the club and the Premier League enough for allowing me to do it and it will be something to tell the grandkids one day."

The Premier League had wanted to include terminally-ill Sunderland fan Bradley Lowery in the trophy ceremony, but the six-year-old was not well enough to make it to London.

Fernando Llorente explained why he opted not to rejoin his former Juve coach at the Bridge when Chelsea made their move in the last transfer window. "I know Chelsea wanted me in January." he confirmed. "I said straight away that I wanted to stay here. We were fighting relegation, there was a cause. I could not go. If a big club comes in for me in the future who knows because every player wants to play for a big club. But I am very, very happy here. I have always wanted to play in the Premier League and I truly believe it is the best league in the world. It is an intense league and it has been a hard season because I am used to winning. But it is also very rewarding when you achieve in this intense situation that we had here."

Speaking to Italian La Repubblica newspaper a forthright Conte confirmed "My objective is to lay the foundations so Chelsea can continue to win. This is already a big club, but it's inconsistent. They won the Champions League, then went out in the first round. They won the Premier League and then finished 10th. Chelsea need to find stability at the top. I will speak to Roman Abramovich soon."

"The lads accepted new methods: very intense training sessions, the diet, the video analysis and importance of details. I feel fortified. I remain intransigent in my work, but I am more flexible.

I learned to turn a blind eye to certain things, like players eating scrambled eggs before a game... you have to accept the traditions of a country. You also need to speak the language, out of respect. I had studied it at school, but had a two-week intensive course. Learning English felt like climbing a mountain: with strong motivation, nothing is insurmountable. The language is irrelevant if you don't know how to transmit emotion: many university professors are not good teachers."

"It's not all happiness and light. The arrival was, but the journey wasn't. With my wife Elisabetta in January we decided that Vittoria would finish school in Turin, even if she was already registered to start in London. However, if I am to stay, then they will come and stay with me. It will be a great opportunity for my daughter to live in a foreign country. I'll tell you one thing for sure, I won't have another year on my own."

Eden Hazard claimed the team struggled last season because of a lack of "motivation and fitness". He told Football Focus: 'That's football. Sometimes you are on the top, two years ago we won also the league, but last season was difficult for some reasons. Sometimes motivation is not on the top, fitness is not on the top, so a lot of things. (This season) we started well and we won the league, but next season we will be in trouble if we don't work hard like we did this season. We need to be ready every year in the same level to be on the top."

Hazard had returned to his best form under Conte, scoring 15 Premier League, and determined to finish a fantastic season in style. "We can't celebrate a lot because we have the FA Cup final, we have to be ready for that, but after West Brom we did a little party together. Even in the dressing room, it was good to see the smile on faces. I think at the end of the season we deserved to win this title. It's not just me, the whole team, all the players they have been fantastic. We won a lot of games. We have one more game and the FA Cup final to play. I hope we can win the Double."

Conte suggested that failing to mount a strong defence of the title, as they did last season, would render them "losers" as he commenced planning for next season.

It was put to Conte that Mourinho's side relaxed after their last title triumph with complacency undermining their defence. "But I hate this word 'relaxed'." he said. "I prefer they use the word 'enjoy' instead. Enjoy your achievement. We had a path, a very difficult path, this season so it's important to enjoy the win with the players, the club and the fans. We worked very hard. But relax? No. I don't like this. I want people who stay, every day, concentrated and preparing for a new win. We must have a winning mentality. If you have that, you want to continue to win every season. It's not easy because, above all in England there are many teams who want to do the same things. But we have to continue to work very hard, maybe stronger than this season, to try to repeat a good season. But if there is someone who is happy to focus on his past, then he's not a winner. He's a loser. The past is good. The past is beautiful if you won. You can always see your past. But, in the present and the future, what you achieved in the past is not important if you are a winner. If you are a loser then you always stay looking behind you and you won't win."

Conte wanted his players to celebrate their achievement on the Sunday night but preparations would begin on Tuesday for the Cup final. The coach planned to return to Italy for a break, but "First we will focus on finishing the league and achieving our targets. Then, together with the club, we will take the best decisions for next season."

SUNDAY, 21 MAY 2017
Chelsea 5-1 Sunderland
Premier League

It was quite a start to the day... N'Golo Kante was named Player of the Year by the Premier League, adding a third individual accolade to his season's collection. He had fended off competition from teammates Eden Hazard and Cesar Azpilicueta, as well as Spurs' Harry Kane, Dele Alli and Jan Vertonghen, Romelu Lukaku of Everton, and Arsenal's Alexis Sanchez to win the award. "It's a huge honour to be named player of the year and I want to thank everyone who voted for me." Kante said in a statement on the league's website. "I work hard in training, I try to give my best and I work with so many very good players; that's why we won the league two times. We played many good games but we won 5-0 against Everton, which was a very beautiful game, and also my goal against Manchester United. It is always good to score and I am happy for these two games."

From that point on it was always going to be an emotional day.

"Thank you from the bottom of my heart for everything you have done for me over the years." John Terry said in a video posted on Chelsea's Twitter feed. "The support picked me up when I was down, the disappointments - it's down to you that I've picked myself up and gone again on the football pitch. When I signed here as a 14-year-old, I never dreamed of doing what I've done in the game. To celebrate today will be sad and really emotional for me and my family but thanks guys, I love you from the bottom of my heart and forever - I will always be a Blue."

Terry described his heartbreak at bringing an end to his time at the club, saying: "This has been the toughest few weeks of my life." Writing his final programme notes, he said: "It is a huge honour for me to become the first player to captain a team to five Premier League titles and I can't wait to go and lift the trophy with Gaz at the end of today's game. It's going to be an emotional game. It's going to be an emotional day, believe me, because I have had so many great memories here, all of them made better by your support. I will never ever be able to thank you supporters enough for your backing along the way, for picking me up when I was down, or singing my name and making me feel like the best defender in the world. It has meant everything to me. Without all of you Chelsea Football Club doesn't exist. So believe me when I say this has been the toughest few weeks of my life. I am, and always will be, extremely grateful for your backing, from when I first stepped onto the pitch at Stamford Bridge for my debut in October 1998 right through to today. From the bottom of my heart, thank you. Today we can become the first team to win 30 games in a Premier League season and we want to make sure we finish with another victory. Then I'll see you at Wembley for the FA Cup final. Let's give it everything we have to make it a Double. Come on the Chels!"

There was a celebratory air at Stamford Bridge, with complimentary prosecco and beer for supporters who arrived early. The Premier League teased Blues fans with a video of the trophy on social media. The Twitter post was captioned "How does this look, Chelsea?" as their team name was being carved onto the roll of honour at the base.

Terry had met supporters at the hotel before kick-off to sign autographs and he offered fans a heartfelt goodbye en route to the ground.

"It's the last time you drive in, walk up the steps and go in the dressing room. I'm going to try and treasure it." he told Sky Sports. Crying already? He wiped his eyes on his sleeve. What he's going to be like at full-time?

Terry started as captain in his final game for the club as 'Tinkerman' Conte, with Ranieri watching from the owners' box, made six changes from the team that beat Watford. Courtois returned, Luiz was restored to centre-back, and Moses and Alonso returned as the wing-backs. Fabregas came into central midfield with Costa up front. Conte, speaking to Sky Sports, explained: "I had to start with

John because he deserves this for this season. John is a legend for this club and he deserves this opportunity."

Aiming to win and set a Premier League record for 30 wins in a season? "It is a target. It is a target for us and also very important. We want to play to win. It is right to celebrate and right to enjoy this moment. It is a great achievement and to celebrate with the club and fans is great."

The sun was shining. In fact it was a perfect day for a send-off, and a presentation ceremony. There was a particularly loud cheer around Stamford Bridge for John Terry as the names in the line-ups were read out.

The Sunderland players formed a guard of honour as Terry lead the team out to huge applause. A massive banner with the words "Captain, Leader, Legend" was passed along the stands. It was not alone as countless banners displayed their appreciation for the departing legend. There was a feeling that his shirt number, 26, could be retired. One banner read: "JT 26: Thank you for everything", another illustrated the number of trophies - 15 in total that Terry had lifted in his 22 years at Chelsea.

Unexpectedly Sunderland, even without the injured Defoe, scored first, Willian equalised, and soon… Cahill was seen warming up. The rumour quickly swept around the Bridge that Terry could be subbed in the 26th minute; the same number as his shirt.

Then Sunderland goalkeeper, Jordan Pickford, cleared the ball straight out of play… and everyone in the ground rose to their feet as the board went up in the 26th minute to show the number 26. He hugged his teammates, who then formed a guard of honour for the visibly touched Terry. On the touchline he handed the captain's armband to Gary Cahill and exchanged a few words with tears in his eyes; there were tears in the stands too. It was an incredibly emotional and moving end to his final appearance at Stamford Bridge.

@GaryLineker - "John Terry's magnificent Chelsea career ends after 26 minutes of his final match. A great defender. A real leader. And a winner."

However, former Spurs striker, Garth Crooks, on BBC's Final Score was not impressed. "I don't know what to make of it, quite frankly. This isn't Hollywood, it's a Premier League fixture. I'm a bit bemused, this has been set up. I'm uncomfortable with it. It's a guard of honour in the middle of a game.

Martin Keown, who spent many years at rivals Arsenal, agreed. "I think it's very unusual to see, I've never seen that before. Okay I know he's a unique player, but yeah, 26 minutes he goes off as he's number 26. Very contrived. Listen, we should forget that. I'm not happy with the way it's been done. We've a great deal of respect with what he's achieved in the game and now of course they can get on with their job now of winning the FA Cup final."

By the end of the match it had become a record-breaking 30th Premier League win for the title-winners as Chelsea became the first English side to register 30 top-flight victories in a 38-game season. Jose Mourinho had held the record with Chelsea after he guided the club to 29 wins in both the 2004/05 and 2005/06 campaigns.

The stats are impressive: 30 wins, 17 out of 19 at home, 83 points from the last 96 available, 85 goals scored, making this their second-best ever Premier League season in front of goal and Conte had led his team to a seven point advantage ahead of second-placed Tottenham.

Chelsea had fallen behind to an early Javier Manquillo (who, presumably, had not been given a copy of the script) strike but hit back quickly through Willian's angled drive. Eden Hazard lashed in his 17th goal of the season to give the home side the lead before his replacement, Pedro, capitalised on a poor backward header from Joleon Lescott to head in. Another substitute, Michy Batshuayi, hit two well-taken finishes late on to end his season with five goals in three games - he'd scored his five Premier League goals from just eight shots on target.

It was most intriguing to watch Diego Costa leave the pitch as he was replaced by Batshuayi - he waved to the crowd with affectionate appreciation. Was it a farewell?

But the match will be fondly remembered for its emotional send-off for John Terry, who had left the field in tears to a guard of honour from his teammates. Contrived, maybe, but it brought a lump to the throat and a tear to the eye to all those who witnessed it. Since making his debut as a late substitute in a League Cup tie against Aston Villa in October 1998, Terry had become synonymous with the success in the Roman Abramovich era; their standout academy player among a raft of big-money buys. Captain, Leader, Legend, one might say.

One by one, the support staff and players filed up the steps to take their positions on the podium. And, with composure regained, for now at least, Terry and his successor, Gary Cahill, were soon able to hold aloft the Premier League trophy amidst a storm of blue and white ticker-tape. Fans and players alike celebrated wildly.

Conte, who suffered a drenching from his coaching staff, got his hands on the silverware and planted a kiss on the trophy before taking his turn to salute the supporters who sung his name. "Antonio, Antonio, Antonio."

One banner read: "Antonio Conte for Prime Minister."

The players brought their families onto the pitch and many of the young children enjoyed the celebration with their champion fathers.

And so to the final farewell - John Terry took the microphone and invited assistant coach Steve Holland to say a few words before he also departed Chelsea, in this case to join Gareth Southgate's England team.

Terry then addressed the fans: "Today is one of the most difficult days of my life, I've been very fortunate to work with some unbelievable players and managers throughout my career. I'm thankful to every single one of them. We all have to thank Roman Abramovich. I'd like to thank him and all the board. He's the best owner in world football. He loves this club from the U8s up, year in year out, to give us best opportunity. On behalf of myself and the fans, thanks."

Abramovich warmly applauded his captain.

"I'd like to thank my wife and my kids for supporting me in this amazing journey I've had."

"Lastly, you guys, the fans, the best supporters in the world without a shadow of a doubt. You have given me everything from the age of 14, picked me up when I was down, sung my name when I have had bad games and disappointed you. Thank you will never be enough, but I will be back here one day, and I will always be supporting the team and players from the bottom of my heart. I couldn't imagine this, you always wonder what this day would be like, I thought I would be alright but I have just melted."

"I'll come back here one day, supporting the team for years to come."

Terry broke down in floods of tears in an embrace with his wife after handing the microphone to Conte, who briefly addressed the fans: "It's an amazing moment for us to celebrate this win, for me and the players. Come on Chelsea, come on!"

On his future, Terry later added: "I'm going to have a few weeks off before deciding anything. Every ex-player says play as long as you can, it is great advice, I want to play, that is why I have called it a day at Chelsea. I didn't want to stand in the way. There are big characters in the changing room, Cahill stepped in and took the armband, David Luiz was good as well and has matured since he came back, Cesc is a big character. I'm looking to the three of them to push the dressing room on."

Conte explained about Terry's 26th minute departure: "I told you that it was very important to find the right solution to celebrate a great champion and a legend of the club. He deserved to start the game and then to have the substitution in the 26th minute. He deserved this celebration because he wrote his Chelsea history. I wish him and his family the best in the future. For me and the club it will be a great loss because he helped me a lot on and off the pitch this season. Now we must respect his decision. I think this idea of my players (the guard of honour) was a great one, to recognise an important career and a legend of the club, one of the best defenders in the world. He deserved this."

He then added that his players' ability to adapt to a new defensive system quickly had been key to their success. "This change was very important for us because we found the right balance and every single player enjoyed this type of situation." he told Sky Sports. "This was a key moment. I have to be pleased because the players had never played with this system and it changed totally. To play three at the back is totally different to playing with four and it wasn't easy. But I found great men and great players."

Conte admitted his achievements in his first season at Stamford Bridge were the stuff of dreams. "I dreamed of this but if you asked me on my first day at Chelsea if I would reach the end of the season celebrating winning the league, and also to be in the final of the FA Cup, it was very difficult for me to imagine. Now, through our work, we have achieved this and it's right to enjoy this moment with our fans. It's amazing for me, for the players and for the club. It's a great achievement for us after a very tough season. Don't forget this. But now it's right to enjoy this moment."

Michy Batshuayi had made Conte think about his future. "I'm pleased for him because Michy had a very difficult season. It's not easy to arrive and play in the Premier League because it's very strong. After one year, working and pushing a lot, and to have great commitment from him, he deserves (to play) the final and for sure he's another weapon. I tried to find the best solution for us to bring all my players in the right form and give more minutes to the players who need to play more, then I have six days to decide the best starting eleven. This season has showed when players came off the bench they were decisive for us. Even today, Pedro and Batshuayi came on and scored three goals. Michy scored at West Brom and Fabregas came off the bench and scored against Watford."

Thibaut Courtois won the Premier League Golden Glove award, holding off competition from Hugo Lloris. He went into the final day of the season with 16 clean sheets to his Tottenham rival's 15, and although hopes of a 17th were dashed inside three minutes, Sam Clucas's 66th-minute consolation in a 7-1 victory for Spurs at Hull City was enough to see the Belgian confirmed as the sole winner. Courtois became only the second Chelsea keeper to win the Golden Glove, though predecessor Cech had claimed it in 2004/05, 2009/10 and 2013/14. A delighted Courtois said: "It's amazing, especially after last year, to bounce back in this way, to be champions, having been top for a long time. Obviously, last year we had a lot of critics, a lot of laughter at us. We had a moment when we were 15th, 16th in the league. People laugh and people get criticised - it's not nice after a season when you won the league. Some criticisms were deserved and others not and if you bounce back winning the title again, that's amazing. They said we didn't want to play any more, they said we were lazy, that kind of stuff, and it's not true. We tried to win our games, but last year was just an off year, especially for a team like Chelsea and the players that were here. Everybody is used to playing for trophies and last year that was not the case and everybody's pride was hurt. I think that is why we wanted to bounce back this season. After the Arsenal game when we lost 3-0 we were in a bad moment again, but we bounced back. And we had an amazing six, seven months. We're very proud about that." Courtois, just 25, has now won four league titles: the Belgian League with Genk, La Liga with Atletico Madrid and two Premier League titles.

Courtois has two years left on his contract and will be staying at the club which needs to challenge for the Champions League, a competition in which he finished runner-up with Atletico in 2014. "I don't think now is the moment to speak about that but, of course, I'm committed to Chelsea. I think next season there is a new goal of the Champions League. It's been a few years since Chelsea won it and I missed out on one (title) in the last minute, so I think a lot of players are hungry for winning that as well. Obviously you need additions because you play on four different fronts, so I think that's important, but I guess the club and the manager know what they're doing. We already have a lot of quality, but maybe sometimes you need a bit more depth because this year we didn't have injuries and you never know what can happen next year. So obviously I guess they will do their work now and hopefully we can finish the season with an FA Cup win as well."

When asked about the in-form N'Golo Kante, David Luiz told Sky Sports: "He's incredible - to have him is unbelievable. He's progressed so much. I'm a bit scared about (Kante), imagine how good he will become if he progresses even more and can score more."

Luiz then paid tribute to all his teammates. "It's been a great year for us. It's never easy to win the Premier League and it was a dream come true to come back here. This was one of my goals. I enjoy football every day, I enjoy it a lot because I love this club."

The defender had endured a mixed spell during his first stint at Chelsea but had been one of the club's stand-out players this season. When pressed on his development, he said: "I'm a bit older now! The day I arrived here, Conte showed me what he wanted me to do."

Some pundits are never satisfied and the latest was Gary Neville: "16 goals - is that as good as it gets, or do you think you can do a lot better? I always want more for you." the Red Devils icon challenged Eden Hazard, face-to-face, on Sky Sports after the match.

"I think I can do better but I need to go step by step, you know." Hazard replied. "If I score too much this season maybe next season will be too much, you know! No, I just try to give everything on the pitch, to score, to create something, then we see. This season was good, we won, so everyone is happy."

The warning signs were there that the competition will be even more fierce come next season - Pep Guardiola will make sure of that. After winning 5-0 at Watford, he commented ominously: "We were under a lot of pressure. Congratulations to Chelsea and to Tottenham, we are so glad to be third. Next season Arsenal cannot be in the Champions League, it shows it is complicated. We made good things during the season. You are judged on results. The gap is too big, we have to play better to be close to them. We are going to try. It is not a club with history of playing in Europe like United or Arsenal. But now we are there five or six years and now we can try to close the gap on the elite. The best team in Europe will be at the Etihad next season. I don't know what we need to add. This is one of the best groups I have ever trained, they never gave up. It was a pleasure to be with them."

Conte was unable to look to next season, his thoughts were instead fully focused on the season finale at Wembley, a match in which he considered Arsenal to be favourites to win the FA Cup. "If you ask me who are the favourites I would say Arsenal. They missed out on the Champions League. Arsenal now has only this possibility to find a good season after a win in the FA Cup. For this reason we must pay great attention. We must find in ourselves the right motivation, the right anger. The game will be very difficult. After I don't know how many years Arsenal missed the Champions League. We must have our antenna very high and prepare in the right way. I'm not talking about a tactical game, I'm talking about motivation, right fire in ourselves, in our soul, in our heart. If we have this in the same proportion as Arsenal, or more, we have the possibility to do the Double. Otherwise we risk a lot. This is the real danger for us, to think that this season is finished. To win the title this season becomes great. This season can become fantastic if we are able to win the FA Cup. We must find the right motivation. It's important for us to celebrate, but then to find the right fire in our soul to be ready to work very hard this week to prepare and to feel in the right way this game. This is a great opportunity to win and to do the Double."

Arsene Wenger, though, had a selection headache at centre-back. Laurent Koscielny can't play after being sent off against Everton and fellow centre-back Gabriel was stretchered off.

MONDAY, 22 MAY 2017

The news at the start of the day was that the Premier League would not investigate the incident when Sunderland, Chelsea and John Terry all colluded allowing the departing captain to be substituted after 26 minutes. However, by the end of a day of non-stop media attention the FA opened an investigation.

It emerged that the idea had originated from Terry with both managers agreeing to what a number of pundits felt was out of order when Sunderland goalkeeper Jordan Pickford kicked the ball out in the 26th minute after being reminded to do so by a Chelsea player. Eventually it took Terry two minutes to leave the field as his teammates gave him a guard of honour, which meant he did not actually leave the field of play until the 28th minute, and curiously there was only one minute of additional time!

Sunderland boss David Moyes confirmed that "Diego Costa asked Jordan to kick the ball out. We knew it was happening."

Terry was not the first to have this treatment in his final game as Didier Drogba's finale at Stamford Bridge set a precedent when he was carried off the pitch by his teammates in the 30th minute of his last game to receive the acclaim of the crowd.

"First of all (Terry) has been an absolute giant of the Premier League, 717 appearances, 15 trophies, but I'm not sure about this." Alan Shearer told the BBC. "Sunderland agreeing to kick the ball out on 26 minutes, I don't think anything should be done that could undermine the integrity of the game. I know it was done with good intentions and he deserves the guard of honour, but it should have been before or after the game or in the last minute."

Critics suggested the arrangement was akin to a spot-fixing stunt but the Premier League said Terry had not broken any rules. Additionally, betting experts suggested that even if there had been a gamble on a 26th-minute substitution then bookmakers would not pay out for such a contrived event.

Paddy Power confirmed they had accepted bets on the specific time of Terry's substitution, giving odds of 100-1, with three punters cashing in having placed money on the change to take place between 26:00 and 26:59. The Irish bookmaker told the Press Association: "We replied to a novelty request for odds on John Terry's substitution - one of hundreds on the Chelsea game - and fair play to the three punters who were on at odds of 100-1. To be honest the only mistake here is we should have clocked sooner there'd be another cringe-worthy Chelsea send-off for JT."

The Press Association spoke to two of the customers who won £2,500 and £1,000 respectively. One punter who attended the game predicted something similar regarding Terry and made an enquiry with Paddy Power before placing a £25 bet on the phone. The punter, who wished to remain anonymous, told the Press Association: "We thought maybe 10-1, 15-1 at most as there was a precedent set (by Drogba). I consider myself relatively lucky." Another punter said he opened an account with Paddy Power in order to place the bet, which was only possible to do over the phone. The Chelsea fan was not watching the game, but says he put on a £10 stake and received his winnings in his account on Monday.

Interestingly, the Twitter page of Chelsea fanzine cfcuk correctly predicted Terry's 26th minute substitution at 2.24pm on the Sunday, over 30 minutes before kick-off. The editor of the fanzine, Dave Johnstone, declined to reveal how the publication obtained the information, saying: "It was fantastic foresight." adding: "Why not do that for one of the best centre-backs this country has ever produced?"

David Luiz enjoyed the London sunshine as he stripped down to his trunks and dived into the swimming pool, enjoying a day off. Posting to his 16.7m Instagram followers, Luiz got a friend to video him scoring the most acrobatic of goals in slow motion. Leaping high into the air, he scissor-kicked the ball into a fun-sized goal at the back of the garden while falling into his pool. It was a highly impressive goal and Luiz celebrated as if he had hit the winner at Wembley.

That evening Conte won two accolades at the 25th annual League Managers Association (LMA) awards: The LMA members voted him as the LMA Manager of the Year 2016/17, sponsored by Everest, and he also won the Premier League Barclays Manager of the Season.

He was presented the newly commissioned Sir Alex Ferguson Trophy by Sir Alex, England Manager and LMA President Gareth Southgate, and Everest Board Member Tony Parsell.

On collecting his award Conte said: "I think I've had a lot of incredible emotions in my first season here in England. I want to say thank you to all the people who voted for me. It's great to receive this award. I hope to deserve this. It's fantastic to read all the names that won this trophy and to stay with these managers is a great achievement for me. I hope to continue in the best way."

LMA Chairman, Howard Wilkinson, said: "This evening's silver celebration LMA Annual Awards Dinner allowed us to reflect on the first 25 years of our association."

"The evening also saw us present the new Sir Alex Ferguson Trophy for the LMA Manager of the Year sponsored by Everest for the first time. This magnificent trophy which was hand-crafted by Thomas Lyte, appointed Goldsmiths and Silversmiths to Her Majesty The Queen, recognises all previous winners of the Manager of the Year award stretching as far back as Sir Matt Busby in 1968, who have received the award at the recommendation of their fellow managers."

"To be honoured by your peers for not merely the achievement itself but also the manner of the achievement cannot be bettered, and this year we have welcomed a new name to the list of top professionals who have won this prestigious accolade."

"For Antonio, to win the Premier League and reach the final of the FA Cup in his first season in England adds further lustre to the praise for a job well done. We are delighted he was able to join us this evening to collect his award and receive the credit from his peers he rightly deserves."

LMA Chief Executive, Richard Bevan, added: "... And of course, it was a special moment to present the Sir Alex Ferguson Trophy to its first recipient, as we crowned Antonio Conte as the LMA Manager of the Year sponsored by Everest for 2016/17."

"Antonio has excelled since joining the Premier League last summer. His tactical expertise, professionalism and desire to win has led to his Chelsea team achieving the greatest number of wins in a Premier League season. He is a truly deserving champion in every sense of the word."

Conte was, of course, also asked about the FA Cup final. "It's important from tomorrow to prepare in the right way for this game against Arsenal, to find the right hunger. Usually in a final it is very important not only to play well and have a good system but to have the right motivation, the right hunger and be ready to fight and show more desire than your opponent. The season is not finished and on Saturday we have another important target against Arsenal. We want to try to win the Double but for sure Arsenal will want to win this trophy. Then we start to prepare for next season and try to do better."

TUESDAY, 23 MAY 2017

Chinese Super League club Tianjin Quanjian announced that it had not made contact with Diego Costa or his agent "during the past six months". Tianjin clarified: "We have no intention of becoming involved in any unhealthy competition and, consequently, paying a premium price."

Juventus confirmed the permanent signing of Chelsea winger Juan Cuadrado in a £17m deal after activating the 'option to purchase' clause within his loan contract. The money was to be paid in three separate instalments.

The Old Lady took to their official website and social media channels to confirm the news, speaking of their delight to have acquired the services of the 28-year-old Colombian international who had signed a three-year deal.

Pat Nevin believed there was an overreaction to John Terry's staged farewell. "It was our party and we had a great time, unfortunately others were looking in and apparently couldn't cope with the fun we were having." Nevin wrote on Chelsea's official site. "So what was the biggest story? Apparently JT leaving the field after 26 minutes to the applause and thanks of the fans and the appreciation of his teammates. I will not add to the nonsense other than to say that there are far more important things to get angry about these days, and I strongly believe that no other player in the game would have received such a negative and, at times, vitriolic reaction from parts of the media and beyond. It seemed personal, targeted, unfair and not a reflection of the day and its emotions."

WEDNESDAY, 24 MAY 2017

Thoughts were, naturally, turning towards the FA Cup final.

Chris Sutton dismissed Conte's theory that the Gunners were favourites as "rubbish" and claimed that Arsenal were some way behind their opponents. "It's a load of rubbish to be honest." Sutton told the Telegraph. "I just think if Chelsea turn up, Arsenal can't live with Chelsea. The gap between the two sides is enormous, it really is."

Pat Nevin, writing on Chelsea's official website, warned of the dangers of switching off. "You could tell by Antonio's demeanour after the match against Sunderland that he wanted to enjoy the moment but it was imperative in his mind that nobody would be allowed to lose any of the hunger for success. He was right to mention that in the press conference because it is human nature to relax just a little after that level of success. If you win the league your brain tells you that the job is done so the fun times and rest and recovery can begin. In fact your body can go into a decline. I was ill within a week of the end of every single season during my 19-year career. Part of it must be psychological and part of it is perfectly natural. As you have been pushing the edge of the fitness envelope for so long, something has to give. Antonio and the staff must be, and will be, on high alert to any dip from any player this week."

Ron 'Chopper' Harris, who still retains the record number of appearances for Chelsea, ahead of the departing Terry, feared Arsenal's return to form will now make it a tough challenge in the final.

In an exclusive interview for ChelseaFan12.com, the original 'Captain, Leader, Legend', said that he can still recall how his Chelsea team in the 1967 FA Cup Final froze in another London derby and ended up losing. Chopper observed: "Not always the best team wins in the FA Cup Final. Some players freeze and it happened to Chelsea in the 1967 Cup Final against Spurs. A month ago I would have been very confident of the outcome against Arsenal in the final, but Arsenal have picked up of late and look a different team than the one even a few weeks ago."

In the same video shoot another former Chelsea legend, Bobby Tambling, disagreed when he predicted: "I have great faith in this manager and his team. That's why I am confident that they will go out and complete the Double." And former Blues' defender, Gary Chivers, chipped in with his view that Chopper's concerns might be justified. Chivers commented: "I am sure that Arsenal will keep Wenger on, and I am also sure that this is going to be a tough, tough game for Chelsea. I also think it's going to be a very good game, and I cannot wait for it."

However, Arsenal were now facing a defensive crisis ahead of the cup.

Laurent Koscielny was ruled out after Arsenal's appeal against his red card was dismissed by the FA. His three match ban starts with the final.

Gabriel Paulista, who left Sunday's game on a stretcher, will definitely miss out through injury, and could even be sidelined for six-to-eight weeks, meaning he would miss the start of pre-season.

And according to Arsene Wenger, Shkodran Mustafi was "still sick" whilst recovering from a suspected concussion.

However, Nevin warned Chelsea not to get complacent. "Obviously the news coming out of Arsenal has been less than positive for our opponents with Laurent Koscielny out and Gabriel also struggling after their win against Everton. Add to that the torment of finally losing out on next season's Champions League involvement and a variety of dilemmas in the upper management and, all in all, it is not a great time for the Gunners. The thing is, that could make them even more dangerous. Their players will certainly be up for it, especially those who think they might be leaving in the summer. They would love to go out on a high with a major trophy and of course they are now serious underdogs in the eyes of most people, which takes the pressure off to some degree. It is also worth remembering that Arsenal are on a good run of form at the moment, with five wins in a row and a combined score of 13-2 during those matches."

David Chidgey, season ticket holder and host of the Chelsea FanCast, wrote an interesting article, talking about Chelsea's recent successes under both Mourinho and Conte, contrasting the two highly successful coaches and going on to state that "...Conte has already reached the popularity level of Mourinho in the space of one season - and that is down to his personality." He also felt "... there is a real sense this is the start of a new era at the Bridge." Time will tell.

Chelsea announced that they had cancelled their victory parade in the wake of the appalling Manchester Arena attack, stating it would be "inappropriate" with the UK terror threat at its highest level after Monday's bombing killed 22 people.

A statement from the club said: "Everyone associated with Chelsea Football Club offers our heartfelt condolences to those affected by Monday's terror attack in Manchester. Our thoughts go out to all the victims, and their families and friends."

"In light of these tragic events, we feel it is inappropriate to go ahead with the victory parade in London on Sunday."

"Given the heightened security threat announced by the Government, and recognising that this is a developing situation, we have given this careful consideration. We strongly believe, in the interests of everyone, this is the correct course of action. We are sure our fans will understand this decision."

"Having consulted with the Metropolitan Police, Hammersmith and Fulham Council and other authorities, we know the emergency services would have been as professional as ever, but we would not want in any way to divert important resources by holding an additional, non-ticketed event on the streets of London."

"Furthermore, as a mark of respect, our players will wear black armbands at the FA Cup Final against Arsenal on Saturday. Chelsea Football Club will also make a donation to a fund supporting the victims of this horrific attack."

Arsenal stated that they would not stage a parade should they win the FA Cup and that a planned screening at the club's Emirates Stadium had been cancelled with fans given full refunds. Chief executive Ivan Gazidis said the safety of supporters and staff was paramount and the club had been in close contact with the security services. "After taking their advice we have reluctantly taken the decision to cancel the screening and potential parade."

A minute's silence was observed before the Europa League final between Manchester United and Ajax in Stockholm, with both teams wearing black armbands. The opening ceremony was toned-down as a mark of respect for the victims.

THURSDAY, 25 MAY 2017

Arsene Wenger contradicted Conte by installing Chelsea as the favourites to win the Cup.

Asked if Arsenal's preparations would be different to their two recent FA Cup finals in light of facing a tougher opponent, Wenger said: "Not much because the pressure is always very high against Hull (2014) and Aston Villa (2015). Especially against Hull because we hadn't won the FA Cup for a long time. We are not favourites, it's quite even or maybe Chelsea are ahead. It's similar to us to what happened against Man City (who Arsenal beat in the semi-final)." The bookmakers agree with Wenger.

Cesar Azpilicueta became only the fourth outfield player to play every minute of a Premier League title-winning campaign - joining Leicester City's Wes Morgan from last year, his teammate John Terry from the season before and Manchester United's Gary Pallister back in the 1992/93 campaign.

Four other players featured in all 3,420 Premier League minutes this season: goalkeepers Ben Foster (Albion) and Fraser Forster (Southampton), and defenders Ben Gibson (Middlesbrough) and Steve Cook (Bournemouth).

Speaking to the Chelsea website Azpilicueta said. "Obviously it's not easy to play every minute and win the league. It's a big achievement. I've tried to do my best to get in the team but I have to be thankful to the manager, he's trusted me a lot. I was always in the team and the only way I could repay his confidence was by working hard which is what I've tried to do since pre-season. In the end we got a big reward but we want a bigger one on Saturday."

Azpilicueta is the Chelsea Player of the Season, according to three former legends, even though N'Golo Kante has run off with all the personal honours. On ChelseaFan12.com 'Chopper' Harris said: "The best two finds of the season have been Moses and Alonso, credit to the manager they had been wondering around at different clubs but he got them making a big impact, but I've got to agree with Chiv (Gary Chivers) Azpilicueta is the most consistent."   Chivers had remarked: "Azpilicueta is the unsung hero of the team. He gives you a seven-and-a-half to an eight out of ten in every signal game. I recall when Salomon Rondon raced clear but Azpilicueta caught him up and made a fantastic tackle, he has great pace, covers well and has been remarkable as one of those three at the back."

Bobby Tambling quipped: "I was going to agree but I couldn't pronounce his name."

"Call him 'Dave', everyone does.", chipped in Chiv!

John Terry "couldn't care less" what people thought about his staged 26th minute substitution. He told the Sun that the reaction hasn't affected him.

"I couldn't care less, I promise you. I couldn't care. All I care about is celebrating with my Chelsea fans. Me and them have an unbelievable rapport and have had for 22 years and no one, whatever you write or someone says or someone's opinion, can ever get in the way of that. So if that's the way I wanted to go out, that's the way I go out. You know what, because I've been 22 years here, won so many trophies, if I wanted to play one minute and come off I would have done. I wanted to play 26 minutes and come off because it's the shirt number."

Terry would be back on the bench for the Cup final as Conte returned to his first-choice back three.

FRIDAY, 26 MAY 2017

Speaking to Italian news channel, Premium Sport, Conte confirmed they were still focused. "The days immediately following our Premier League victory were beautiful because it's only fair to enjoy such the victory after a year. But at the same time, we wanted to keep the tension high because the season isn't over yet and we want to finish it in the best way. When you're at a big team, you must breathe the right air, have a winning mentality and always play to win. I just want to do the best I can with my team. I always thought about the club and not myself. The important thing is to work well and improve the club you work for. After that, if you win, better still."

He was asked about the challenges of the Champions League. "In football you can't just get up one day and win it. I did it for the first time with Juventus after winning my first Scudetto and we were eliminated by Bayern, who then won the competition. In the following year, we went out to Galatasaray in the group stage and got to the semi-finals of the Europa League. I had the pleasure of coaching in the Champions League for two years, but these are competitions in which you have to have an important foundation. Winning isn't easy, in order to win, you must follow a path that only a few know about."

Gianluca Vialli called on Conte to emulate Sir Alex Ferguson and stay at Stamford Bridge for 25 years. The former Chelsea striker and manager told Sky Sports: "I think Antonio loves the club and wants to play in the Champions League. There was a rumour about him going to Inter Milan, rather than Juventus, but if I was him then I would be staying a bit longer, fall in love with London, Premier League football and Chelsea and stay for 25 years like Alex Ferguson did."

Vialli, who used to be a teammate of Conte's at Juventus, was impressed with the way his compatriot had managed to change Chelsea's fortunes. "It's been fantastic. To recover from a situation that wasn't ideal, he managed to turn things around. He did it, especially when he made that tactical change after about seven or eight games. That really changed the season. Chelsea played really effective football, but also entertaining. I think they deserved the title in the end."

Cesc Fabregas was braced for Wembley heartbreak as Conte prepared to recall Nemanja Matic. The former Arsenal captain who, no doubt, would relish the chance to complete the Double against his former club was likely to be used as an impact sub, which had been his speciality in recent months.

Matic had not started since Chelsea clinched the title at West Brom but was expected to return to partner Kante in midfield. Conte had yet to reveal his starting line-up but trained his team in a formation without Fabregas.

Victor Moses could hardly believe he was on the threshold of a possible Double, as he admitted: "That would be a great achievement for me. We've got a new manager here who's willing to give everyone an opportunity. He gave me that opportunity and I didn't look back after that. I'm very pleased with that and I just want to keep improving in every game I play. It's a new role for me and I'm still getting used to it. I'm more focused now than ever. I'm enjoying my football again. The more games you play the more experience you get and I'm enjoying that so far this season. It's from the manager, he's given me a lot of confidence. Not just me personally, but the other boys as well. He gives every single one of us confidence to go out there and enjoy our football."

Moses admitted the champions were still thinking about the 3-0 defeat they suffered at Arsenal back in September. It was the game that changed the season. Now they will use it as motivation again. "We still think about it." Moses said. "We felt very sad after that game. Now we want the Double."

David Luiz's decision to take a pay cut and return to Chelsea was vindicated for the 30-year-old Brazilian who had previously joined Paris Saint-Germain for £50m in 2014, having won the Champions League, FA Cup and Europa League with Chelsea. He then won three consecutive Ligue 1 titles before returning for £34m. "I don't always like the easy life. That's why I took a risk and I'm very happy. It was the right decision. I love the risk. In your life if you don't take a risk you're not going to taste something new. Not just in your professional life, I think it's every day. I cut my salary to come back here. But it's OK. God has given me a lot so I'm very happy with this. I was winning in Paris. I went to Paris for two years and won all the titles in France. I had a great life. I had a great credibility with the club, I had everything in Paris and then I took a risk to come back to one country that was not that happy with me."

Luiz has an FA Cup winners' medal but missed the 2012 final against Liverpool with a hamstring injury before returning to the side as Chelsea won the Champions League on penalties. "I don't want to miss this one. I want to play. I want to try to give my best for the team. I have the ambition. I want to win the next title, we have the opportunity this season and then let's see."

Chelsea were seeking the Double for only the second time in their history and Luiz credited Conte for masterminding the campaign. "Conte is a great person, a great character and he's passionate - he loves football. The day I arrived here we talked together and he tried to explain his philosophy to play football. He said to me: 'You are the player I want in my team and to improve my team.' And then I said to him: 'I'm going to work hard for you and for the team.' And that's it."

Former Chelsea midfielder Claude Makelele, who spent five years with Chelsea, winning two titles, two League Cups and an FA Cup, heaped praise on N'Golo Kante.

With Kante's domination of the midfield over the past two seasons there were natural comparisons between the two, and the current Swansea assistant manager Makelele was expecting even more success. "People talk about the Makelele position, but I am old and it is time everybody called it the Kante position. N'Golo deserves that." he told official Chelsea website. "Every time I watch N'Golo, I see so much desire in him, so much focus and so much determination to make himself a better player with every game. He was the heartbeat of the Leicester team, but it was also like taking a bulldog for a walk, you had to keep pulling him back because he had so much energy. Now N'Golo has added intelligence. He appreciates the position of his teammates more and how to play in a more sophisticated system where it is not all about running and tackling, but the decisions he makes. Some players are meant to be superstars, but some - like N'Golo and myself - must be happy making other people look good. Next season we will see him become even better because he will have the challenge of the Champions League. He is also part of a fantastic generation of young players coming through for France, which will also see him develop."

Conte had claimed that Arsenal were favourites for the cup despite finishing a whopping 18 points behind their London rivals in the league and Victor Moses added: "We don't feel any pressure, we're just taking this game as it comes. If he says Arsenal are the favourites, then… I don't know. But we've got good players who can win us games. We think we're good enough to beat Arsenal but it's not going to be an easy game. We've got the league title and they're going to want to win because they missed out on top four. We're going to try and stop them because we want the Double."

Gary Cahill admitted the players would be affected by the Manchester bombing as they try to enjoy a Cup final amidst heightened security. The club increased their own security around the squad, and on the day of the final Cahill expected his family to be at Wembley and believed the players would try to carry on as normal. "Before talking about the game, it's important to show our respect and send our condolences to the families that have been affected in Manchester. We've all got families and I can't imagine how they're feeling right now. I lived close to Manchester, it's a great city and I'm sure they'll pull together. It's difficult. There's an element of trying to live your life in a normal way. Everyone speaks about trying to make sure it doesn't affect you, but it's impacted everyone in England, especially the families. It's a tragedy, like when we played at Wembley after the bombings in Paris. It's horrible. We send our best wishes to everyone involved and I'm sure the security will be top drawer at Wembley on Saturday. We're going to try and enjoy it as much as we can. I try not to worry. I'm sure there's a lot that goes on behind the scenes that we don't know about, but it's very difficult to stop absolutely everything. These aren't normal situations. When you see these things happen around the world it has a huge impact, but when it happens in your own country it's even more devastating. You can't let it affect everything you do in your life. We have to pull to together as a country and a city like Manchester. My family want to come and support me on Saturday, so we're treating it as a normal game."

Cahill had nearly joined Arsenal. "It was close. It broke down on the fee, nothing to do with me. Chelsea came in after that and the rest is history."

He had joined Chelsea from Bolton in January 2012 and within five months had won the Champions League and FA Cup. A year later, he added the Europa League. Then the League Cup and Premier League in 2015 followed. "It becomes like an addiction to win more. When you have that feeling of winning a trophy you just want it again and again. Outside my family and my kids being born, it's the best feeling ever and it was again when we lifted the Premier League trophy the other day. Your career is short and you want to achieve as much as you can. If you have no goals then what is the point of playing? The FA Cup for me, it's what I used to watch growing up. People say to me the shine has gone off the Cup and I reply: 'Are you crazy?' It's the best cup you can win."

Eden Hazard was determined to lift the trophy for the first time since moving to Stamford Bridge in June 2012. "We want more, you always want more. For Chelsea, for such a big club like this, you need to win one, two, three trophies every season if you can. Now we have the possibility to win another trophy so all the players are ready for that. It's such a great competition for the fans."

He was noncommittal over the question of where he ranks among the world's best. "People are always talking, but I don't care about that. I try to be the best I can. I don't know if I am top five, top 10, top 20 in the world. It's not my target. I just want to enjoy my football. Players like Ronaldo and Messi are leaders. People that want to be better every day. That's why they have been at the top for the last ten years. They need to prove, we all need to prove every day. But I don't think too much about that. I just concentrate on myself, on football, on the pitch, on the training ground. Then I see what comes. When I signed for Chelsea in my head it was to win titles. Maybe not like this - I have already won two Premier Leagues, one League Cup, one Europa League. It's not bad - but it can be better. The FA Cup and Champions League, why not?"

Hazard believed a Wembley win would lay down a marker for what Chelsea hope to achieve next season. "We have this new manager, we have a couple of young players so everything is ready to build something. The last ten years in Chelsea have been great. Now it's like a new generation. Frank Lampard is finished, Didier Drogba is finished, Ashley Cole, and now John. It's a new generation, and we want to prove that the club is one of the best in the world. For next season, the FA Cup is a good opportunity to put pressure on Arsenal and all the other opponents. To show what we can do next season."

As for leaders, Hazard admitted: "We have a couple of players who can be leaders. I am in my fifth year at Chelsea. We have some guys who have a lot of experience, so we are ready. I try to be a leader on the pitch. John is a legend for us, the club, for all the fans. Next season he's not here anymore, but some of the guys are ready to take this opportunity."

Willian pledged his future to Chelsea. "Yes (I will be a Chelsea player next season)." Willian told the Evening Standard. "I have a contract with Chelsea until 2020 and I am very happy here. I have a great relationship with all the people that work at Chelsea and the fans too. They have been great to me since I joined. Chelsea are back in the Champions League next season and I am looking forward to playing in it again. It is a big, big target for us and we have to look to win that trophy next year."

He echoed similar sentiments when speaking to Brazilian TV channel SporTV: "Of course money is important, no one can survive without money. But money is not everything. If I can get this British citizenship - I can start to do documents next year. You have to take a test to get that passport too. Surely this passport can open doors in the future. I can get my passport and I can get it for my family too. That's the purpose I have. Besides the objectives on the pitch, besides enjoying the country, getting this passport would be another prize for me."

Willian knew the Gunners would provide a "difficult" test. "We want to end the season with the Double. We have the Premier League but we want the FA Cup too. This is a big game for us. It will be difficult against Arsenal and we have to be ready. We have to be focussed and play in the same way we have all season."

Bertrand Traore wanted to stay at the club following his season-long loan at Ajax. The 21-year-old had shone in the Eredivisie, reaching the Europa League final where their youthful side lost 2-0 to Manchester United. He planned talks after going on international duty with Burkina Faso. "I will go with the national team and after that take some rest. Then I will go back to Chelsea and have a talk - we will see. That's my hope (to be at Chelsea next season).That was the key when I came to Ajax - play as many (games) as I could, do well, and try to go back to Chelsea. I think I had a great season but I don't decide to stay at Chelsea or move. I will see what my future will be."

Conte conducted his final news conference of the season at Stamford Bridge.

He started by offering his thoughts and solidarity to the victims of the Manchester bombings. "Tomorrow we have to play an important game, and try to win an important trophy, but I don't want to forget what happened in Manchester, and we are very close to the families of the people who have died." He added, "This situation, for sure, creates a bit of difficulty in your mind. If you start to think we are always in danger, then we have died before we die. A game of football or a concert is a moment you must live with passion, with passion and enthusiasm. When this type of situation happens, for sure, you are a bit scared. But we must continue to live and face every situation in the right way."

He was eager to extend his contract. "If the club give me the possibility to stay here and to extend my contract, for sure I am available to do this. But we have the same idea about the future. The way we have to do things together, to improve the squad and the team. But, I repeat, I'm happy for this season and am happy to stay here. I hope to stay here for many years." Vialli had earlier called on Conte to emulate Sir Alex's lengthy tenure at United to which Conte replied. "It would be great to do this. For a coach, that's the best solution - to stay for a long time at the same club and build, with the club, something important. But you know very well that modern football is dangerous. Our job depends a lot on the results. I think the only way that I know, to convince the club I should stay a long time, is to work very hard with my players. For sure, that is my hope."

Wenger was now into his 21st year as Arsenal manager. "When you stay for a long time at the same team - we're talking about a great team, not a small team - we must consider him like one of the best managers in history." Conte said. "For sure, I don't trust that tomorrow will be the last game for Arsene. I think he deserves to work with Arsenal because he showed, in these 20 years, he is a good manager. He did a good job. Only this season they missed out on the Champions League. In England, this target, sometimes you can undervalue this."

It was, of course, certainly John Terry's farewell. "Our target, our aim, is to reach another trophy and to see him lift this trophy. I have this dream. Also, my players have this dream." Asked if Terry might feature one final time, Conte said: "For sure John will be with us and for sure he will be on the bench, and then we'll see what the game requests in the moment we are playing."

Conte said his side must now forget about their league exploits as Arsenal were out to save their season. "I saw a lot of concentration from all my players in training, we trained very well despite the heat. I guess they are calm, it is impossible for me to not trust my players after this season, but for 120 minutes plus penalties we have to forget we won the league."

Wenger's team had a great FA Cup pedigree, winning in 2014 and 2015, 12 times overall and Conte again insisted that Arsenal started as favourites. "We could start as the underdog, as we won and celebrated league, but the side we face are a team that lost the Champions League next season and have this possibility to save their season. We must pay great focus and show great desire. I trust a lot in my players as they showed great concentration to win the league. It will be a tough game for both teams, and we are ready to fight, play a good game and try to win the trophy."

Conte revealed that he had tried to watch Wenger on the training ground in early 2015. At that time Conte, who was Italy's head coach, met up with Pochettino at Tottenham's training base and additionally paid a visit to Chelsea and West Ham. He also requested permission to watch one of Wenger's training sessions, but the only chance he got to see Arsenal was in their 3-1 defeat at home to Monaco in the Champions League. "Honestly, I tried to contact Arsenal during my experience in England when I visited Chelsea, West Ham and Tottenham, but in that moment they were very busy. I saw when they lost at home to Monaco in the Champions League, but I didn't have the opportunity to see Wenger during a training session. I would've liked it, but it wasn't possible."

He relived his lowest moment in his first season and how it all changed. "After that Arsenal defeat, I was angry." reflected Conte. "It was difficult for me to accept. For two days, it was not easy for my family to live with me, but they understand. But I channelled my anger in the right way. I tried to change the situation." Roman Abramovich had been demanding answers but, "Honestly, I was very calm. I knew that I was putting all of myself, all my strength, into this new job. Myself and my staff were working so hard. To find the right solution quickly is not easy. You must be very good, very prepared, but also lucky. You must have the players to give you the possibility to impose your ideas. I was lucky to have a group who put themselves into my idea of football, and we put ourselves in a position where we could secure a fantastic title. The owner came for three days to watch our sessions, watch the video analysis, to stay with us. He supported me. He never showed me he was angry. The club always trusted me. I never thought the club was thinking about sacking me."

The defeat by Arsenal had put all thoughts of winning the title out of his mind. "It was very difficult to think about winning the League after that and that we'd be celebrating at the end. We had a lot of problems. I don't like speaking about winning the Double before we win. If you win, then speak about it. It won't be easy." However, he did promise himself a celebratory cigar if his team lifted the Cup, even though he doesn't smoke! "We have to make it a fantastic season. There's only one way to do that, by winning. I don't smoke, but I'm ready to smoke a cigar if we win."

Following the press conference Conte hosted a nice little 'do' for journalists by way of an apology for his persistent lateness throughout the season. He had become well known for running late at his Friday media briefings but he put on a buffet in a corporate box next to the one used by Roman Abramovich. The Premier League trophy was brought out for pictures and Conte spoke openly about adjusting to life in London, about bringing his family to England in the summer and, once again, confirming his desire to stay with the newly crowned Premier League champions. He then rushed off to make the team bus for Wembley.

Alan Shearer speaking on BBC Radio 4 said, "Antonio Conte has been hugely impressive at Chelsea in the way he got the dressing room together, his signings have been brilliant and the way he handled the Costa situation. He hasn't criticised anyone in public, everything has been handled within the club. Every decision he has made has worked for him."

Frank Lampard, who got his hands on the trophy four times with Chelsea, summed up: "The FA Cup final is a big occasion anyway but when you get this close to the Double you realise how hard they are to come by and you want to finish the job. I think it is very clear that Chelsea are favourites, looking at their league form and how consistent they have been. They have a stronger team and a stronger squad than Arsenal at present, but I am still expecting a tight game. You cannot disrespect Arsenal. They have players who can hurt you and they have been in better form recently themselves. But in Conte they have a very strong manager who will have had his eye on this game from the moment they won the title at West Brom. He has quite cleverly rotated the team in the past two games to give everyone minutes, and their training will have been very focused towards Saturday too. As we know, they are always well organised and a fantastic team unit, and are very confident because they know they can rely on one of their high-quality attacking players to win games. If they are on form and the team works as it has worked all year, then Chelsea will win."

Ian Wright, a two-time winner with the Gunners, added: "Arsenal's situation now makes them dangerous too. Rather than being on a downer after missing out on the top four last weekend, I think it is more a case that they have got nothing to lose. Chelsea are favourites this time but not by much. The thing with Conte's team is that they are very experienced and they will know exactly what to expect from Arsenal. But the fact Chelsea are so good makes it even better if Arsenal can beat them. Chelsea have been by far the best side in the Premier League this season, so beating them would go a long way to showing that Arsenal have got a team that can compete against the best and that they should be doing a lot better in the league. Chelsea are the masters of this formation at the moment, and Arsenal are going up against the best with a weakened team."

SATURDAY, 27 MAY 2017
Arsenal 2-1 Chelsea
FA Cup Final

The day began on a high note with newspaper headlines universally in agreement that Conte was staying for sure; no doubt based on his briefings as well as comments from yesterday.

Apparently he will sign a new £9.5million-a-year contract after the final, committing his future to the club until 2021 after rejecting interest from Inter Milan. He planned a short break after today's game before returning for meetings and a move to London with his wife and daughter, while also taking more advanced English lessons. Conte said: "I have two more years' contract with the club. Then, if the club give me the possibility to stay here and to extend my contract, for sure I am available to do this. We have the same idea about the future, the way we have to do things to improve the squad and the team."

He intended to expand his squad and build a team "to be ready for the Champions League. This year we had a base of 13-14 good players. Next year with the Champions League we have to increase in numbers and in quality. The base is here, now we must put on the cherries. I am happy for this season and I am happy to stay here. I hope to stay for many years."

Chelsea were now into their twelfth final having already won seven. Since 1999 both Arsenal and Chelsea had won the competition five times, but Chelsea had slightly the better FA Cup record by virtue of one more quarter-final appearance. Whoever won would be the best FA Cup team of the 2000s.

Arsenal were now the first club ever to appear in the FA Cup final a total of 20 times and victory would set a new competition record of 13 FA Cup wins; almost 10 per cent of all the times the trophy had been lifted. Seven of the last eight ties between the clubs had been won by Arsenal. Chelsea came out on top in the last meeting - a 2-1 semi-final win in 2009 - but that was their only FA Cup victory against the Gunners in the past 70 years. This was only the second FA Cup final in 35 years to feature two London clubs - the other was in 2002 when Arsenal beat Chelsea to claim the Double.

For the first time ever, the FA Cup was streamed live online from the Spider camera; offering a unique perspective with a birds eye view of the pitch with virtual graphics.

And Martin Keown, on BBC's Football Focus, offered his opinion from two opposing angles: "Eden Hazard's dribbling is up there with the best in the game - Messi, Ronaldo, Bale. The players just bounce off him as he dribbles up the field. Once he starts those runs, you just can't stop him."

"I think Alexis Sanchez is tailor made for a pitch like this. He has that great athleticism, he is an opportunist, he is full of confidence and he is a defender's nightmare. You cannot give him a moment's space. He really is a match winner for Arsenal."

Jody Morris, now youth team manager at Stamford Bridge, offered a little snippet: "David Luiz is a huge character. He goes over to talk to the young players and is interested. He is a funny guy and likes having a joke but John Terry told me he has given some really good speeches in the dressing room."

Frank Lampard, on BBC One, was summing up, "Antonio Conte took on a team in a bad place and there were a few individuals who had their worst seasons in Chelsea shirts and he fixed it. Mid-season there were rumours that Eden Hazard was being a bit difficult on the training field but Conte dealt with it immediately. He came down on it with an iron fist and then he put an arm around him and that has brought the best out in him. With the older players, you just want honesty from the manager and that is what has happened with John Terry - he laid it on the line early with John and that has really helped with his season. Makelele was a great player, Kante is him and some. Claude would patrol at the half-way line, didn't really go forward or unleash in the other half - Kante can do that. In this Chelsea team, he's the difference for them. They were a bit pedestrian last year but he's brought energy to the team." (Perhaps a case of the 'commentators' curse' but Kante, in the final, would lose concentration from the restart, after 10-men Chelsea had equalised, to give Ramsey the freedom of the penalty area to score the winner - then again nothing much went right!).

Alan Shearer, also on BBC One. "I've never seen anyone cover as much grass in a 90-minute game as N'Golo Kante. There's no denying Eden Hazard's ability but it's no coincidence he's had his best goalscoring season with Kante in the team. Kante snuffs out moves from the opposition. He's so good at it. That means Hazard doesn't have to track back. There's not as much responsibility on Hazard, so he can concentrate on doing his job up front. That is a huge ask for Per Mertesacker to come in after playing 53 minutes of the season or so. I think Conte will target that back three. He'll tell Diego Costa to get into that back three as soon as he can."

Ruud Gullit added. "I think Chelsea will win 2-1. Chelsea are secure in themselves because they have won something. Arsenal, it's a difficult season for them. Chelsea have talked about the dangers of complacency. But this will be the icing on the cake if they win this match. Conte has a good team and they are all professionals. Be aware that some players can get easy-going. David Luiz is like that. But Conte is on the team all the time to make sure that doesn't happen. If you win, it's OK. If not, it can irritate players. We saw that with Jose Mourinho and Eden Hazard."

Just before the game Conte spoke to the BBC. "I think in this type of game, it's difficult to tell if there is a favourite. Arsenal will be motivated but we have worked very hard this week and also in the mentality that we must keep great concentration. It's very important to keep the right concentration because when you win the league in this way, it is possible you can become relaxed. But we have tried to work very well. I'm excited and nervous. It's my first final in England and I'm enjoying this. But also I have great concentration, because I'm here to win."

Conte and Wenger proudly lead their teams out ahead of captains Gary Cahill and Per Mertesacker.

The customary 'Abide with me' rang out at Wembley. There was a brass band, a choir and, of course,

the colourful fans. It was the most traditional of English football matches kicking off at…
5.30pm! Not 3.00. Travesty!

Arsenal won the FA Cup for a record 13th time in a thrilling final, beating 10-man Chelsea.

Arsene Wenger had now become the most successful manager in the competition's history with
seven victories as the Gunners took a hugely controversial lead in the fifth minute through Alexis
Sanchez. The striker clearly handled - with both hands - to bring the ball under control, but the
linesman had his flag up for Aaron Ramsey who was stood in an offside position. Ramsey did not
touch the ball, allowing Sanchez to run through and slot in; but the referee, Anthony Taylor, had
missed the bigger picture - the deliberate handball.

It handed Arsenal the initiative and gave them an enormous confidence boost to go on and totally
dominate the first half. Danny Welbeck struck the woodwork with a header, Ramsey chested the
ball against the post on the follow-up. Captain Cahill made two goal line clearances and Arsenal
could have led by three or four at half time.

Chelsea's players had taken to the field of play without the black armbands, worn as a tribute
to the victims of the Manchester bombing. Gary Lineker, fronting BBC's coverage, explained
at half-time: "Many of you are wondering why Chelsea aren't wearing black armbands. Apparently
it was an error, they just forgot, and they will be wearing them in the second half." It was a genuine
mistake, explained the Chelsea press officer. They were on jackets but they got changed into
a different jacket.

Victor Moses forced David Ospina into a fine save in the second period, before the Chelsea
wing-back was given a second yellow card on 68 minutes for diving in the penalty area; that was a
good decision by the referee. Conte had answered the call from the crowd to send on Cesc Fabregas
in an attempt to exert more control, only seven minutes before the sending off, and so he never
really got the chance to find that killer pass that had marked so many of his substitute appearances.

However, with 14 minutes remaining, Chelsea clawed their way back through Diego Costa's
deflected shot. But Arsenal regained the lead less than three minutes later as Ramsey headed in,
what turned out to be the winner, having scored the crucial goal in the 2014 cup final against Hull.
Costa struck the ball from close range straight into the chest of Ospina, who did so well to keep
composure and make himself big for an important save in Chelsea's one big chance to force extra
time.

In the end it was just one game too far for Conte, who had failed once before to complete the
Double with Juve.

Conte reflected: "I think the first goal was very strange. The first half we didn't start well, we didn't
have the right approach and we suffered in first 25 minutes. We started to play better in the second
half and the red card was decisive. I didn't see the incident on the TV and it was difficult
to understand. Honestly it is difficult to discuss this situation, I didn't see. I don't want to make
a mistake without to watch this situation. The reality is we lost the game. The first goal, the player
had his hands attached to the ball with two hands. Offside or not is not important. I don't know
if my players had the time to recover, I need to look at the goal, but there is a clear handball, but
I don't know why the referee didn't decide to whistle. It can happen. A player makes a mistake, the
referee makes a mistake. I think that we were unlucky."

"My players put all themselves in the game, our start wasn't good and the approach wasn't good.
They pushed at the start, we paid for the start. Arsenal started very well with great determination.

They surprised us a bit but I repeat our first 25 minutes weren't good. At our best moment, the referee decided to give the red card. It is very difficult to tell because I saw a contact with Moses and the defender but not sure if it was enough. It was one of the key moments. Then we let in after one moment and it was the key moment for our loss. We created another chance with Diego, but Ospina made a good save."

"I put Cesc on after 60 minutes because we wanted to try to have more quality in the passes to find the situation with vertical passes. For sure Matic played a really good game, if you see our past and sometimes I make this change when we are losing or drawing to have more quality, when the rhythm is lower."

"There is disappointment for the final result but it can happen and there was a lot of pressure. Victor Moses has been good and played an important season."

Thibaut Courtois commented: "We are obviously disappointed but I want to say congratulations to Arsenal. They played a good game. The first goal should never have been allowed - it was clearly a hand ball and then Ramsey was offside because he was interfering in play. After that goal, we tried to play but they deserved it. Then we went down to ten men and the red card was correct. Victor Moses doesn't need to apologise. I wouldn't say we were surprised because for the last four or five games in the league Arsenal upped their game so we expected a hard game. When you score, you get momentum and can build on that. We tried but obviously not enough."

Former England midfielder Jermaine Jenas on BBC Radio 5 live said: "The Chelsea players were hanging their heads but they had an unbelievable season. On the day, not enough players turned up, they did not deserve to win. Man for man, they were much better than Chelsea. I cannot believe how ordinary Arsenal made Chelsea look. The Premier League champions could not handle Arsenal's footballing ability in the middle of the pitch. They could not get any rhythm or get on the ball. It was their best display of the season."

An emotional Ian Wright commented: "Chelsea have won the league but will have a bit of a downer now. Arsenal have had a terrible season but have now won the FA Cup and they will go into the summer with a bit of an upper. You wouldn't have expected Chelsea to be as poor as they were, but you've got to take advantage of that. Eden Hazard has been brilliant all season, but he didn't turn up today."

Frank Lampard put it all into perspective when he made it clear, while the players and fans would be leaving bitterly disappointed, they should not lose sight of a magnificent title triumph.

There was small consolation in the fact that Nemanja Matic's stunning strike in the semi-final against Spurs was voted on the BBC as best FA Cup goal this season.

Social media, of course, was busy soon afterwards:

@ChelseaFC - "Not our day, but what a season we have had…"

@thibautcourtois - "Disappointed with the loss today, but let's not forget the amazing season we had! Premier league…"

@_Pedro17_ - "It's been a shame not to win another Title for all of you Blues. Thanks a lot for your support this season. Come On @ChelseaFC"

@CesarAzpi - "Disappointed with today's result but proud of being part of this club and this amazing season! Next season we'll go for more. Thanks! #cfc"

@mbatshuayi - "Bad end to a wonderful season... but no regrets we can still be proud of what we achieved as a team"

John Terry dreams of returning to the stadium as a manager, but was still undecided about his future. "I am going away, I need a good week away just to reflect. It doesn't help because it's heart-breaking, going out like that and losing. It's the last time probably at Wembley as a player. Hopefully one day I'll be back here as a manager, that's kind of the ambition. It has been difficult for me actually as a player because I've been looking to do coaching for the last year. Every time we get a day off, you've got a coaching session planned and then you think 'OK, I am going to spend it with the family'. The next thing you know, the season has finished and you've kind of missed out on a few sessions and everything. But, if I do stop or if I do carry on playing, I will press on in that regardless. I do want to be a manager. I think I've got too much to give and I've learned too much not to pass that on, whether that's initially to a younger generation or eventually at this level. Listen, this is the target - being here, managing a top side."

Terry had already cleared out his locker at the Cobham training ground ahead of the final. "That was an emotional one, my last day clearing out the locker. It kind of makes you feel a little bit empty when you're putting everything, your possessions over the year and pictures of your kids into a bag."

Last word of the day though, and there were many of them assessing the true worth of a memorable season, goes to the man who made it happen, Conte of course:

"Our season was incredible to win the league in this way, it was great but now it's important to look forward and to restart. Now the most important thing is to give a correct evaluation on our season It was incredible for us. Every player performed 120 per cent, we didn't have injuries and it is important this. This season for us was incredible because every single player worked very hard and next season we must pay great attention to understand that we have to improve, numbers in the squad and quality. It's very important. We must be cold to evaluate this situation. If I have to be worried it is because in the mind of my players this defeat, but we started the season at 10th place and it has been a great season for us. To win after 30 wins and reach the final of the FA Cup with not a big squad, a normal squad, I think it was incredible. My players must remain in the mind our fantastic season and the final. You have to reach this point and it is a pity we didn't win. We must be proud of this."

SUNDAY, 28 MAY 2017

It was a day of reflection as well as looking forward.

Glenn Hoddle observed in his Mail on Sunday column: "There were two big refereeing decisions for Anthony Taylor. The second one, sending off Victor Moses, was easy. He was waiting for the touch from Alex Oxlade-Chamberlain instead of getting on with it, creating space and whipping in a cross or a shot. He was negative in waiting for a tackle that never came. The referee got it right because you don't want to see a player falling like that. Moses let himself down. Arsenal's first goal should have been chalked off for two reasons. First, it was handball by Alexis Sanchez in the build-up; his hands were up above his head. But even if the officials hadn't seen that, Aaron Ramsey was offside and interfering with play because he took two steps towards the ball before Sanchez reached it. The linesman's flag went up and of course that influenced the Chelsea goalkeeper and the defenders. It was in their minds that Ramsey was going to turn the ball in. The referee should have stuck with the linesman's decision of offside."

"Chelsea have been so professional this season but they will be kicking themselves for equalising with ten men and then conceding again so quickly. I think they probably over-celebrated. David Luiz didn't look over his shoulder at Ramsey's run through the middle. Mentally they were still thinking about being 1-1. Having said that, few neutrals would begrudge Arsene's historic moment at the final whistle. What was a great final also had a perfectly observed minute's silence for the victims of the Manchester bombing."

Thibaut Courtois revealed that FA Cup final referee, Anthony Taylor, had visited Chelsea's Cobham training ground at the start of the season as a matter of course to explain various rules. "I think it is clearly hands. At the beginning of the season, they call us in to Cobham to explain the rules. It was even the same referee this year (Taylor). They say that the hands should always be in a natural position. If he has his hands next to him and he gets the ball to the arm, he cannot do anything about it. But now he actually does a volleyball block. It's one of the best blocks I've seen." Clearly stating that is was a definite handball under the rules as they had been explained to players and staff.

Courtois also felt Ramsey should have been flagged for offside as he would have got to the ball before Sanchez. "Ramsey is out of control and bothering me, because if he's not there I can get out and get the ball before Alexis. Because he's standing there, I stop and stop the defence. It's clear that he interrupts the game for me, that he participates in the game, and it's clear hands."

Victor Moses had been universally condemned for his blatant dive, which happened on the eve of his wedding, but Conte declined to join the chorus of criticism. "Honestly, I did not see the situation. I don't know for sure, but there is a lot of attention on this moment." Conte said. "Sometimes I think it could be tiredness. We are at the end of the season and a lot of players are tired and then there is a lot of pressure. For sure, it is not a good situation to dive, it is true. But Moses is an honest player and if there was this situation he was tired and he didn't want to cheat the referee."

Despite the final defeat Cesc Fabregas insisted Chelsea's campaign should still be classed as a success. "It wasn't easy to lose, but it was still a good season. We go home with a bad taste. But we would prefer to win the Premier League to the FA Cup, so it is still a good season."

As for being left out of the starting line-up, and his future, he added: "I am not upset and I have nothing against Antonio. He has done a fantastic job. I think I have a very good relationship with him. He has been honest with me, and me with him. I understand his idea of football very, very well. I like it a lot. Every player wants to play more. This is in the genes of a winner. I am one of them and I will never put my head down or hands down. I want to fight. (I'm) not necessarily (wanting to leave Chelsea), but, in football, you can never say never. Everything can happen. I feel loved by the fans here. Every time I have played, I have shown I can play at the top level in this team, by far. It is all about trying to change the manager's decision, but he wants what's best for the team."

Paul Merson believed that Chelsea will now be determined to win the Champions League under Conte. Writing in his column for the Daily Star, Merson said: "I think next season they will go hard for the Champions League. Some of those players have won the league in two of the last three years. They will want to win in Europe now - and so will Conte because he's never won it. You wouldn't bet against them either."

Certainly Conte now planned big changes. The major question was whether he would continue to trust Diego Costa, who had made it clear that he would only consider leaving the club if it was to his former side Atletico, the striker confirming, "I will only leave Chelsea for Atletico. If not, I will stay here. I'm not interested in other clubs. I have a contract and no intention of leaving, but if there are changes to be made that might reduce my chances, if the coach won't count on me anymore or is to give space for another striker, I know that I'll have to leave. Everyone knows what my preferred club is, there's nothing to hide. Money is good, but I'm grateful for what I have right now and I have other things to look forward to, like playing the next World Cup. I know that I have a chance to be called if I'm playing well and at a high level, that's something I want." Costa had scored his 21st goal in the final but he confessed: "I guess we were a little off coming into the match, while Arsenal showed they wanted to win it. They scored once and had the chance for a second during the first 45. We came better for the second half and scored the equalizer, but they went ahead soon after. It happens. I want to congratulate them for the fine display."

Speaking to Belgian newspaper, Het Nieuwsblad, about what Chelsea needed to do to prepare for a return to Europe's premier club competition, Eden Hazard said: "The Champions League is definitely a goal for the club. There are not many players in this team who have already won it. The coach hasn't, either. It's a goal for everyone. We'll see which players are coming in. Hopefully, there are some big players."

Southampton's Virgil van Dijk was one the primary targets with competition from Manchester City and Liverpool, but the 25-year-old Dutch international favoured a move to Stamford Bridge.

The club felt they had the edge on Manchester United in the pursuit of Monaco's Tiemoue Bakayoko for central midfield while, up front, Real Madrid's Alvaro Morata was Conte's first choice as striker. However, some within the hierarchy wanted to bring back Romelu Lukaku, but with a £75m price tag, Morata was the better option as he was not getting regular football at the Bernabeu. There was also a chance of reviving interest in Fernando Llorente as well as investigating a move for Dries Mertens as the forward - but it seemed Napoli were determined to keep the Belgian.

Clearly, along with Asmir Begovic, others would have to leave to help fund the possible £200m signings, with Chelsea considering an offer from Manchester United for Willian as Jose Mourinho remained keen to be reunited with the player he had brought to the Bridge.

Eden Hazard capped a magnificent return to form by being named Player of the Year at the club's end-of-season awards ceremony at Battersea Evolution. He also scooped the Goal of the Season for his solo strike against Arsenal and vowed to remain at the club when picking up his prize.

Hazard was also nominated for his goal against West Ham at the London Stadium, joking: "Just to make sure which one is the best, I scored two!" He added "Nemanja my friend, unlucky!" after Matic missed out with his wonder strike against Tottenham in the FA Cup semi-final.

N'Golo Kante won the Players' Player of the Year and said: "It's been a great season (for the team) and hopefully next season we will be even stronger. To be chosen by the other players is something special, I want to thank them."

Former players were also in attendance, with Michael Ballack announcing Hazard as the winner, among an audience that included the Class of '97 - 20 years on from their FA Cup success against Middlesbrough.

The current players came out to loud applause, as Terry and Cahill carried in the Premier League trophy, with the first-team squad following them to their seats.

@ChelseaFC - "There is one more thank you tonight, one more goodbye... #CFCAwards17"

The night ended with an acknowledgment of the departing captain. Frank Lampard led the tributes in a video reel of tributes from former players, saying: "He leaves the legacy of being the most successful captain in our history, and the most successful captain in Premier League history taking over from Roy Keane. What he's done off the pitch, involving himself with the fans and with the academy… those are legacies that match his performances on the pitch."

@ChelseaFC - "What a reception for our #CaptainLeaderLegend! #CFCAwards17"

John Terry collected his Special Recognition award, presented by former manager Claudio Ranieri, and made an emotional appearance on stage, saying: "Chelsea's my life and it has been for 22 years and it'll never go away. The fans mean everything to me, the memories will live with me forever. I couldn't be here without you and I thank you from my heart. I hope to be back here in the future. The club have made it clear that the door is always open. I'm going to go away for a week and will decide my future, whether that's playing or finishing. I'm finding it hard to even consider playing for another club at the moment, but that was the desire for why I'm leaving so we'll see what happens, and see what the future brings."

It was an emotional end to a gruelling but hugely successful first season under Antonio Conte. With more questions than answers, 2017/18 was going to be compelling viewing.

KING CONTE

It was always going to be a fascinating season with no clear-cut favourite for the title. Leicester City, as reigning champions, were never really considered as serious contenders although, under Claudio Ranieri, stranger things had happened. Arsenal had been the perennial top-4 finishers for the past two decades, Jurgen Klopp now had significant Premier League experience and was ominously moulding his Liverpool side, Tottenham were edging ever closer to the pinnacle of English football under Mauricio Pochettino, Pep Guardiola at Manchester City was a serial winner wherever he went and, of course, there was the ex-Special One, Jose Mourinho, who was spending an absolute fortune at Manchester United. Surely the 2016/17 Premier League champions would be one of the above.

However, it was an Italian who flew into England under the radar and turned a team that had finished 10th the previous season, in what was an abject defence of their crown, into the champions of England.

Antonio Conte had achieved an amazing feat of football mastery, through unbelievable diligence, sheer hard work, masterful problem-solving, acute tactical awareness, and immense self-belief.

In hindsight most of us should have taken more notice, after all his record in Italy was highly impressive to say the least. And, of equal significance, Chelsea did not have the resource-stretching challenges of the European stage. But we were blinded by the bright managerial lights already within our game; they would now be more determined than ever to shine next season.

So, as the season - in which a new special one arrived, a legend retired and the Premier League was won - is consigned to glorious football history Chelsea fans could now look forward to an even greater challenge… 2017/18 would see competition in two domestic cups, a defence of the Premier League title, and the brutal challenges of the Champions League. It will be a season to savour.

King Conte - he came, he saw, he switched to three at the back, and he conquered! Hail Conte!

2016/17 SEASON RESULTS & STATS

MONDAY, 15 AUGUST 2016, PREMIER LEAGUE

Chelsea   2-1   West Ham United

Hazard (47' pen), Diego Costa (89')   Collins (77')

POSSESSION: 62% · SHOTS (ON TARGET): 16 (6) · OPPONENTS SHOTS (ON TARGET): 7 (3)
REFEREE: Anthony Taylor · ATTENDANCE: 41,521

LINE-UP: 13 Courtois, 2 Ivanovic, 24 Cahill, 26 Terry, 28 Azpilicueta (booked 75'),
7 Kante (booked 3'), 22 Willian (substituted for Pedro 80', booked 90'),
8 Oscar (substituted for Batshuayi 85'), 21 Matic (booked 90'),
10 Hazard (substituted for Moses 85'), 19 Diego Costa (booked 19')

SUBSTITUTES: 1 Begovic, 4 Fabregas, 11 Pedro, 14 Loftus-Cheek, 15 Moses, 23 Batshuayi, 34 Aina

SATURDAY, 20 AUGUST 2016, PREMIER LEAGUE

Watford   1-2   Chelsea

Capoue (55')   Batshuayi (80'), Diego Costa (87')

POSSESSION: 62% · SHOTS (ON TARGET): 13 (4) · OPPONENTS SHOTS (ON TARGET): 6 (2)
REFEREE: Jonathan Moss · ATTENDANCE: 20,772

LINE-UP: 13 Courtois, 2 Ivanovic, 24 Cahill (booked 20'), 26 Terry, 28 Azpilicueta, 7 Kante,
11 Pedro (substituted for Moses 71'), 8 Oscar (substituted for Batshuayi 73'), 21 Matic
(substituted for Fabregas 78'), 10 Hazard (booked 90'), 19 Diego Costa (booked 56')

SUBSTITUTES: 1 Begovic, 4 Fabregas, 14 Loftus-Cheek, 15 Moses, 23 Batshuayi, 29 Chalobah, 34 Aina

TUESDAY, 23 AUGUST 2016, EFL CUP - SECOND ROUND

Chelsea   3-2   Bristol Rovers

Batshuayi (29', 41'), Moses (31')   Hartley (35'), Harrison (48' pen)

POSSESSION: 54% · SHOTS (ON TARGET): 28 (12) · OPPONENTS SHOTS (ON TARGET): 7 (3)
REFEREE: Keith Stroud · ATTENDANCE: 39,276

LINE-UP: 1 Begovic, 34 Aina (substituted for Terry 77'), 2 Ivanovic, 24 Cahill, 28 Azpilicueta,
4 Fabregas, 21 Matic, 15 Moses, 14 Loftus-Cheek (substituted for Oscar 82'),
11 Pedro (booked 48', substituted for Hazard 75'), 23 Batshuayi

SUBSTITUTES: 8 Oscar, 10 Hazard, 13 Courtois, 19 Diego Costa, 26 Terry, 29 Chalobah, 41 Solanke

SATURDAY, 27 AUGUST 2016, PREMIER LEAGUE

Chelsea 3-0 Burnley

Hazard (9'), Willian (41'), Moses (89')

POSSESSION: 60% · SHOTS (ON TARGET): 22 (10) · OPPONENTS SHOTS (ON TARGET): 6 (0)
REFEREE: Mark Clattenburg · ATTENDANCE: 41,607

LINE-UP: 13 Courtois, 2 Ivanovic (booked 44'), 24 Cahill, 26 Terry, 28 Azpilicueta, 7 Kante,
22 Willian (substituted for Moses 77'), 8 Oscar (booked 31'), 21 Matic,
10 Hazard (substituted for Pedro 81'), 19 Diego Costa (substituted for Batshuayi 80')

SUBSTITUTES: 1 Begovic, 4 Fabregas, 11 Pedro, 14 Loftus-Cheek, 15 Moses, 23 Batshuayi,
34 Aina

SUNDAY, 11 SEPTEMBER 2016, PREMIER LEAGUE

Swansea City 2-2 Chelsea

Sigurdsson (59' pen), Fer (62')   Diego Costa (18', 81')

POSSESSION: 55% · SHOTS (ON TARGET): 28 (7) · OPPONENTS SHOTS (ON TARGET): 6 (2)
REFEREE: Andre Marriner · ATTENDANCE: 20,865

LINE-UP: 13 Courtois (booked 59'), 2 Ivanovic, 24 Cahill, 26 Terry (booked 90'), 28 Azpilicueta,
7 Kante, 22 Willian (substituted for Moses 77'), 8 Oscar (substituted for Batshuayi 88'),
21 Matic (substituted for Fabregas 76'), 10 Hazard (booked 89'), 19 Diego Costa (booked 41')

SUBSTITUTES: 1 Begovic, 3 Alonso, 4 Fabregas, 11 Pedro, 15 Moses, 23 Batshuayi, 30 David Luiz

FRIDAY, 16 SEPTEMBER 2016, PREMIER LEAGUE

Chelsea 1-2 Liverpool

Diego Costa (61')   Lovren (17'), Henderson (36')

POSSESSION: 53% · SHOTS (ON TARGET): 12 (4) · OPPONENTS SHOTS (ON TARGET): 13 (5)
REFEREE: Martin Atkinson · ATTENDANCE: 41,514

LINE-UP: 13 Courtois, 2 Ivanovic, 24 Cahill, 30 David Luiz, 28 Azpilicueta, 7 Kante,
21 Matic (substituted for Fabregas 84'), 22 Willian (booked 45', substituted for Moses 84'),
8 Oscar (substituted for Pedro 84'), 10 Hazard, 19 Diego Costa

SUBSTITUTES: 1 Begovic, 3 Alonso, 4 Fabregas, 11 Pedro, 15 Moses, 23 Batshuayi, 34 Aina

TUESDAY, 20 SEPTEMBER 2016, EFL CUP - THIRD ROUND

Leicester City 2-4 Chelsea

Okazaki (17', 34'), Wasilewski (sent off 89')   Cahill (45'+2), Azpilicueta (49'),
Fabregas (92', 94')

POSSESSION: 67% · SHOTS (ON TARGET): 27 (11) · OPPONENTS SHOTS (ON TARGET): 8 (3)
REFEREE: Robert Madley · ATTENDANCE: 29,899

LINE-UP: 1 Begovic, 28 Azpilicueta, 24 Cahill, 30David Luiz (booked 109'), 3 Alonso,
21 Matic (booked 83'), 4 Fabregas, 15 Moses, 14 Loftus-Cheek (substituted for Diego Costa 67'),
11 Pedro (substituted for Hazard 89'), 23 Batshuayi (substituted for Chalobah 80')

SUBSTITUTES: 7 Kante, 10 Hazard, 13 Courtois, 19 Diego Costa, 22 Willian, 29 Chalobah,
34 Aina

SATURDAY, 24 SEPTEMBER 2016, PREMIER LEAGUE

Arsenal 3-0 Chelsea

Sanchez (11'), Walcott (14'), Ozil (40')

POSSESSION: 51% - SHOTS (ON TARGET): 9 (2) · OPPONENTS SHOTS (ON TARGET): 14 (5)
REFEREE: Michael Oliver · ATTENDANCE: 60,028

LINE-UP: 13 Courtois, 2 Ivanovic (booked 28'), 24 Cahill, 30 David Luiz, 28 Azpilicueta, 7 Kante,
22 Willian (substituted for Pedro 70'), 4 Fabregas (substituted for Alonso 55'), 21 Matic,
10 Hazard (substituted for Batshuayi 71'), 19 Diego Costa (booked 83')

SUBSTITUTES: 1 Begovic, 3 Alonso, 8 Oscar, 11 Pedro, 15 Moses, 23 Batshuayi, 29 Chalobah

SATURDAY, 1 OCTOBER 2016, PREMIER LEAGUE

Hull City 0-2 Chelsea

Willian (61'), Diego Costa (67')

POSSESSION: 59% · SHOTS (ON TARGET): 22 (9) · OPPONENTS SHOTS (ON TARGET): 8 (2)
REFEREE: Anthony Taylor · ATTENDANCE: 21,257

LINE-UP: 13 Courtois, 28 Azpilicueta, 30 David Luiz, 24 Cahill,
15 Moses (booked 35', substituted for Pedro 85'), 21 Matic (booked 41'), 7 Kante, 3 Alonso,
22 Willian (substituted for Chalobah 89'), 19 Diego Costa, 10 Hazard (substituted for Oscar 81')

SUBSTITUTES: 1 Begovic, 2 Ivanovic, 4 Fabregas, 8 Oscar, 11 Pedro, 23 Batshuayi, 29 Chalobah

SATURDAY, 15 OCTOBER 2016, PREMIER LEAGUE

Chelsea 3-0 Leicester City

Diego Costa (7'), Hazard (33'), Moses (80')

PPOSSESSION: 55% · SHOTS (ON TARGET): 16 (6) · OPPONENTS SHOTS (ON TARGET): 5 (0)
REFEREE: Andre Marriner · ATTENDANCE: 41,547

LINE-UP: 13 Courtois, 28 Azpilicueta (booked 51'), 30 David Luiz, 24 Cahill,
15 Moses (substituted for Aina 82'), 7 Kante, 21 Matic, 3 Alonso, 11 Pedro
(substituted for Chalobah 68'), 19 Diego Costa, 10 Hazard (substituted for Loftus-Cheek 82')

SUBSTITUTES: 1 Begovic, 14 Loftus-Cheek, 23 Batshuayi, 26 Terry, 29 Chalobah, 34 Aina,
41 Solanke

SUNDAY, 23 OCTOBER 2016, PREMIER LEAGUE

Chelsea 4-0 Manchester United

Pedro (1'), Cahill (21'), Hazard (62'),
Kante (70')

POSSESSION: 44% · SHOTS (ON TARGET): 14 (6) · OPPONENTS SHOTS (ON TARGET): 16 (5)
REFEREE: Martin Atkinson · ATTENDANCE: 41,424

LINE-UP: 13 Courtois, 28 Azpilicueta, 30 David Luiz (booked 41'), 24 Cahill, 15 Moses, 7 Kante,
21 Matic, 3 Alonso (booked 66'), 11 Pedro (booked 1', substituted for Chalobah 71'),
19 Diego Costa (substituted for Batshuayi 78'), 10 Hazard (substituted for Willian 78')

SUBSTITUTES: 1 Begovic, 8 Oscar, 22 Willian, 23 Batshuayi, 26 Terry, 29 Chalobah, 34 Aina

WEDNESDAY, 26 OCTOBER 2016, EFL CUP - FOURTH ROUND

West Ham United 2-1 Chelsea

Kouyate (11'), Fernandes (48')   Cahill (90'+4)

POSSESSION: 53% · SHOTS (ON TARGET): 16 (4) · OPPONENTS SHOTS (ON TARGET): 13 (7)
REFEREE: Craig Pawson · ATTENDANCE: 45,957

LINE-UP: 1 Begovic, 30 David Luiz, 24 Cahill, 26 Terry, 34 Aina (substituted for Pedro 67'),
7 Kante, 29 Chalobah (substituted for Hazard 63'), 28 Azpilicueta, 22 Willian,
23 Batshuayi (substituted for Diego Costa 54'), 8 Oscar

SUBSTITUTES: 3 Alonso, 10 Hazard, 11 Pedro, 19 Diego Costa, 21 Matic, 37 Eduardo, 41 Solanke

SUNDAY, 30 OCTOBER 2016, PREMIER LEAGUE

Southampton 0-2 Chelsea

Hazard (6'), Diego Costa (55')

POSSESSION: 45% · SHOTS (ON TARGET): 13 (7) · OPPONENTS SHOTS (ON TARGET): 10 (1)
REFEREE: Mike Jones · ATTENDANCE: 31,827

LINE-UP: 13 Courtois, 28 Azpilicueta, 30 David Luiz, 24 Cahill,
15 Moses (substituted for Ivanovic 87'), 7 Kante, 21 Matic, 3 Alonso,
11 Pedro (substituted for Willian 78'), 19 Diego Costa (substituted for Batshuayi 89'), 10 Hazard

SUBSTITUTES: 1 Begovic, 2 Ivanovic, 8 Oscar, 22 Willian, 23 Batshuayi, 26 Terry, 29 Chalobah

SATURDAY, 5 NOVEMBER 2016, PREMIER LEAGUE

Chelsea 5-0 Everton

Hazard (19', 56'), Alonso (20'),
Diego Costa (42'), Pedro (65')

POSSESSION: 60% · SHOTS (ON TARGET): 21 (9) · OPPONENTS SHOTS (ON TARGET): 1 (0)
REFEREE: Robert Madley · ATTENDANCE: 41,429

LINE-UP: 13 Courtois, 28 Azpilicueta, 30 David Luiz, 24 Cahill (substituted for Terry 84'),
15 Moses, 7 Kante, 21 Matic, 3 Alonso, 11 Pedro (substituted for Oscar 71'), 19 Diego Costa,
10 Hazard (substituted for Batshuayi 80')

SUBSTITUTES: 1 Begovic, 2 Ivanovic, 8 Oscar, 23 Batshuayi, 26 Terry, 29 Chalobah, 34 Aina

SUNDAY, 20 NOVEMBER 2016, PREMIER LEAGUE

Middlesbrough 0-1 Chelsea

Diego Costa (41')

POSSESSION: 58% · SHOTS (ON TARGET): 13 (3) · OPPONENTS SHOTS (ON TARGET): 12 (1)
REFEREE: Jonathan Moss · ATTENDANCE: 32,704

LINE-UP: 13 Courtois, 28 Azpilicueta (booked 51'), 30 David Luiz (booked 64'), 24 Cahill,
15 Moses (substituted for Ivanovic 90'), 7 Kante (booked 73'), 21 Matic, 3 Alonso, 11 Pedro
(substituted for Chalobah 80'), 19 Diego Costa, 10 Hazard (substituted for Oscar 90+2')

SUBSTITUTES: 1 Begovic, 2 Ivanovic, 4 Fabregas, 8 Oscar, 23 Batshuayi, 26 Terry, 29 Chalobah

SATURDAY, 26 NOVEMBER 2016, PREMIER LEAGUE

Chelsea 2-1 Tottenham Hotspur

Pedro (45'), Moses (51')   Eriksen (11')

POSSESSION: 46% · SHOTS (ON TARGET): 9 (5) · OPPONENTS SHOTS (ON TARGET): 12 (6)
REFEREE: Michael Oliver · ATTENDANCE: 41,513

LINE-UP: 13 Courtois, 28 Azpilicueta, 30 David Luiz (booked 19'), 24 Cahill,
15 Moses (substituted for Ivanovic 81'), 7 Kante, 21 Matic, 3 Alonso, 11 Pedro
(substituted for Oscar 83'), 19 Diego Costa, 10 Hazard (substituted for Willian77', booked 85')

SUBSTITUTES: 1 Begovic, 2 Ivanovic, 4 Fabregas, 8 Oscar, 22 Willian, 23 Batshuayi, 29 Chalobah

SATURDAY, 3 DECEMBER 2016, PREMIER LEAGUE

Manchester City 1-3 Chelsea

Cahill (45' og)   Diego Costa (60'), Willian (70'),
Aguero (sent off 90'+6),   Hazard (90')
Fernandinho (sent off 90'+7)

POSSESSION: 39% · SHOTS (ON TARGET): 10 (4) · OPPONENTS SHOTS (ON TARGET): 14 (5)
REFEREE: Anthony Taylor · ATTENDANCE: 54,457

LINE-UP: 13 Courtois, 28 Azpilicueta, 30 David Luiz, 24 Cahill, 15 Moses, 7 Kante (booked 49'),
4 Fabregas (booked 90'), 3 Alonso, 11 Pedro (substituted for Willian 50'), 19 Diego Costa
(substituted for Chalobah 85, booked 90'), 10 Hazard (substituted for Batshuayi 90'+4)

SUBSTITUTES: 1 Begovic, 2 Ivanovic, 8 Oscar, 22 Willian, 23 Batshuayi, 29 Chalobah, 34 Aina

SUNDAY, 11 DECEMBER 2016, PREMIER LEAGUE

Chelsea 1-0 West Bromwich Albion

Diego Costa (76')

POSSESSION: 67% · SHOTS (ON TARGET): 12 (2) · OPPONENTS SHOTS (ON TARGET): 6 (1)
REFEREE: Mike Dean · ATTENDANCE: 41,622

LINE-UP: 13 Courtois, 28 Azpilicueta, 30 David Luiz, 24 Cahill, 15 Moses
(substituted for Fabregas 74'), 7 Kante (booked 48'), 21 Matic (booked 88'), 3 Alonso, 11 Pedro
(substituted for Willian 63'), 19 Diego Costa, 10 Hazard (substituted for Ivanovic 79')

SUBSTITUTES: 1 Begovic, 2 Ivanovic, 4 Fabregas, 22 Willian, 23 Batshuayi, 29 Chalobah, 34 Aina

WEDNESDAY, 14 DECEMBER 2016, PREMIER LEAGUE

Sunderland 0-1 Chelsea

Fabregas (40')

POSSESSION: 66% · SHOTS (ON TARGET): 19 (6) · OPPONENTS SHOTS (ON TARGET): 8 (3)
REFEREE: Neil Swarbrick · ATTENDANCE: 41,008

LINE-UP: 13 Courtois, 28 Azpilicueta, 30 David Luiz, 24 Cahill, 15 Moses (booked 90', substituted for Ivanovic 90'+3), 7 Kante, 4 Fabregas, 3 Alonso, 22 Willian (substituted for Chalobah 89'), 19 Diego Costa, 11 Pedro (booked 56', substituted for Matic 76')

SUBSTITUTES: 1 Begovic, 2 Ivanovic, 5 Zouma, 14 Loftus-Cheek, 21 Matic, 23 Batshuayi, 29 Chalobah

SATURDAY, 17 DECEMBER 2016, PREMIER LEAGUE

Crystal Palace 0-1 Chelsea

Diego Costa (43')

POSSESSION: 46% · SHOTS (ON TARGET): 13 (6) · OPPONENTS SHOTS (ON TARGET): 6 (2)
REFEREE: Jonathan Moss · ATTENDANCE: 25,259

LINE-UP: 13 Courtois, 28 Azpilicueta, 30 David Luiz, 24 Cahill, 15 Moses (substituted for Ivanovic 79'), 7 Kante (booked 60'), 21 Matic, 3 Alonso, 22 Willian (substituted for Fabregas 64', booked 90'), 19 Diego Costa (booked 22', substituted for Batshuayi 89'), 10 Hazard

SUBSTITUTES: 1 Begovic, 2 Ivanovic, 4 Fabregas, 5 Zouma, 11 Pedro, 23 Batshuayi, 29 Chalobah

MONDAY, 26 DECEMBER 2016, PREMIER LEAGUE

Chelsea 3-0 Bournemouth

Pedro (24'), Hazard (49' pen),
Cook (90'+3 og)

POSSESSION: 44% · SHOTS (ON TARGET): 14 (4) · OPPONENTS SHOTS (ON TARGET): 7 (3)
REFEREE: Mike Jones · ATTENDANCE: 41,384

LINE-UP: 13 Courtois, 28 Azpilicueta, 30 David Luiz, 24 Cahill, 15 Moses (substituted for Aina 90'), 4 Fabregas, 21 Matic, 3 Alonso, 22 Willian (substituted for Chalobah 83'), 10 Hazard (substituted for Batshuayi 90'+4), 11 Pedro (booked 63')

SUBSTITUTES: 1 Begovic, 2 Ivanovic, 5 Zouma, 14 Loftus-Cheek, 23 Batshuayi, 29 Chalobah, 34 Aina

SATURDAY, 31 DECEMBER 2016, PREMIER LEAGUE

Chelsea   4-2   Stoke City

Cahill (34'), Willian (57', 65'),   Martins Indi (46'), Crouch (64')
Diego Costa (85')

POSSESSION: 60% · SHOTS (ON TARGET): 18 (7) · OPPONENTS SHOTS (ON TARGET): 5 (2)
REFEREE: Robert Madley · ATTENDANCE: 41,601

LINE-UP: 13 Courtois, 28 Azpilicueta, 30 David Luiz, 24 Cahill, 15 Moses (booked 24',
substituted for Ivanovic 82'), 4 Fabregas (booked 59', substituted for Matic 73'), 7 Kante,
3 Alonso (booked 70'), 22 Willian (substituted for Chalobah 84'), 19 Diego Costa, 10 Hazard

SUBSTITUTES: 1 Begovic, 2 Ivanovic, 5 Zouma, 14 Loftus-Cheek, 21 Matic, 23 Batshuayi,
29 Chalobah

WEDNESDAY, 4 JANUARY 2017, PREMIER LEAGUE

Tottenham Hotspur   2-0   Chelsea

Alli (45'+1, 54')

POSSESSION: 55% · SHOTS (ON TARGET): 11 (2) · OPPONENTS SHOTS (ON TARGET): 9 (2)
REFEREE: Martin Atkinson · ATTENDANCE: 31,491

LINE-UP: 13 Courtois, 28 Azpilicueta, 30 David Luiz, 24 Cahill (booked 38'), 15 Moses (substituted
for Batshuayi 85'), 21 Matic, 7 Kante (substituted for Fabregas 79'), 3 Alonso (substituted for
Willian 65'), 11 Pedro (booked 18'), 19 Diego Costa, 10 Hazard

SUBSTITUTES: 1 Begovic, 2 Ivanovic, 4 Fabregas, 5 Zouma, 22 Willian, 23 Batshuayi, 29 Chalobah

SUNDAY, 8 JANUARY 2017, FA CUP - THIRD ROUND

Chelsea   4-1   Peterborough United

Pedro (18', 75'), Batshuayi (43'),   Nichols (70')
Willian (52'), Terry (sent off 67')

POSSESSION: 64% · SHOTS (ON TARGET): 35 (13) · OPPONENTS SHOTS (ON TARGET): 12 (3)
REFEREE: Kevin Friend · ATTENDANCE: 41,003

LINE-UP: 1 Begovic, 5 Zouma, 26 Terry (sent off 67'), 24 Cahill (substituted for Aina 57'),
2 Ivanovic, 29 Chalobah, 4 Fabregas (booked 24'), 14 Loftus-Cheek (substituted for
Azpilicueta70'), 11 Pedro, 22 Willian (substituted for Kante 73'), 23 Batshuayi

SUBSTITUTES: 7 Kante, 10 Hazard, 15 Moses, 19 Diego Costa, 28 Azpilicueta, 34 Aina, 37 Eduardo

SATURDAY, 14 JANUARY 2017, PREMIER LEAGUE

Leicester City   0-3   Chelsea

Alonso (6', 51'), Pedro (71')

POSSESSION: 65% · SHOTS (ON TARGET): 8 (3) · OPPONENTS SHOTS (ON TARGET): 7 (2)
REFEREE: Andre Marriner · ATTENDANCE: 32,066

LINE-UP: 13 Courtois, 28 Azpilicueta, 30 David Luiz, 24 Cahill, 15 Moses, 7 Kante, 21 Matic,
3 Alonso, 22 Willian (substituted for Batshuayi 84'), 10 Hazard (substituted for Fabregas 79'),
11 Pedro (substituted for Loftus-Cheek 84')

SUBSTITUTES: 1 Begovic, 2 Ivanovic, 4 Fabregas, 5 Zouma, 14 Loftus-Cheek, 23 Batshuayi,
29 Chalobah

SUNDAY, 22 JANUARY 2017, PREMIER LEAGUE

Chelsea   2-0   Hull City

Diego Costa (45'+7), Cahill (81')

POSSESSION: 53% · SHOTS (ON TARGET): 9 (5) · OPPONENTS SHOTS (ON TARGET): 9 (4)
REFEREE: Neil Swarbrick · ATTENDANCE: 41,605

LINE-UP: 13 Courtois, 28 Azpilicueta, 30 David Luiz, 24 Cahill, 15 Moses, 7 Kante (booked 43'),
21 Matic, 3 Alonso, 11 Pedro (substituted for Willian 71'),
19 Diego Costa (substituted for Batshuayi 87'), 10 Hazard (substituted for Fabregas 71')

SUBSTITUTES: 1 Begovic, 4 Fabregas, 5 Zouma, 6 Ake, 22 Willian, 23 Batshuayi, 29 Chalobah

SATURDAY, 28 JANUARY 2017, FA CUP - FOURTH ROUND

Chelsea   4-0   Brentford

Willian (14'), Pedro (21'), Ivanovic (69'),
Batshuayi (81' pen)

POSSESSION: 60% · SHOTS (ON TARGET): 22 (8) · OPPONENTS SHOTS (ON TARGET): 6 (2)
REFEREE: Michael Oliver · ATTENDANCE: 41,042

LINE-UP: 1 Begovic, 5 Zouma, 26 Terry, 28 Azpilicueta (substituted for Kenedy 71'),
11 Pedro (substituted for Diego Costa 76'), 4 Fabregas, 29 Chalobah (booked 89'), 6 Ake,
22 Willian (substituted for Ivanovic 64'), 23 Batshuayi, 14 Loftus-Cheek

SUBSTITUTES: 2 Ivanovic, 10 Hazard, 15 Moses, 16 Kenedy, 19 Diego Costa, 21 Matic, 37 Eduardo

TUESDAY, 31 JANUARY 2017, PREMIER LEAGUE

Liverpool 1-1 Chelsea

Wijnaldum (57')   David Luiz (24')

POSSESSION: 38% · SHOTS (ON TARGET): 8 (2) · OPPONENTS SHOTS (ON TARGET): 7 (3)
REFEREE: Mark Clattenburg · ATTENDANCE: 53,157

LINE-UP: 13 Courtois, 28 Azpilicueta, 30 David Luiz, 24 Cahill, 15 Moses, 7 Kante, 21 Matic,
3 Alonso, 22 Willian (booked 79', substituted for Fabregas 83'),
19 Diego Costa (substituted for Batshuayi 90'+4), 10 Hazard (substituted for Pedro 72')

SUBSTITUTES: 1 Begovic, 4 Fabregas, 5 Zouma, 11 Pedro, 23 Batshuayi, 26 Terry, 29 Chalobah

SATURDAY, 4 FEBRUARY 2017, PREMIER LEAGUE

Chelsea 3-1 Arsenal

Alonso (13'), Hazard (53'), Fàbregas (85')   Giroud (90'+1)

POSSESSION: 42% · SHOTS (ON TARGET): 13 (6) · OPPONENTS SHOTS (ON TARGET): 9 (5)
REFEREE: Martin Atkinson · ATTENDANCE: 41,490

LINE-UP: 13 Courtois, 28 Azpilicueta, 30 David Luiz, 24 Cahill,
15 Moses (substituted for Zouma 88'), 7 Kante, 21 Matic (booked 70'), 3 Alonso, 11 Pedro
(substituted for Willian 84'), 19 Diego Costa, 10 Hazard (substituted for Fabregas 84')

SUBSTITUTES: 1 Begovic, 4 Fabregas, 5 Zouma, 22 Willian, 23 Batshuayi, 26 Terry, 29 Chalobah

SUNDAY, 12 FEBRUARY 2017, PREMIER LEAGUE

Burnley 1-1 Chelsea

Brady (24')   Pedro (7')

POSSESSION: 72% · SHOTS (ON TARGET): 13 (2) · OPPONENTS SHOTS (ON TARGET): 7 (4)
REFEREE: Kevin Friend · ATTENDANCE: 21,744

LINE-UP: 13 Courtois, 28 Azpilicueta, 30 David Luiz (booked 75'), 24 Cahill,
15 Moses (substituted for Willian 72'), 7 Kante, 21 Matic (substituted for Fabregas 67',
booked 89'), 3 Alonso, 11 Pedro (substituted for Batshuayi 87'), 19 Diego Costa, 10 Hazard

SUBSTITUTES: 1 Begovic, 4 Fabregas, 5 Zouma, 6 Ake, 22 Willian, 23 Batshuayi, 29 Chalobah

SATURDAY, 18 FEBRUARY 2017, FA CUP - FIFTH ROUND

Wolverhampton Wanderers 0-2 Chelsea

Pedro (65'), Diego Costa (89')

POSSESSION: 65% · SHOTS (ON TARGET): 13 (4) · OPPONENTS SHOTS (ON TARGET): 8 (2)
REFEREE: Jonathan Moss · ATTENDANCE: 30,193

LINE-UP: 1 Begovic, 5 Zouma, 26 Terry, 6 Ake, 15 Moses, 4 Fabregas, 29 Chalobah,
11 Pedro (booked 49', substituted for Azpilicueta 73'), 22 Willian (substituted for Kante 80'),
19 Diego Costa, 10 Hazard (substituted for Loftus-Cheek 86')

SUBSTITUTES: 7 Kante, 14 Loftus-Cheek, 16 Kenedy, 23 Batshuayi, 24 Cahill, 28 Azpilicueta,
37 Eduardo

SATURDAY, 25 FEBRUARY 2017, PREMIER LEAGUE

Chelsea 3-1 Swansea City

Fàbregas (19'), Pedro (72'),   Llorente (45'+2)
Diego Costa (84')

POSSESSION: 66% · SHOTS (ON TARGET): 16 (5) · OPPONENTS SHOTS (ON TARGET): 3 (2)
REFEREE: Neil Swarbrick · ATTENDANCE: 41,612

LINE-UP: 13 Courtois, 28 Azpilicueta, 30 David Luiz (booked 75'), 24 Cahill, 15 Moses
(substituted for Zouma 85'), 7 Kante, 4 Fabregas, 3 Alonso, 11 Pedro (substituted for Matic 76'),
19 Diego Costa, 10 Hazard (substituted for Willian 85')

SUBSTITUTES: 1 Begovic, 5 Zouma, 14 Loftus-Cheek, 21 Matic, 22 Willian, 23 Batshuayi, 26 Terry

MONDAY, 6 MARCH 2017, PREMIER LEAGUE

West Ham United 1-2 Chelsea

Lanzini (90'+2)   Hazard (25'), Diego Costa (50')

POSSESSION: 48% · SHOTS (ON TARGET): 9 (4) · OPPONENTS SHOTS (ON TARGET): 11 (2)
REFEREE: Andre Marriner · ATTENDANCE: 56,984

LINE-UP: 13 Courtois, 28 Azpilicueta, 30 David Luiz, 24 Cahill, 15 Moses
(substituted for Zouma 76'), 4 Fabregas (booked 45'), 7 Kante, 3 Alonso, 11 Pedro
(substituted for Matic 65'), 19 Diego Costa, 10 Hazard (substituted for Willian 75')

SUBSTITUTES: 1 Begovic, 5 Zouma, 14 Loftus-Cheek, 21 Matic, 22 Willian, 23 Batshuayi, 26 Terry

MONDAY, 13 MARCH 2017, FA CUP - SIXTH ROUND

Chelsea 1-0 Manchester United

Kante (51')   Herrera (sent off 35')

POSSESSION: 73% · SHOTS (ON TARGET): 20 (5) · OPPONENTS SHOTS (ON TARGET): 4 (1)
REFEREE: Michael Oliver · ATTENDANCE: 40,801

LINE-UP: 13 Courtois, 28 Azpilicueta, 30 David Luiz, 24 Cahill, 15 Moses
(substituted for Zouma 89'), 7 Kante, 21 Matic, 3 Alonso, 22 Willian (substituted for
Fabregas 81'), 19 Diego Costa (booked 87', substituted for Batshuayi 90'+4), 10 Hazard

SUBSTITUTES: 1 Begovic, 4 Fabregas, 5 Zouma, 11 Pedro, 23 Batshuayi, 26 Terry, 29 Chalobah

SATURDAY, 18 MARCH 2017, PREMIER LEAGUE

Stoke City 1-2 Chelsea

Walters (38' pen),   Willian (13'), Cahill (87')
Bardsley (sent off 90'+5)

POSSESSION: 64% · SHOTS (ON TARGET): 20 (7) · OPPONENTS SHOTS (ON TARGET): 5 (1)
REFEREE: Anthony Taylor · ATTENDANCE: 27,724

LINE-UP: 13 Courtois, 28 Azpilicueta, 30 David Luiz, 24 Cahill, 15 Moses (substituted for
Fabregas 70', booked 90'), 7 Kante, 21 Matic (substituted for Loftus-Cheek 82'), 3 Alonso,
22 Willian (substituted for Zouma 88'), 19 Diego Costa (booked 17'), 11Pedro

SUBSTITUTES: 1 Begovic, 4 Fabregas, 5 Zouma, 6 Ake, 14 Loftus-Cheek, 23 Batshuayi, 29 Chalobah

SATURDAY, 1 APRIL 2017, PREMIER LEAGUE

Chelsea 1-2 Crystal Palace

Fabregas (5')   Zaha (9'), Benteke (11')

POSSESSION: 73% · SHOTS (ON TARGET): 24 (11) · OPPONENTS SHOTS (ON TARGET): 8 (3)
REFEREE: Craig Pawson · ATTENDANCE: 41,489

LINE-UP: 13 Courtois, 28 Azpilicueta, 30 David Luiz (booked 83'), 24 Cahill (booked 79'),
11 Pedro, 4 Fabregas (substituted for Loftus-Cheek 90'+7), 7 Kante, 21 Matic (substituted for
Willian 59'), 3 Alonso (substituted for Batshuayi 74'), 10 Hazard, 19 Diego Costa (booked 50')

SUBSTITUTES: 1 Begovic, 5 Zouma, 14 Loftus-Cheek, 22 Willian, 23 Batshuayi, 26 Terry,
29 Chalobah

WEDNESDAY, 5 APRIL 2017, PREMIER LEAGUE

Chelsea   2-1   Manchester City

Hazard (10', 35')   Agüero (26')

POSSESSION: 39% · SHOTS (ON TARGET): 10 (4) · OPPONENTS SHOTS (ON TARGET): 17 (7)
REFEREE: Mike Dean · ATTENDANCE: 41,528

LINE-UP: 13 Courtois, 5 Zouma (substituted for Matic 45'), 30 David Luiz, 24 Cahill,
28 Azpilicueta, 4 Fabregas (substituted for Willian 81'), 7 Kante (booked 90'), 3 Alonso,
11 Pedro, 10 Hazard (substituted for Loftus-Cheek 90'), 19 Diego Costa

SUBSTITUTES: 1 Begovic, 6 Ake, 14 Loftus-Cheek, 21 Matic, 22 Willian, 23 Batshuayi, 26 Terry

SATURDAY, 8 APRIL 2017, PREMIER LEAGUE

Bournemouth   1-3   Chelsea

King (42')   Smith (17' og), Hazard (20'), Alonso (68')

POSSESSION: 49% · SHOTS (ON TARGET): 15 (5) · OPPONENTS SHOTS (ON TARGET): 11 (1)
REFEREE: Andre Marriner · ATTENDANCE: 11,283

LINE-UP: 13 Courtois, 28 Azpilicueta, 30 David Luiz, 24 Cahill, 15 Moses (booked 8',
substituted for Zouma 90'+2), 7 Kante (booked 58'), 21 Matic, 3 Alonso, 11 Pedro (booked 74',
substituted for Willian 88'), 10 Hazard (substituted for Fabregas 84'), 19 Diego Costa

SUBSTITUTES: 1 Begovic, 4 Fabregas, 5 Zouma, 22 Willian, 23 Batshuayi, 26 Terry, 29 Chalobah

SUNDAY, 16 APRIL 2017, PREMIER LEAGUE

Manchester United   2-0   Chelsea

Rashford (7'), Herrera (49')

POSSESSION: 54% · SHOTS (ON TARGET): 5 (0) · OPPONENTS SHOTS (ON TARGET): 9 (3)
REFEREE: Robert Madley · ATTENDANCE: 75,272

LINE-UP: 1 Begovic, 5 Zouma (substituted for Loftus-Cheek 83'), 30 David Luiz, 24 Cahill
(booked 48'), 15 Moses (substituted for Fabregas 54', booked 90'), 7 Kante, 21 Matic (substituted
for Willian 66'), 28 Azpilicueta, 11 Pedro, 10 Hazard, 19 Diego Costa (booked 33')

SUBSTITUTES: 4 Fabregas, 6 Ake, 14 Loftus-Cheek, 22 Willian, 23 Batshuayi, 26 Terry, 37 Eduardo

SATURDAY, 22 APRIL 2017, FA CUP - SEMI-FINAL

Chelsea   4-2   Tottenham Hotspur

Willian (5', 43' pen), Hazard (75'),   Kane (18'), Alli (52')
Matic (80')

POSSESSION: 37% · SHOTS (ON TARGET): 8 (5) · OPPONENTS SHOTS (ON TARGET): 13 (4)
REFEREE: Martin Atkinson · ATTENDANCE: 86,355 (Wembley Stadium)

LINE-UP: 13 Courtois, 28 Azpilicueta, 30 David Luiz, 6 Ake, 15 Moses, 7 Kante (booked 90'),
21 Matic, 3 Alonso (booked 45'), 22 Willian (substituted for Hazard 61'), 23 Batshuayi
(substituted for Diego Costa 61'), 11 Pedro (substituted for Fabregas 74')

SUBSTITUTES: 1 Begovic, 4 Fabregas, 5 Zouma, 10 Hazard, 19 Diego Costa, 26 Terry, 29 Chalobah

TUESDAY, 25 APRIL 2017, PREMIER LEAGUE

Chelsea   4-2   Southampton

Hazard (5'), Cahill (45'+1),   Romeu (24'), Bertrand (90'+4)
Diego Costa (53', 89')

POSSESSION: 48% · SHOTS (ON TARGET): 17 (7) · OPPONENTS SHOTS (ON TARGET): 12 (4)
REFEREE: Lee Mason · ATTENDANCE: 41,168

LINE-UP: 13 Courtois, 28 Azpilicueta, 30 David Luiz, 24 Cahill, 15 Moses (substituted for
Terry 86'), 7 Kante (booked 40'), 21 Matic, 3 Alonso, 4 Fabregas (booked 49', substituted for
Pedro 77'), 10 Hazard (substituted for Willian 90'), 19 Diego Costa

SUBSTITUTES: 1 Begovic, 6 Ake, 11 Pedro, 22 Willian, 23 Batshuayi, 26 Terry, 29 Chalobah

SUNDAY, 30 APRIL 2017, PREMIER LEAGUE

Everton   0-3   Chelsea

Pedro (66'), Cahill (79'), Willian (86')

POSSESSION: 51% · SHOTS (ON TARGET): 11 (5) · OPPONENTS SHOTS (ON TARGET): 12 (3)
REFEREE: Jonathan Moss · ATTENDANCE: 39,595

LINE-UP: 13 Courtois, 28 Azpilicueta (booked 40'), 30 David Luiz (substituted for Ake 82'),
24 Cahill (booked 35'), 15 Moses, 7 Kante, 21 Matic, 3 Alonso, 11 Pedro (substituted for
Fabregas 82'), 10 Hazard (booked 75', substituted for Willian 85'), 19 Diego Costa (booked 56')

SUBSTITUTES: 1 Begovic, 4 Fabregas, 5 Zouma, 6 Ake, 22 Willian, 23 Batshuayi, 29 Chalobah

MONDAY, 8 MAY 2017, PREMIER LEAGUE

Chelsea 3-0 Middlesbrough

Diego Costa (23'), Alonso (34'), Matic (65')

POSSESSION: 57% · **SHOTS (ON TARGET):** 21 (7) · **OPPONENTS SHOTS (ON TARGET):** 2 (1)
REFEREE: Craig Pawson · **ATTENDANCE:** 41,500

LINE-UP: 13 Courtois, 28 Azpilicueta, 30 David Luiz (substituted for Terry 84'), 24 Cahill, 15 Moses, 4 Fabregas, 21 Matic, 3 Alonso, 11 Pedro (substituted for Chalobah 81'), 10 Hazard (substituted for Willian 72'), 19 Diego Costa

SUBSTITUTES: 1 Begovic, 5 Zouma, 6 Ake, 14 Loftus-Cheek, 22 Willian, 26 Terry, 29 Chalobah

FRIDAY, 12 MAY 2017, PREMIER LEAGUE

West Bromwich Albion 0-1 Chelsea

Batshuayi (82' minutes)

POSSESSION: 68% · **SHOTS (ON TARGET):** 24 (5) · **OPPONENTS SHOTS (ON TARGET):** 7 (2)
REFEREE: Michael Oliver · **ATTENDANCE:** 25,367

LINE-UP: 13 Courtois, 28 Azpilicueta, 30 David Luiz, 24 Cahill, 15 Moses (substituted for Zouma 86'), 4 Fabregas, 21 Matic, 3 Alonso, 11 Pedro (substituted for Batshuayi 76'), 10 Hazard (substituted for Willian 75'), 19 Diego Costa

SUBSTITUTES: 1 Begovic, 5 Zouma, 6 Ake, 7 Kante, 22 Willian, 23 Batshuayi, 26 Terry

MONDAY, 15 MAY 2017, PREMIER LEAGUE

Chelsea 4-3 Watford

Terry (22'), Azpilicueta (36'), Batshuayi (49'),
Fabregas (88')

Capoue (24'), Janmaat (51'), Okaka (74')
Prodl (sent off 90'+2)

POSSESSION: 47% · **SHOTS (ON TARGET):** 24 (9) · **OPPONENTS SHOTS (ON TARGET):** 9 (3)
REFEREE: Lee Mason · **ATTENDANCE:** 41,473

LINE-UP: 1 Begovic, 5 Zouma, 26 Terry, 6 Ake (booked 30'), 28 Azpilicueta, 7 Kante, 29 Chalobah (booked 58', substituted for Fabregas 79'), 16 Kenedy (substituted for Aina 75'), 22 Willian, 10 Hazard, 23 Batshuayi (substituted for Pedro84')

SUBSTITUTES: 3 Alonso, 4 Fabregas, 11 Pedro, 19 Diego Costa, 24 Cahill, 34 Aina, 37 Eduardo

SUNDAY, 21 MAY 2017, PREMIER LEAGUE

Chelsea 5-1 Sunderland

Willian (8'), Hazard (61'), Pedro (77'),
Batshuayi (90', 90'+2)

Manquillo (3')

POSSESSION: 71% · SHOTS (ON TARGET): 28 (8) · OPPONENTS SHOTS (ON TARGET): 7 (3)
REFEREE: Neil Swarbrick · ATTENDANCE: 41,618

LINE-UP: 13 Courtois, 28 Azpilicueta, 30 David Luiz, 26 Terry (substituted for Cahill 28'), 15 Moses, 4 Fabregas, 7 Kante, 3 Alonso, 22 Willian, 10 Hazard (substituted for Pedro 71'), 19 Diego Costa (booked 38', substituted for Batshuayi 62')

SUBSTITUTES: 1 Begovic, 5 Zouma, 11 Pedro, 21 Matic, 23 Batshuayi, 24 Cahill, 29 Chalobah

SATURDAY, 27 MAY 2017, FA CUP FINAL

Arsenal 2-1 Chelsea

Sanchez (4'), Ramsey (79')

Moses (sent off 68'), Diego Costa (76')

POSSESSION: 48% · SHOTS (ON TARGET): 18 (5) · OPPONENTS SHOTS (ON TARGET): 16 (6)
REFEREE: Anthony Taylor · ATTENDANCE: 89,472 (Wembley Stadium)

LINE-UP: 13 Courtois, 28 Azpilicueta, 30 David Luiz, 24 Cahill, 15 Moses (sent off 68'), 7 Kante (booked at 59'), 21 Matic (substituted for Fabregas 61'), 3 Alonso, 11 Pedro (substituted for Willian 72'), 19 Diego Costa (substituted for Batshuayi 88'), 10 Hazard

SUBSTITUTES: 1 Begovic, 4 Fabregas, 5 Zouma, 6 Ake, 22 Willian, 23 Batshuayi, 26 Terry

2016/17 SQUAD APPEARANCES (+ SUBSTITUTE APPEARANCES) AND GOALS

	Player	Premier League		FA Cup		League Cup		Total	
		Apps	Gls	Apps	Gls	Apps	Gls	Apps	Gls
28	Cesar Azpilicueta	38	1	3 (+2)	0	3	1	44 (+2)	2
11	Pedro	26 (+9)	9	4	4	2 (+1)	0	32 (+10)	13
24	Gary Cahill	36 (+1)	6	2	0	3	2	41 (+1)	8
10	Eden Hazard	36	16	2 (+1)	1	0 (+3)	0	38 (+4)	17
19	Diego Costa	35	20	2 (+2)	1	0 (+2)	0	37 (+4)	21
7	N'Golo Kante	35	1	2 (+2)	1	1	0	38 (+2)	2
22	Willian	15 (+19)	8	5	4	1	0	21 (+19)	12
15	Victor Moses	29 (+5)	3	3	0	2	1	34 (+5)	4
21	Nemanja Matic	30 (+5)	1	2	1	2	0	34 (+5)	2
13	Thibaut Courtois	36	0	2	0	0	0	38	0
30	David Luiz	33	1	2	0	2	0	37	1
4	Cesc Fabregas	13 (+16)	5	3 (+2)	0	2	2	18 (+18)	7
3	Marcos Alonso	30 (+1)	6	2	0	1	0	33 (+1)	6
23	Michy Batshuayi	1 (+19)	5	3 (+1)	2	3	2	7 (+20)	9
2	Branislav Ivanovic	6 (+7)	0	1 (+1)	1	1	0	8 (+8)	1
29	Nathaniel Chalobah	1 (+9)	0	3	0	1 (+1)	0	5 (+10)	0
26	John Terry	6 (+3)	1	3	0	1 (+1)	0	10 (+4)	1
5	Kurt Zouma	3 (+6)	0	3 (+1)	0	0	0	6 (+7)	0
14	Ruben Loftus-Cheek	0 (+6)	0	2 (+1)	0	2	0	4 (+7)	0
8	Oscar	5 (+4)	0	0	0	1 (+1)	0	6 (+5)	0
1	Asmir Begovic	2	0	3	0	3	0	8	0
34	Ola Aina	0 (+3)	0	0 (+1)	0	2	0	2 (+4)	0
6	Nathan Ake	0	0	3	0	0	0	3	0
16	Kenedy	0	0	0 (+1)	0	0	0	0 (+1)	0

BARCLAYS PREMIER LEAGUE TABLE 2016/17

	Team	P	W	D	L	F	A	W	D	L	F	A	W	D	L	F	A	GD	Pts
1	Chelsea	38	30	3	5	85	33	17	0	2	55	17	13	3	3	30	16	52	93
2	Tottenham Hotspur	38	26	8	4	86	26	17	2	0	47	9	9	6	4	39	17	60	86
3	Manchester City	38	23	9	6	80	39	11	7	1	37	17	12	2	5	43	22	41	78
4	Liverpool	38	22	10	6	78	42	12	5	2	45	18	10	5	4	33	24	36	76
5	Arsenal	38	23	6	9	77	44	14	3	2	39	16	9	3	7	38	28	33	75
6	Manchester United	38	18	15	5	54	29	8	10	1	26	12	10	5	4	28	17	25	69
7	Everton	38	17	10	11	62	44	13	4	2	42	16	4	6	9	20	28	18	61
8	Southampton	38	12	10	16	41	48	6	6	7	17	21	6	4	9	24	27	-7	46
9	AFC Bournemouth	38	12	10	16	55	67	9	4	6	35	29	3	6	10	20	38	-12	46
10	West Bromwich Albion	38	12	9	17	43	51	9	2	8	27	22	3	7	9	16	29	-8	45
11	West Ham United	38	12	9	17	47	64	7	4	8	19	31	5	5	9	28	33	-17	45
12	Leicester City	38	12	8	18	48	63	10	4	5	31	25	2	4	13	17	38	-15	44
13	Stoke City	38	11	11	16	41	56	7	6	6	24	24	4	5	10	17	32	-15	44
14	Crystal Palace	38	12	5	21	50	63	6	2	11	24	25	6	3	10	26	38	-13	41
15	Swansea City	38	12	5	21	45	70	8	3	8	27	34	4	2	13	18	36	-25	41
16	Burnley	38	11	7	20	39	55	10	3	6	26	20	1	4	14	13	35	-16	40
17	Watford	38	11	7	20	40	68	8	4	7	25	29	3	3	13	15	39	-28	40
18	Hull City	38	9	7	22	37	80	8	4	7	28	35	1	3	15	9	45	-43	34
19	Middlesbrough	38	5	13	20	27	53	4	6	9	17	23	1	7	11	10	30	-26	28
20	Sunderland	38	6	6	26	29	69	3	5	11	16	34	3	1	15	13	35	-40	24

ACKNOWLEDGEMENTS AND SPECIAL THANKS

My special thanks go to Jules Gammond at G2 Entertainment publishers, Paul Clark at ChelseaFan12 (@Fan12Chelsea) and my long-suffering editor Sean Willis.

My appreciation and acknowledgements go to the wealth of information from Chelsea TV, the BBC Sport website, Mail online, but most importantly the fans, the manager and the players for their contribution on social media.

HARRY HARRIS

Harry Harris is a Double winner of the British Sports Journalist of the Year award, British Variety Club of Great Britain Silver Heart for 'Contribution to Sports Journalism', Double winner of the Sports Story of the Year award, the only journalist ever to win the Sports Story of the year accolade twice. He has won a total of 14 industry awards.

Harry has appeared regularly as an analyst on football on all major TV news and sports programmes and channels, including Richard & Judy and Newsnight, BBC News and ITV News at Ten, Sky, Setanta, plus Radio 5 live, Radio 4, and talkSPORT. He has been interviewed on Football Focus, appeared on the original Hold The Back Page, and Jimmy Hill's Sunday Supplement on Sky.

Harry is arguably the most prolific writer of best-selling football books of his generation. Among his 75 books are the highly acclaimed best seller Pele - His Life and Times, 'Gullit: The Chelsea Diary', 'All The Way Jose', Chelsea Century, Chelski, 'Wayne Rooney - The Story of Football's Wonder Kid'. Autobiographies on Ruud Gullit, Paul Merson, Glenn Hoddle, Gary Mabbutt, Steve McMahon, Terry Neill, Bill Nicholson: 'Glory, Glory - My Life With Spurs.' Biographies on Roman Abramovich, Jurgen Klinsmann, Sir Alex Ferguson, Jose Mourinho, Terry Venables, Franco Zola and Luca Vialli. He wrote George Best's last book, and best seller, 'Hard Tackles and Dirty Baths', and 19 - a history of Manchester United's record league titles.

Harry has written one of the most influential football columns in the country for three decades and is regarded as one of the best investigative journalists and perhaps the best news gatherer of his generation. He worked for the Daily Mail, Daily Mirror, Daily Express, Daily Star, Sunday Express and Star on Sunday, and as ESPNsoccernet Football Correspondent: 35 years as the No.1 football writer.

Current books: Down Memory Lane, Leicester City: The Immortals, Jose Mourinho: The Red One, and Kerry Dixon: Up Front.

ChelseaFan12.com
THE #1 UNOFFICIAL CHELSEA FANSITE

SHOP ⚽ NEWS ⚽ STATS